Carolyn & Jerry – thank you for always being there for us. Your guidance has been invaluable throughout the many "miles" we have traveled together.

Susan

LEADING
THE PUBLIC UNIVERSITY

To Gerald AND Carolyn Blaney,
Carolyn + Jerry;
you helped in a meaningful way to shape the modern university. Your friendship and steadfast support have meant much to us personally and to WVU.

David Hardesty

LEADING
THE PUBLIC
UNIVERSITY

Essays, Speeches, and Commentary

David C. Hardesty Jr., J.D.
PRESIDENT AND PROFESSOR OF LAW,
WEST VIRGINIA UNIVERSITY

WITH Susan B. Hardesty
FOUNDER, MOUNTAINEER PARENTS CLUB

 West Virginia University

MORGANTOWN 2007

Published by the West Virginia University Press for West Virginia University

© 2007 West Virginia University Press, Morgantown 26506

First edition published 2007 by West Virginia University Press

Printed in the United States of America

15 14 13 12 11 10 09 08 07   9 8 7 6 5 4 3 2 1

ISBN-10 1-933202-30-0

ISBN-13 978-1-933202-30-3

(alk. paper)Library of Congress Cataloguing-in-Publication Data

Leading the Public University. / by David C. Hardesty, Jr.

        p.   cm.

1. Education, Higher--Social aspects--United States. 2. Education, Higher--Aims and objectives-
-United States. 3. Universities and colleges--United States. 4. West Virginia University--History.I.
Title. II. Hardesty, David C, Jr. III.

IN PROCESS

Library of Congress Control Number: 2007939222

For Susan,

my partner in life and my partner in leadership of our alma mater,
and for Ashley and Carter,
who have shared fully in our joys and tribulations.

For the men and women of West Virginia University,
and all who support their vital work.

For the students of the university, and their parents,
who have informed and inspired us.

CONTENTS

V   PREFACE

1   INTRODUCTION · FOLLOW YOUR INSTINCTS

9   PART ONE · LESSONS LEARNED:
        LEADERSHIP PRINCIPLES AND PRACTICES

11   1   RECOGNIZING LESSONS LEARNED AT THE TURN OF THE
             CENTURY: THE FINAL STATE OF THE UNIVERSITY ADDRESS

25   2   TEN CHARACTERISTICS OF A HIGHLY EFFECTIVE
             ORGANIZATION

32   3   LIFELONG LEARNING FOR LEADERS AND ORGANIZATIONS

46   4   BUILDING LEADERSHIP CAPACITY

56   5   LEADER OVERLOAD: THE OPERATIONAL RISKS OF A
             ROBUST ORGANIZATIONAL AGENDA

71   6   CAN EDUCATION BE RUN LIKE A BUSINESS?

78   7   LEADING CHANGE: REMARKS TO THE NATIONAL
             ASSOCIATION OF STATE UNIVERSITIES AND LAND-GRANT
             COLLEGES

89   PART TWO · MISSION, VISION, AND VALUES:
        THE PRESIDENT AS UNIVERSITY ADVOCATE

91   7   GETTING STARTED: THE INAUGURAL ADDRESS

105   9   MARKING PROGRESS IN THE STATE OF THE UNIVERSITY
             ADDRESSES

165   10   A Plea for Public Support of Higher Education

171   11   The Joy of Teaching, Inside and Outside of the Classroom

176   12   Involving Parents in Support of the Mission: The West Virginia University Mountaineer Parents Club
By Susan B. Hardesty

186   13   The Vital Role of the Private Donor: West Virginia University's Randolph Cancer Center Gala

189   14   The Role of Women at West Virginia University
By Susan B. Hardesty

199   15   The Value and Perils of Intercollegiate Athletics

208   16   The Meaning of Social Justice

214   17   Priests of the Temple

239   **Part Three · Teaching Moments: A President's Call to Action**

241   18   Remarks after September 11

255   19   Remarks to New Citizens of the United States at a Naturalization Ceremony

260   20   Finding Wisdom in the Information Age

270   21   Champion for Youth Development Programs

281   22   Celebrating Volunteers: First Annual Conference on Volunteerism

290   23   Encouraging Student Success

308   24   Supporting Productive Communities

335   PART FOUR · EDUCATION AND EXPERIENCE: PREPARING FOR LEADERSHIP

338   25   REFLECTIONS ON OUR JOURNEY TO SERVICE
354   26   REFLECTIONS ON UNDERGRADUATE GROWTH: FOR THE 125TH ANNIVERSARY OF WOODBURN HALL
363   27   REFLECTIONS ON THE OXFORD EXPERIENCE: RESIDENTIAL EDUCATION AS PREPARATION FOR LEADERSHIP
373   28   LEADING LAWYERS: WHY LAWYERS LEAD IN AMERICA
387   29   THE EDUCATION OF A VOLUNTEER: REPORT OF THE CHAIRMAN TO THE UNIVERSITY SYSTEM BOARD OF TRUSTEES
401   AFTERWORD · BRINGING CLOSURE, TIME TO SAY GOODBYE: A LETTER OF FAREWELL TO THE UNIVERSITY COMMUNITY

405   CONCLUSION

408   APPENDIX 1 · TIMELINE OF SPEECHES
411   APPENDIX 2 · THE NUMBERS AT WVU

413   BIOGRAPHICAL INFORMATION
415   REFERENCES AND CITED WORKS

PREFACE

On July 1, 1995, I assumed the presidency of West Virginia University, my undergraduate alma mater, a comprehensive, multi-campus, public research university. The institution is a vibrant and significant learning community, which has served its many constituencies since 1867. It was founded shortly after the Civil War, in a state born of the war, and since that time, it has served its host state through periods of war, depression, civil conflict, and economic transformation and growth. West Virginia University is one of the public colleges and universities called "land-grant" institutions. They have this designation because they were established through the sale of federal lands given to the states in order to generate money to fund higher education. Originally, land-grant institutions were established through acts of Congress to serve society through the extension of knowledge and skills to the people and communities of a growing America. Gradually, many have expanded their mission. Today, the university I served also engages in research and medical education.

West Virginia University is a very large and complex organization, and it is often designated as one of the nation's flagship universities. For twelve years, I was privileged to serve as its president and primary spokesperson. Over those years, my understanding of the president's role as a leader within the university, as a member of the community, and as a public figure throughout the state—even across the nation—has evolved. The president must be held accountable, not only to the academic community he or she leads, but also to the community at large.

Leading a public university is, in every sense, an act of leadership in the public sector. Every university president's speeches and writings share with the public the essence of the university's mission, vision, and values. The speeches demonstrate changes in culture and policy and serve as verbal or written pictures of various moments in the life of ever-evolving campuses. They solicit political, philanthropic, and volunteer support. They offer words of encouragement and celebration. Of course, behind each of the presidential messages are the strategic planning exercises, statutory mandates, meetings, personnel choices, events, and other factors that help to formulate those messages.

Toward the end of my tenure, it became apparent to me that my writings portrayed a unique portrait of my university and could also contribute to the dialogue about relationships between institutions of higher education and the communities they serve.

My speeches and essays were premised on my belief that a university president must be a public leader. As a president, I interacted not only with students and faculty in the academy but also—just as importantly—with public officials, legislators, business leaders, donors, and alumni. I represented to these constituencies the benefits and objectives of post-secondary public education in order to garner support for my university from the state and the community.

As a matter of course, I nearly always prepared written remarks for presentations at public events. Perhaps this is because I am a lawyer by profession and accustomed to a written record of oral presentations, or perhaps it is because the remarks that a president is called on to make convey policy determinations, serve to memorialize events and people, and record the history of our institution. They are frequently printed and subjected to scrutiny by many individuals and their representatives. My writings represent the communications tools by which I sought to make cultural changes and advance toward achieving the university's official agenda.

Leadership is far more complex than written or oral communications, and leadership skill involves far more than public speaking or writing skills. But rhetoric and public-speaking skills, with the logical presentation of ideas, remain an essential element of the power of the modern higher education presidency.[1]

For the most part, this book is a compilation of speeches, essays, and articles written during my twelve-year tenure as a president (1995–2007). This period of service was roughly twice the national average tenure for major university presidents and the longest in the history of our university. It also occurred at the turn of the century, a time of significant change in American higher education.

During this period, my wife, Susan, also a graduate of West Virginia University, was an active partner and leader of the university in every sense of the word and I acknowlege that partnership throughout the book by referring to our ideas, actions, and decisions. She joined me as a spokesperson for the university throughout the period and became known as the founder of a new and dynamic organization, the Mountaineer Parents Club. We have been privileged to serve our alma mater as partners in leadership, just as we are partners in life. Susan, who engaged the campus since the day I was appointed, is the author of several segments of the book, including the essays "West Virginia Daughter of the Year," "Involving Parents in Support of the Mission," and "The Role of Women at West Virginia University." The book also contains a few speeches written prior to my appointment as president. They are included because I think they will give the reader some insight into the development of my skills and values over time.

The individual speeches and writings contained in this collection are not, individually, works of scholarship in the traditional sense. But taken as a body of work, it is my belief that they offer an in-depth examination of the nature of the leadership that must be exhibited by the modern public university president.

The challenges we faced and responses of our leadership team are faithfully documented in what follows.

Rather than arranging these speeches and publications by date of their delivery, I have chosen to group them by the aspects of leadership they represent. The introduction sets the stage for the speeches and essays included in this book by reflecting on my background, my vision for the university immediately after my appointment, and my view (from the end of my presidency) of my role in the dynamic growth and changes the intuition has experienced over the past twelve years.

Part 1 of this book, "Lessons Learned: Leadership Principles and Practices," examines both the challenges our leadership team faced and the lessons we learned while pursuing a very active agenda of positive change and growth. The first speech is my final State of the Campus Address, which explains our leadership approaches and also provides a glimpse of the university's growth during my tenure. (university statistics providing a comparison of the state of the university at the beginning and end of my presidency can be found in Appendix 2.) Our experiences and leadership research offer an introduction to the leadership required of a university president and provide a more general introduction to leadership theory.

Part 2, "Mission, Vision, and Values: The President as University Advocate," explores a president's responsibility to focus the institution's attention on its mission, vision, and values. Key university speeches range from the inaugural address to the State of the University addresses. This section also includes addresses to important constituents of the university and acknowledges the important contributions of many beloved individuals who helped to build our university. Such figures exist at every institution of higher education in the United States, and these remarks are offered as examples of how such people can and should be celebrated.

Part 3, "Teaching Moments: A President's Call to Action," represents my attempts to learn, and help others learn, from events, both expected and unexpected, and to address concerns raised by our various constituencies. This part, for example, includes my remarks to the university community after September 11.

Part 4, "Education and Experience: Preparing for Leadership," describes the ways our families, education, and experiences shaped our values and leadership styles.

A few words about style will also be helpful. Each segment is introduced with a personal assessment (in italics) of the context for its delivery and a statement of its intended purpose. The style of the speeches varies somewhat, due to my own maturation over the years, my assessment of the occasion and audience, the contributors and editors involved, and other factors. But it will be evident to the reader that my lawyer's tendency toward advocacy and logical presentation frequently manifests itself. I have always been inclined to make writing and speaking points in "threes, fives, and tens," which can be a help to an overworked judge trying to get to the essence of a case or a hindrance to an avid fan of fiction and more serious literature.

While the remarks that follow were written to speak directly to the many constituencies of West Virginia University, they are fairly typical of the efforts made by institutional leaders across America to mobilize their campuses in an effort to educate their students, assemble new knowledge through scholarship and research, and serve the nation's communities. Thus, they address the concerns of many leaders across higher education in America at the turn of the century, the dawn of a new millennium. I offer these speeches and essays as a modest guide for new and aspiring presidents of higher education institutions, as well as a record of public leadership with its successes and its challenges.

ACKNOWLEDGMENTS

Speaking in London in 1949, after authoring an extraordinary number of books and articles, former British Prime Minister Winston Churchill said:

> Writing a book is an adventure. To begin with it is a toy and an amusement. Then it becomes a mistress, then it becomes a master, then it becomes a tyrant. The last phase is that just as you are about to be reconciled in your servitude, you kill the monster, and fling him about to the public.[2]

This book is about the public utterances of a university president and the president's spouse. We therefore want to acknowledge the many invitations we received to speak throughout our state and nation during our tenure and the kind invitations to submit articles for publication, usually in a guest editorial format. Much of what we have written resulted from those invitations.

Also, we recognize that in many ways this book chronicles the events, programs, and achievements of every person associated with our university at the turn of the century. Our students and their parents have inspired us from the beginning, and many of the remarks published here touch on our efforts to envision a student-centered learning community.

We also want to recognize the many members of the faculty and staff and administrators we have come to know and respect, especially those with whom we worked on a daily basis. These persons include men and women in the president's office and at Blaney House, home of the president of West Virginia

University; executives and staff in our hospital system, foundation, and alumni association; the vice presidents and deans of the university; our formal and informal faculty, staff, and student advisors; and the dedicated chairs and members of the various governing boards who offered us the rare opportunity to serve our alma mater. Their hard work, advice, and counsel led to many of the programs described in this book, and many offered helpful suggestions and comments on the speeches I gave at the time of delivery.

Several former university presidents, alumni, philanthropists, and donors offered special support during our years of service, and our various contacts, partnerships, and travels with them ripened into real friendships that will last a lifetime. In many ways, they have made the programs described in this book possible. Carolyn Eberly Blaney, herself a speech major at West Virginia University, was always helpful in providing feedback, usually positive and encouraging, when she was present at our presentations.

We have also served with legislators elected to six different sessions of congress and the West Virginia legislature and four governors of our state, each of whom cared about higher education and West Virginia University and supported regular and special appropriations to higher education. We owe special thanks to our United States senators John D. Rockefeller IV and Robert C. Byrd, whose acumen, skill, and personal generosity are revealed in several of the speeches that follow.

Several accomplished and experienced friends read the manuscript of this book in various forms, including Dr. Jennifer Fisher, who served with us for twelve years as a top presidential assistant, policy analyst, and chief of staff; Dr. Gerald E. Lang, provost and vice president for academic affairs; David's childhood friend and author Meredith Sue Willis; former president Dr. Gene Budig; and Dr. Robert DeClerico, a distinguished member of our political science faculty. Each offered helpful insights and suggestions that improved the text and brought clarity to our effort.

As mentioned later, several people worked every day on our public communications efforts, including three chiefs of staff in the president's office, David Satterfield, Margie Phillips, and Dr. Jennifer Fisher; Vice Presidents Carolyn Curry and Chris Martin; various university editors; and Sara Master, Ginny Petersen, and Gloria Bowers in the Office of the President. Amy Quigley, who has written broadly for both of us, deserves special mention. She listened well, found our voice, and helped us to write numerous articles and speeches over the years.

We need to thank and recognize the hard work, research, and writing skills of Dr. Jessika Thomas, who works in the WVU office of academic affairs. Her thoughtful assistance in reading and editing several drafts brought a new level of clarity to our thinking and writing.

Finally, we both have been privileged to study public speaking and writing with dedicated teachers in our high schools and four different institutions of higher learning. They encouraged us to find our voices, introduced us to great orators and authors, and helped us to develop our communications skills, asking nothing in return but that we do the same for others at some future time. We owe them much, as do thousands of others who learned under their tutelage.

INTRODUCTION

FOLLOW YOUR INSTINCTS

CREATING THE VISION

On July 1, 1995, I assumed the presidency of West Virginia University, a comprehensive, land-grant, multicampus, public research university. It is the flagship of the West Virginia higher education system. It was a fulfilling and emotional moment for my wife Susan and me.

Both members of the WVU class of 1967, Susan and I found that much of our lives were invested in the university. In fact, Susan was raised on the campus, the daughter of a lifetime faculty member at the university. I served as student body president as an undergraduate. We both volunteered throughout our lives for the institution, serving on various committees, boards, and advocacy groups.

On the first working day of my appointment, I announced that our university would put students at the center of its strategic thinking. It was an instinctive move that was, on the whole, well received. Over the next few years, our efforts to become a more student-centered school became more intense and elaborate, resulting in the investment of millions of dollars and thousands of hours in what proved to be the central strategy of the early years of my presidency. The vision statement we developed, which appeared on my business cards for more than a decade, insists that the university is "a student-centered learning community meeting the changing needs of West

Virginia and the nation through excellence in teaching, research, service and technology."

During the early months of my presidency, I asked alumnus Glen H. Hiner, then chairman of Owens Corning, "What is the single best piece of advice you can give a university president?" He thought a long time and finally said, "Follow your instincts. They got you the job!" By that I think he meant that the designation of someone to lead any major institution is a matter of trust in the designated leader's integrity, abilities, *and* instincts on the part of the governing board and those they represent. And trust in our instincts is exactly what we did.

Only in retrospect have I tried to examine the source of my instincts. In part, the answer is found in my background. Susan's influence on our campus cannot be underestimated. She is a full partner in my life. Susan was a public school teacher; she has always had student progress and success at the top of her priority list. I have observed and learned from her for thirty-eight years. At the time of my selection, we had two teenaged children. They informed us as only children can. We also had a feel for the people and culture of the state of West Virginia. We lived in a rural community, but I worked in the capital city, Charleston.

In addition, in my first career as a lawyer, I had been a volunteer for higher education, our community foundation, business associations, and our children's public schools. Our situation and these experiences gave us a feel for today's students and their parents, as well as other constituencies of the university.

The university also had a long history of good teaching and had valued student success since its founding in 1867. I soon learned that several successful major corporate presidents and chairs, other college presidents, nonprofit-sector leaders, professionals, military leaders, and other prominent Americans were among our alumni. In contrast to the school's image as a large, somewhat impersonal college whose students seemed to value social activities more than academic life, the institution has a history of student centeredness. Our board of trustees and other governance groups also urged us to "take on" this image, preparing us for a return to our roots.

Further, I had been student body president at the university and had come to believe over the years that what I had learned outside the classroom rivaled what I had learned in the classroom. In fact, Dr. Harry B. Heflin, who had served as president when I was a student leader, and a few of the student affairs professionals who were at the university when I arrived as a student, were still on campus. I trusted their advice and counsel as I considered our future.

I also had served my alma mater as a member of its local advisory board and governing board for many years. As a result, I came to believe that what separates a university from a social services organization or research company—what makes a university distinctive and worthy of public support—is its commitment to educating the next generation of citizens and their leaders. Just a year or so later, the National Association of State Universities and Land-Grant Colleges issued a clarion call for student centeredness in the first of several task force reports funded by the Kellogg Foundation.[3] Interestingly, it was called *Returning to our Roots*. It had been initiated while I was a member of the governing board, and I was aware of its early findings.

Of course, I consulted with others whose advice I sought and trusted, and they advised me to focus my thinking on a strategic vision that could be widely understood.

George B. Bennett, a WVU alumnus and prominent consultant and entrepreneur now living in the Boston area, volunteered his time early on in my tenure to visit the university and consult on leadership matters. George has an extraordinary ability to size up a complex situation and pose the essential problem to the decision maker. During the course of his consultation, George held up the children's book *Where's Waldo?* and said to our management team,

"In every complex organization there are a limited number of problems, which, if addressed successfully, hold the key to success. Look for Waldo!" The little figure in the child's bedtime book, so hard to find among the other images until discovered but then so evident, became a powerful metaphor for organizational vision and leadership. This made all the sense in the world to me. As a lawyer, I knew that in every case, there are only a few pivotal facts or legal principles upon which every negotiation or trial depends.

A year later, James O'Toole, author of *Leading Change*, a book about organizational change strategies, visited our campus.[4] He made a similar point, noting that shared values give an organization its character and must be part of the leader's vision for the future.

The vision of student centeredness, therefore, may not have been instinctive in the sense of spontaneity or rashness. Perhaps it should be seen as the logical progression of things. But I did something that I now realize in retrospect was an entrepreneurial and even risky move. I made a major personal and institutional commitment to a strategic vision on my first day on the job. While I had talked formally about the thrust to the student body president, my primary transition advisors, the dean of students, several members of the cabinet, selected faculty, and a few family members, friends, and other close personal advisors, the vision of becoming a more student-centered university was not the result of a lengthy strategic planning exercise. It was the result of a lifetime of education and experiences, and of listening to the valued advice of those who cared as much about the university as I did. Because it was based on the needs of those we served, it struck a chord with the university's many constituencies.

ADVOCACY FOR CHANGE

The student-centered commitment of West Virginia University involved a five-point plan of action aimed at putting students at the heart of the university. "Students are the reason we exist," I told the university community. I was an outsider to the academy, but for the most part, the campus embraced the vision. As money was reallocated, some resistance was encountered, based on both theoretical grounds and human nature. The criticism was ultimately helpful and improved our programs.

American higher education, at the turn of this century, was looking for Waldo, hunting for the meaning of its existence at the dawn of a new age. New competitors, exploding information, the global economy, changing societal mores, and many other factors challenge the leaders of our colleges and universities to choose from a great number of possible investment strategies in a time of rising costs and limited resources. Many believed that creating and sustaining a more student-centered environment was the key to preserving the important role of our colleges and universities. I was just one such person.

As president of our university, I was privileged to watch as many people worked long hours to transform our institution into one that is, in fact, much more centered on student success than it was previously. They saw the vision as clearly as I saw it, sometimes more clearly, and our students, faculty, staff, and state are better off because they did. They formulated the strategies, planned for our future, assembled the resources necessary to fund our vision, and established and eventually reached the goals and objectives that transformed our institution.

We had some help. The move was not opposed, and was quietly supported by my predecessor and many other leaders on our campuses. For several years, West Virginia University had taken the quality movement seriously and had applied the principles of the quality movement to daily life at the university long before my tenure. The university was ready for change.

We also faced an atmosphere of urgency. Enrollment was predicted to decline due to the demographics of our state, from which a significant portion of our students come. As a university focused primarily on traditional students, the enrollment challenge threatened our financial situation and motivated us to find ways to keep our finances stable. In addition, our state legislature had mandated a strategic planning exercise that ultimately required the realloca-tion of tens of millions of dollars on our campuses. These factors created a sense of crisis that attracted intense interest from the university's constituencies.

In recent years, the national associations of colleges and universities have been interested in the topic of student life, especially for undergraduates, on large campuses. This interest has resulted in a flurry of books, reports, and ar-ticles that have inspired and informed us. Because I was new to higher educa-tion leadership, I read widely during the early years of my presidency, and the richness of the literature on presidential leadership has guided our reforms.

In short, the time was right. The need was great. Action was possible. People off campus and on campus were ready and willing to lead and to act in an entrepreneurial fashion.

Asking for change is easy. Changing is hard. It requires knowledge, integ-rity, and transparency; the identification of strategies, goals, and objectives; reinforcement; change champions; courage; reassessments of old traditions and values; and much more.

There is an evident need to think more globally; compete in new ways; invest in technology; address the modern family's search for meaning; termi-nate outdated programs and create new ones; address rising costs, tuition, and attendants' demands for accountability; make education more available; think more strategically; change business processes; and address other issues—but each concern requires change.

This book chronicles how one institution was called upon by its president to transform itself at the turn of the century. The men and women who make up that institution accepted the need for change and became comfortable changing. In addition to efforts to become more student-centered, the uni-versity embraced the need for many other changes across our many programs and locations: research became more focused, private funds have been substantially increased, buildings have been renovated and built, and programs have been eliminated and added.

The transformation is far from complete. Toward the end of my service as president, I came to realize an American university's agenda can never truly be complete. As society changes, which it inevitably will, universities must change, and they inevitably will. In one important sense, the leader of a modern university campus must be a change agent, generating a constant state of change.

GIVING THE "ROAR"

Of course, not all public rhetoric of university presidents advocates the need for change. Often, presidents are called upon to remind constituents of important traditions and values of the university for which they are stewards, and asking that these traditions and values be maintained and supported over the years. Presidents may also be seen as trustworthy repositories of insight, analysis, and expertise. For this reason, they are often invited to speak at a wide variety of conferences and meetings on subjects of interest to the host group. In such cases, the president may use examples from the university in order to increase understanding of and support for higher education. This book contains many examples of such remarks, given on a wide variety of occasions to a number of different groups.

In short, the president's role is both to lead and to represent the university. Aside from integrity, no other skill is more important to this role than formulating the strategic messages to be delivered on and off of the campus and speaking to and on behalf of the institution.

On the occasion of his eightieth birthday in 1954, Winston Churchill, refuting the claim that he had inspired the nation to victory over the Nazi menace, discussed the power behind his rhetoric. He rejected "what many people have kindly said, namely that I inspired the nation." He insisted that the nation's "will was resolute and remorseless, and as it proved, unconquerable" and that, even though its people were "dwelling all round the globe," they "had the lion's heart." Churchill attributes to himself only "the luck to be called upon to give the roar."[5]

University presidents are challenged to roar for their institutions every day and, in doing so, urge action by suggesting a vision and strategies that will advance the institution. What follows is a record of how one president attempted, in a small way, to roar on behalf of his university.

NOTES

1   For further discussion of the role of communication in leadership, see Howard Gardner and Emma Laskin, *Leading Minds: An Anatomy of Leadership* (New York: Basic Books, 1996), 34, 39.

2   Winston Churchill (1949), quoted in Jack House, *Winston Churchill: His Wit and Wisdom* (London: Hyperion Books, 1965), 135.

3   The commission began meeting in January of 1996 and produced six reports over the next four years. See further the Kellogg Foundation, *Returning to Our Roots: Executive Summaries of the Reports of the Kellogg Commission on the Future of State Universities and Land-Grant Colleges* (Washington, DC: National Association of State Universities and Land-Grant Colleges, Office of Public Affairs, 2001).

4   James O'Toole, *Leading Change: The Argument for Values-Based Leadership* (San Francisco: Jossey-Bass Publishers, 1996).

5   Winston Churchill, The Nation Had the Lion-Heart, speech at Westminster Hall, November 30, 1954, in Winston S. Churchill, *Never Give In! The Best of Winston Churchill's Speeches* (New York: Hyperion, 2003), 490.

PART ONE

LESSONS LEARNED

LEADERSHIP PRINCIPLES AND PRACTICES

The American university presidency is a position of public leadership. This is especially true of state universities. Although higher education may be caricatured as an ivory tower separated from the realities of daily life, a public university president interacts not only with students and faculty in the academy, but also, and just as importantly, with public officials, legislators, business leaders, donors, and alumni. A president must demonstrate the benefits and objectives of post-secondary public education in order to garner support from the state and community. In order to address institutional needs effectively, a president must also relate to the many constituents within the university and develop a broad base of support for change. A public university president also must be a leader of business, the state, and local communities, as well as a leader of the communities that exist within the university.

Given these responsibilities, it is not surprising that a 2005 survey of university presidents, conducted on behalf of the *Chronicle of Higher Education*, emphasized the importance of leadership abilities. Half of the presidents surveyed suggested that "strong leadership ability" was the attribute most important to the success of their presidency.[1] Two other traits frequently selected by the survey participants were "strong interpersonal skills" and "a strong vision," both of which are strongly related to leadership acumen.[2] Clearly, presidents perceive their successes to be most directly related to their leadership abilities.

During my twelve years as president of West Virginia University, I grew as a leader through participating in leadership activities, reading about leadership theory and practice, discussing leadership with my administrative team and colleagues around the county, and personal experience. The collective work of many others on the nature and sources of leadership has informed our methods for developing and achieving university goals. I have come to believe that thoughtful and deliberate leadership strategies increased the possibility of success with regard to each endeavor.

Because leadership principles and practice were so important during my tenure as president, I frequently reflected on my own experiences as the head of a leadership team in public forums. This section deals with the topic of leadership, addressing it from a number of perspectives. While my experiences are specific to higher education, the models and practices described are relevant to a wide range of leaders.

ONE

RECOGNIZING LESSONS LEARNED AT THE TURN OF THE CENTURY

THE FINAL STATE OF THE UNIVERSITY ADDRESS

2006

Good leaders pause periodically to consider lessons learned. The military has an established practice of doing the "after action review." As part of the review, officers and enlisted soldiers alike look back over their actions during a campaign or battle and collectively ask, what can we learn that we can pass on to the next group undertaking a similar mission? Other tools, such as retreats and institutional research, accomplish the same purpose.

Recognizing lessons learned is only part of the practice. Passing the lessons along to others through written and oral communication is equally important. My final State of the University address, which looks back over more than a decade of work as president, is the most reflective. It was titled Lessons Learned at the Turn of the Century. In a sense, this book begins with the clarity that only hindsight offers.

Allow me to begin by stating the obvious. This is the twelfth time I have addressed you to offer my assessment of the state of West Virginia University. While we may be together other times in the coming year, this is my last formal opportunity to share my thoughts on the state of the university with you.

During times of transition, we all feel compelled to say all that we are thinking in the little time that we have. As I drafted my remarks, so many thoughts, images, and memories of my lifetime connection with WVU, and aspirations for the WVU community, came to mind.

For some strange reason, a phrase I learned in high school in Latin class came to the fore: *habere in animo*. I think it means "to have in mind." Suffice it to say that I will not say all I am thinking, and that is good for me and excellent for you.

How could I possibly begin without saying thanks to you and to our other colleagues in the university community for your support and generosity of spirit toward WVU over the past eleven years? Presidents who serve their undergraduate alma maters are rare, but they each know what a privilege it is to serve the institution that launched them in life. This is especially true in our case, because Susan and I met and married here, our children have been educated here, and we have spent the most productive years of life in service to a place we love. We are, therefore, grateful to the governing boards of the university and the broader university community for giving us the opportunity to serve, and for supporting us during our service. During this time, you, the members of the university community, have taught us much, offered excellent advice and counsel, and listened when we have asked for your attention. You have worked hard to improve our programs and to bring even greater recognition to WVU.

This you have done by your collective efforts, but also through your individual efforts to be the best that you could be. You have helped to lead us from one place to another, and it has required hard work and passion. You have shared tough times with Susan and me, making them more bearable. You have shared in the joys that we experienced as well. I will always have a deep and heartfelt respect for the faculty, staff, and administration of WVU. My first message is, therefore, very simple: thank you for all you have done and will continue to do.

In drafting my remarks, I was forced to reflect on the challenges we have faced together during my tenure as president and the manner in which WVU has met those challenges. Our time in service together at WVU has included both the turn of the century, a marker reached only twice in the history of the university, and a new millennium, a marker not reached in the history of American education.

During my tenure, American higher education has truly been at a crossroads. Looking back a decade, it is clear that WVU faced many transition issues: state funding cuts required us to increase both tuition and enrollments in order to maintain excellence; state and federal funding priorities changed: and health care, prison reform, public works, and economic development efforts began to compete with education for adequate funding. We faced new competitors, around the world and within the United States. We crossed the infamous Y2K barrier and invested millions of dollars in required new technologies. High school enrollments declined dramatically in West Virginia, requiring a new emphasis on recruitment. Buildings needed to be replaced or repaired, and infrastructure and new facilities were required. Our constituents demanded more and more, sometimes creating competing demands. In the midst of our transition, the events we now collectively call "9/11"—and the resulting economic restructuring—presented us with new demands. It truly has been a tumultuous turn of the century and an auspicious launch of the new millennium.

It is fair to ask, how have we, WVU's turn-of-the-century stewards, done in terms of piloting this flagship and navigating for our shipmates and others in the fleet over the past several challenging years? I have no idea how history will judge us—such a judgment requires wisdom and insight only the passage of time will afford. But I believe that we can say we have done the best we could under the circumstances.[3] Enrollment across our campuses grew by 25 percent. Research funding grew 100 percent. Extension clients grew 110 percent. Patients served by our hospitals and practice plan grew by 50 percent. Our private foundation assets grew 493 percent, and our endowment grew 290 percent.

Together with our sister campuses and health-care system hospitals, we have built or launched nearly $1 billion in new construction, renovations, and infrastructure improvement. We have achieved national recognition for excellence of leadership, teaching, research, and service in several existing and new fields. Our faculty, staff, students, and departments have brought home numerous awards, which have in turn lifted the profile of our university. Our alumni recognition is as strong as it has ever been, which I was reminded of this past week at the inauguration of WVU graduate and four-star general Doc Foglesong, as the president of Mississippi State. Whole systems have been reworked and changed, from the way we purchase, to the way we compensate, to the way we govern ourselves. And, as our fans know, we have become an even better sponsor of intercollegiate athletics—it is no accident that today we are considered a premier intercollegiate athletic program.

And so I assert that we, the turn-of-the-century stewards of WVU, have accomplished much in which we can take great pride. And you, as well as many of our colleagues, have played an important role in meeting the challenges we confronted.

As I prepared my remarks for today, an important question—perhaps the most important question—kept recurring in my mind. I know the challenges we have confronted together, and I know what we have accomplished together, but what have we learned together? What are the lessons we should pass on to the next generation of professional and volunteer leaders at West Virginia University? I want to suggest five such lessons to you today.

First, we have learned that we must achieve the level of excellence necessary to be truly competitive in a global economy. When I was a student here, waiting for Susan after class at the wall in front of Stewart Hall, I would often hear the phrase, "What does that have to do with the price of eggs in China?" It meant that someone just said something unrelated to the group discussion topic, because nothing here—in Morgantown, in West Virginia—could have anything to do with the price of eggs in China. If that were ever true, it is no longer true. Today, the peoples of the world are linked by satellite communications, the Web and related technologies, increasing cultural awareness, shared values, international research agendas, international education programs, energy consumption patterns and consequences, global-reach companies, and more.

In this global village, university degrees must be markers of global excellence. Our faculty and students know this. Even after 9/11, more students study abroad and travel from other countries to study here than ever before. Our graduates living in Shanghai shed tears when they hear "Country Roads" because they appreciate the value of the education we afforded them. We are helping to found a medical school in Oman, and one of our graduate students is leading an economic development program in Chile. Students in China and Morgantown exchange places to learn the ceramic arts and business strategies. Many of our colleagues, including some of our best faculty, are immigrants to our country. Our students are showing intense interest in learning relevant foreign languages, working in the national security arena, serving in the military, living in our new international house, and doing more to learn all that they can learn about the world in which we live.

To this end, I am very excited to announce today a $2 million gift from the estate of J. Vance and Florence Highland Johnson that will establish a

Chinese Studies Program at West Virginia University. It will be housed in the Eberly College of Arts and Sciences and appropriately named the J. Vance and Florence Highland Johnson Chinese Studies Program. The endowment will support the multidisciplinary program with four fundamental components: two professorships—one in the teaching of Chinese in the Department of Foreign Languages and one in Chinese Studies—a student support fund for study abroad, and a library fund. In the study-abroad program, students will spend the equivalent of one academic year studying in the native language at a Chinese university. Participants will be known as Johnson Scholars. The library fund will build and maintain a quality Chinese collection to support faculty and students in the Chinese Studies Program. Courses will be offered in a variety of academic areas such as language, culture, history, and politics.

This initiative spotlights the great importance of offering opportunities for our students to understand and compete for jobs in this global village. It also embodies the principle of interdisciplinary work, complementing initiatives in the College of Business and Economics and the Office of International Programs. On behalf of the entire university community, I thank the Johnson family, longtime residents of Clarksburg, WV, for their generosity, and I congratulate the foundation, Dean Mary Ellen Mazey, and the Department of Foreign Languages on this landmark announcement. Through this new program and in all that we do, we must keep this truth in mind—yes, we live, work, and compete in a global economy, and it will always demand standards of excellence worthy of the best players in an arena of global competition.

Second, our actions must exhibit strategic thinking. We must seek to understand the big picture and make principled decisions based on our mission, vision, and values. We must constantly push ourselves in our colleges and programs to see the big picture.

Vanderbilt Chancellor E. Gordon Gee spoke last week on campus and said, "In today's universities, no department or college can be intellectually self-sufficient." We have done much on our campus to become more interdisciplinary, and we understand that we avoid such efforts at our peril. Many of our successes over the past ten years were based upon the work of the task forces we mounted, our strategic planning efforts, the expert perspectives of people from within and outside the institution, our collaborations with other campuses, our adherence to an identified mission, and our vision to be a more student-centered learning community.

All of these efforts enabled us to see the big picture. In my first year as president, we invited a prominent engineering alumnus, George Bennett, to visit campus. A widely known consultant, he urged us to "look for Waldo" in our planning efforts. Using a popular children's book of the 1990s as a metaphor, he insisted that we identify that thing or those few things which, if we could accomplish them, could truly change our position as a university. In the book, Waldo is hard to find in the clutter on the page, but once you find him, it is obvious every time you look at the picture.

Our "Waldos," too, have commanded strategic investment, but they have changed our university. They have included collaborations with other universities and groups as diverse as the Pittsburgh Symphony and the National Energy Technology Laboratory. Strategic thinking led us to new programs in forensic science, biometrics, integrated marketing, Chinese business, neurosciences, neurosurgery, and the Resident Faculty Leader Program, as well as renewed emphasis on energy and the environment (including the Industries of the Future Program). They also led to a new library, recreation, and science facilities; strategic partnerships with federal and state agencies; the parents club; improved 4-H; and more.

Our work has led us to seek new sources of revenue and investments in innovation that will enhance learning, research, and service on all of our campuses. Competition for funds and human leadership resources will always be intense. Almost by definition, leadership is the allocation of scarce resources. There is never enough money to go around. Strategic thinking and principled decision-making offer a reasoned way to get stronger despite resource limitations.

In short, the second lesson is this: only strategic thinking and decision making based on mission, vision, and values offer a principled way to decide what our future will be. Always ask, what is the big picture in this situation, and how can we best allocate the limited resources we have for maximum effect?

Third, we must welcome the many demands for accountability and use the energy they generate to constantly improve our organization. We live in an age of accountability. Our students, parents, funding sources, donors—all those we serve—were raised with "800" numbers to call if they were dissatisfied, and guarantees of satisfaction for services rendered. Today, families save for years and students pay back debt over a large part of their lifetimes to attend WVU. The sacrifice of this investment must be honored through the value of the opportunities we provide. The rest is up to the student to do his or her part.

I am told that purveyors of the martial arts do not try to stop the force behind the thrust of an opponent. Instead they use that force to accomplish their own ends and, ultimately, victory. We need to think of judo when thinking about accountability to our constituencies. We must ask how can we use the force of accountability coming at us to gain new resources, to change our institution for the better, to improve the lives of those we serve?

An essential element of this lesson is the notion of transparency, or seeking to provide those we lead, both on and off of campus, with a principled explanation of what we are trying to do and why we are trying to do it. Transparency involves continuous communications. But even more, transparency is a form of trust shared with those we serve. In the end, most of our constituencies know the value of the university. We simply have to offer up our insights, and learn from theirs, in order to reach common ground.

I believe these lessons of accountability, transparency, and trust are what account for the tremendous growth and positive impact of the Mountaineer

Parents Club, which began with a few believers and grew under the leadership of my wife, Susan, to an organization of fifteen thousand families around the nation and on three continents. Together with the parent advocate, the parent newsletter, and programs such as the Parent University and Parents Weekend, we have harnessed the brute force of parent-demanded accountability to improve our institution and change it for the better. Today, parents help us recruit, offer ideas for continuous improvement, participate by the thousands in university events, and give us true insights into the quality of the education we provide.

I heard recently that one university has a "parent bouncer" whose job it is to keep parents out of the university's business. In my opinion, that university is taking every "accountability body-blow" frontally. Our experience has shown us a different and more effective strategy. Similarly, I think many of our faculty members have wisely connected our research activity to the cries for economic development and the needs of communities within our state. As a result, we have seen better recognition that our research mission is very relevant to the needs of the state's citizens.

Nowhere could this be clearer than in the health sciences, where high-quality jobs, rural medicine programs offering the best of health care through MDTV and distributed clinics, and a new health care system of hospitals and providers have firmly linked progress in local communities to the flying WV logo. Our health sciences enterprise answered the call for accountability years ago, and the tremendous advances and support they have garnered underscore the value of embracing the push to stand accountable for the resources invested in us. In years to come, we need to continue harnessing the demands for accountability and leverage them to improve our university.

Fourth, our organization must become and remain a learning organization. To do that, we must learn constantly, in every way possible, and share what we have learned throughout the organization. Those of us who work in a university environment surely provide leadership to society whether we recognize our leadership role as such, or not. In its most elemental form, teaching is leading, as is adding to the body of knowledge in a discipline and sharing lessons learned. The reason we have self-selected into a university community reflects an innate curiosity and a passion for the vibrancy that can be found when the debate of ideas, the sharing of knowledge, and the search for discovery are part of the core mission. The example we set in front of a classroom, our reports of the results of our scholarship and research, our advice to student organizations, our work in the communities of this state, our work in the clinics, our partnerships around the nation and around the world, and in fact, nearly all of our work is seen by others as a leadership activity. As such, we should model —and you should encourage those you advise to lead—a learning lifestyle.

We ourselves must struggle to continue to be lifetime learners; encourage, reward, and require learning in our departments and divisions; celebrate collective and individual learning milestones; listen to those we serve for their insights into what we do right and wrong; borrow ideas across domains of expertise; and preserve for others what we have learned. To this end, we have worked hard in recent years to modernize the personnel systems on our campus and to foster a culture of development and career advancement that will make this a better place to work and a better servant of society. But there is much, much more to be done. To paraphrase Robert Frost, the woods through which we will travel are lovely, dark, and deep, and we have miles to go before we sleep.[4]

Recently, Margie Phillips, former chief of staff, was asked to lead a new vice presidency for personnel. My hope is that she can, with our help, improve the learning and advancement support we give those with whom we work and upon whom we rely as members of our team.

I readily acknowledge that appropriate pay for work performed is part of this equation. Very few of us feel overpaid, no matter how much we make. Part of this feeling is just human nature, but part of it is the reality of competitive pay comparisons. The fact is that the global economy about which I spoke earlier will require that, over time, this university pay its faculty, staff, administrators, and student workers on a national scale for the work they perform. After years of state-driven budget cuts, part of the challenge of the next few years will be finding revenue resources to regain the ground lost to our peers and provide adequate salaries. In short, we must be a learning organization.

Finally, we have learned that everyone associated with WVU wants to find meaning in their contribution. We must constantly invest in praise and recognition of the meaning of our individual and collective work. This is a lesson that has been demonstrated on our campuses, time and time again, over the past decade. Our colleagues have responded to challenges, time and time again, and rightly want recognition for doing so. Our graduates seek our confirmation of their lifetime accomplishments. Our civic leaders want to be associated with our institution in a positive way.

All of this is easily recognized when we confer an award, send out a congratulatory letter, lift up a name in our speech, thank a student for an outstanding comment, induct a deserving graduate into a hall of fame, promote a deserving colleague, or in some other way confer praise or some symbol of our respect on those we lead. We all seek meaning in our lives, and we seek a sense of belonging and meaning where we work. This age-old principle has been documented by those who study psychology and those who study leadership.

Most recently, this entirely natural human craving was recognized by leadership experts James Kouzes and Barry Posner in their book, *A Leader's Legacy*: "No one likes to be an assumption. Everyone wants to be significant."[5] The key, here at WVU, is that we all want to feel valued and to find meaning in our life's work, and we want to know that our university recognizes that we do our job well.

To summarize, I submit that we have learned at least five major lessons at the turn of the century: (1) The work that we do must achieve the excellence necessary to be truly competitive in a global economy. (2) Our actions must exhibit strategic thinking. (3) We must seek to understand the big picture and make principled decisions based on our mission, vision, and values. (4) We must welcome the many demands for accountability, and we must use the energy they generate to constantly improve our organization. (5) Our organization must become and remain a learning organization. To do that, we must learn constantly, in every way possible, and share what we have learned throughout the organization. Everyone associated with us wants to find meaning in their contribution. We must constantly invest in praise and recognition.

Over the past decade—the turn of the century—West Virginia University (and, in fact, all of higher education) has again tried to reinvent itself, to meet the needs of a rapidly changing world. I am sure there are more lessons to be learned from our experiences, more lessons to be documented for posterity. I know I have not captured all the lessons that we have learned. But I hope I have you thinking: what have we learned? How can we pass it on?

The future is filled with uncertainty and the unexpected. But while there is much uncertainty ahead, there is one truth of which I am very sure: West Virginia University, with all of its complexity and challenges, will confront those uncertainties, and it will continue to serve society. This is because WVU is a student-centered learning community meeting the changing needs of our state and nation through a commitment to excellence in teaching, research, service, and technology. This is clearly one humbling, undeniable, and important truth that welcomes your next president.

Several years ago, in a State of the University address, I related an analogy from Mark Twain's *Life on the Mississippi*.[6] I have found myself reflecting on it again. Mark Twain writes about his own experience as a riverboat pilot who began his first day with wonder in his eyes, standing aboard his riverboat in awe of the mighty Mississippi.[7] He marveled at the trees forming a canopy over the river. He admired the ripples on the water, and as the day ended, he was thrilled at the beauty of the sunset melting crimson across the horizon. He felt like the luckiest person in the world—because he knew he would get to enjoy the Mississippi River every day and get paid for it.

As the years went by, the magic faded. The canopy of trees meant low-hanging branches that could fall and get caught in his wheel. The ripples in the water that were once so peaceful now reminded him that rocks were underneath the surface and could damage his boat. The beautiful sunset was now just a cue that he'd soon be piloting the riverboat in the dark. The riverboat captain lost sight of why he went to the river in the first place—he forgot his dream.

When I talk about *Life on the Mississippi*, the lesson for any of us, no matter our career, is to remember our dream and why we pursued it in the first place. I remember my first year like it was yesterday and can honestly say I have never forgotten why I was so excited and honored to be president of my alma mater. It is most clear at commencement, when the pride of the graduates is matched only by the joy of their families. When I shake the hand of an M.D. who I remember recruiting out of a rural West Virginia high school, I remember why I am a part of this great university. When I see Becky McCauley, a first-generation college student from West Virginia, rise to become the only student in the nation to win two of the country's most prestigious scholarships—the Goldwater Scholarship and the Truman Scholarship—I remember why we work so hard. I hope when you hear her thank the people of the university who mentored her, you will be reminded of how important you are in the lives of our students.

Whether you are the faculty advisor, the person who processes the research grants, or the dining-staff member who gives a smile when a student is overwhelmed in midterms, you make a difference every day; your job here is important. I challenge you to always remember why you came to the "river"—

why you wanted to make your life's work in higher education. I challenge you to remember the great privilege we enjoy. Granted, there are frustrations—sometimes it's the traffic, or the rush of advisees during registration time, or the long days to audit our accounts. But we should not lose sight of the "river," of what WVU is all about, and how many people depend upon us to help them realize their own dreams.

I plan to work hard this year—as hard as I ever have—never forgetting why I came to work here eleven years ago and why I came as a student some forty years ago. I hope you will continue to do all you can to keep our momentum going this year and beyond. People expect nothing less from those who constitute a flagship university.

NOTES

1   Rita Bornstein, "The Nature and Nurture of Presidents," *Chronicle of Higher Education* 52, no. 11 (2005), http://chronicle.com (accessed November 17, 2006).

2   Bornstein, "The Nature and Nurture of Presidents."

3   See appendix 2 for a chart comparing statistics from my arrival in Fall 1995 with the most recent data.

4   Robert Frost, "Stopping by the Woods on a Snowy Evening" in *The Poetry of Robert Frost*, ed. Edward Connery Latham (New York: Holt, Rinehart, and Winston, 1969), 224–225.

5   James M. Kouzes and Barry Z. Posner, *A Leader's Legacy* (San Francisco: Jossey-Bass Publishers, 2006), 11.

6   See "Staying on Track (1997)" in chapter 9.

7   Mark Twain, *Life on the Mississippi* (1883; Pleasantville, NY: Reader's Digest Association, 1987), 68–69. Citations are to the 1987 edition.

TWO

TEN CHARACTERISTICS OF A HIGHLY EFFECTIVE ORGANIZATION

2003

Since my undergraduate years, I have been very interested in the subject of leadership. I began reading leadership literature in earnest in 1976, after the publication of James MacGregor Burns's book, "Leadership."[1] On an increasing number of occasions over the years, I have been asked to speak on the topic. I have tried to summarize the lessons learned by our leadership team and pass them along to interested audiences. In doing so, I have drawn upon not only my own research and that of the many experts we have invited to campus in recent years, but also the practical experiences of the leadership team at West Virginia University. Eventually, the university, along with other organizations, sponsored a statewide conference to discuss the "best practices" of today's leaders.

With the help of our leadership team, I developed five major addresses on leadership and delivered them at the conference.

The first speech was called "Ten Characteristics of a Highly Effective Organization." I delivered it, in some form, to many diverse audiences over the past several years, always to groups of leaders, and always customized to the needs of the audience. Despite its rather simple format, it was recognized as one of the most important messages of my presidency. I think its appeal lay in its usefulness as a checklist for leaders with a new assignment.

After its presentation at a state leadership conference in 2003, this version of the speech was published by "The State Journal," a West Virginia weekly business magazine; it is representative of the content of the speech, which was the most requested presentation I was called upon to make during my presidency. On various occasions, these remarks were offered to several national audiences, often as a convention keynote address. Even smaller groups, such as the governing boards of not-for-profit organizations and the officers of the Mountaineer Parents Club, requested the presentation and used it in their volunteer efforts.

Since the mid-1970s, when James McGregor Burns wrote *Leadership*, his classic treatise on leadership, I have been fascinated by the subject of how some individuals are able to motivate others to act in their own self-interests.[2] Since Burns's book, leadership literature has grown voluminously. I have tried to read what I could of this genre of research and experience-based books. In addition, I have had experience in government, the private sector, and public higher education. I have made enough mistakes for one lifetime and have had the privilege to work with leaders in almost every sector. Over time, I have come to believe that there are characteristics that most highly effective organizations exhibit. These characteristics are consciously talked about by the leaders of the organizations and taught and modeled by the cadre involved in taking the organization from point A to point B.

Here are those characteristics:

1. *Clarity of the Organization's Mission*—The word "mission" has religious roots, and according to *The New Shorter Oxford English Dictionary*, the word is "an instance of being sent, especially to perform some function or service." I like a subsequent definition better: "a journey with a purpose."[3] The importance

of mission clarity cannot be overestimated. A sound mission tells you not only what the organization will do but also what it will not do. Mission creep is rampant in organizations as various units of the organization attempt to spread their wings. On occasion, the result can be disastrous, especially if the organization is not well-heeled enough to be "all things to all people," which very few are.

2. *The Power of the Leadership Vision*—In the movie *Apollo 13*, there is a scene in which one of the astronauts is asked by a congressman, "How did we get to the moon? Was it a miracle?"[4] The astronaut replies, "We just decided to do it, and millions of people helped us to get there." John Kennedy, our president in 1962, had set forth the vision clearly: "We will put a man on the moon and bring him back within ten years."[5] I remember watching him give that statement on television. What a vision. It had the effect of energizing not only NASA but also the country. In fact, the vision was realized in less than ten years, and the national need to energize the scientific community after Sputnik was realized because of that vision.

3. *Adherence to Shared Values Throughout the Organization*—In his book on leadership, James O'Toole talked about "Rushmorian character."[6] What he meant by this is that organizations can acquire and exhibit values which, over time, give them real character, just as the figures carved in stone on Mount Rushmore were admired for their true character. The point is that to be truly shared and held throughout the organization, values must be enforced by its leaders.

4. *Cohesive, Balanced Team of Leaders*—The biggest mistake organizations make is hiring someone just like the person who retired, was terminated, or left for another job. The point of hiring should be that it can be used to change the organization for the better. Therefore, we should ask the question, "What does the organization need right now?" That is the talent that should be hired. More importantly, leaders should never hire people just like themselves. Teams need to be balanced. We all have different talents. The author Bernice McCarthy argues that some of us can imagine the future, others are doers, others have

analytical minds, and others are people-oriented.[7] A good leader will assemble a balanced team and then build trust within it.

5. *Clear and Measurable Goals and Objectives*—Effective organizations establish clear and measurable goals and objectives for most people within the organization. It is not uncommon for an excellent board to work with its CEO to establish goals and objectives, which are then cascaded throughout the organization to create a sense of the importance of accomplishment, not just the effort.

6. *Mechanisms for External Feedback and Input*—Peter Drucker has often pointed out the importance of staying in touch with customers. In fact, he would argue that a significant percentage of every executive's time must be spent in understanding the customer base of the organization and its changing needs.[8] I know in my own work I am struck by how often our students change because society is changing and their parents are changing. Mechanisms such as free hotlines, focus groups, and problem solvers are common in highly effective organizations.

7. *A Desire to Learn Continuously*—As many, including motivator Norman Vincent Peale, have said, "When you stop learning, you stop growing." A good organization will have continuing education as one of its priorities. It will be modeled by the leading executives of the organization, but practiced throughout. Ossification is the death knell of an organization.

8. *Pursuit of Excellence*—Excellence is often the result of thoughtful determination of the organization's mission, vision, values, goals, and objectives. When the organization believes it is doing the right thing, it can persevere in the face of crises and criticism and meet almost any challenge. I am reminded of Winston Churchill, who was once asked to state the most significant lesson of World War II. His answer: "Never, never, . . . never give in."[9]

9. *Competent Planning and Decision-Making Processes*—Here there is room for improvement with practice. Have the right people been consulted?

Are customers included on task forces? Do we use both inside and outside points of view in making a decision? Are the people who are going to be held accountable for a solution involved in the decision to go forward? Are people being pushed hard enough? Or in the words of Ron Heifetz and Marty Linsky, authors of *Leadership On the Line*, are the leaders able to get up on the balcony and look down at the busy dance floor?[10] Strategic planning, strategic thinking, retreats, and other forms of planning and decision-making processes all have one thing in common—they are a conscious effort by the organization's leaders to do better.

10. *Periodic Celebrations of the Nobility of the Work, and of Collective Accomplishments*—We all like to be praised, and we all like to celebrate our successes. Competent organizations do this on a regular basis. At every commencement at West Virginia University, we recognize those who have given service to the university, created outstanding academic records while students at WVU, and exhibited the highest ideals of the academy. All effective organizations do the same thing. To paraphrase Victor Frankl, author of *Man's Search For Meaning*, if we but find the "why's" in life, the "how's" will take care of themselves.[11] Frankl was quoting an earlier philosopher, but his point was this: people are motivated when they understand the meaning of their work; people yearn for an alignment of their joys in life and their work. As one Chinese philosopher said, "Find a job that you love, and you will never work a day in your life."[12]

To these characteristics could be added many more. The important thing is that we think about how our organization can become more effective. We need good leaders in West Virginia and in this country, now more than ever. To a certain extent, leadership is an art, and people are born with charisma and talent. But leadership also comes with practice and conscious thinking about what we can do to make our organizations better. I hope this list of ten characteristics of a highly effective organization stimulates thought about how your organization can serve its role in society more effectively.

NOTES

1   James MacGregor Burns, *Leadership* (New York: Harper and Row, 1978).

2   "Leadership over human beings is exercised when persons with certain motives and purposes mobilize, in competition or conflict with others, institutional, political, psychological, and other resources so as to arouse, engage, and satisfy the motives of followers" (Burns, *Leadership* [New York: Harper and Row, 1978], 18).

3   *New Shorter Oxford English Dictionary on Historical Principles*, 5th ed. (Oxford: Oxford University Press, 2002), 1796.

4   *Apollo 13*, produced by Brian Grazer and directed by Ron Howard (Universal Pictures, 1995).

5   John F. Kennedy, Moon Speech at Rice University Stadium, Houston, Texas, September 12, 1962.

6   James O'Toole, *Leading Change: The Argument for Values-Based Leadership* (San Francisco: Jossey-Bass Publishers, 1996).

7   Bernice McCarthy, *4MAT in Action: Creative Lesson Plans for Teaching to Learning Styles with Right/Left Mode Techniques* (Oak Brook, IL: Excel, 1981).

8   Peter Drucker, *The Essential Drucker: Selections from the Management Works of Peter F. Drucker* (New York: HarperBusiness, 2001), 181–188; see also pages 20 and 24–25.

9   "[N]ever give in, never give in, never, never, never, never—in nothing, great or small, large or petty—never give in except to convictions of honor and good sense" (Winston Churchill, Never Give In! speech at Harrow School, October 29, 1941, in Winston S. Churchill, *Never Give In! The Best of Winston Churchill's Speeches* [New York: Hyperion, 2003], 307).

10   Ronald A. Heifetz and Marty Linsky, *Leadership on the Line: Staying Alive through the Dangers of Leading* (Boston: Harvard Business School Press, 2002), 51–73.

11   Victor Frankl, *Man's Search for Meaning: An Introduction to Logotherapy*, trans. Ilse Lasch, 3rd ed. (New York: Simon and Schuster, 1984), 9, paraphrasing Friedrich Nietzsche.

12   Confucius.

THREE

LIFELONG LEARNING FOR LEADERS AND ORGANIZATIONS

2004

This speech, the second in the West Virginia Leadership Conference series, emphasizes the importance of lifetime learning, not just for leaders, but also for the organizations they lead.

During my first year of college, the distinguished president of our university, Paul Miller, admonished those of us in the first-year class, "Continue learning across your entire lifetimes." I heard the words, but the convocation at which I heard them was so colorful, those first days in class so challenging, and the anticipation of our first football weekend so intense that I simply did not internalize them. As I progressed through my undergraduate years, I occasionally caught a glimpse of what he was suggesting to us.

But now, with three degrees and three careers behind me, I understand what he meant. I see it written large on a big screen and hear it repeated in imaginary surround sound. President Miller's admonition is one of the few important lessons of my lifetime of study and work. I see clearly now the importance of developing the skills of lifetime learning and honing the resultant intellectual curiosity. The value of lifetime learning is both ageless and time-less. I think this was true one thousand years ago, and I think it will be true one thousand years from now.

LEARNING TO LEARN, BOTH INSIDE AND OUTSIDE THE CLASSROOM

The ability to learn across one's lifetime is furthered through one's formal education. I was fortunate to have good teachers in the public school system of my state, and at West Virginia University, Oxford University, and Harvard Law School.

But I have always thought that learning outside the classroom was important. As a WVU student, I learned much from student activities. More recently, I premised many reforms at WVU on my belief that lifetime learning begins outside the classroom. After all, students at a traditional college usually attend class between fifteen and eighteen hours each week, and while those hours are critical, much more time is spent studying, socializing, participating in clubs, and attending campus events. During our first-year orientation program, we stress the importance of making choices about what to do with time outside the classroom.

LIFETIME LEARNING SKILLS

Among the most important lifetime-learning skills are the ability to comprehend and analyze information and the closely related intellectual confidence to read or hear original works and develop one's own interpretation of their meaning. Lifetime learning involves the confidence to attempt to apply what one knows in the workplace. It also includes the ability to exchange ideas with others through written and oral communication; time-management skills, which enable one to set aside time for learning; and the courage to risk making mistakes and learning from them. Lifetime learning depends upon fact-finding skills, including the ability to collect and analyze information before acting. Doing so becomes second nature to a lifetime learner. Sitting in meetings, the best leaders will learn as much as they can before making a major decision.

We all do this to some extent. Parents learn to check out a number of colleges before committing to paying tuition. Young home-buyers look at the market before taking out a mortgage. Then, as life goes by, we begin to rely on data accumulated on prior occasions. Gradually, our intuition becomes more and more informed. We think before we act, but it takes less time because of our experiences.

HARD WORK REQUIRED

It's not easy to keep learning. For example, public speaking requires practice and a teacher to nurture and encourage you. Mastery of oral communication is critical to the success of the modern leader. Winston Churchill, for example, saved a nation (perhaps the Western world as we know it) with his words. He practiced writing and speaking throughout his lifetime and was truly prepared when, in his sixties, it was time to remind England that he had "nothing to offer except blood, toil, tears and sweat."[1] When requesting the lend-lease program, he told FDR, "Give us the tools, and we will finish the job."[2] After one important battle in Egypt, Churchill said, "This is not the end. It is not even the beginning of the end. But it is, perhaps, the end of the beginning."[3] Words like these don't come easily.

Analytical skills don't come easily either. I am sure that I frustrated my high school and college teachers, who taught me to use more than instincts and precepts learned by rote memory when addressing an issue. When I was a student at Oxford, there were roughly seventy-five professors of philosophy. Logic and precision were valued, not just in the one-student-per-class tutorials and weekly papers, but during dinner, in social discourse, and even in the pubs. It was an amazing place, where thinking clearly was part of the fun, not just an activity used to earn a grade.

Harvard Law School, like all law schools, takes the analytical process even further, demanding that law students come to a reasonable degree of certainty about the consequences of a legal argument or a factual pattern they have never seen before. Years after law school, I came to understand that the ability to judge risks associated with a proposed action is a learned skill, not an inherited trait. Patients and clients entrust their life and property to professionals, and depend upon professional judgments gained from a lifetime of learning when they put their futures into the hands of someone else.

BENEFITS OF LIFETIME LEARNING

While lifetime skills are tough to obtain, once acquired they bestow many benefits—wisdom and perspective, better decisions, better health, and joy—upon our lives.

PERSPECTIVE

As a result of our learning inside and outside the classroom, we gradually acquire perspective. Understanding the context in which we live, learn, and lead is very important, and it is an acquired skill. This is the skill Heifetz and Linsky, authors of *Leadership on the Line*, call "getting on the balcony," or gaining a perspective on what is happening in one's field or in the larger society.[4]

Gradually, as we learn, we become better at making decisions at work and in our personal lives. We also learn to make decisions more quickly. We learn the value of learning from our mistakes. Experience makes us wiser if, and only if, we continue to learn. Experience only counts if we have learned from it. New information gained by lifetime learning, added to life's biggest teacher—experience—tends to make us better at what we do the longer we do it.

HEALTH BENEFITS

The aging process slows some things down, notably coordination, strength, and stamina. But there are opera singers, athletes, violinists, and actors who believe the notion that to get older is to slow down mentally.

Scientists have found there is an added benefit to lifetime learning: it may help us preserve our memory. They are now telling us to continue using our brain by doing everything from reading to working crossword puzzles. A study conducted at the Rush Alzheimer's Disease Center found that frequent participation in cognitively stimulating activities is associated with a reduced risk of Alzheimer's disease.[5]

ENJOYMENT

Of course, the big bonus paid to lifetime learners is the true enjoyment and happiness that a habit of lifetime learning brings. If, when we travel, we seek to understand the culture visited, not just observe it, our journeys will be more exciting. Our reading can take us to times in the future and in the past and to places near and far. What joy I have found in reading about the founding fathers, Churchill, Plato, and Caesar. I am becoming more and more interested in the marvels of poetry.

In short, I want to learn more as life goes by, primarily because I enjoy the very act of learning so much. I have an image in my mind as I approach my sixties. It involves me hooking up a wire from my head to the heads of my children and transmitting all I know—good and bad—into their brains. Oh, if I could only share so easily! Alas, it took a lifetime to learn what I know, under tutelage from teachers, mentors, coworkers, and friends. Trying new things and making mistakes was part of the process. Only now do I see the opportunities that I missed to learn even more and the good fortune I had to learn what I did.

Education, Cicero said, is the greatest gift we can give the Republic.[6] But a good education is, as Dr. Miller suggested, acquired across our lifetimes—not just in school. Lifetime learning is an attitude about how we intend to lead our lives—"I will get as much out of this class, out of this relationship, out of this job, out of this book, and out of this visit as I possibly can. I will make lifetime learning a habit."

To Cicero's admonition I would add that lifetime learning is the greatest gift we can give ourselves. So read, explore, travel, and make new friends across your lifetime. Dr. Miller was right: lifetime learning is an important habit for leaders.

ORGANIZATIONAL LEARNING

The benefits of lifelong learning are not confined to individuals. I believe that an organization can become a perpetual learner if its members constantly seek to absorb and apply new information. The commitment to build a learning organization starts at the highest levels of leadership. If organizational leaders establish a culture of lifetime organizational learning, it will radiate downward throughout the organization. Creating a learning organization, in my experience, can be surprisingly straightforward.

TEN WAYS TO CREATE A LEARNING ORGANIZATION

1. *Engage in regular retreats as a part of the strategic planning process.* Effective organizations engage in planning and have competent planning processes. My own view is that such processes must provide for periodic assessment of the competitive environment in which an organization operates. Every day, we are bombarded with phone calls and e-mails demanding our attention, and our calendars are filled with important meetings and events. The day-to-day work of an organization is vital, but sometimes its relentless demands make it difficult to step back and see the big picture.

Retreats and planning are intertwined. It has been said that planning is learning followed by action.[7] The learning process often involves an environmental scan of the organization and external trends affecting it, as well as an analysis of the data uncovered.

The best way to address such issues is to retreat to a place away from the workplace. Typically, the simple act of meeting in a new environment inspires people to look at problems in new ways, and inventive solutions result.

Planning retreats enables organizational leaders to examine data, share information and concerns, and build consensus regarding the organization's direction. During the past year, we have held several strategic planning retreats for members of our leadership team. In turn, our vice presidents and executive officers often discuss the insights from these retreats—and ways to implement them—at subsequent retreats with the key leaders reporting to them, who in turn hold retreats with staff members from our individual units.

2. *Give your customers a prime seat at the table.* It is absolutely vital to seek feedback from your customers, your clients, your patients, and others you serve. Such feedback is not always readily available, so it is important to establish a vehicle for obtaining it.

Students and their parents are very important "customers" for WVU. The education of students is central to our purpose as a university, and the quality of education we provide is the ultimate standard of our success or failure as an organization.

For this reason, it behooves us to pay close attention to the concerns of students, parents, and their ideas for improving the university. Focus groups are one way to seek student and parental input, and I regularly lead such focus groups myself.

A phone line we instituted for parents who have questions or concerns has provided an even more effective way of gathering parental input. The Mountaineer Parents Club Helpline is answered by a parent advocate who responds to parents' concerns within one business day. She also listens to their suggestions and passes them along to appropriate institutional leaders. These suggestions are taken very seriously.

For example, we once received a flurry of calls complaining about the confusing format of our student bills. After meeting with parents and discussing the problem, we simplified the format, and the complaints stopped. Simplifying the bills' format also led to a significant saving in resources.

3. *Listen to others who care about and support the organization.* I also believe it is important to spend time listening to people outside of the organization who have a genuine concern for its future and expertise pertinent to its effective operation. Obviously, we try to listen to the governor, the members of the legislature, and to other state policymakers.

On our campuses, we have numerous groups whose members give us direction, offer fresh perspectives, and render crucial advice. The most important of such groups is our governing body, the WVU Board of Governors. Its members are exceptionally talented people who have built successful careers in diverse fields. They have an awareness of trends that may affect us and problem-solving approaches that we would not have considered.

WVU also has a network of visiting committees—purely advisory bodies whose several hundred members meet regularly to advise leaders of each WVU college, school, and other university programs. College and school visiting committees are generally populated by those who have distinguished themselves in the career fields associated with the college or school. Who better to advise deans and faculty members on such issues as the preparation that employers are seeking in new graduates? Information clearly flows in the other direction as well—to advisory board members from university leaders. As board members learn more about the university, they make more informed decisions. This strengthens the organization's effectiveness and can lead to good results.

4. *To the extent possible, keep everyone in your organization in the information loop.* Open, participatory meetings of senior staff members assure that organizational leaders are knowledgeable and cooperative. Because such meetings encourage a collaborative decision-making process, they create "buy-in" for the organization's vision and direction.

At WVU, I meet twice each week with vice presidents and our other key leaders. A flip chart is in place in the conference room, and I generally begin the meeting by writing down the topics I want to address. As they come in the door, meeting participants are free to add topics that they believe the group should discuss.

A typical meeting involves a thorough discussion of the most important of these issues. Each member of the group gains an understanding of the issue in question and contributes to the decision-making process. The transparent nature of this process assures that senior leaders feel fully invested in critical decisions facing the university. We absorb all the information that should be considered before we decide on an issue. As a result, individual decisions made outside our joint meetings are better and more informed.

By encouraging senior members of an organization to offer input into our future, participatory planning meetings create a sense of teamwork. This activity, in turn, encourages the organization's leaders to adopt similarly participatory practices with their own staff members, and for those staff members to do the same with their employees, until an open communication style permeates the entire organization. At a large organization such as WVU, keeping individual employees informed about the organization's goals—and seeking their input on ways to meet those goals—is a challenge. Formal channels of communication with employees (which at WVU include the Faculty Senate, our classified Staff Council, student government, an Intranet, e-mail bulletins, and a twice-monthly publication) help to foster communication.

5. *Aggressively seek to learn industry best practices.* I strongly encourage senior WVU leaders to attend national meetings and conferences in their fields—but only with the clear understanding that they will formally share the ideas they discover with their colleagues when they return.

As president of WVU, I participate in meetings of the groups representing universities in Washington, the Big East, the BCS, and the National 4-H Council; meetings called by state and federal agencies; and retreats of presidents sponsored by charitable foundations. All have proven valuable, not just to me, but also to the organizations I lead. Let's just call the payoff "the information dividend." Vice presidents and executive officers also attend national conferences and share the information they glean from them with their employees.

Often, WVU administrators are asked to give national conference presentations about their own innovative approaches, such as successful revitalization of the student living- and learning-environment on campus. Being asked to make such a presentation is an honor, which elevates the stature of the entire state. However, what we learn while preparing these presentations is their most valuable aspect.

6. *Be receptive to advice when it comes from outside the organization—especially when it comes from people who have distinguished themselves as experts in their fields.* I have already told you about the planning conducted by our senior university leaders. I have found that this group's meetings are also an excellent venue for professional development. From time to time, I invite an expert from outside the university to share management wisdom with group members. Our leaders enjoy the opportunity to hear from well-known experts, and they respond enthusiastically.

Recently, for example, former WVU president Gene Budig—a Princeton University professor who is also the former president of Major League

Baseball's American League—spoke about leadership issues. Other speakers have included Fortune 500 executives, government leaders, consultants, and a variety of leaders in fields other than education. I invited these people on the theory that leadership issues cross over various "domains of expertise," to use the words of Howard Gardner.[8]

The value of guest speakers is not limited to upper management, however. Senior university officials often invite guest speakers to address their employees. If you want to generate excitement among your employees, I urge you to consider the role guest speakers could play in your organization.

7. *Encourage acquisition of new skills, and update the old.* WVU has helped to sponsor the Entrepreneurial Leadership Conference, which is a great example of continuing education. The format of this conference—in which participants read a book that forms the basis of breakout sessions and then attend a talk given by the book's author—has promoted rich discussion on all aspects of leadership. The fact that participants represent a diverse range of professions makes our discussions particularly interesting. I know that I will return to campus with a bevy of new ideas to share with my colleagues.

8. *Hire lifelong learners.* Obviously we try to hire people who have demonstrated outstanding leadership at other organizations. From within, we find people such as Chris Martin, our new vice president for institutional advancement, who started at WVU as an assistant professor and most recently served as our journalism dean. An experienced journalist and award-winning teacher, she is contributing new approaches to promoting WVU around the state and nation.

From outside the organization we welcome people like Marie Foster Gnage, the first woman president of WVU at Parkersburg. Dr. Gnage, formerly the senior vice president for academic affairs at Raritan Valley Community College in New Jersey, has demonstrated the qualities needed to strengthen WVU Parkersburg's presence in its region.

The university's social justice program assures that we hire highly qualified people from a variety of backgrounds, who enrich our university with their unique perspectives. Diversity in the workplace is a great teacher!

In addition to professional expertise and proven leadership ability, we seek one thing in all our candidates for high-level positions—a true excitement for continuous lifetime learning. We are looking for people who believe they still have things to learn, and who inspire others around them to do the same. These people, in turn, hire and promote employees who share their love of learning and, in this way, help to extend the culture of lifetime learning.

9. *When you learn something new, share it.* As a leader, I constantly seek information that can help me do my job better. When I find it—whether in books, in journal articles, in reports from other universities, in news items, or just from insight—I make a point of sharing it with appropriate members of my management team.

I know that they, in turn, share it with their colleagues and employees, and more importantly, they follow my example by sharing their own discoveries with me, their peers, and their staff members. If you want your employees to share interesting ideas with you and with each other, be sure to act as a model by sharing the things you're learning with them.

10. *Celebrate practitioners of the art of lifetime learning.* To maintain the culture of learning, we regularly celebrate the organization's collective accomplishments and the nobility of its work. These celebrations enable us to reward individuals whose achievements have made an impact on WVU. By lifting up learning and innovation, we motivate others to continue learning and improving.

I won't say that we have succeeded in fully implementing a learning culture in all areas of WVU, but by following the ten practices I have outlined—and particularly by hiring people who love learning—we are moving closer to that goal every day.

CONCLUSION

The National Council on Competitiveness, which is composed of leading business, government, and education executives, believes that America's future strength will be in its ability to foster innovation faster than other economies.[9] Innovation is fostered by learning and discovery. Organizations and leaders who continue to learn are critical to America's future. Lifetime learning, I have tried to suggest, is a worthy value for both leaders and the organizations they lead. Lifetime learning is not always easy; it requires a lifetime of work and change—an investment well worth the dividend.

Two of the better known athletes from WVU are basketball greats "Hot Rod" Hundley and Jerry West. A fan once asked Hundley, "Who was the better player—you or Jerry West?" Hundley said that coming out of high school, he was clearly the better player. Having played basketball with a passion throughout his childhood, he came to college with phenomenal skills.

But, he said, in college, Jerry West practiced above and beyond the call of the coaches every day. When they went pro, West continued to learn all he could about the game and to learn from every mistake (most of which he didn't make twice). A few years into the pros, Hundley noted, "I was looking for a radio job and Jerry West's silhouette was used as the logo for the new National Basketball Association. Why? He got better every day he played!"

There is a lesson here for all of us. We all need to get better every day we lead.

NOTES

1   Winston Churchill, Blood, Toil, Tears and Sweat speech to House of Commons, May 13, 1940, in *Churchill, Never Give In!*, 206.

2   Winston Churchill, Give Us the Tools, broadcast by the BBC, February 9, 1941, in *Churchill, Never Give In!*, 262.

3   Winston Churchill, The Bright Gleam of Victory speech at Lord Mayor's Luncheon, Mansion House, London, November 10, 1942, in *Churchill, Never Give In!*, 342.

4   Ronald A.Heifetz and Marty Linsky, *Leadership on the Line: Staying Alive through the Dangers of Leading* (Boston: Harvard Business School Press, 2002), 51–73.

5   R. S. Wilson, L. L. Barnes, and D. A. Bennett, "Assessment of lifetime participation of cognitively stimulating activities," *Journal of Clinical and Experimental Neuropsychology* 25 (2003): 634–642.

6   Cicero said, "What greater gift can we offer the republic than to teach and instruct our youth?"

7   See Arie P. De Gues, "Planning as Learning," *Harvard Business Review* 66.2 (1998): 70–74.

8   Howard Gardner, *Leading Minds: An Anatomy of Leadership* (New York: Basic Books, 1996).

9   Council on National Competitiveness, "Compete Home Page," http://www. compete .org/ (accessed January 19, 2007).

FOUR

BUILDING LEADERSHIP CAPACITY

2006

The next presentation in the leadership conference series deals with the topic of attracting, retaining, and developing leaders within an organization and, therefore, how to build organizational leadership strength. Using the Socratic Method so common in colleges of law, I decided to format these remarks as a series of questions.

The reaction to this format from a very diverse audience, which ranged from MBA students to chief executive officers of major corporations, was mostly positive. The original speech was delivered from an outline. What appears below is the result of converting the outline to text format.

Let's begin with an obvious question: Why take up your time to discuss the topic of leadership development?

The more I thought about this question, the more obvious it became that every organization, large or small, public or private, must think about how to attract and retain a competent leadership team and work continuously to make it more effective. In fact, leadership is a skill that should be taught and valued throughout the entire organization. Intense global competition has made it much less certain that boards and chief executive officers can count on lifetime loyalty to the organization. In addition, as I have suggested elsewhere, leader fatigue is common due to the robustness of competition in the global economy. These trends are exacerbated by the emergence of more headhunter firms and ease of mobility within, and even among, industries.

To a significant extent, out-migration of leaders is inevitable. It is simply impossible for everyone to find themselves at the top of the organization, even the most respected members. I was told by a friend in a position to know that when Jack Welch retired as chairman and CEO of General Electric, there were three announced candidates to succeed him: Jeff Immelt, the ultimate choice; Bob Nardelli; and Jim McNerney. When the selection process was concluded, Nardelli left immediately to become chairman and CEO of The Home Depot. At the same time, McNerney became chairman and CEO of 3M, and he later went on to the same position at Boeing. Before that, when Welch was selected to replace Reg Jones, he was selected over three other candidates, all internal to the company. One, Ed Hood, stayed with the company and became a vice chairman. The other two candidates, Stan Gault and Tom Vanderslice, left to become CEOs of other companies (Gault went to Rubbermaid and then Goodyear; Vanderslice went to a computer company). Obviously, all of these individuals were fine men and excellent leaders, but there can be only one CEO at General Electric.

Every organization needs new ideas. Old-fashioned attitudes at the top may inhibit progress on many fronts. The emergence of new leaders and the sharing of leadership duties provides new ideas and new insights into strategic planning efforts and execution strategies; ethics and organizational culture are guided by leaders at all levels. Finally, when a crisis occurs, leadership cannot be in short supply.

What are the consequences of failing to embrace a leadership development approach in your organization? The failure to recognize the need for leadership development obviously leads to many adverse events: attrition of the best leaders, less readiness and change resiliency, low morale, higher recruiting and training costs, lack of self-direction, destructive competition within the organization, myopic outlooks, wrong-headed attitudes, and failures of ethics and legal compliance.

The failure to develop leadership at almost any level may impact the entire organization. At our university, hundreds of us work at increasing enrollment because it is the lifeblood of our university finances. All it takes is one person to answer the phone and not be helpful, or one encounter with a professor who speaks discouragingly about the institution, or one failure to follow up and send information to a prospective student to change a person's mind about applying to WVU. In short, the work of hundreds can be undone by one.

If you don't think leadership development at every level is important, here's another example. Think about Abu Ghraib, where young soldiers who were shielded from scrutiny made decisions that apparently lacked judgment and were even illegal. The results clearly show us why developing leadership at *every* level of the organization is crucial; the decisions of a few relatively low-ranking soldiers ended *right on top of the desk of the president of the United States.*

What those of us attending this conference have in common is that we need all people in our organization to act as leaders. My message is straightforward: as a leader in your organization, you must internalize the importance of leadership development, and you must make a commitment to developing future leaders and leadership capacity. How can leadership development be made a part of organizational culture? Well, to say something Yogi Berra might say, it all begins in the beginning! Leadership development begins by recruiting persons with a desire and capacity to lead.

By hiring certain people, leaders send a powerful signal to others in the organization. Brad and Geoff Smart call it "Topgrading" in their book by the same name.[1] The most important leadership skill is building a highly talented team.

Topgrading means identifying A players for every open position, not just for a few key slots. According to *Topgrading*, A players hire other A's, but B's hire C's.

If you have too many B players in your middle management, you'll have too many C players in your workforce, and this will not help succession planning in your organization. Brad and Geoff Smart estimate that the cost of a failed hire is fifteen times the base salary of the position. Peter Drucker has asserted that personnel decisions are the most consequential and the hardest to "unmake."[2] So, here are some questions to think about:

- How involved are you in the recruitment process?
- Do you interview candidates for most important positions?
- If not, at what level of positions in the organization do you interview candidates?
- How do you screen candidates for their passion to lead?
- Does character matter to those who hire in your organization?
- How do you find out what a person is truly like and how they are likely to react under pressure?

Another way an organization can emphasize leadership development is to make sure that organizational job descriptions match their corresponding job assignments. It is the leader's job to make sure that each employee has a reasonable chance of success in the job they are chosen to do. Job descriptions set expectations, which can only be exceeded if they are known. One authority calls this matching process "Job Sculpting," which he defines as the art of matching people to jobs that resonate with the activities that make them truly happy.[3] Too often, says Douglas McGregor of Harvard, we fail to recognize that people work because they want to reach job-related goals, not because they are forced to work by a commanding management-structure.[4]

Here again, there are questions that are pertinent:

- Are job descriptions important in your organization?
- What expectations do job assignments set for employees?
- Can a leader be truly evaluated without a job description or job assignment?
- Do job descriptions in your organization contemplate risk taking and creative activity?

It is also important to build a culture of diversity among organizational leaders. The culture of your organization should reflect diversity of present and future leaders. Diversity strengthens the culture of leadership. Diversity here includes not just race and gender but a variety of backgrounds and aptitudes.

Working women often have a tough time facing the challenges presented by the modern workplace. They need to demonstrate their value in a male-dominated culture by gaining access to challenging assignments and being given appropriate support. They need mentors and other support as much as anyone else.

Persons of color face their own challenges. Often feeling alone and unsupported, they face pressure to act as role models, act as mentors, and combat historical prejudice. "First generation" professionals from lower economic and social strata also face workplace challenges. Their cultural backgrounds are often worlds apart from the norm, so networks are lacking, and there are frequently too few role models who empathize with their backgrounds and values.

Generational differences present some challenges in the workplace. Workers under thirty-five tend to be less loyal to a company or brand, want to be able to give input right away rather than work their way up a chain, are not afraid to make decisions, and are eager to network. The most talented will be in great demand.

A very important related point is this: organizational decisions should reflect the input of multiple leaders. The logic of a new book called *The Wisdom of Crowds*, by James Surowiecki, is compelling: under almost all circumstances, teams make better decisions than do individuals.[5] At a lecture on our campus, Surowiecki argued that this is true for team estimates of both present and future situations, and that the conclusion holds for complex problems as much as for straightforward ones. He argues that "group think" can result from a lack of diversity in the workplace.

I believe that differences of opinion, based on differences in background, improve decision making in the context of team decision making. You need a devil's advocate in your group. You need the perspective of someone with an "elite" education, as well as someone who scrapped their way through community college and a state university. You need the point of view of someone who is a new citizen of this country. Being part of a minority gives a person one perspective, and being part of a majority gives him or her another. Diversity is not only a matter of fairness; it is a matter of effective decision making. Can you answer these questions?

- Do you know your team, really?
- Is it truly diverse?
- Do you care if it is?
- Do you value each member for what he or she adds?
- Did you invite to this conference anyone from your organization who needs a boost in order to climb the leadership ladder?

Potential leaders need opportunities to demonstrate their talents and build their confidence through special and challenging assignments. From time to time, talented people need special assignments that push them outside of their comfort zone, help them gain confidence, and give them a chance to lead others from different departments and fields. Such experiences help people at different levels in the organization gain a more global perspective, and will also help those in the top administrative positions better understand the organization's potential.

Challenges help people to learn, to find solutions to problems, to use strategic lenses, to face adversity, to become better leaders, to gain self-respect, to be more sensitive to others, to determine one's own limitations, and to become more flexible. Challenging assignments are analogous to physical exercise— strength training, flexibility, and aerobics. "No pain, no gain," as a physical trainer would say. Often, talented people are doers, and for that reason, leaders in positions of authority tend to lean on them. But do thinkers get a chance to lead in your organization?

There is another very important reason to give more people in your organization a turn at leading. The pandemic-flu warnings suggest that 40 percent of your workforce could be affected. Suppose 40 percent of your workforce was out for an extended period. Suppose *you* are out for an extended period of time. Ask yourself these questions:

- Do you delegate real challenges even though you might handle them better and more quickly yourself?
- Who are your go-to people? Are there others you never ask to undertake special assignments?
- Could you do more to provide them with leadership-development opportunities?
- Could you do more to challenge non-performers?

Leaders at the top should model personal growth and a goal orientation for other leaders to see. Tools such as goal-setting start at the top. Your goals should include technical-skill development as well as interpersonal-skill development. New-member orientation is also very important as a means of teaching employees that the mission and vision of the organization is critical. Similarly, good leaders offer their team members feedback collected from multiple sources. In a lecture on our campus, Buzz Shaw, a former president of Syracuse University, argued that individual plans for improvement are best. They avoid generalities, focus on specific behaviors, and suggest specific improvements.

Good potential leaders will want to know their own strengths and weaknesses as seen by others. Here are some questions to ponder:

- What are your own strengths and weaknesses?
- Do you have personal goals for yourself?
- Do you expect others in your organization to have goals?
- Do you have formal reviews of employees?
- Are these about future development, past performance, or both?
- What informal cues do you send about what you value in employees?
- Are your employees comfortable giving you, a leader, feedback?

Potential and rising leaders within the organization need the opportunity to grow through personal interaction with senior leaders, leaders in other domains of expertise, and organizational peers. Such opportunities can be created by simply riding with an up-and-coming leader to a conference and chatting about lessons learned in life. More formal opportunities are available, including seminars and organizational retreats. Today, some firms are offering to pay for formal coaching and are encouraging informal networking through the payment of dues and sponsorships. Ironically, although these opportunities are rare in most organizations, they are utilized by college basketball teams; players study film together; talk about offensive schemes at the chalkboard; and participate in skills practices, individual coaching sessions, and team dinners. Should your future leaders be given the learning opportunities that college basketball players enjoy?

Look to other groups and fields for benchmarks and examples. Too often we limit our points of comparison to prior years' results or the efforts of other divisions within our own organization. Yet we all have much to learn from other industries. If you run a residence-hall system, ask why your favorite hotel is successful. If you have significant relationships with customers, ask yourself how you determine your own favorite products. Do you make your choices, at least in part, based on the service you enjoy when you buy or return certain merchandise? Think of one business you go to often (a restaurant, a bank, a store), and ask yourself why you go there. Think of someone you admire. What qualities make that person so rare? Can you or others develop those qualities?

Finally, good leaders always acknowledge and celebrate leadership initiative and skill when they see it. This can be done both formally and informally. Universities are known for giving awards to donors and scholars, but how often do we honor workers on campus? Public-recognition awards, personal e-mails from the boss, and listings in a public place can be a cost-free way of saying thanks for a job well done. But bonuses, pay raises, and promotions really get others' attention. Is your reward system adequate? Do your rewards include both monetary incentives and recognition awards?

To conclude, I suggest to you that all leaders must recognize a duty or obligation to develop the leadership capacity of their organizations. In one sense, these actions—leadership-development activities—are a moral responsibility of competent leaders. If leaders fail in these activities, they are focusing on themselves rather than on the organizations they are leading into the future. In all great organizations, more than one leader is present. Recognition of this fact is more than humility; it is recognition of the true nature of leadership. It is an interactive process among leaders.

To paraphrase James MacGregor Burns, true leaders stand on the shoulders of those they lead.[6] Generals must rely on privates and sergeants to take the lead. Coaches must rely on players who are leaders. Businesses must rely on division managers to boost profits. University presidents must rely on deans and faculty chairs to ensure quality across disciplines. If we truly care about our organizations, we will want to see the young lieutenants develop—they are future generals. We will want to see players mature—they are future floor coaches. We want our division managers to do well—they are future CEOs. And we want faculty and deans to do well—they are the future vice presidents and presidents. This leads to one final question: What are three things you can start doing in your organization that will develop the leadership capacity in everyone who wants to lead, and thereby make your organization more effective?

NOTES

1   Bradford Smart and Geoff Smart, *Topgrading: How Leading Companies Win by Hiring, Coaching and Keeping the Best People* (Paramus, NJ: Prentice Hall Press, 1999).

2   Peter Drucker, *Classsic Drucker: Essential Wisdom of Peter Drucker from the Pages of Harvard Business Review* (Boston, MA: Harvard Business School Publishing, 2006). See also Peter Drucker, *The Effective Executive* (New York: Harper and Row, 1966), 32–33.

3   Timothy Butler and James Waldroop, "Job Sculpting: The Art of Retaining Your Best People," *Harvard Business Review* 77, no. 5 (1999): 144–152.

4   Douglas McGregor, *Human Side of Enterprise* (New York: McGraw Hill, 1960) 45–57.

5   James Surowiecki, *The Wisdom of Crowds: Why the Many Are Smarter than the Few and How Collective Wisdom Shapes Business, Economies, Societies, and Nations* (New York: Doubleday, 2004).

6   "The role of the 'great man' . . . is all the more legitimate and powerful if top leaders help make their followers into leaders. Only by standing on their shoulders can true greatness in leadership be achieved" (James MacGregor Burns, *Leadership* [New York: Harper and Row, 1978], 443).

FIVE

LEADER OVERLOAD

THE OPERATIONAL RISKS OF A ROBUST ORGANIZATIONAL AGENDA

2005

Our leadership team was a strong and experienced group of dedicated people. It was aggressive, and it developed an aggressive agenda to advance the university. After many years together, the team members decided to reflect on the operational risks of a robust agenda.

This speech, another in the series delivered to the West Virginia Leadership Conference, is the result of that reflection and a limited review of literature devoted to this topic.

INTRODUCTION

In most organizations, large and small, and in every sector, "leader overload" is a common occurrence. It sometimes spreads like a contagious illness. A normally competent leader's inappropriate behavior, inability to determine correct priorities, and inability to execute effectively usually lead to organizational stress and ineffectiveness. At times, organizations become ineffective simply because their leaders are overloaded.

Most of us have read President Teddy Roosevelt's well-known observation that genuine leaders climb into the arena of life and eagerly take the risks associated with being an active decision-maker.[1] Over the past decade, we have certainly been active at West Virginia University, and we have had our share of both successes and failures. Both have informed us, but failure has taught us more. These remarks are offered in a spirit of humility, in the hope that sharing what we have learned will prove useful to you in your own efforts to lead.

At WVU, the discussions that have followed instances of overload have informed all of us, and today we are focusing on preventing overload. While we will never be entirely successful, we are better off for having spent time thinking about the subject. My colleagues deserve much of the credit for the concepts in this paper. Credit should also be given to the research and thinking of Dr. Jennifer Fisher, who has been on the staff of the WVU president for a decade and who is keenly aware of the characteristics of effective leaders. She has assisted us for more than a decade as we have sought a better understanding of the characteristics of good, effective leaders. Credit is also due to Chad Proudfoot, a graduate assistant in the WVU Office of the President, who searched through ten years of *Harvard Business Review* journals to add authenticity and color to our own anecdotal understanding of this subject.

RECOGNIZING LEADER OVERLOAD

Assuming that an organization, whether small or large, is effective at developing a relevant agenda, and assuming the leaders of the organization exhibit drive and ambition, a robustness of operations will become the norm over time. As the organization gets very busy, confidence and optimism will be part of its collective personality, resources will begin to flow in to fund initiatives, and associates will offer to "partner" in new ventures. And, of course, the unexpected will inevitably occur, presenting new opportunities and challenges.

It is at "this moment in time," to use a musical phrase, that the operational risks of a robust agenda will emerge. There is an iceberg nature to leadership overload. The signs that an organization is getting out of control may seem like several discrete problems arising at the same time, but it is much more likely that what has developed is a more chronic and underlying condition of leader overload. When leaders are overloaded, the organization as a whole becomes overloaded. When leaders are overloaded, their effectiveness declines. Here are a few signs of overload:

1. *Loss of focus by team members*: Loss of focus is really our failure to discriminate among competing priorities. Often overload is present when team members begin working equally hard on unequal tasks; focusing on urgent, but unimportant tasks; and giving inadequate attention to important tasks.

In 2002, an article in the *Harvard Business Review* asserts, "Fully 90% of managers squander their time in all sorts of ineffective activities. In other words, a mere 10% of managers spend their time in a committed, purposeful, and reflective manner."[2] The author cites loss of focus as one key manifestation of this particular symptom of overload.

2. *Poor execution by leaders who are normally competent and reliable*: When your best managers begin making common mistakes, leader overload may be present. Signs of poor execution include cost overruns, lawsuits arising during execution, missed deadlines, assignments of impossibly short deadlines, agenda clutter, corners being cut, and just simple carelessness.

3. *Excessive optimism and lack of serious scrutiny of projects*: When normally competent managers begin routinely overestimating their capabilities, overload is probably part of the reason. When we are pressed, it is more popular to be an optimist with the boss than a skeptic. The results can be unexpected failures (such as the Challenger disaster), underestimation of costs, frequent

internal arguments over accountability for outcomes, difficulty reaching consensus, and the frequent need for redesign or rescheduling of projects.

Why are we overly optimistic? First, good leaders foster an optimistic and
"can do" attitude. After a few successes, we all begin to believe that we can take
on more and more work. Second, strong team members do not want to let
the boss down. Third, leaders can inadvertently foster excessive optimism. As
Edward M. Hallowell asserts, "Companies that ask their employees to do too
much at once tend to reward those who say yes to overload while punishing
those who choose to focus and say no."[3] This inevitably leads to some members of the organization being overloaded, in part due to their inability to say
no. We are often our own worst enemy.

4. *Customer abandonment*: Customer abandonment leads to loss of income,
declining reserves, and the inability to act when necessary for lack of funds.
There are numerous examples in the business world of companies that diver-
sify their products so much, they lose their identity and the loyalty of their
customer base. Most of you saw the recent Hardee's commercials that told us
the chain had strayed and was back to focusing on hamburgers, so they hoped
customers would come back to what they used to love about Hardee's.

The discipline it takes to focus energies on the core mission of the organization can be the difference in a company's survival. When leaders see a loss
of resources or decline in support, there is a possibility that the mistakes and
problems from an overloaded agenda have taken a toll on the organization's
support base.

5. *Abandonment of organizational values*: Overload is present when leaders use poor judgment about matters important to the organization's values.
Manifestations of this symptom include external editorial criticism, poor labor
relations, falsified reports, unexpected resignations from respected colleagues,
and a leader's sleepless nights and self-doubt about whether he or she is doing the right thing. When a leader sees these things happening, it is time to

examine whether the organization has abandoned, or inconsistently applied, its values.

6. *Loss of leadership stamina, low morale, and loss of organizational energy*: Reports of low morale, lack of participation in meetings, and frequent illness among employees and staff indicate that leaders are tired and that the organization is suffering. This is especially notable when a normally productive employee shows signs of adverse change or frustration.

7. *Loss of board and stakeholder alignment and support*: Board micromanagement and public displays of division within the team or lack of alignment among stakeholders can be symptomatic of the overload illness. These usually signal inadequate attention to communication due to the press of business (i.e., the robustness of the agenda).

Of course, there is much more to leadership failure than leader overload. I have suggested these problems just to stimulate your thinking. No doubt Ram Charan's talk at this conference on the need for attention to the execution of plans has stimulated your thinking as well.

The key point here is this: Lack of focus, poor execution by normally excellent managers, excessive optimism, loss of customers, abandonment of values, lack of alignment, and low morale may signal overload, an illness that undermines the effectiveness of any leader and his or her organization.

PREVENTING OVERLOAD

What can leaders do to prevent overload? Senior leaders at WVU talk openly about the overload issue. We have increased, and in some cases doubled, almost every metric at WVU during the past decade. Our enrollment has grown dramatically, imposing increased workloads on our employees. Research projects impose new levels of work and performance on our campus. Donors expect and deserve follow-through after a successful capital campaign. Government at all levels expects us to be ever more accountable. Parents of our students want to be involved. Our students see themselves as customers and expect high levels of technology and responsiveness.

At WVU, we plan to continue growing for the next several years. We could find ourselves overloaded in the not-too-distant future. To avoid problems, we have talked about the difference between a healthy and robust agenda and one that is clearly overloaded. We have also asked the question: what should we do when we find an overloaded leader or unit?

QUESTIONS AND SUGGESTIONS

Here are some basic questions and suggestions for leaders. We have taken this information away from our discussions, and it may prove helpful in preventing and addressing overload:

First, do we have the right people in the right jobs? Leaders must give the highest priority to hiring the right people in the first place. Clear job descriptions and clear goals and objectives are a very high priority. Robust agendas require robust leaders who are motivated, visionary, experienced, and "change resilient," in the words of last year's speaker, CLG CEO Julie Smith.

When the going gets tough, we all plow ahead with the team we have in place, which means to me that a high-quality, functional team must be in place before the agenda becomes fully robust. It is much better to ask who you want in your foxhole, rather than waiting until you are actually in the foxhole and looking around to see who is there.

Key employee selection is a slow process but one worth the extra time. Creating the best possible job description, expanding the pool of applicants, having a good interview process, and seeking needed talents not currently represented on the team are some of the mini-lessons I take away from our experience at WVU. As we say, try never to just fill a position; that is appointment by default. Rather, we ask what talent is needed and hire the person needed today, who might be a differently skilled person than was required the last time that position was vacant. Jim Collins, the well-known author of *Good to Great*, gives succinct advice on this point: the good-to-great leaders began the transformation by first getting the right people on the bus (and the wrong people off the bus) and then figuring out where to drive it.[4]

Jack Welch, in his new book, *Winning*, suggests several key traits to look for in evaluating job candidates: positive energy, the ability to energize others, the courage to make tough yes-or-no decisions, the ability to execute and finish the job, and passion for the work.[5] He also argues that for top leaders there are even more proclivities to look for: self-confidence and convictions, the ability to see around corners, a strong penchant for surrounding themselves with people better and smarter than they are, and the resilience to learn from their mistakes.[6] The people who have these traits will have tendencies that help them, and those around them, avoid overload. They will also have the ability to detect overload and pull the organization out of it before long-term damage is done. In Collins's words, "When in doubt, don't hire—keep looking. When you know you need to make a people change, act. Put your best people on your biggest opportunities."[7]

Says Collins, "The old adage 'People are your most important asset' is wrong. People are not your most important asset. The right people are. Whether someone is the 'right person' has more to do with character traits and innate capabilities than with specific knowledge."[8]

Finally, we can draw a great example from WVU basketball coach John Beilein. He assembled the right group of players and incarnated the well-known cliché that the whole can be greater than the sum of its parts. Getting the right people on the bus is the first part of the challenge, but how you facilitate their development as a team quickly becomes the next challenge.

Second, are we working on the right things? Leaders must continually enforce adherence to the mission of the organization, which, after all, instructs as to what we will and will not do. When we are overloaded, we need to get back to basics.

Collins talks about the fox-and-the-hedgehog parable. Time and again, the fox spends his days stalking the hedgehog. When the hedgehog finally comes out of his hole, he once again sees the fox ready to make the attack. The hedgehog goes into a ball with his sharp spikes protecting him. The fox is, of course, unable to attack, and thus he has wasted valuable time and energy going after the unattainable. The hedgehog, on the other hand, relies on the one thing he does best to survive and, indeed, beats the fox every time.[9]

The same applies to organizations: What does your organization do best? What drives its profits? What can it do better than others? What can it not do better than others? Drifting off mission is natural but very detrimental to effectiveness. When people begin to spend time on tasks that are not critical, the consequences of overload will become apparent.

Third, do all employees understand our expectations for their performance? Leaders should establish and constantly reinforce expectations within the organization. Once the team is assembled, and its collective job is made clear, each member should be thoroughly acquainted with organizational expectations for his or her performance. Both goal setting and formal leadership development programs, which are frequently a low priority, have a very high cost/benefit ratio in any organization.

From third-party evaluations of prospective employees, to systematic development of multiple layers of leadership throughout the organization, growth of organizational capacity through growth of individual capacity can be a tremendous investment.[10] Furthermore, various forms of orientation and alignment— new employee orientation, the use of specific goals and objectives, formal and informal feedback mechanisms, judicious use of consultants, retreats that foster alignment, and other traditional tools—are good investments. These tools have gained their reputations for a reason.

Finally, as an important expectation, we must encourage people to ask for help when they need it. Questions, comments, and sharing of feelings should be welcomed in order to improve the organization and, importantly, to offer early warning of pending leader overload.

Fourth, are we leading in accordance with the mandates of our values? Leaders must exhibit and enforce espoused organizational values, even when they themselves are under stress.

But how are values enforced? To begin with, leaders should always try to explain their decisions. We should follow the example of the American legal system. In the long run, judges rely on their oral and written explanations for support of their decisions. Leaders are no different—people want to know "why?" To paraphrase writer Victor Frankl, find the why's in life, and the how's will take care of themselves.[11]

Next, leaders must enforce values, even when it is painful and difficult to do so. This is easy to say and hard to do—but of utmost importance. Punishment is part of any values system. Conversely, rewards are necessary to convey the true meaning of excellence and vision for the organization. Jim Kouzes, last year's speaker, admonishes us, "People become exhausted, frustrated, and disenchanted. They're often tempted to give up. Leaders *encourage the heart* of their constituents to carry on. Genuine acts of caring uplift the spirits and draw people forward."[12]

Finally, one value—integrity—is the ace of trump in the leadership game. It is the one nonnegotiable value. In the words of Jim Kouzes:

> In almost every survey we've conducted, honesty has been selected more often than any other leadership characteristic; overall, it emerges as the single most important ingredient in the leader-constituent relationship . . . What we found in our investigation of admired leadership qualities is that more than anything, people want leaders who are credible. Credibility is the foundation of leadership.[13]

Fifth, are we exercising discipline in operations? Leaders must achieve a proper balance between control and freedom to act. At times, the distance between micromanagement and excellence of oversight is very short. Good leaders can tell the difference.

Again, we hear from Mr. Collins, who argues for organizational discipline:

> A culture of discipline involves a duality. On the one hand, it requires people who adhere to a consistent system; yet on the other hand, it gives people freedom and responsibility within the framework of that system. A culture of discipline is not just about action. It is about getting disciplined people who engage in disciplined thought and who then take disciplined action.[14]

According to Gary Yukl, a professor at State University of New York at Albany and author of *Leadership in Organizations,* participatory models for decision making range from autocratic decision-making to consultation to joint decision-making to delegation. The right model must be chosen for the right job.[15] Delegation, of course, is a frequently used mode—all good leaders must delegate. The question is what to delegate, how much to delegate, and what guidance to give in terms of deadlines and required outcomes. Delegation is not a matter of shouting, "You do it!" as you pass someone in the hall. Sometimes, we just have to impose our decisions, while on other occasions we have the luxury of consulting. Choosing the right model for participation should be a conscious decision.

Related to the balance of control and freedom is the frequently noted concept of transparency. The perceived need for confidentiality is a frequently given reason for delegation not being used within an organization. I believe that in most contexts, control of strategy and information has outlived its usefulness. Modern organizations tend to value transparency of procedures and delegations while keeping only business secrets confidential. In large organizations, lack of transparency is evidence of lack of trust.

Internal audits and external audits should be seen as supportive of effective execution. They should be welcomed, not feared, if people are trying to do the right thing, because audits provide external validation of a job well done.

Sixth, are we learning continuously? Leaders should undertake systematic post-action reviews and seek perspective on their work. The Army War College calls its efforts along these lines "after-action reviews." In recent years, the army has included interim reviews as part of its process as well. Imagine officers and enlisted men together, under fire, asking, "Why is this thing not working!" There are perhaps no other organizations as steeped in hierarchy as the military, so if army privates can openly provide constructive feedback to their superiors, there is no reason we in other organizations should stifle feedback from "the ranks." When the ranks are telling you they are tired or a plan won't work, consider whether the agenda is simply overloaded before perceiving their remarks as lack of cooperation.

We need to achieve a culture of candor. The freedom to speak openly about how an operation failed or why it unexpectedly succeeded is of critical importance to organizational health and growth. In his new book, Welch devoted an entire chapter to candor.[16] He reflects that he has always been a big proponent of candor but underestimated its rarity. True candor, Welsh posits, is speaking frankly and engaging in a straightforward debate. Respect and candor are not enemies. Candor can actually facilitate more respect among people who work closely together.

Leaders need to accept, praise, exemplify, and expect candor. Avoiding the realities of an issue can bring about leader overload simply because people are unwilling to challenge someone's idea. Perhaps such reviews can give the perspective that Ron Heifetz, our 2003 conference speaker, suggested we should seek when he urged us to get off of the dance floor and "climb on the balcony." Other metaphors for the same concept are "taking time to sharpen the saw" or "making sure we see the forest in spite of the trees." Climbing on the balcony in order to gain perspective can be difficult for those on the dance floor who are frantically moving their arms and legs to keep up with the music.

It is a leader's job to remind others of the big picture. When we are working hard, we sometimes forget that others are also working hard. We also forget, as one of our senior team members reminded me recently, just how much we are getting accomplished.

Seventh, are we anticipating the problems associated with the implementation of our decisions? Good leaders always focus on effective implementation. As Ram Charan suggested this year at the conference, churning out ideas and plans simply places them on the agenda. The subsequent work it takes to achieve the called-for improvements or to assimilate growth cannot be overlooked.

Don't confuse people by asking too much. Maintain clear priorities. If a leader puts so many things on the agenda that employees cannot tell what task has priority and what does not, overload will take root. It is good to have ideas, but it is critical to distinguish those that are truly important to the core mission of the organization. Look to employees, customers, and stakeholders for cues as to what fits that criterion.

At WVU, we believe strongly in having those whose job it will be to implement a plan be part of the planning process. What we call "task forces" or "work groups" take projects from the conceptual stage through to completion, and often an implementation schedule is affixed to a plan and an "implementation team" reports back to the appointing authority, for up to two years, on progress toward implementation of plans.

Clearly, a focus on how an organization will do something helps the leader predict the speed and ease with which it will be done. To avoid overload, leaders must monitor to make sure that there are not too many major initiatives going at once and also that the same people are not being stretched across too many initiatives.

Similarly, if responsibility to implement plans continually falls on the same people, there could be significant overload, and a logjam will occur. Given the certainty that some employees will feel compelled to take on every assignment, a leader has to share in the responsibility of balancing the workload against what is truly essential to the organization's goals. This can be done by ensuring appropriate staffing in the key places within the organization and, of course, through prioritization of initiatives.

Eighth, is your gut telling you something is wrong? Our instincts play a role in our leadership efforts. When attempting to deal with overload, you should trust your instincts to take corrective action, at least to the point that you create a presumption that needs to be rebutted, or, at a minimum, thoroughly examined when your gut tells you the organization is overloaded. Experience matters. Your gut can be wrong, but usually it is not.

I was impressed by Malcolm Gladwell's new book, *Blink*.[17] In it, he argues that some of us, and at times all of us, can discern problems or information in a highly complex environment without the need for lengthy investigation. He argues that we do in fact glean the most important bits of information from a barrage of information streams. Part of this ability is in the way our brain works, a science we do not yet fully understand. Coaches can sense that a move will not work before the results are seen. An expert can detect a fake antique before it is proven to be inauthentic. Counselors can tell a marriage is not working in just a few minutes with a couple. Leaders can tell something is not working before the formal reports are prepared. Leaders can fix problems without knowing exactly why they are there. Good leaders develop and trust their instincts.

CONCLUSION

Remember, overload is not a character flaw. We have all been overloaded. It is part of being an active leader. When overload strikes, our organizations suffer. In a sense, they become infected with an organizational influenza. The illness must be treated. The list of symptoms and cures presented here is not exhaustive, but hopefully it will help you to think about how organizations can best avoid the overload illness.

In the end, the doctor's prescription for overload is always the same: hire good people, adopt a clear and unambiguous mission, establish clear expectations, adhere to values that give the organization character, strike a proper balance between control and freedom, review and reflect frequently, focus on execution and implementation, and trust your instincts to do the right thing when you know something is wrong.

Remember: the overload illness can be treated, but it is easier to prevent. For this reason, the best prescription for overload is good preventive medicine.

NOTES

1   Theodore Roosevelt, Citizenship in a Republic speech at the Sorbonne, Paris, April 23, 1910.

2   Heike Bruch and Sumantra Ghoshal, "Beware the Busy Manager," *Harvard Business Review* 80, no. 2 (2002): 62–69, 64.

3   Edward M. Hallowell, "Overloaded Circuits: Why Smart People Underperform," *Harvard Business Review* 83, no. 1 (2005): 54–62, 61.

4   Jim Collins, *Good to Great: Why Some Companies Make the Leap . . . and Others Don't* (New York: HarperCollins, 2001), 41.

5   Jack Welch and Suzy Welch, *Winning* (New York: HarperBusiness, 2005).

6   Welch, *Winning*, 84–90.

7   Collins, *Good to Great*, 63.

8   Collins, *Good to Great*, 64.

9   Collins, *Good to Great*, 90–91.

10   See, for a discussion and examples, Cynthia D. McCauley and Ellen Van Velsor,

eds., *The Center for Creative Leadership: Handbook of Leadership Development*, 2nd ed. (San Francisco: Jossey-Bass, 2004).

11   Victor Frankl, *Man's Search for Meaning: An Introduction to Logotherapy*, trans. Ilse Lasch, 3rd ed. (1959; New York: Simon and Schuster, 1984), 9, paraphrasing Friedrich Nietzsche.

12   James M. Kouzes and Barry Z Posner, *The Leadership Challenge: How to Get Extraordinary Things Done in Organizations*, 3rd ed. (San Francisco: Jossey-Bass Publishers, 2003), 19.

13   Kouzes, *The Leadership Challenge*, 27, 32.

14   Collins, *Good to Great*, 142.

15   Gary Yukl, *Leadership in Organizations*, 5th ed. (Delhi, India: Saurabh Printers, 2002) 81.

16   Welch, *Winning*, 25.

17   Malcolm Gladwell, *Blink: The Power of Thinking without Thinking* (New York: Little, Brown, and Company, 2005).

SIX

CAN EDUCATION BE RUN
LIKE A BUSINESS?

1994

This article was written for the inaugural issue of the West Virginia School Board Association's newsletter the year before I became a university president. I was asked to contribute because I was chairman of the School Improvement Council of Ripley High School and a member and former chair of the University System of West Virginia Board of Trustees.

At the time, I was also a partner in the law firm of Bowles, Rice, McDavid, Graff, and Love in Charleston, West Virginia, and the chairman of the West Virginia Roundtable Inc., a business trade association comprising major business executives in West Virginia. The purpose of the article was to ask one of the more frequently posed questions about higher education: can education be run like a business?

First, congratulations are in order to the West Virginia School Board Association upon the launching of its new newsletter. This publication is destined to become an important vehicle for communication, not only among the members of the education community, but to those beyond as well. I am very pleased to have been asked to contribute to this inaugural issue and have selected as my topic the relationship between the business community and the public education community.

About the time I graduated from the public schools of Harrison County, President John Kennedy said that our progress as a nation can be no faster than our progress in education. I think most members of the business community accept this proposition as a commonsense way of stating that the goals and aspirations of the business community in America are closely tied to our public education access and quality.

My viewpoint, for the purposes of this article, is that of the chairman of the West Virginia Roundtable Inc. (Roundtable). A nonprofit corporation, the Roundtable has members who are many of the leading business executives in the state of West Virginia. Founded in the mid-1980s, the Roundtable has since been involved in and pushed for reform in several important public policy areas: education, taxation, at-risk children, venture capital formation, economic development, health care, government organization, and management, as well as other areas. The goals of the Roundtable can be stated quite simply:

- To maintain a network for major business executives in the state in order to facilitate good communication and the interchange of ideas among the business leadership in West Virginia
- To develop issues that should be part of the public agenda, to study those issues, and to present findings and suggestions to appropriate public-policy makers
- To contribute to the economic development of West Virginia by helping to develop and to foster job-creating policies and activities.

At the heart of the Roundtable is an implied vision for our state, which includes good government, a sound and diversified economy, and excellent public education and higher education systems.

Most business executives in the state maintain important linkages with the education community. Some of these linkages are natural. For example, business leaders serve on school boards, have children in the schools, participate in school improvement councils, maintain business partnerships, recruit from the public education systems and colleges of our state, and participate in economic development activities with educational institutions. The list goes on and on. Suffice it to say that there is significant interaction between the business community and the education community and that this interaction is important.

It is often said that government (including its education function) should be "run like a business." To me, this statement is overly simplistic and misses the fundamental point that business and government are different. Public decision-making is different from private decision-making. The goals of private businesses are derived differently than those of public bodies—like school boards and the State Board of Education. Nevertheless, I think it is fair to observe that there are important expectations that the business community has for the education community.

Let me try to state these expectations, in no particular order:

"CUSTOMER" ORIENTATION

Today, more and more business leaders are reengineering and reinventing their businesses in an effort to achieve "customer orientation." Recognizing the customer's important role in the life of any organization leads quickly to a focusing of the efforts of that organization. It appears reasonable, therefore, for the business community to ask the education community to keep its eye on its customers.

The question then becomes, who are the customers of the education community? For public school systems, most business people would immediately agree that the customers are the students. Promoting students' interests should be at the heart of every school system. Obviously parents, future employers, employees, and taxpayers are also customers of the system, but the primary customer of every school system is its student population.

ACCOUNTABILITY

Accountability has at least two prongs: financial accountability and program accountability. In terms of financial accountability, the business community would expect any school board to have reasonable systems in place to ensure the proper application of funds, and it would expect the system to have a budget and live within it. As for program accountability, businesspeople tend to look at test scores, job placements, and college admissions as indicators of whether the public education system is doing its job. Processing of mandates from the legislature and the State School Board are not nearly as important to the business community as the outcomes of the processing are.

PLANNING

Every business has to plan, and if it doesn't, it will encounter problems. For this reason, most businesspeople expect other organizations to have some sense of where they are headed in both the long and short term. Planning fosters better delivery of services, maintenance of facilities, training, recruitment, and program development. It also fosters the establishment of reasonable goals and objectives that are clearly understood, not only by the board of directors, but also by the employees of any system, whether it be a business or a public education system. For this reason, most businesspeople would expect the education community to spend time developing its goals and objectives.

EFFICIENCY AND RESPECT FOR THE TAXPAYER

Much of the business community has recently experienced competitive pressures that have led to enormous changes in the culture of American economic life. International competition, the changing of our society into an information technological society, and the insistence of the American consumer on better products at lower prices have led to a substantial change in the culture of American business. In the business community, words like "total quality management," "strategic planning," "customer orientation," and "efficiency" are not just words; they are the means by which businesses will survive in the twenty-first century. Pressures on profits are significant. For this reason, businesspeople ask for respect for the taxpayer; that is, they ask that public spending demonstrate respect for the taxpayer, and his or her tax dollars, by being efficient, thoughtful, and prudent.

SOUND DECISION-MAKING PROCESSES

Everyone knows that you can't take the politics out of government. But there is an expectation that politics can be minimized in education governance. Because education can involve large bureaucracies, the politics of that bureaucracy can sometimes alter what businesspeople expect—rational decision-making processes. The boards of education of this state are largely the connecting link between the public and the public education system. Business people understand that decisions cannot always be made rationally, but the hope and expectation is that most often they will be.

LEADERSHIP

At the heart of every business organization is leadership. This talent is expected not only of the CEO but of the other major actors in the business and, in many cases, of every single employee of the business. Most private-sector employees are called upon to lead at different times in their lives, whether it be by developing a new product, satisfying a new customer, making systems more efficient, or otherwise helping the business to grow and prosper.

The business community, therefore, looks to school boards, superintendents, principals, and important state-office holders who focus on education for leadership. When an issue cries out to be addressed and is not, the natural query is, where is the leadership that should be applied to this situation?

QUALITY PRODUCT

Increasingly, American businesses are aware that they must offer quality products or fail. For example, there have been tremendous turnarounds in the automotive industry recently. Chrysler, a failing corporation a few years ago, now offers a product line that customers find exciting. Ford has spent large sums of money redesigning its product line to be relevant to modern American lifestyles. GM, feeling these competitive pressures, is making significant changes in the way it does business. The Japanese automakers, taking their lead from the "quality" gurus of total quality management some years ago, try to offer quality products.

This evidence of the importance of quality in business tends to cause business leaders to expect that what they receive from public education will also be of quality. There is significant concern about this issue in the business community. State School Superintendent Dr. Henry Marockie (who, by the way, is a member of the Roundtable) came from a system that actually gave a "guarantee" to employers that his system was offering a quality education. Hopefully this kind of thinking is part of public education today, as business leaders clearly expect it.

GOOD COMMUNICATION

No business leader can succeed without good internal and external communications. Public education is no different and should view itself as having a responsibility to share its goals, aspirations, and achievements with its customers, their parents, employees, and taxpayers. Too often public policy fails because people have spent too little time informing others of what they intend to do and are doing.

SOUND ADMINISTRATION

Business leaders observe the administration of the public school systems with their eyes open. While they may not always understand the legal requirements facing administrations and boards, they do understand good administration. It is as simple as "knowing it when you see it." Business leaders would therefore urge that sound administrative structures and management principles be used in managing the millions of dollars that are put into public education in this state.

LINKAGES

I want to end this article where I began by focusing on the fact that business leaders clearly do recognize that public education, vocational-technical education, and higher education are among the most important functions of state and local government in America. A higher percentage of volunteer time is probably spent by business leaders on education than on any other concern. The linkages that have been developed by and among the State School Board, the county school boards, the university and college systems, and the business community are numerous and commendable. Business leaders accept such linkages and expect them to grow.

These expectations are reasonable and achievable. To the extent that these expectations seem to be recognized and acted on by the education community, the business community of this state is likely to be even more supportive of public education efforts in West Virginia than it has been in the past. Business leaders, like President John Kennedy, see the future of the American economy as being largely dependent on the quality of and access to public education in America.

SEVEN

LEADING CHANGE

REMARKS TO THE NATIONAL ASSOCIATION OF STATE UNIVERSITIES AND LAND-GRANT COLLEGES

2000

What follows is a summary of my remarks during a panel discussion for college and university presidents on the subject of strategies for change on the American public university campus. These remarks were delivered on November 14, 2000, at the annual meeting of the National Association of State Universities and Land-Grant Colleges. The presentation is an effort to synthesize lessons our leadership team has learned over a number of years, during which we were engaged in significant efforts to change our campus culture. Admittedly, these remarks are more informal and less precise than later efforts I made to summarize our progress. A later piece, called "Changing Campus Culture," written for the "Encyclopedia of Applied Developmental Science," with Drs. Larry S. Cote and Larry LeFlore, is a more comprehensive effort to summarize our efforts to make West Virginia University more "student centered."[1] I also reflect on this topic as part of a response to remarks by Dr. Albert Yates, president emeritus of Colorado State University, in "University Presidents as Moral Leaders."[2] *All indicators of progress mentioned in these remarks advanced over the next several years, including enrollment, Parents Club membership, private support, and reductions in negative indicators.*

My wife Susan and I got our dog Monty (short for the Latin word for *mountaineer*) the day after the *Princeton Review* named WVU the country's number one party school. This designation was not welcomed and, in the opinion of many, unwarranted, and it thrust the institution into an unfavorable national spotlight. The result was a firestorm of commentary and controversy on our campus. Monty offered unconditional love—and did we ever need it that day!

Within days, national television programs and magazines were portraying the schools on the party-school list as subpar in academic quality, and even dangerous. Some companies actually put newsletters out to their employees, warning them not to recruit students graduating from the adversely branded schools. These kinds of generalizations were unfounded and unfair to our faculty and students. But, as on other campuses with large concentrations of undergraduates, the truth is, to the extent that a culture of alcohol and substance abuse exists, it undermines our efforts in the classroom and detracts from public support.

Prior to becoming president of my alma mater, I had decided that changes in undergraduate life were needed. Then, and now, I believed that quality inside the classroom cannot be achieved without careful attention to life outside the classroom.

Years earlier I had read Derek Bok's book *Higher Learning*, in which he recalled the words of a mentor: "Your most creative ideas about the future of Harvard will come in the next few months, before you take office and get embroiled in your official duties."[3] As I looked over the landscape after I was appointed president, but before I went to Morgantown, I identified several potential problems. For starters, I felt that the abandonment of *in loco parentis*, the philosophy that colleges and universities should substitute their authority for those of parents of undergraduate students, had been taken too far on America's college and university campuses.

Fortunately, with the help of private support from the Kellogg Foundation, NASULGC was looking at issues related to undergraduate life. I found the early proceedings of that task force both instructive and informative. With help and input from others on campus, on my first day as president, July 5, 1995, I held a press conference to outline a plan for change at the institution. The central theme was that we needed to become a much more "student centered" institution. At the press conference, I announced several initiatives:

1. *We established a new vice presidency, the vice president for student affairs, to serve as a student advocate, coach, and mentor. (The chief student affairs officer had formerly reported to the provost.)*

To fill this position, we successfully recruited a person with a nontraditional background. Major General Kenneth Gray was the army's assistant judge advocate general, a position in which he dealt with millions of young people. He was also a West Virginia native, a WVU Law graduate, and a parent of two WVU students. He was not a student affairs professional by training, but he understood how to organize, lead, and effect change. As importantly, he cared about our university.

2. *We created a parent organization to tap into parents' cries for accountability and concerns about campus life.*

We explicitly solicited parents' help in the change effort. With early help from Texas A&M, and under my wife's personal leadership, the Mountaineer Parents Club was formed to involve parents in student success on our campus. It has grown into something that uniquely suits our institution. Among its more important innovations is a parent advocate's office with a toll-free line and a full-time employee. Today, the Mountaineer Parents Club is more than eight thousand families strong and one of our most valuable mechanisms for constituent communication. The Parents Club is a student-support organization, not a fund-raising organization.

3. *We charged a broad-based student affairs task force to identify our biggest problems and offer ideas for improvement.*

Later, we reported on our efforts to implement the task force's ideas until the group was satisfied that we had adequately addressed their recommendations. The use of noncampus members in the group was critical to its success. We also established a student affairs visiting committee to provide continual input on our efforts.

4. *We radically changed the first-year experience to foster a stronger sense of community.*

The underlying principle for our efforts was that if students get off to a good start, retention will improve, as will the overall student experience. I was particularly influenced by the book *The Abandoned Generation*, by William H. Willimon and Thomas H. Naylor. In it, the authors argue eloquently for more efforts to create communities within our campuses.[4] After I became president, Dr. Willimon visited our campus to speak at a winter convocation and meet with our leadership team.

Our most significant effort to give students a community within a larger institution was the development of a faculty leader program for the residence halls. This type of program is not unique to WVU, and we have learned from ideas tried at other institutions. For each residence hall, we constructed adjacent homes for faculty in-residence and new seminar rooms, computer labs, and meeting spaces for students. Today, our resident faculty leaders organize enrichment programming in the halls, teach orientation courses, call students with mid-term grade reports to discuss academic progress, advise students on academic goals, meet with parents, and generally serve as mentors for students.

5. *We reestablished a new student convocation that had been abandoned years earlier.*

The purpose of the convocation was to orient students to our expectations of them in the freshman year. For about five years now, the pace of change on our campus has been breathtaking. The results are evidence of great progress and increased confidence among our stakeholders. Enrollment is up. Our program was a financial success. Mid-term grade reports for freshmen have improved markedly in the last few years. Our private foundation's cash receipts have reached new highs, signifying increased support from alumni and friends. Our endowments per student have doubled. Calls from legislators on behalf of frustrated parents have virtually ended, thanks to our Parents Club helpline.

Our yield of in-state students is increasing despite a decline in the number of West Virginia high school graduates due to a changing economy. Retention is improving, especially among students classified as academically at-risk. We are increasingly focused on academics at the undergraduate level. A student–faculty task force recently recommended an increase in academic requirements for graduation and the creation of capstone experiences in every major. We have earned a number of safety awards and rankings in national publications.

Our town–gown relations are markedly improved. The university has joined with the city in numerous initiatives, such as "parent perks," a rails-to-trails project, and riverfront development. This year, Morgantown was named the "Best Small City in America" by *Demographics Daily*.

Through polling, we know that in our region the words "student centered" are now strongly associated with WVU. In recent years, approximately one hundred colleges and universities have come to campus or specifically asked for information in order to learn firsthand what we are doing to improve undergraduate student life. Finally, anecdotal feedback tells us we are on the right track.

Because of time constraints today, I can only focus on our efforts to become a more student-centered institution, but that is only one area in which we engaged in change. Additionally, we have focused our research agenda, improved outreach and service, and invested heavily in technology infrastructure—all with equal challenge and equally encouraging results. With great humility, I suggest the following lessons learned:

1. *Announce, and be transparent about, your intentions when change is really required.*

The campus will respond to leadership initiatives if they are perceived to be necessary. Boldness is rewarded. Timidity is not.

2. *Look outward. Listen to the people you serve and involve them in the change process.*

An "outside" perspective was key to our ability to perceive the need for and ask for change. For example, we never would have implemented the resident faculty leader program had we not listened to the concerns of parents sending their children to live in the residence halls. We were able to build on these perspectives by asking for advice from the people affected most by our actions.

Any leader can do this regardless of his or her background. Ask for feedback and involvement from the people you serve, inside and outside the organization. They will tell you where the problems are, and as they gain confidence in the institution's responsiveness, the institution will reap rewards.

3. *Make and document the case for change.*

A leader has to build the case when change is needed. This is time consuming but very important. It requires facts, data, and personal involvement. Indeed, the case for change in higher education is sometimes more difficult because the urgency is not felt in the university towers in the same way as in the private sector. Short of severe financial crisis, paychecks are not dependent upon the financial success of the organization. While there are good reasons for this in academia, it does make the case for change less direct. With enrollment dropping and legislative mandates to reallocate financial resources, we wanted to avoid a financial crisis and thus tried to share information that helped show why change was so important before such a time came that it would become urgent.

One of the simplest things that built the case for change was the day that two administrators stood in one of those long registration lines and monitored student and parent reaction as they moved toward the front. After half a day in line, it didn't take long for a solution to be found. By the next semester, the lines were eliminated, and today most students simply register by phone. It wasn't that anyone thought the long lines were acceptable, but there hadn't been a linkage of the lines, declining enrollments, and the institution's financial stability.

4. *Build, mold, balance, and nurture a strong change-leadership team.*

Our vice president for student affairs is just one example of the administrative team at WVU. The strengths and talents of the team have been critical to our success in the last several years. Our provost, communications director, extension director, dean of students, and counselors deserve special mention. They have special talents for leading change, focusing on goals, and producing results in record time.

5. *Persevere.*

Winston Churchill is quoted as saying "never give in."[5] When you know you are on the right track, stay the course despite pressures to give up and leave the status quo in place. It was not easy to propose the idea of a faculty residence program. Opposition became extremely vocal when we began to spend money on the project. Many of us spent countless hours hosting open sessions on campus, talking about the need to reengineer our freshman-year experience.

One of the most memorable meetings was with a group of faculty who were launching every conceivable criticism at the program. Finally, I asked how many in the group had a son or daughter in college. A few raised their hands. I then asked of those people how many had children enrolled at WVU and living in our residence halls. Just two kept their hands up and one said, "Put this program in place as fast as you can—we need it." This single "confession" gave me the courage to keep trying.

Two years after we began our first student-centered initiatives, the first Kellogg Commission report focused all public institutions on becoming more student-centered. This articulation of NASULGC's position validated our efforts. We totally embraced the tenets of this report. Perhaps most importantly, the Kellogg report gave us courage to persevere.

6. Don't be afraid to actually allow change to occur.

We knew the infamous back-to-school block party had to end, and the city police were prepared to make sure that happened. Fearing the reaction to a law enforcement crackdown, a group of students developed an idea for a block-party alternative called "FallFest." It was important to work together, so the administration was supportive despite some criticisms. In just a few short years, Fall Fest has turned into a very popular and safe welcome-back mixer that attracts about thirteen thousand of our students, without the problems of the old-style block party.

Another program, WVUp All Night, was originally suggested by students. The program required reallocation of funds. Student Affairs was willing to give it a try, so central administration supported their creation. Vice President Gray and many others, particularly from Student Affairs, pitched in to help keep the student union open until 3 AM on weekends. The program has become successful: it has attracted corporate support, been featured on ABC's *Good Morning America*, and most recently been honored among the best strategies in the nation for providing students with alternatives to the bar scene. Most importantly, student evaluations of the program are positive.

7. Communicate and celebrate successes.

Leading change requires storytelling. Stories make the abstract more real and personal. It was important for us to identify the right problems and have strong internal and external mechanisms in place to communicate both problems and solutions. We provided constructive means for input along the way and took time to celebrate successes.

8. *Get lucky. Expect some bad breaks.*

In short, when making change, expect curveballs, relapses, and resistance. Don't expect things to go smoothly. Many events are beyond our control, so we must react as best we can. My partner in law practice once told me, "Things are never as bad as they feel, or as good as they feel." The designation as the "number one party school" was no doubt bad, but it was not as terrible as it seemed on the day we got Monty. It did cast a lot of negative publicity on the institution, but, on the other hand, the ranking helped underscore the case for change with greater urgency. Within a year, we were not on the top-ten list of party schools. More importantly, the culture had turned the corner.

We are not done at WVU. We do believe in ourselves and know that change on campus is possible. There are countless individuals who have contributed their time, energy, and ideas. Change takes that kind of input and help, and it takes time.

These are WVU's lessons for change: state your intentions regarding change; look outward; make the case for change and document it; build a good leadership team; stay the course; allow change to occur; communicate and celebrate changes; expect the unexpected; and allow time for changes to happen.

Change is never easy. The truth is that there is a constant need for change on campuses. The point of presidential leadership is to identify the areas where change is most needed and then provide a vision for how it can come about.

NOTES

1   David C. Hardesty Jr., Lawrence S. Cote, and Larry LeFlore, "Changing Campus Culture" in Handbook of Applied Developmental Science: Promoting Positive

Child, Adolescent, and Family Development through Research, Policies, and Programs, eds. Richard M. Lerner, Donald Wertlieb, and Francine Jacobs (Thousand Oaks, CA: Sage Publications, 2003) 4: 13–34.

2   David C. Hardesty Jr., "A Response to President Yates' Essay: 'Vision, Transparency, and Passion,'" in University Presidents as Moral Leaders, ed. David G. Brown. (Westport, CT: Praeger, 2006), 129–134.

3   Derek Bok, *Higher Learning* (Cambridge, MA: Harvard University Press, 1986), 8.

4   William H. Willimon and Thomas H. Naylor, The Abandoned Generation: Rethinking Higher Education (Grand Rapids, MI: William B. Eerdmans Publishing Co., 1995), 142–162.

5   Winston Churchill, speech at Harrow School, October 29, 1941, in Winston S. Churchill, Never Give In! The Best of Winston Churchill's Speeches (New York: Hyperion, 2003), 307.

PART TWO

MISSION, VISION, AND VALUES

THE PRESIDENT
AS UNIVERSITY ADVOCATE

Every academic president must speak with clarity about the mission of the institution he or she leads, the vision that has been established to inspire the institution, and the values that will be enforced during his or her presidency. The successful president is, above all, an advocate for the mission, vision, and values held dear within the university community.

This advocacy almost always begins in the first major address to the university community, often called the inaugural address. However, there are many more opportunities to teach the mission, vision, and values of the institution, to mark the progress on the journey that is the life of the public university, and to stop and reflect upon the collective work of the university community. One of the most notable occasions is the annual state-of-the-university address, typically delivered in person to the faculty assembly during a meeting to which other constituencies are customarily invited.

In addition to the formal inaugural and state-of-the-university addresses, a university president advocates the university's mission, vision, and values during speaking engagements with specific constituent groups and when celebrating the contributions of members of the campus community. This section includes speeches given to a wide variety of audiences on a number of occasions, but all highlight the value to society of the university and our institution's unique attributes.

EIGHT

GETTING STARTED

THE INAUGURAL ADDRESS

1995

By custom, the inaugural address is the most significant speech delivered by the president at the beginning of his or her term. While some are more modest and informal than others, the "inauguration," "investiture," or "first academic convocation" is a good venue for a major speech because it assembles most constituencies of the university to celebrate the transition to a new president and to hear what the new campus leader has to say. In most such cases, at least in the cases of public universities, greetings are offered by public officials, board representatives, faculty representatives, and often a presidential colleague.

At my own inauguration, my remarks followed those of our governor, a United States senator, the chair of the Board (later West Virginia's Secretary of Education), the president of the Massachusetts Institute of Technology (a fellow graduate of West Virginia University), the faculty senate chair, a student, and others. The event was held on a beautiful day in front of Woodburn Hall, the signature building on campus. My selection as the first nontraditional president in decades was controversial in some quarters. I knew it would be important for me to be clear about my understanding and endorsement of all elements of the university's mission, my aspirations for the institution, and the values I held dear.

In this address, I tried to recognize all three elements of the university and demonstrate my appreciation for each, express values that I would enforce as president, and recognize the important role of the university in society.

I was assisted in the drafting process by several people, but two stand out in my mind. The late Rev. Jerry Rector, a former United Methodist pastor who became a speech writer for Senator Robert C. Byrd, volunteered to help. He was home, and very sick, at the time, but he shared his talents as a gift to Susan and me; we were in his discussion group at Wesley United Methodist Church as students. I am also indebted to Dr. Jack Byrd of our industrial engineering faculty, a man with a sensitive and well-rounded intellect who suggested that I quote my old friend Dr. Ruel Foster at the end of the speech. The quote concluded the speech with a forcefulness that is still remembered by some more than a decade later. Dr. Foster had been my Rhodes Scholarship coach, or advisor, when I was a student.

In retrospect, I can now see clearly how the story of my own life, and the story of several faculty members and graduates, was important to the speech, and how the stories intertwined to clarify the nature of the institution's mission elements.

About the same time I delivered the address, I read Howard Gardner's book, "Leading Minds."[1] In it, Gardner, in collaboration with Emma Laskin, notes the critical importance of stories to the leader's ability to communicate. He also notes how powerful it is when the leader speaks of his experiences. The book's impact on my understanding of the commitment and emotion I felt at the beginning of the term as president of my alma mater is hard to overestimate. I have cited it in many contexts over the years and tried, in an effort to reach the widest possible audience, to include stories that explained the central points of a speech whenever possible .

This past Fourth of July, I represented West Virginia University in a parade in Morgantown. As Susan and I stepped from the vehicle to take our position on the speakers' platform, I was greeted by an elderly gentleman who said to me, "Mr. President, I wanted to meet you. You see, I didn't go to college myself, but I sent all eight of my children to WVU."

As Basil Callen's eyes filled with pride in the accomplishments of his family, my heart filled with emotion. In his eyes, I saw the eyes of my parents. At that moment, I was again reminded of both the extraordinary importance of the institution I had been chosen to lead and the challenges this position presents to the person who is privileged to be its president.

Thirty-two years ago this month, I arrived in Morgantown, the son of loving parents, the product of our public school system, and one who had been nurtured by the people of Shinnston, a beautiful small town located on the West Fork River just forty miles from where we gather today. I left four years later, prepared to meet the rigors of Oxford and Harvard universities and the workplace beyond. My mind had been opened to the world of ideas by the distinguished faculty of this institution. I was transformed by this institution and by the thousands of taxpayers and volunteers who supported it while I was here.

It is, therefore, with a deep sense of gratitude and humility that I stand before you today as this university's twenty-first president. Mere words seem inadequate to express my thanks to those who taught and mentored me while I was a student here and to those who have made it possible for me to assume the mantle of leadership today.

My wife, Susan, was one of my classmates here, and I would like to take a moment to pay tribute to her and to my children, Ashley and Carter. Susan and I have made our journey through life together, and we will serve our university together. Our children will share in our joys during my service here. They will also share in our trials and tribulations. Their steadfast love supports me and enables me, and I want them to share in this inaugural moment with me.

This university makes a true difference for the better in the lives of those who spend time on its campuses. And as I stand before you today, I am reminded of the words of our friend Dr. Maurice Brooks, set forth so eloquently in his book about our region, called *The Appalachians*. He wrote, "In some manner, a mountain country places its mark on those who dwell within its shadows. Scots carry with them a Highland pride of birth and place, even though they may wander thousands of miles from heather-covered moors. Natives of Switzerland see the Alps, although those peaks are far below the horizon. And thus it is with those nurtured in Appalachia—they leave, but they look back, remembering pleasant things. The land has claimed them, and its ties will not be severed."[2] So it is with our mountains, and so it is with our university. It has claimed us. Our ties are strong—they will not be severed— and they beckon all of us to serve it when we are called.

One of our most illustrious graduates, Jerry West, recently said, with simplicity and humility, that as he looks back on his life, he realizes that almost all of his personal dreams have come true. He went on to say that the roots of his good fortune were firmly planted at West Virginia University.What is notable about his remarks is that they are representative of testimonials that can be given by leaders in almost every walk of life in our society. Our 120,000 living alumni know that dreams come true at, and because of, WVU.

ON THE MISSION OF LAND-GRANT UNIVERSITIES

Our alumni are not alone in their realization. The citizens of our state and region are touched daily by our service and research. This is the true greatness of the comprehensive university. This is the historical significance of land-grant universities.

Since 1867, West Virginia University has served society, especially West Virginia and the region of which it is a part. It has always had the same mission: teaching, research, and service. The manner in which it has met its mission, however, has in large measure been determined in the context of events influencing it at various times in its history.

Our generation of leadership at West Virginia University is challenged today, just as prior generations of leadership have been challenged. We will succeed in moving the university forward in our time, just as prior generations have in theirs. We will succeed for three reasons.

ON THE TEACHING MISSION OF WEST VIRGINIA UNIVERSITY

First, we always have and we still do care deeply about students, teaching, and learning on our campuses. We want our students to have rich and rewarding experiences while they are with us. We want them to learn about the world of ideas and how to think, to communicate, to respect others who are different from them, to participate in the international community, to lead, to serve, to address ethical problems, and to accept civic responsibility. We want our students to have bold dreams and to believe that they too can make a difference. We believe we will prepare them to do just that.

There are roughly twenty-two thousand students at all of the campuses of WVU. We care about each and every one of them. We care about what they learn and how they learn it. We care about the quality of their experience while they are with us. We care about their ability to learn continuously throughout their entire lifetimes. This is the message Presidents Paul Miller and Harry Heflin put forth while I was a student here. This is my message as well. Students are the primary reason West Virginia University exists.

We will support this caring attitude toward our students by providing them with the best faculty available to us and by supporting that faculty with the libraries, laboratories, and other resources necessary to provide students with an education that enables them to compete in a technologically advanced, global economy.

We will also express our caring attitude toward students by enriching the learning environment inside and outside our classrooms. We will aspire to offer exceptional student living experiences. And in everything that we do, we will foster student success. As Cicero said so succinctly, there is no greater gift that we can give the Republic than the education of its people.

ON SERVICE BY WEST VIRGINIA UNIVERSITY

Our second message is that we will vigorously serve our state, our region, our nation, and our global community. We care about those we are charged to serve. As a land-grant institution and as a comprehensive research university, we are supported by the people of our state and nation. They expect us to serve, and we will meet their expectations.

We will provide exceptional rural health care, we will foster community development, we will look for ways to assist our public system of education, we will address the quality of life of those around us, we will continue the education of professionals, we will provide useful and practical knowledge to the people of West Virginia through our extension service, we will foster new industries and revitalize older ones in order to provide meaningful work for future generations, we will assist our governments, and we will help those whose circumstances require helping hands.

We will, every day, make service a priority, and by so doing, we will earn the respect of those we serve. We will enter into partnerships with those we serve, to help make their dreams come true.

ON RESEARCH AT WEST VIRGINIA UNIVERSITY

Finally, we will extend the frontiers of knowledge. Our research will be meaningful, competitive, useful, and relevant. Our more than twenty centers and institutes, which now return over ten dollars to our campuses for every one dollar provided by our state, will continue to work to expand our understanding of our environment, our natural resources, our bodies, our minds, and worlds both past and future.

Our professorate and their departments will look for ways to teach better, to use technology better, to live better, to serve better. Forty percent of our research is engaged in finding cures for disease and health problems. Much is devoted to our natural resources. Some research is applied; some is basic to our understanding of human and natural processes, and we know not where it will lead. But it is all important.

We will, therefore, remain a comprehensive research university. We will do so because it is important to our teaching and service missions, because it is important to our state and nation, and because it is important to future generations.

ON THE RELATIONSHIP OF TEACHING, RESEARCH, AND SERVICE AT WEST VIRGINIA UNIVERSITY

We urge the citizens of our state and nation to ponder with great care the interrelated nature of the teaching, research, and service elements of the mission of universities like ours.

My father-in-law, Clifford Brown, taught at WVU for thirty years. He held many positions, including chair and assistant dean, but his first love was teaching. He was a mentor and teacher of the first rank. He loved nothing more than to witness the successes of his students. One such student was a young man from nearby Pennsylvania who came here in the late 1950s. In Phil Faini (currently dean of creative arts on this campus), he saw great promise. He nurtured Phil and worked hard to help him achieve success. Phil later said that he considered Professor Brown the "grandfather" of his students.

Dean Faini, picking up the torch, became interested in expanding our knowledge of percussion, especially the instruments and rhythms of East Africa. His research, now widely recognized as seminal in the world of percussion artists, eventually infused our campus with beats and sounds rarely heard on this continent before. Our bands, groups, and ensembles became well known for their excellence in percussion.

Phil Faini has himself mentored dozens of young artists and teachers. One, David Satterfield, became interested in service and extending the College of Creative Arts into our state. One of his projects involved sharing the exciting rhythms of the Pride of West Virginia Drumline with the high schools of West Virginia. During one of David Satterfield's outreach visits, a young man from Ripley watched from the sideline while his high school band was instructed. He had decided against college. His future was uncertain. As he watched the WVU band that day and talked with Mr. Satterfield, he was inspired to dream again about what could lie ahead. He decided, then and there, to enroll at WVU and to become a part of the Pride of West Virginia.

Robert Dehart decided to succeed. He completed his bachelor's degree in history, and this fall when Mr. Dehart is awarded his master's degree in secondary education, he will be the product of three generations of teaching, research, and service at our university.

Thus, today I reaffirm, without reservation, the three-part mission of this great land-grant, comprehensive university. I am confident in its future because I know those it serves care about it as much as those it comprises care about those they serve.

ON CAMPUS VALUES THAT FOSTER LEADERSHIP AT WEST VIRGINIA UNIVERSITY

As we move forward into the next millennium, exceptional leadership across our university will be essential. How is it to be fostered? To lead effectively, it seems to me that all of us must execute our mission, and demonstrate our caring attitude, by exhibiting behavior that demonstrates our commitment to a clear set of values. They must be shared by those who constitute our university. The complexity of our times and the scope and breadth of activity at each of our campuses make it impossible for university administrators, including the president, to make every decision.

Leadership is not accomplished by unilateral action or micromanagement. It is not accomplished by detailed proscription or prescription. None of us can solve every problem or address every issue that is raised within the university. What we can do when we have the opportunity, however, is to help establish values by which others may lead, select people with leadership potential, and hold those selected accountable to those values. I suggest, therefore, that the following values guide our actions in leading the university into the twenty-first century.

ON EXCELLENCE

First, we must foster excellence and continuous improvement at our university. We are, of course, very proud of the achievements of our faculty, staff, and students. And we are pleased to note the extraordinary contributions to society and this institution of our graduates, friends, and contributors. But excellence is a journey, not a destination. We must never be comfortable with our achievements.

Improvement is a never-ending process. We must foster a culture that keeps asking questions, challenges how and what we do, and creates bold new approaches. We must foster an atmosphere in which quality is rewarded and all of our employees feel empowered to effect positive change. We cannot afford to let any worthwhile idea go unstated or unused. We must continuously improve, inside and outside the classroom.

To achieve true quality, it seems to me that we must attract to this institution the strongest faculty, the best students, and the most competent administrators and staff that we can. The best will also be people who care about West Virginia, its people, and its flagship university. In the years to come, our excellence will come from our focus. Our focus will come from our obligation to preserve and transmit knowledge, and it will come from society's needs as we find them.

ON STEWARDSHIP

Second, we will exhibit stewardship. The men and women who lead our university bear a special responsibility for assuring that it moves forward constantly. We are stewards and guardians of this wonderful place.

Our responsibility for stewardship is particularly apparent when one reflects upon the achievements of those who have gone before us. From our first president—Alexander Martin, a Methodist minister from Scotland—to our twentieth president, Neil Bucklew, each of our presidents has left his mark upon the institution. So it is with those who have taught since 1867 in the halls in which we sit, and so it is with those who have supported them. WVU is great today because of the contributions of countless persons, some well known and some unheralded.

Our stewardship will take the form of sound administration, prudent budgeting, effective planning, collaboration within our institution and with other institutions, holding ourselves accountable, efforts to preserve our culture and traditions, and efforts to ensure that we offer value to those who pay our tuition and fees. Good stewardship both inspires generosity in support of our efforts and honors our obligations to those who have preceded us and the generations to come.

ON OUR CAMPUS COMMUNITY

Third, we will foster a close university community. At a commencement address here in 1963, Dr. Henry Steele Commnger said, "It is a primary duty of the university to instill in all of its members . . . a sense of membership in and responsibility to the larger community."[3]

I agree completely, knowing full well that the effort to foster community will require much more effort today than it did some three decades ago.

Building a sense of community today involves more than acquainting each member of our community with the backgrounds and aspirations of the others. It involves developing a sense of trust among members of our community and developing trust between those on our campuses and those served by them.

Like building excellence, building a sense of community is not a one-time task but a continuing challenge, rooted deeply in our mission and values. Mindful of the similarities and differences of those represented in the community, we must—each of us—accept responsibility to and for our community. We must encourage freedom of expression in dealing with difficult issues in ways that bridge our differences. We must continue to find ways to increase tolerance and to foster collective aspirations and pride.

Our community must involve shared goals, freedom of thought and expression, justice for each member, self-discipline, a caring attitude, and a celebration of the heritage of this institution. As we go forward, let us all resolve to act with integrity in all that we do and to create the trust upon which a true community can be built. Dreams come true when members of a community resolve to help each other achieve them.

ON INNOVATION

Next, we will foster innovation. Derek Bok, former president of Harvard University, has said:

> More and more, therefore, the United States will have to live by its wits, prospering or declining according to the capacity of its people to develop new ideas,

to work with sophisticated technology, to create new products and imaginative ways of solving problems. Of all our national assets, a trained intelligence and a capacity for innovation and discovery seem destined to be the most important.[4]

If this is true of our country, it is also most assuredly true of our university. True, we are part of a tradition that is a thousand years old. My room at Oxford was built in 1344. Exploring ideas is not new to our planet, but we must find new ways to do our ageless tasks.

We must innovate in the classroom, the laboratory, the library, the office, the dormitory, and everywhere else. We must embrace technology and use it not only to educate ourselves and our students but also to serve. We may need to ask others to free us to innovate and find new means of accountability. We may need to invest at times when investment dollars are hard to come by. We may need to reeducate ourselves and others. We may need to adopt new administrative methods.

But innovate we must. We must model innovation and creativity for our state and region. Our future and the future of those we serve depend on our willingness to be bold, or as some say, to go "outside the traditional box" to find solutions.

ON COMMUNICATIONS

Finally, our individual and collective dreams will best be realized if we talk to one another effectively. All that I have mentioned today—teaching, research, service, excellence, stewardship, community, and innovation—can best be fostered and achieved if we communicate our ideas to one another effectively. We must reach out to one another, to those we serve outside the university community, and to the society beyond.

Last month I told our new students that I believe there is clearly a limit to how far they will progress in the workplace if they do not learn to communicate their ideas to others. The same is true of our university. It must be a place where communications are effective and complete. Our progress depends upon it. Our challenges require it.

In short, we must each do our part to lead the university. We must offer our students an exceptional learning experience, inside and outside the classroom. We must reach out to our state and nation with vigorous service. We must press forward into the frontiers of knowledge. And in all that we do, we must foster excellence, stewardship, community, innovation, and good communication. We are all called to lead. We are all called to serve. We must all accept the call.

THE UNIVERSITY AS A PLACE WHERE DREAMS ARE REALIZED

I would like to close my remarks by reminding us all what a wonderful university this is. It is truly the crowning achievement of the people of West Virginia. It binds us together as a state; it fosters progress; it paves the pathways to the future. But most of all, it opens minds to the world of ideas, and in doing so it opens the way for dreams to come true. Is it any wonder, then, that one university president said that a university campus is hallowed ground? Is it any wonder, then, that "our hearts with rapture thrill" as we contemplate the magnificence of our university? In writing about our campus in Morgantown, Ruel Foster, one of our most beloved emeriti professors, who came to Morgantown in 1941 and is still here today, once said:

> Look on these buildings, these paths, these students, and in imagination tread again the heel-gnawed steps, the myriad walks, and see again the faces that once were with you in this place . . . May we not say that the university . . . is, in a manner of speaking, the collective dream of all the past and present

generations of students—students who in their . . . tenure have left pieces and patches of their lives on this . . . campus?

As you leave today, and every time you walk across our campuses, look into the eyes of the students you encounter, and just imagine. Will you see a future faculty member who is, more than anything else, dedicated to teaching future generations of our students? Will you see a future public servant who may change the course of history? Will you see a young man or woman who will by his or her research relieve others of misery? Will you see our next major athlete or a social activist who will bring justice to our society?

See if you can find the budding novelist who will achieve national recognition. See if you can find the next Fortune 100 CEO. See if you can find the next president of a university. Just as important, see if you can find a successful parent, friend, neighbor. Look hard. They are all here, in the form of dreams yet to be realized.

I accept the mantle of leadership of my alma mater, and as I do so, I ask you to join with me in helping to make dreams come true at West Virginia University.

NOTES

1   Howard Gardner, in collaboration with Emma Laskin, *Leading Minds: An Anatomy of Leadership* (New York: Basic Books, 1996).

2   Maurice Brooks, *The Appalachians* (Boston: Houghton Mifflin, 1965), 331.

3   Dr. Henry Steele Commager, Commencement Address, Morgantown, WV, June 3, 1963.

4   Derek Bok, *Higher Learning* (Cambridge, MA: Harvard University Press, 1986), 5.

NINE

MARKING PROGRESS IN THE STATE OF THE UNIVERSITY ADDRESSES

During my time as president of West Virginia University, I delivered twelve formal State of the Campus, or State of the University, addresses. Such speeches are often mandated by the rules of the faculty senate or university assembly, and the mandate clearly makes sense. Campus leaders and external constituencies deserve an update on the president's thinking. More importantly, however, such remarks serve many different legitimate purposes related to campus leadership. They serve to benchmark beginning points in a presidency, establish mile markers along the way, and summarize lessons learned that should be incorporated into the campus culture.

Our State of the University addresses were often printed and sent to university community leaders. They were also reformatted for use in shorter presentations at off-campus locations (for example, in Washington, DC, and Charleston, WV). Perhaps more importantly, they were carefully researched and crafted, and their content formed the basis of ongoing remarks "on the stump" at alumni events and similar gatherings throughout the year.

I have included five State of the University speeches in this book, two from very early in our administration, when the challenges seemed mighty and the future less certain. They each sustain the tone of the inaugural address and repeatedly ask for support and recommitment to the mission during a difficult time. Early State of the University addresses continue the mission, vision, and values contained in the inaugural address, assess the current environment in which the campus operates, and point to specific planning efforts and budgeting priorities. Two later speeches exhibit a growing confidence and the increasing clarity that comes with successful completion of many elements of our agenda. The final State of the University address is included as Part 1, Chapter 1.

While I usually outlined, and sometimes drafted, all or part of what I wanted to see in the State of the University speeches, these addresses were clearly the product of a team. Presidential assistants and all vice presidents participated in suggesting format and content statements. Their input ensured compliance with university policy and crafted policy pronouncements and budget priorities in the proper fashion. Editing was accomplished by a number of editors and staff writers at the university.

A STUDENT-CENTERED VISION

1996

This speech addressed four questions that I often asked during my presidency: Who are we? Where are we? Where are we headed? How will we get there? It also launched several early programs, suggested several strategic aspirations, and attempted to define "quality" as it applied to higher education. The speech followed a six-month listening and policy-development period. It launched a series of initiatives that were largely accomplished over the next decade, including the establishment of the Mountaineer Parents Club, the construction of new library facilities, the use of modern business practices, and a clear student-centered vision.

INTRODUCTION

Since assuming the presidency, I have been privileged to view this institution from a unique vantage point. You have given me a six-month review, which has included written and oral briefings from most deans and directors; visits to academic units and regional campuses; numerous meetings at Jackson's Mill with leaders of the faculty, classified staff, students, and administrators; tours of athletic facilities, hospitals, and residence halls; visits with alumni throughout the region; visits with our state's elected leaders; visits to Capitol Hill; and review of hundreds of letters about the university, often containing suggestions for improvement. In short, I have gotten an advanced degree in "WVU."

By way of sharing with you what I have learned, I would like to begin today by posing a few simple questions relating to our identity as an institution: Who are we? What is West Virginia University? Why are we, who make up WVU, at this moment in time devoting our most productive years to working at this institution, in its many locations?

In one sense, the answer to these questions can be simply stated: We constitute a public, land-grant, comprehensive, research university. As such, we are supported by our students and their families, our state, our nation, our private donors, and our research clients. We are here to teach, to discover, and to serve. Yet, surely we can be seen as being more distinctive than this. Are we not, in some sense, special? I believe that we are. Let me tell you why.

OBSERVATIONS ABOUT OUR UNIVERSITY

First, this university has offered, and always will offer, opportunity and hope to its students. In most cases, the expectations of our students are raised after they join us, and their hearts embrace new dreams that could not have been imagined before they arrived on this campus. The most eloquent and striking testament to the magic that happens when faculty and students are brought together was delivered recently by West Virginia University's twenty-fifth Rhodes Scholar, Carolyn Conner.

Carolyn is a native of Valley Fork, West Virginia. She is the daughter of Jack and Margo Conner, a school bus driver and a teacher's aide respectively. Carolyn Conner has excelled at the university, perhaps beyond her own wildest expectations. She not only achieved what amounts to a perfect academic record while at WVU, but she has also now been awarded a Rhodes Scholarship to study at Oxford, bringing honor to herself, to her family, to us, and to her state. Carolyn will study philosophy and physics, and I am confident that she will become a leader in her chosen field in the years to come. When I introduced Carolyn to the governor and the state press corps in Charleston, she said:

> All of my life, people have said that I could succeed. My parents said that I could. My teachers in Clay County said that I could. My professors at WVU said that I could. And gradually I came to believe that I could, and I did. And I want to be a college professor, and the rest of my life, I too will tell young people, "You can!"

In her simple and sincere statement, Carolyn spoke insightfully about what we do best at this university. No doubt, words as eloquent could be spoken by thousands of our students, past and present. We teach. We open minds. We lead by raising expectations. We inspire. We offer hope. We yield up opportunity to those who come to us to learn, and in doing so, we lead, and we add value to the lives of each succeeding generation. Perhaps Henry Adams stated it best: "A teacher . . . can never tell where his influence stops."[1]

Secondly, we serve West Virginia. I have seen how the university reaches out to the people of our state and region, providing true leadership through public service. One of the best examples lies in our Robert C. Byrd Health Sciences Center, which has turned its attention to improving the delivery of rural health care. Every day, our students, staff, and faculty members provide high-quality health care in rural locations, and the people of West Virginia are responding. Thanks to Governor Caperton, our legislature, the Kellogg Foundation, and the people who are West Virginia University, the Rural Health Initiative of the Robert C. Byrd Health Sciences Center is today far reaching.

I want to publicly thank Governor Caperton for his recognition and ringing endorsement of the quality of West Virginia University last week in his State of the State address. Governor Caperton has again recommended a substantial investment in higher education as well as monies for various projects that best exemplify our service to our citizens. The Rural Health Initiative, of which I just spoke, was bolstered by the governor with an additional appropriation of $1.5 million to ensure we may continue to provide health care to citizens in rural areas.

Additionally, Governor Caperton enthusiastically recommended the expansion of a WVU Extension Service program—Energy Express. This program allows disadvantaged children to continue learning and developing their academic skills in a structured atmosphere throughout the summer. Although it is quite an ambitious challenge, Governor Caperton has provided funds for the WVU Extension Service to lead this effort while expanding this landmark initiative to all fifty-five counties.

I have also seen the quality of our regional campuses, which increased enrollments this year, and the Charleston Division. The commitment to excellence has prompted another institution—West Virginia Institute of Technology—to consider joining us as a third regional campus. We also serve through the Office of Service Learning and its many student service projects, individual faculty efforts, cultural events, distance education efforts, and participation in consortia related to job development. There are very few lives in West Virginia that aren't touched by WVU. West Virginia University's commitment to reach out in our state is without peer.

Third, we engage in scholarship and research. I have been privileged to see many of our research efforts at work and to explore with the principal investigators and center directors the hope and promise their work offers for West Virginia. I have seen our researchers working to develop new construction materials and engineered wood products that offer hope to the forestry industry in our state. I have seen the Carbon Products Consortium efforts to develop useful new products from high-sulfur coal.

Our Geographic Information System Laboratory in the Department of Geology and Geography has teamed up with the State Geological Survey and the West Virginia Department of Environmental Protection on a five-year project to develop a geographic information mapping system. This partnership exemplifies how WVU can work cooperatively with state agencies through legislative-sponsored activities to serve West Virginia. The end result of this project will undergird the long-term economic development efforts of West Virginia. Time and again I have seen the great value that our university scholarship and research adds to the lives of the people it serves.

Fourth, I have seen how this university is part of the greater international community of scholars. This year I have visited with representatives of colleges in China, Japan, the Ukraine, and South America who are familiar with our work and welcome what we can do for their countries. In doing so, we learn much that is valuable to us. I have gotten to know a young student from Malaysia. She chose WVU because our standards for achievement were higher than those of other universities in the United States and because our campus continues to be among the safest in the country. I have watched our College of Business and Economics open its doors to the leaders of Shanghai. Their initiatives will bear fruit for the people of China as well as those of West Virginia. We are an important part of the international system of higher education.

Finally, I have seen how the university is a repository of knowledge and culture for this and future generations. I have visited our major library facilities. I have become familiar with the University Art Collection. I have seen student performers at work in the arts. I have seen how our senior members of the faculty are themselves significant repositories of knowledge. In Japan, they would be called "national treasures."

In the January 1996 issue of *Discover* magazine, the top one hundred science stories for 1995 were listed. One of these stories is about the work of Dr. Kenneth Showalter, Eberly Distinguished Professor of Chemistry. Dr. Showalter's research in chemical nonlinear dynamics was highlighted as one of the top four research stories in chemistry for the past year. Dr. Showalter is one of the many "national treasures" that exist among the faculty here at WVU.

We are a quality institution. We are a leading institution. And in all that we do, our foundation, our alumni, our fans, our governing board, and numerous other individuals who love this institution are extraordinarily supportive. I am proud to be your president, and I am proud of you. This, then, is who we are. It follows that we should ask, where are we?

OBSERVATIONS ABOUT OUR SOCIETY

We have arrived at our own time in history, but just as in times past, we face a set of challenges that will test our character and leadership. Consider the words of WVU President Irvin Stewart. He told the Class of 1947 that they were "entering an unsettled world. There is change, and the promise of change, everywhere . . . [C]hange, like the game of musical chairs we played as children, gives the newcomer his opportunity. It is a challenge to the graduate who has the energy and imagination to put his intellectual equipment and training to best use."

The challenges of change are certainly not new to this university. For the record, here are just a few of the challenges that are converging upon us as we enter the twenty-first century: federal funds for higher education, health care, and other programs in West Virginia will be reduced by hundreds of millions of dollars over the next several years. As a result, the state has limited funds and many competing priorities. We are mandated to give well-deserved salary increases. We are feeling the impact of a general increase in societal problems such as alcohol and drug abuse, lack of civic responsibility, and crime. Current expenses will continue to grow.

Each year fewer students are graduating from West Virginia high schools. The number of high school seniors in West Virginia will drop more than 20 percent over the next ten years. Additionally, many high school graduates are not opting for a traditional college education. The main campus is losing enrollment. At the same time, both traditional and nontraditional (older and place-bound) students are demanding increased access to higher education, insisting on new outlets like the Bridging the Gap effort.

All over America, people are demanding more accountability from higher education. Distressingly, increasing numbers of Americans see a higher education as a private good, something that should be paid for by those who are privileged to receive one. And, perhaps most importantly, our economy is now marked by three important attributes: globalization, enhanced technology (and new means of communication), and a seemingly never-ending search for quality. WVU must respond to all of these changes.

This will not be easy. We were all trained, educated, and socialized as members of a university community in a different era—a time of rising expectations justified by rising tuition and fees, rising federal support for research and student aid, and rising student populations.

We now must operate in a different era. Federal funds are shrinking, state funds are limited, enrollments are declining, and we are expected—in the midst of all of this—to adjust to what amounts to gigantic shifts in our economy. The impact of all of these forces creates a swirling sea of change that we must navigate. As good stewards of this institution, *we must strengthen* WVU in the midst of today's significant challenges. We cannot lower our standards. We cannot accept less than high quality. We cannot stop investing in the future. We have no choice but to change ourselves, and we are charting a new course. I should point out that higher education is often criticized for not changing fast enough. Consider these remarks by Dr. Robert Zemsky of the University of Pennsylvania and Dr. William F. Massey of Stanford University:

> There is a growing sense that colleges and universities have become too set in their ways to change—the last hold outs against the restructuring that is recasting the America enterprise. What banks, retailers, manufacturers of every description, insurance companies, hospitals and governments have undertaken has some how remained beyond the reach and will of higher education.[2]

ON STRENGTHENING OUR UNIVERSITY

What course shall we chart in the context of our times? The answer, I believe, lies in understanding that most of our students and parents, our research clients, our taxpayers, and others we serve view us as providing a variety of services to them, primarily through teaching, research, and outreach. For us, then, the future must involve improving the quality of our services. We must begin to think of better quality as involving better service to those who look to us for help, hope, opportunity, and leadership.

QUALITY OF THE STUDENT EXPERIENCE

First, it is clear—very clear to me—that we must stay the course. In the years to come, we must focus more on the needs and expectations of our students and the quality of their campus experience. Given increases in tuition and the differentiation of colleges based on their marketing strategies, parents and students today select a college or university based on the reputation (perceived quality) of the institution. The perceived quality of our institution, in turn, is based on how well we perform in providing three levels of service: the basic level, the performance level, and the excitement level.[3]

I should admit that Susan and I have a vested interest in the quality of the student experience at WVU. Our daughter, Ashley, will be attending WVU as a freshman beginning in the fall of this year. Like us, other students and parents have a set of basic expectations from this or any institution. Parents and students expect to encounter:

- a safe campus,
- residence halls conducive to study,
- available courses in students' majors,
- helpful and supportive advising, and
- an environment where students are treated with respect.

If we fail in these, we will lose students because their basic expectations are unmet. We will also lose prospective students if the word gets out that we can't meet even the basic needs of our students. I submit that we must excel at meeting these basic needs if we are to halt declines in our enrollment in Morgantown. This is why we provided a safe alternative to what had become a dangerous block party, launched our student initiatives, and tried to project a more student-centered image of the university. I would be remiss if I failed to take this opportunity to state how proud I am of the leadership shown by Student Body President Pat Esposito and the student administration in developing FallFest '95 as an alternative to the block party. These mature student leaders showed tremendous courage and perseverance and have my utmost respect and admiration.

"Performance level" quality indicators are those aspects of an educational experience that students and their parents consider most when making decisions about which higher education institution to attend. These include:

- high-quality instruction,
- excellent job placement,

- graduate school acceptance,
- reasonable cost, and
- a pleasant campus environment.

Should we not meet expectations in these areas as well? Are these not reasonable expectations? I believe they are.

But what excites our students? What makes them urge others to join us at WVU? I believe that excitement comes from exceeding our students' expectations, primarily through demonstrations of genuine concern. For example, excitement could come from a simple act like a faculty member calling a student at home to show concern about absenteeism or a poor grade. Most of the time, excitement doesn't cost anything, but it can be a major contributor—making us a role model for other institutions.

Today, I am presenting you with the final report of the student affairs task force. This report is the product of the hard work of a dedicated group of faculty, students, and staff. I publicly thank them for their efforts in improving the student experience.

In an effort to continue to build quality, I am accepting their recommendations in principle and am appointing Dean Herman Moses as the project manager to ensure the recommendations are implemented as quickly as possible. He will head a committee that will include the provost and my chief of staff. I would like to share with you, and endorse, the report's student-centered vision for WVU:

- We will exceed our students' expectations in everything we do.
- We will actively recruit students capable of succeeding at WVU.
- We will become one of the leaders in retention among land-grant universities. Every employee at WVU will become involved in retention, and all of our employees will understand how they can help our students meet their academic goals.

- We will improve our living and learning environment. Our residence halls will set the tone for the entire campus in shaping student behavior and helping students adjust to an academic environment that is, in many cases, far different from what they experienced in high school.
- Our support processes will be efficient and designed for students.
- We will be an exemplary service organization that treats students with respect.
- We will invest in student success. Although our financial challenges are great, we must invest in programs and facilities that enhance student academic success.
- We will invest in bringing more student service technology to our campus, especially to our residence halls and to our classrooms.

WVU has always been a campus that cares about its students. The recommendations outlined in the task force report will build on our past achievements to create a student success environment. At the same time, I want us to focus on the needs and expectations of those who assist in paying for the education of our students. Most of our students have parents and other loved ones who help to pay their tuition and fees. Many of these same parents and other loved ones are also West Virginia taxpayers. Shouldn't we focus on those who pay the bills and ask what we should offer them?

Our Mountaineer Parents Club is a direct response to a bona fide need for campus contact with the parents and families of our students. It is designed to help our students succeed. The Parents Club has been well received and is in the process of forming chapters all around the country. To date, more than 1,200 families have joined. I expect that number to climb in the years to come and to reach approximately half of the family units who support students here. Our Parents Club should be a primary foundation upon which student success is built.

To better inform and better connect parents and families with our campus, I am pleased to announce the beginning of a benchmark parent service—the

Mountaineer Parents Club Helpline. The Helpline is a toll-free phone number for the use of parents when they are in need of information or assistance related to WVU. The Mountaineer Parents Club also encourages our students' parents to share their candid comments, criticism, or praise through this mechanism.

We will try to respond to every call within one business day and sincerely hope this initiative helps WVU to better connect our students' parents and families to their university experience. We are implementing this service to make WVU an accessible, helpful, responsive, and less confusing institution to our students and their parents.

I thank and congratulate the WVU Alumni Association and my wife Susan for their leadership and tireless efforts for the Mountaineer Parents Club.

I remind you again that over half of our parents have not attended college and sometimes find it difficult to relate to a seemingly large and complex institution like WVU. But regardless of their own experience, and despite our size and complexity, there is one thing that parents do understand, and that is a caring spirit and attitude on our campus. We have that caring spirit and attitude, and I hope that we can project it into the home of every student.

Recently I received a letter from Ann and Bob Cadran of Cary, North Carolina, the parents of Erika Cadran, a sophomore student at WVU who died here in 1995 after a severe asthma attack. Many parts of the university came together to help Erika's family through a very difficult time. The Cadrans wrote me to express their appreciation. They wrote:

> At the conclusion of the memorial service, the hundred or so in attendance walked solemnly to Oglebay Hall and to the mast of the USS *West Virginia* where a bell tolled 21 times for Erika. It was a ceremony fit for someone of greatness. Yet she was just an ordinary student beginning her sophomore year at WVU. Apparently, nobody is just an average student at WVU.

When WVU shows that it cares, people respond! The Cadrans care about us because we cared about them. It is just that simple.

THE RESEARCH ENVIRONMENT

Secondly, we must address changes in the research environment. As we focus on research, we will want to apply many of the same principles of quality and customer satisfaction that we are applying in student services. Over the last fifty years, thanks to partnerships among government, business, and academic institutions, the United States' record of technological innovation has been the envy of the world.

Compared with other major nations, our investment in research is falling behind. As companies and government seek to economize, research funding is an easy target, and research grants are being cut. It is expected that significant cuts in funding of research will continue for some time. We already have carved out a few key areas for research that have been successfully funded—in rural health, telemedicine, software, carbon sciences and products, and world music.

We must be relentless in seeking funding for our important work. We must develop a strategy that recognizes where the research dollars are, focuses our research, carves out some niches to concentrate on, and delivers high-quality research at a competitive price. We must identify partners who have compatible interests, develop effective policies for research centers and institutes, and continually focus our efforts.

We also need to address the needs of researchers in the arts, humanities, and social sciences who contribute to the social, cultural, and intellectual growth of our citizens. While their limited sources of research support are drying up, their value is not diminished, and their research must be supported. Therefore, I have created and charged a research task force to help formulate a university-wide research strategy, including the development of policies for research centers and institutes, and to submit recommendations for incentives to encourage research at WVU in all areas—the arts, the humanities, and the sciences. The members of our task force will be highly talented and broadly respected. As we revise our research strategies, we must focus on the needs and expectations of those we serve. I will charge the task force to ask the following questions:

- Whom do we serve as a research institution?
- What are their needs and expectations?
- How we can exceed their expectations?

I have requested that the group provide me with a report by the end of this academic year. We can continue to have a high-quality research program here, one that is, in some respects, world class.

OUTREACH PROGRAMS

Thirdly, it will be important for us to improve the quality of our outreach programs. Again we must ask the basic questions, whom do we serve, what are their needs and expectations, and how can we exceed them? We must serve the public, not just through our Extension Service and Health Sciences Center, but throughout the entire university, in all of its locations.

In the twenty-first century, it will be important for us to embrace outreach in every college and school and to make it a part of what we do daily. It will also be important for us to reward and compensate those engaged in outreach. Extension, outreach, and public service are the most compelling and significant ways that we can demonstrate to the West Virginia taxpayers who support us that we care about them and are worthy of their support. Our presence must be felt in every county and every segment of our state.

CORE FACILITIES

Fourthly, I think we should take great care that we do not neglect the core facilities of our university, including our libraries. We must instead think of our university library system as being a major building block upon which our quality—and, hence, future opportunities for our students and for ourselves—must be built. They are critical to the basic quality of this institution. We must not think of our libraries, for example, as an entity competing with individuals for salaries and benefits. The library has been a vital part of this university since its beginning. In a report to the governor, outlining the most pressing needs for the new university, WVU's first president wrote simply, "The necessity of a suitable college library is so evident that we need but only refer to it."[4] By the end of the century, WVU had what was referred to at the time as a "model library." It contained nearly twenty thousand books and periodicals. Unfortunately, our libraries today are in need of serious attention. I believe this situation must be seriously addressed—and it is best addressed through serious actions rather than words. I have authorized Provost Lang to develop and oversee implementation of a plan to modernize WVU's libraries. This will be a monumental undertaking, and it will require us to answer new questions:

- Is it worth maintaining a collection of books that are never used?
- Is it worth maintaining books that are rarely used in open stacks?
- Is our collection focused on the actual needs of those who use the library?
- What role will technology realistically play in the twenty-first-century library?
- Are we devoting sufficient study areas for students, staff, and faculty?

I have more questions and few answers, but I do recognize that, at every turn, the libraries of our institution are at its heart. Our libraries must remain strong if our university is to remain strong. Governor Caperton demonstrated his recognition of the critical importance of our libraries and their need for further support in his State of the State address last week. In the executive budget he presented to the legislature, the governor recommended a $2 million investment to improve the WVU libraries. Today I am making a multiyear commitment of at least $25 million in support of WVU's libraries. Fulfilling this commitment will require board approval. Through my commitment, I want to assure each of you that the library challenges are among my highest priorities.

We must also improve the quality of other facilities and invest in new ones. Our master planners have just completed reviewing the programmatic requests of what you perceive our facilities needs and opportunities to be. I am very interested in new downtown classrooms and labs, new technological investments, major renovations in agriculture and forestry, a new shell building and women's gymnastics center, a creative arts "gateway" to our campus, and student recreational facilities.

I can tell you that current expectations exceed the university's ability to pay. Thus, we will have to establish priorities, and we will need private help to meet our priority needs. It is likely that future planning activities, including those to plan facilities, will take the form of additional task forces, which will comprise university community members with varied interests. We are entering a time when priorities will have to be realistic.

WORKPLACE QUALITY

Finally, it is imperative that in these times of financial challenge, we find ways to improve the quality of our workplace. We will need to:

- benchmark various levels of productivity,

- establish reward systems that appropriately reward desired behaviors,
- use technology in instruction and in the delivery of services on campus,
- devise new systems that are user friendly and refuse to tolerate systems that are not
- change our curriculum when necessary to meet the needs of our disciplines and our society.

This may require a different way of thinking. Too many times since I have come to campus, I have been told, "I would like to do that because I know it is right, but the money is simply not available." There is a lot of money spent at WVU. I fear that our cost allocation mechanisms, methods of accounting, and, most importantly, our patterns of thinking preclude us from doing what we know we should do when we see a need.

The successful university of the future will be service oriented. It will focus on the needs of those served, and it will act responsibly when a need is identified. This may mean curtailing some current activities that have lost their effectiveness or that have a lower priority than the new priorities that have been established.

The final report of the administrative task force will be completed and broadly distributed near the end of this month. As you review it, you will note that much of its content is devoted to a call for changes in the administrative culture of WVU—from a rigid, rule-based culture to a principle-based culture; from hierarchically based interaction to cross-functional communication and decision making; and from an introspective organizational focus to a culture of community, cooperation, and collaboration with the citizens who support WVU.

Today, I too call for a change in the culture of the institution—an evolutionary change, but a clear change nevertheless. The change must be toward a more service-oriented university, one that constantly seeks to improve its quality by ascertaining the needs of those it serves, providing leadership by working with them to establish appropriate expectations for the level of service we provide, and then exceeding these expectations once they are established. I see a service-oriented culture as one that will help us to establish clearer priorities in the context of our times, and I see exceeding the expectations of those we serve as the only means by which we can hope for increased public funding in the future and enhanced external support for the programs we offer.

It is in serving better that we will be perceived as offering higher quality and leading better. It is by following the focused star of service to others that we will be able to competently navigate the swirling seas of change. Thus, in everything that we do, we must seek the answer to three questions:

- Whom do we serve?
- What are their needs and expectations?
- How can we meet those needs and exceed those expectations?

CONCLUSION

I have said it before, and I will say it again today: this university is the crowning achievement of the people of West Virginia! As a land-grant university, it is one of the pillars upon which the future of our country is based. The privileged look you have offered me during my initial six months of service as your president has clearly convinced me that even in the challenging times in which we live, we will strengthen this university. The extraordinary assets of this university, especially the people who constitute it and support it, will make that happen. Therefore, in the midst of significant change, we should move forward together with great confidence.

STAYING ON TRACK

Piloting River Boats, Wiggling Free, Finding Waldo, and
Following in the Footsteps of St. Patrick

1997

The mission and vision of the university were again reaffirmed in this State of
the University address. Individual and collective achievements were noted, and
a more specific strategic agenda was announced. This speech also reminded the
members of our university community of the vital importance of their work.

Every day I am reminded of the strengths of this extraordinary institution and each individual who is a part of it. Each of us here is called to different work. We hail from many traditions. We adhere to many creeds. We have many different ideas. Whatever may appear on the surface to divide us is far outweighed by our common devotion to the work of higher education. It is that commitment that binds us together.

The spirit of learning and service thrives in the hearts and minds of the good, talented, creative, and caring people of WVU. Today, our university touches every town, every county, and every citizen in West Virginia. Examples abound of how our faculty and staff move West Virginia and WVU forward.

Let us not forget our retirees' influence on each of us. For many of them, the hope of a better university, a better West Virginia, a better nation, was a life's work.

Our students come from all fifty-five counties in West Virginia, all states in the nation, and eighty-seven foreign countries, reflecting our fundamental goal to broadly educate to the best of our abilities. Some of these students you know well: Carolyn Conner, our twenty-fifth Rhodes Scholar; Trish Kalbaugh, our fifteenth Goldwater Scholar; *USA Today* scholar Brian Caveney; and Carmella Evans, a WVU pharmacy student who, just last week, was named to the *USA Today* all-academic team.

Others may not always capture the headlines, but they capture the excitement of our teaching—students like those in our nationally ranked engineering honorary and advertising classes; students who help flood victims or volunteer at a Habitat for Humanity house-building over their Thanksgiving break.

Add to these faces our 130,000 alumni from all fifty states and sixty-seven foreign countries who are a continual source of pride. These alumni include athletic superstars like Jerry West and "Hot Rod" Hundley, and academic and professional superstars like Charles Vest, the current president of MIT, and Terry Wimmer, a winner of the 1996 Pulitzer Prize for journalism.

Thousands of donors and fans support our institution. Their gifts, added to the growth in endowment funds, made this the most successful year ever for the WVU Foundation.

It was well publicized that our Gator Bowl berth was due, in part, to this university's phenomenal fan support. More than twenty-five thousand Mountaineer fans packed the stands in Jacksonville to prove it.

Members of the faculty and staff, thank you for all that you do! I have taken the time to share these snapshots of our university community in the hopes you will recall them often. At times, WVU may seem large and complex. We sometimes get caught in the daily routine of our duties, but I hope that from time to time you will take a moment to step back and reflect on the importance of what you do.

Mark Twain, in *Life on the Mississippi*, writes about how he sometimes "pitied" doctors. He remembered his early days as a riverboat captain and how exhilarating it was to be on the river, experiencing the beautiful elements of nature on the mighty Mississippi. Later in his life, however, he came to regard the eddies, the water, and the branches over the river as constant threats to his boat. He had forgotten what drew him to the river in the first place: he loved the work! He then pondered the medical profession. He worried that doctors would concentrate too much on medical problems and not enough on the joy of serving others.[5] Clearly, hundreds of other faculty and staff have not forgotten.

Ladies and gentlemen, believe in what you do. You are part of something extraordinary.

THE CHALLENGE OF CHANGE

As I have mentioned on several occasions, a number of changes are converging on our college campuses at the same time. These include the globalization of the economy, with its incessant drive for competitive quality in every service and product; the transformation of our state's economy; rapid advances in technology; a possible decline in this nation's social capital; accountability efforts; changing patterns in research funding; more competition; and enrollment challenges, to name a few.

In this context, I think it is important for each of us to remember that often change is no one's fault. Tolstoy once wrote an essay on leadership, in which he pondered what the "cause" was when an apple fell from a tree.[6] Was it the wind? Was it gravity? Was it the apple's increasing weight? Was it the sun ripening the stem? Tolstoy reminded us, as did Homer, that fate is the one thing not one of us can escape. Change is, in a historical sense, involuntary, but it does present opportunities. We can either shape change or suffer change. We can lead or be led. Let us decide to lead and lead together.

Abraham Lincoln enjoyed telling the story of a frog mired in the mud of a country road one spring. The frog called upon his many influential friends for help. They responded enthusiastically and spent an enormous amount of energy attempting to free their friend. But alas, he could not be moved. The next day, the friends were all shocked to see this frog happily croaking at a nearby farm pond. "We don't understand," they said. "When we couldn't help you yesterday, we thought you would die there. What happened?" The frog explained that he, too, thought death was certain. Suddenly, a wagon approached from down the road. As he heard the wagon wheels barreling toward him, as he heard the pounding of the horses' hoofs, he suddenly mustered the energy to wiggle free. To survive, he had made the seemingly impossible possible.[7]

Clearly, this is a defining moment for WVU. We must muster the energy to "wiggle free" and take charge of our own destiny.

CREATING AND CONNECTING THE VISION

This is easier said than done, but we can meet the challenges of change. To do so, we must first adopt a clear vision of what we want to achieve together. This collective understanding must be supportable and mobilizing, grounded in believable hope, and reflective of what the people of this state think our university should do.

To this end, a cross section of people helped develop a vision for WVU; it encompasses our tradition, knowledge, and insights from many of you. In the spirit of serving this institution, we offer it as reflection of how WVU's people are responding to the needs and opportunities at hand. We believe it echoes what matters most to us as we face a future that is ours to create.

West Virginia University is a student-centered, learning community meeting the changing needs of the people of West Virginia and the nation through teaching, research, service, and technology.

Knowing the direction in which to lead is only the first step. We must also build a leadership culture capable of realizing the promise of our vision. In truth, each of us is a leader. As individuals, we must realize the responsibility of change lies not just within the institution but within each of us. We must take care to not focus so deeply on our own specialized environments that we lose sight of our collective mission and interdependence. We must communicate better laterally and vertically. We must be more open and honest with each other to build mutual trust. We must exhibit a spirit of generosity when we give our time, praise, and information to others. And we must set and exemplify high ethical standards. Woven together, such behaviors strengthen the very character of West Virginia University.

As we look to the future, we should recognize that we have made considerable progress. WVU reached a significant milestone when it was recently designated a Truman Scholarship Foundation Honor Institution, one of only seventeen institutions so recognized. The full-time freshmen who enter WVU consistently have the highest SAT and ACT scores in West Virginia. Our recent retention and graduation rates are also the best of any college or university in West Virginia. While there is room for improvement, we are attracting higher-quality students and are working to see that these students graduate. There is clear value added through the educational experience at WVU.

WVU also understands and takes the challenge of technology seriously. Through our MDTV program, which links specialists in Morgantown and Charleston with physicians in rural clinics, West Virginians can access quality health care. If we can deliver medical services effectively using technology, then surely we can deliver quality education as well. We are making inroads. A new course is being offered in Morgantown by faculty from Parkersburg. A statistics course for WVU is being developed on the World Wide Web. I know of other courses in history and music that are under development, and I applaud all of these efforts. Rooms like this Project 320 classroom we gather in today and our RuralNet initiative further help educators teach in engaging ways. Importantly, our faculty received about $650,000 from the state's vice chancellor for technology to develop new courses. Internet connections and cable networks are planned to be in our residence halls by next fall. We have completed the fiber-optic backbone for the Morgantown campus and will soon complete the "wiring" of all major buildings. This crucial part of the infrastructure has cost us more than $10 million, an essential investment if we are to be successful in our vision for the twenty-first century. Our technology growth also extends to the newly developed Institute for Software Improvement, representing a collaborative arrangement with the state and the West Virginia High Technology Consortium Foundation. Clearly, WVU is playing a role in shaping the new environment in which we will work and educate students.

We have also made significant progress this year in stabilizing enrollment, addressing the need for a modern library system for our campuses, enhancing the freshman year experience, increasing faculty and staff salaries on the main campus by more than $13 million in the last two fiscal years, and focusing our important research agenda.

Running through these achievements and others is the recognition that quality must pervade all we do. Every day, for example, we must think through issues of academic and program quality. The recent debate in the faculty senate about writing across the curriculum is a good example of our need to continually reexamine pedagogical issues that form the base of our academic programs.

We now have the opportunity to build on the progress we have achieved. To maintain our momentum, we will take the following five action steps:

ACTION 1: REMAIN STUDENT CENTERED

First, we must remember always to look to those we serve for guidance—students, patients, clients, and research sponsors. Above all, we must remain student centered. If we are to preserve the public trust, students must remain our primary focus. Feedback suggests we are on the right track.

I want to thank all those working on Operation Jump-Start. This program has been aimed at personalizing the freshman experience, and people are noticing. Although our effort is new, the initiative has already garnered national attention, including features in the *New York Times*, the *Pittsburgh Post-Gazette*, the *New York Newsday*, the *New Hampshire Union Leader*, and other publications across the country and throughout West Virginia. Results are encouraging. We have exceeded predicted enrollment in the freshman class, and students who have been touched by our programs in advising and tutoring tell us that our freshman efforts are worthwhile.

David Stewart, one of seven resident faculty leaders, credits Jump-Start with helping 102 freshmen improve their midterm grades in Boreman Hall alone. The other resident faculty leaders have similar testimonials. We invite you to join us in sharing this progress at our first ever Sophomore Launch in April during Spring Parents Weekend and our Weekend of Honors.

Our outreach to parents has had some impressive first-year results. The Mountaineer Parents Club Helpline receives and processes dozens of calls weekly. Our goal to eliminate long registration lines met with resounding success. I want to thank the staff who worked hard to change the process last year and who continue to make improvements to bring next fall's registration online. Our students regularly work alongside faculty on projects that range from learning the unique art of making steel drums to researching and ameliorating some of the nation's most difficult environmental problems.

All of these examples, among others, rightfully keep students at the heart of our efforts. Whether we call it student centered, patient centered, or even research-client centered, the message should be clear: WVU, first and foremost, commits its energies to the needs and concerns of those we primarily serve. We are not self-centered—we are "other centered."

ACTION 2: ENGAGE SOCIETY

Second in our five action steps: we must further engage society by better serving it. Charles E. Hathaway, chancellor of the University of Arkansas, warns us that "the university must not stand apart from its society and its immediate environment, but must be an integral part of that society."[8] We simply have not been as aggressive on this front as the times demand. We are not always seen, for example, as addressing the number one issue consistently identified by West Virginians: obtaining jobs for the unemployed and underemployed. Welfare reform amplifies this concern. President John F. Kennedy said that our progress as a nation can be no greater than our progress in education. I sincerely believe our progress as a university can be no greater than our service to the entire state.

We are making strides. Five initiatives, in particular, demonstrate our efforts to become engaged.

First, the extension task force reaffirmed the importance of the WVU Extension Service as the critical link connecting the university to the citizens of West Virginia. The vision statement for the Extension Service asserts that the organization is founded upon a partnership of researchers and educators who develop and communicate sound, research-based knowledge to address critical issues in West Virginia. We welcome Dr. Lawrence Cote from Penn State to lead our Extension Service. Dr. Cote has a strong record of past achievement; his appointment has been well received within the institution, and we await his official arrival on March 15.

Second, as you know, we have a solid history of support from the Kellogg Foundation through our Health Sciences Center. Because of our past success, we were invited to submit a new proposal for community partnership activities to the foundation. Provost Jerry Lang and Professor Lei Bammel proposed community–university partnerships that would transform our students through community involvement. This program has been likened to a "student Extension Service" in that it would provide students with a culminating experience aimed at helping communities solve problems. We are optimistically awaiting word from Kellogg about the status of this exciting public service concept.

Third, we have been reexamining the notion of a self-sustaining science and technology park in Morgantown. This issue has been discussed often, but I want us to revisit it once again in light of our need to support both our research efforts and our efforts to aid economic development in north central West Virginia.

Fourth, the executive MBA program in the College of Business and Economics represents one of our successful academic ventures to bring the expertise of the university to the people. Enrollment has been growing, and we are simultaneously reaching out to various population centers throughout West Virginia. I encourage other colleges and schools to examine how they might also reach out.

Fifth, we must extend ourselves to major employers, as we have with the chemical industry through the Polymer Alliance and with the federal government at the NASA and FBI facilities in Fairmont and Clarksburg. At NASA we have established a joint research partnership, known as the Institute for Software Improvement, with the state and the High Technology Consortium Foundation. This institute will be dedicated to working on problems of software reuse and software validation. Additionally, Professor Michael Yura will lead a team of university employees to visit the FBI center to better see how our resources can address the concerns of our neighbors.

Fifty years ago, President Irvin Stewart said that the state is our campus. We must demonstrate to all of West Virginia our clear intention to view the state as our campus and to become more valuable to our state and the nation.

ACTION 3: FOCUS RESEARCH

Our third action step is to focus our research. WVU's research mission cuts across every segment of the university and has increasingly been at the core of our land-grant institution's activities. It is our mechanism for learning and developing our knowledge base. But just as change is forcing us to better direct our other missions, so too must we maximize the quality of our research and its relevancy to pressing state and national issues. We simply cannot be all things to all people. Waning dollars demand more focus on our campuses. As our research task force recommended, WVU should invest its discretionary research resources in focus areas and areas of excellence where its research activities can become internationally competitive. These focus areas should reflect the history, the culture, and the social and economic needs of West Virginia.

After broad input and extensive deliberation, the associate deans for research are implementing this recommendation by suggesting these six research focus areas:

- Advanced materials
- Energy and environment
- Human development and culture
- Information technology
- Local and regional economic development
- Molecular and biomedical sciences

These areas were chosen based on existing strengths, potential for funding, state-industry needs, and potential for community and economic development. Together they represent a concerted way WVU can improve the quality of life for West Virginians and society in general. I applaud the faculty, staff, and students involved in this process for their vision and bold determination. These evolving foci will need to be constantly assessed in terms of current conditions and change. Our intent to focus research does not diminish the importance of research efforts in other areas. Our goals are to continually capitalize on our strong research tradition, encourage cooperative ventures, and build the strongest national and international reputation possible.

ACTION 4: IMPLEMENT THE MASTER FACILITIES PLAN

Our fourth call to action is to implement the facilities master plan. Recently approved, the planning process was unique in its formulation, its direction, and its result. Involving hundreds of people over two years, the planning process squarely emphasizes academics. Four major academic buildings will be thoroughly renovated, greatly improving our ability to teach and to do research.

New space will also be added to campus. It is academic space in the form of library, laboratory, classroom, research, and teaching areas, and it includes a new 180,000-square-foot academic building. It is student space in the form of meeting, study, and recreation areas. It is space that allows us to meet the needs and expectations of all who come to our campus pursuing education, contribution, and growth. The plan integrates well with the city of Morgantown, offering opportunities to partner in recreation and riverfront development.

Although ambitious, our master plan is feasible and can be accomplished within a reasonable period without unduly taxing university resources. Funding will come from either monies set aside by law for building and construction or from private gifts. The operational monies of this institution will not be diverted. That means salary, supply, and travel funds will be unaffected. Neither will tuition increase as a result of the master plan, with the exception of a proposed recreation-center fee to be voted on by the students.

As we work to make this plan a reality, we will look to our facilities and services professionals for effective guidance through the design and construction process, we will look to the West Virginia University Foundation for fundraising and community support, and we will look to our faculty and staff for continued input to ensure a consistent link between our facility improvements and strategic direction.

ACTION 5: IMPROVE COMMUNICATIONS

A fifth and final call to action is to improve our communications, internally and externally. As we strive for quality, we must explicitly differentiate WVU's strengths and attributes from those of our competitors. With increasing competition for students, research dollars, and other resources, we can no longer afford to be misunderstood, overlooked, or confused with others. We must have a unified and distinguishable message, supportive of our overall vision.

A prominent WVU graduate, George Bennett, is one of America's leading thinkers on the subject of organizational change. Amidst so much change and information, he encourages us to "look for Waldo." You know Waldo, the hard-to-find character in a child's book hidden among thousands of other figures? George prompts us to ask, where's WVU? What characteristics define our quality? Both our strategies and our messages must convey focus and quality.

Better communication can lead to many positive outcomes: a national reputation for our faculty, increased research funding, increased enrollment of high-quality students, strong state support, better faculty and staff recruiting returns, internal harmony, trust, and increased pride. We know WVU is distinctive. Our task is to be sure that when others are asked to describe us, words like "impersonal," "party school," or "huge campus" are forever replaced by words like "innovative," "high quality," "cost effective," "caring," and "academically distinguished."

These five actions—remaining student-, patient-, and client-centered; engaging in society; focusing our research; implementing our facilities master plan; and communicating more effectively—point us toward our highest aspirations.

We have a lot going on at West Virginia University. Many positive paths are being forged. The strategic development that I describe does not necessarily equate increased expenditures, but it does mandate a redirection of current expenditures. There are important decisions to make. We are molding and shaping the university to meet the demands of our time, much as it was developed by others before us as they faced the challenges of their day. These strategies will take more thought to develop. They will need teamwork to achieve and a willingness to be bold. But the strategies are achievable, and in their successes, the students, faculty, and staff of WVU and the citizens of West

Virginia will accrue the benefits. Above all, we should continually remind ourselves that the fundamental goal of our strategies is to improve as an academic institution so that we can serve society better.

CONCLUSION

Over the semester break, I read a book that reminded me of just how important great centers of learning like ours are, not just for students passing through them, but also for civilization itself. I read the story of Ireland's heroic role, from the fall of Rome to the rise of Medieval Europe in Thomas Cahill's book *How the Irish Saved Civilization*.[9] Rome, the mightiest empire the world had even seen, fell in only seventy-five years. Whole communities—systems of law, education, culture, agriculture, and commerce—disappeared in a little over a generation. Whole nations that flourished under Rome fell in a matter of years.

A little-known story during Rome's fall centers on a Roman named Patricius who was converted to Catholicism. Later known as St. Patrick, he brought civilization to Ireland. In his thirty short years, Patricius created a series of monasteries and places of learning in Ireland that not only adopted his belief system but also fostered education and learning among the people. The clergy he energized turned their efforts toward education, copying and studying books by daylight and candlelight that were written by the great thinkers of Rome, of Greece, and of the early Christian Church.

Thus, even as mighty Rome fell, Ireland's culture and educational levels rose. Even as Europe fell into the abyss of the Dark Ages, learning was not lost. And when Europe later stabilized, the Irish emerged to resettle the rest of the British Islands and Europe, creating more abbeys, monasteries, and universities. To quote Cahill, "Wherever they went, the Irish brought with them their books, many unseen in Europe for centuries . . . Wherever they went, they brought their love of learning and their skills in bookmaking. In the bays and valleys of their exile, they reestablished literacy and breathed new life into . . . Europe."[10]

Are there not many lessons for us here from the work of Patricius? One person *can* make a difference. Civilization *can* fall in a very brief time. Most of all, we should glean the importance of education and learning to any society.

WVU's role as an engaged university is critically important to West Virginia. Learning and education is inexorably tied to successful government, commerce, culture, and law. As educators and scholars, we play a central part in maintaining the means by which society can disseminate, discover, and apply knowledge. Education is an essential element in the progress of our nation. I can think of no higher calling or more noble work. Great public universities like ours are the pillars upon which the future of our nation is based.

Each of us can be a St. Patrick. We can each make a difference writing our story of success, large or small, in the soil of WVU, West Virginia, America, and the world.

Let us resolve to work together to meet the demands of these times. Let us appreciate one another for our year of achievement, for being who we are, and for serving constantly and unselfishly. I am convinced that individually and collectively we are the right people at the right place at the right time. Where our nation goes, land-grant public universities will forge the path. Wherever West Virginia is going, WVU must go first.

In the life of this university, as in the life of each person, there are certain defining moments. There are periods of uncertainty, and then suddenly, the way seems clear. It's time to act. WVU's moment has arrived. Today we are offered the opportunity to stand up, take responsibility, and become what we are meant to be. In the twenty-first century, our public universities will show the way to a lasting, productive, civilized culture, full of opportunity and intellectual riches for all who so aspire. These moments are not entrusted to the timid. They belong to the bold.

Let it be said that when the challenges were greatest, WVU answered in kind. When the hour struck, WVU was there to ring in the new millennium for the people she served.

THE NEW UNIVERSITY

2001

By 2001, the results of pursuing the agenda that had been established years earlier were becoming evident on our campus. The next two speeches reported on the progress being made and encouraged the university constituencies to continuing stretching to reach the new goals that had been established. One part of the first speech focused on the presidency of Paul Miller, who was president when I was at WVU and who had become, since my inauguration, a mentor and role model for me. He and Harry Heflin, acting president when I was student body president, are mentioned several times in my speeches. Dr. Miller visited the campus, and I used his eyes to help the campus see West Virginia University from the perspective of someone who had not been on campus in several years. It was a "fresh eyes" approach to marking progress.

In later years, I would write an outline for the State of the University address, which would then be supplemented by the chief of staff in the president's office, the provost, and others. Then, a draft would be written by Amy Quigley in the Office of University Advancement and Marketing, edited, and returned to me for further revisions. The final version was usually posted on the university Web site on the day of delivery. Thus, the State of the University speeches both set forth my personal thoughts and served as a vehicle to announce university policy.

Later State of the University addresses were often supplemented by video presentations, on the theory that video can convey commitment and emotion through the voices of others more effectively than through any one spokesperson.

I am pleased to present to the faculty senate and others today my annual State of the University address. In addition to my remarks, I am distributing three publications as evidence that the state of our university is strong, and getting stronger. One of these presents a sampling of our recent university-wide achievements. Another tells about our plan for new facilities on the Morgantown campus. The third outlines how we are implementing the recommendations of the commission on academic standards and expectations.

In each of our focus areas—teaching, research, service, and technology—West Virginia University is thriving. Moreover, the financial position of the institution is strong, largely because of our ability to leverage the dollars we get from tuition and state appropriations and also due to our success in attracting external support. But before I go into this, I would like to tell you about an experience I had recently.

In July, Paul Miller, WVU's fifteenth president, and his wife, Francena, who was a prominent member of the faculty here, visited the campus in Morgantown. Susan and I feel a strong bond with Dr. Miller. He was president here in 1963, and he delivered the convocation address to Susan, me, and the other members of our class when we sat where the 3,700 current WVU freshman students sat this fall. We had a wonderful day of touring the Morgantown campus. We toured the Mountainlair and the downtown campus, Evansdale, the Law Center, the PRT, the Health Sciences Center, the new athletic facilities, and the new Student Recreation Center.

Dr. Miller was instrumental in developing the Evansdale campus, and he takes great pride in the evolution that has occurred at WVU since he was its president nearly forty years ago. On the green expanses of Evansdale, facilities have risen that seem so much a part of today's WVU as to have been there forever: the Creative Arts Center, the Towers, Percival Hall, Allen Hall. Yet, when Paul Miller was inaugurated in 1962, not one of them had even been sketched out on a note pad.

More important than the facilities themselves is the evolution in WVU's teaching, research, and service that they helped enable. Physical improvements such as those achieved by the Miller administration are directly linked to improvements in WVU's curriculum, research capacities, student life, and public service and outreach.

Try to imagine WVU without the Mountainlair, for example. The current facility was built during the Miller and Harlow administrations and expanded during Neil Bucklew's tenure. Several generations of WVU students have known it as a central part of their college experience. Yet, there was a time not so long ago when this vital facility did not exist, nor did the excellent educational programs and gathering spaces it shelters exist. Today, they are part of our university's fabric.

When we look further back into WVU's history, we see the two-building campus of 1867. We see the all-male student body with its corps of cadets and the bearded professoriate. We see the first women degree-candidates arriving in 1889, the first African American undergraduate student receiving his degree in 1954, the first coed marching band in 1972. There is Jerry West leading his team to victory at the old field house, and Carolyn Conner becoming the most recent in our legacy of Rhodes Scholars from WVU.

This progression of changes at WVU shows us that, as in nature, human organizations evolve. They adapt to meet the inevitable changes and challenges in their environment. As they do, they not only survive but become stronger. When we consider the natural world, we tend to think of evolution as a very slow process, something that occurs over epochs and eons. When we consider human organizations, however, evolution is something that can occur rapidly—in years, months, even days. Such has been the case at West Virginia University.

Six years ago, I was inaugurated as president of a very different WVU than the one we know today. I promised at that time to make every effort to ensure that WVU is a place where dreams can be realized, where the future is always in our sights even as we respect the past and work to overcome present challenges. Since then, working together, we have transformed WVU into a stronger university with new and updated facilities; a focused and balanced mission; a commitment to core values, including student-centeredness; and a clearer view of the present and future needs and goals of the people we serve. We are in a period of accelerated change that is strengthening and improving our university in many important ways. The result of our work is a new West Virginia University. Yet, our traditions are intact. Our history remains that of a land-grant university fulfilling its mission to serve the people of our state. Things are happening at WVU now that will benefit individuals and society in ways never imagined in 1895 or 1995—and in many ways we cannot imagine today. The university, of course, is older than any of us will ever be. It is probably wiser than any of us, and it will outlive every one of us. Everything we do now to advance the institution helps to guarantee the advancement of generations to follow. Ours is a noble cause, and a vital one.

The most obvious and inescapable evidence of the new West Virginia University that is rising upon well-established foundations is the new look in facilities here in Morgantown. The buildings taking shape downtown and in Evansdale are not replacements for structures that have outlived their usefulness. They are state-of-the-art facilities designed to give new capabilities to a rapidly evolving, student-centered research university. The new downtown library complex will be technologically advanced to meet the research needs of the twenty-first century. The life-sciences building will foster collaboration among two important disciplines: biology and psychology. These superb facilities, along with the recently opened Student Recreation Center and computer laboratories, and the soon-to-open interactive Visitors Resource Center at One Waterfront Place, demonstrate our commitment to our students' success.

Moreover, each is a new point of pride. Each makes an unequivocal statement that West Virginia University is among the nation's forward-thinking, progressive institutions. This truth is echoed by improvements at our regional campuses across the state. The new West Virginia University dispels old stereotypes. It replaces these with newfound awareness of West Virginia's vibrant culture, economic potential, and growing commitment to excellence.

Even as these new structures rise, dramatically changing the face of our campus, we are reminded of our past and our traditions by the stately older buildings standing beside them. Woodburn Hall, Oglebay Hall, Colson Hall—these facilities and others resound with the footsteps of past generations. We owe a debt of gratitude to my predecessor, President Neil Bucklew, and his administration for their efforts in preserving these historic facilities for use by new generations of WVU students.

Accelerated evolution is occurring in many other areas of the university also. Our new capacities in research would astound the bearded professoriate of a century ago—and even the faculty who served their tenure in more recent times.

In the 2000–2001 fiscal year, we set a new record for sponsored programs at WVU: $88.7 million. The figure is up 14 percent over the previous highest level, $79 million in 1993. This achievement is due in part to the significant improvements in WVU's research infrastructure that we have fostered, led by Dr. John Weete and the Research Corporation's board of directors. More importantly, the new record is the result of the path-breaking work of outstanding faculty members in our research focus areas.

Evolution has changed WVU's public service programs for the better as well. Our rural health care programs are a model for the nation. They link tertiary care here in Morgantown with numerous rural health delivery sites across the state. In economic development, business expansion and retention, community planning and design, firefighter training, 4-H and child-development programs, and numerous other capacities, we serve thousands across our state and nation.

New forms of technology have also evolved. They help our campus run more efficiently and foster computer literacy among our students and faculty. Ours is one of America's most "wired" campuses. Last year, 83 percent of students brought a computer into the residence halls, and the Technology Support Center had all these students connected to the campus network within four days. In an exciting new development this winter, we will launch the Mountaineer Information Express, a WVU-only Web portal that links students to each other and to the faculty, as well as to the world outside.

We also have attracted private support, which would have been undreamed of just a few years ago, to help achieve the university's mission. The foundation's capital campaign, Building Greatness, is proving a great success. We are on target and on track to raise $250 million in new gifts and endowments for the university. As of today, the campaign has attracted $175 million. These funds—which are given to us mainly by generous alumni and friends—support endowed professorships, graduate and undergraduate scholarships, new program development, facility enhancements, and many other improvements.

Just last week, I was pleased to announce an extraordinary $18.4 million gift from two Morgantown sisters, Gladys Gwendolyn Davis and Vivian Davis Michael. In their wills, they made the largest donation from individuals in WVU's history: $16.2 million for the College of Agriculture, Forestry, and Consumer Sciences, and $2.2 million for the College of Law, the College of Creative Arts, and the new downtown library. In honor of the sisters and their mother, Estelle Conaway Davis, WVU is now home to the Davis College of Agriculture, Forestry, and Consumer Sciences. We are very grateful for the Davis family's loyalty and support of WVU over many years.

As our institution evolves, we are finding new, more holistic ways to educate students, inside and outside the classroom. Among these are distributed education, Web-based courses, service learning, and the student-centered programs of Operation Jump-Start. Educational needs, delivery methods, and content must evolve, but at the heart of each new learning initiative remains the treasured relationship between student and teacher.

Gail Galloway Adams, who has influenced many students in the WVU creative writing program through her outstanding teaching and guidance, shared a noteworthy observation with the student affairs task force several years ago. "In the move to a student-centered university," she said, "the first thing to remember is that students in ancient times met in a square, under a tree, on a hill, to engage in conversation with a single teacher who hoped to convey the joy of ideas, the deep satisfaction of the intellectual life."

As WVU changes to meet new needs, as we grow stronger and are called upon to deliver more and different services to more people, we will not forget that we are first and foremost an institution of higher learning. This commitment to education is the fundamental essence of our being. It is present in everything we do, everywhere we go.

Today, I urge everyone to think about the ongoing evolution of West Virginia University. Think about making dreams come true. Think about how WVU might better fulfill its vision of being a student-centered learning community and meeting the changing needs of West Virginia and the nation through teaching, research, service, and technology. It is interesting and even fun to speculate as to what our university might become.

SPECULATIONS

Here are my own speculations:

I foresee that the demand from our constituencies and governing bodies for increased accountability will grow even greater. According to the College Board, tuition and fees at public, four-year colleges increased 53 percent over the last ten years.[11] This is creating serious concern about the value of a college education. As Professors Willimon and Naylor wrote in their book *The Abandoned Generation*:

> Faced with decades of unrelenting tuition increases, more students and their parents are asking, "What are we getting for our money?" . . . It is unwise for faculty and administrators who have asked students to go into considerable debt and to make major financial sacrifices to criticize [them] for asking, "Is college worth the sacrifice?"[12]

We will make certain that the educational experience we offer at WVU is one that truly merits spending one's life savings or going into debt in order to attend our university. While the student will retain ultimate responsibility for making the most of what we offer, our offerings must be ones that students need to achieve their educational and future career goals. And while they are enrolled here, we must take care to provide a comfortable, safe, supportive environment for our students. The Mountaineer Parents Club, 8,300 families strong, is just one mechanism whereby we can gauge how we are doing on a daily basis and act rapidly to improve.

In addition to taking good care of our students, we will make certain that we continue to be good stewards of the public's investment in us through state appropriations. I should note here that, since state appropriations and tuition account for only about half of our revenues, we have built the magnitude of this university largely by earning the confidence of external sponsors, donors, and others. However, being accountable to the state remains vitally important. In fact, it is now required of us, through mechanisms such as the campus compact we presented to the Higher Education Policy Commission earlier this year.

High-performance leadership will be required to keep WVU's academic, administrative, and service functions operating at peak efficiency. When we consider that the WVU system with its medical centers and hospitals includes almost thirty thousand students and about twelve thousand employees, it is easy to see how important leadership is to us. I foresee an increasing need for faculty and staff to learn "best practices" for what they do, and to model them for colleagues, students, and the people of the state. Universities are complex organizations, and they are getting more complex, so it is inevitable that the leadership practices that make them run well will become more valued—inside higher education and in organizations outside our campuses.

I foresee the evolution of more nationally recognized research and service centers and institutes at WVU. In the future, we will see more and more benefits accruing from our leadership in leveraging the investments made in us. Just like the vision we had for developing a world-class health sciences center years ago, we now have, for example, the seeds for the Center for Renewable Resources and Economic Development.

Like the current centers, the new ones will achieve excellence by focusing on areas that are important to the state and nation, such as economic development, health, technology, and the arts and humanities. At the heart of these centers will be dedicated faculty members, including some who are new and some who have been here a long time. The result of their efforts will be dollars for the university, jobs, patent income, spin-off businesses, social progress, cultural enrichment, and many, many more benefits for the institution, state, and nation.

As this transfer of technology and knowledge occurs, our university will gain wider recognition as an economic engine for West Virginia, facilitating job creation and community enhancement throughout the state. This will be an important part of our mission in the future, because the public will demand it of all public universities across the nation. WVU is uniquely positioned for this role in our state. We offer the collective strength of our multicampus system, expertise in issues with local and regional implications, and educational programs that meet economic needs. At last count, in 1998, the economic impact of WVU's people and programs in the state and region totaled $1.3 billion.

The National Association of State Universities and Land-Grant Colleges released a report in August that highlighted some of WVU's economic impact, including a $4.78 return on every state tax dollar spent on WVU and the generation of 6,368 jobs in addition to the approximately 12,000 that are directly related to the university. There is no question that having a vigorous, responsive flagship institution improves the fortunes of West Virginia.

Additionally, I foresee West Virginia University evolving into a more inclusive, diversified educational center. It will always provide traditional student experiences, but it will also be a vibrant enterprise comprising many distributed, customized, and technologically advanced systems.

A freshman from Shinnston may sit in a residence hall room and take a class with a nontraditional student from California. Their classmates may be from China, Mexico, and Germany. Technology will bring them together, and the result will be a global wheel of knowledge with its hub at WVU. Of course, we will not undermine the residential programs of the university, but as new ways of learning evolve, we will make good use of them at WVU.

Related to this broadening of our reach, I foresee a change in our conception of WVU. In the future it will be not just a place but also a community of interested persons connected across their lifetimes in an enterprise worthy of financial support.

The Alumni Association and the foundation will be instrumental in creating a positive attitude toward the university and higher education that brings alumni and supporters into a symbiotic relationship with WVU. We have much to share with one another. Through it all, while much will change, I foresee that the core mission, vision, and values of the university will remain the same as they are today. They are enduring and worthy of constancy. WVU is a student-centered learning community. It is meeting the changing needs of West Virginia and the nation. Our goal remains to do an excellent job in each of our mission areas and to be better recognized nationally as a group of individuals and an institution that has achieved appropriate balance in teaching, research, and service. WVU's enhanced reputation will bring many benefits to individuals and society.

Now that you have heard some of my ideas on the subject, I ask you, how do you anticipate your role in WVU's future? I invite you to share your ideas with me, your colleagues, your students, anyone with an interest in keeping WVU strong in the future. All great ideas were once new ideas.

West Virginia University is surely a marvelous place. It is self renewing and constantly renewing, and one of the joys of service to the institution is to see that the university is constantly evolving. I hope that my message today has helped you to recognize some of the many ways it is, indeed, becoming a new West Virginia University.

"What is now proved was once only imagined," said William Blake.[13] I looked into Dr. Miller's eyes that day as he gazed across the Evansdale and Health Sciences campuses. I saw in them tears of joy at the recognition that he and his generation, good men and women doing their best, played an important role in the evolution of West Virginia's flagship institution. Their dreams of a stronger, more capable university have come true.

I trust that forty years from now, you will have the same feeling when you see what has become of the institution you are transforming by your ideas and actions today. With continued hard work, devotion to helping others, and commitment to achieving greatness, your dreams, too, will come true. May we never stop dreaming of a better West Virginia University.

QUALITY MATTERS

2005

By 2005, I was using my own perspective as an alumnus who had been associated with WVU for over forty years to encourage faculty, staff, and administrators to savor their accomplishments and rekindle their determination to accomplish even more in the years to come.

First, let me thank you all for coming today and for all you do, individually and collectively, for West Virginia University.

This past July 1 marked the tenth anniversary of the day I became president of West Virginia University. It has been an honor for Susan and me to serve you and our alma mater. Like other milestone occasions, this particular anniversary was a natural time for us to reflect on the past decade at WVU.

Our memories include many great days for the university, such as the announcement of our partnership with the FBI in creating the forensic and biometric initiatives. We also vividly recall some of the more challenging times, such as the day seven thousand people (mostly students) stood in Woodburn Circle to contemplate and memorialize the September 11, 2001, terrorist attacks. I had the responsibility of finding the words to give the tragedy some perspective for our students. I remember other special moments as well, like the first time I saw a student whom I had helped to recruit out of a small West Virginia high school walk across the stage to receive a medical degree.

These and similar experiences constantly remind me of how profoundly West Virginia University transforms the lives of students, just as it has transformed many of our own lives. We have collectively traveled a long way over the past ten years. The enrollment growth, successful capital campaign, and increased sponsored project funding have enabled us to weather a turbulent economy and still manage to make investments in our human resources, technology, programming, libraries, and infrastructure. Perhaps it is worth all of us looking back, if just for a moment.

In 1995, a number of challenges were converging on us. At the time, they seemed quite daunting.

First, globalization was increasingly evident, thanks to a relatively peaceful world, rapid advances in communications, and the inevitable impact of market forces at work in the global economy. Together we correctly saw what lay ahead—ever-closer connections among the peoples of every nation, international competition for business and ideas, the rise of the American military, and the growth of new economies that would challenge our own, especially in China and Europe.

We saw concomitant changes in the local economy, especially what was perceived at the time as the decline of the basic building blocks of the Appalachian economy—coal, steel, glass, and other key industries.

Second, the growing importance of information technology was recognized as a trend that would change the world, connecting us instantly with anyone, anywhere, and making it possible to search for even the most obscure data by calling up the new search engines of the Internet. The Y2K problem loomed large. We knew that investment would be required and that, in the future, job descriptions would take for granted a familiarity with technology unknown to our parents and even many of us at that time. While the investments were important, they were difficult given the many demands on our resources.

Third, we heard new demands for accountability from our parents and students, the public, and state and federal government agencies. All were asking more and more from colleges and universities. At the same time, public funds were being demanded by prison systems, the health care industry, and other government and private sectors, so resources were limited. We faced the proverbial, and perhaps perpetual, challenge of "doing more with less." In West Virginia, the best expression of this movement was the passage of Senate Bill 547 in the spring of 1995. This bill called for increased salaries but only provided partial funding for them.

We were asked to serve more people through our teaching, research, and service programs while we were also reallocating operating funds toward meeting the salary targets. Because of our land-grant service mission, we were urged to get more involved in southern West Virginia and the Eastern Panhandle, and to focus on economic development in new and more intensive ways than ever before. Similarly, parents—the baby boomers—who had been raised in a consumer-driven era were asking for more accountability in the quality of academic programs, in the responsiveness and convenience of services, and in the amenities of campus. As tuition was raised markedly at public, and especially private, universities, these demands for accountability were amplified.

Fourth, we could see new competitors on the horizon—for both students and research grants. We saw the lightning speed with which these competitors—from private schools and laboratories to increasingly aggressive public universities in other states—would emerge, and we witnessed their ability to react and adapt as the competitive environment changed. Entrepreneurs entered the not-for-profit world and went after the same projects as our principal investigators and Extension agents, but without the heavy regulation imposed upon public universities. This made it vital to cut out any self-imposed red tape and seek changes that would enable more effective procedures. Competition for students, by other campuses and new kinds of online education providers, posed a heightened concern because of the forecasted decline in West Virginia high school enrollments. We recognized that the university would have to change to meet the challenges of the new competitors and that the changes foreseen were costly and significant.

Fifth, we anticipated changes in the way we were going to go about our business in the years to come. Most of our constituencies off campus—industry, alumni, donors, and partners—expected higher education to move toward a more "businesslike" model because of their successful experience with the total quality movement, reengineering, and cost-reduction measures in their worlds of work. We sensed an impatience with higher education and began to see changes in the support systems at many institutions. The way hospitals, physicians, and other instructional health care providers were reimbursed for their work changed dramatically. Tenure was called into question; our governance structure was challenged; the absence of a merit system for compensation was debated; paper-driven processes were criticized; complaints about student housing, lines, and registration intensified; and other evidence of past practices were not only questioned but called unacceptable. We were asked to develop new programs in what seemed to us an incredibly short time period. Finally, we saw correctly that the new costs imposed by the drive for global quality and ubiquitous technology on our campuses could not be met by state funds alone.

We knew that all public universities would have to raise more private dollars, find more research and sponsored program support, raise tuition and fees, and charge more for services, all in a very tough and competitive market. We knew there would have to be a capital campaign led by the WVU Foundation and that the research establishment on campus would have to step up and dramatically increase revenues.

Globalization, the technology boom, demands for accountability, new competitors, expectations for more efficiency, and other changes shaped our work here at WVU. We were not alone. All of higher education has confronted the same challenges over the past decade.

I think most of us saw what was coming, to one degree or another. We also saw that our individual and collective capacity to change would play an ever-increasing role in our lives if we were going to survive, let alone thrive, in the changed environment of the new millennium.

Looking back, with the clarity that ten years of hindsight affords us, what is amazing is not only that the predicted trends developed, which they most assuredly did, but that they developed so quickly and with a much larger impact than most foresaw at the time. It hasn't been the direction in which we were headed that surprised us but the turbulence and speed of the trip.

Fortunately, we were able to meet these challenges head on, with task forces, new programs, new systems, campus mergers, reorganized programs and functions, new personnel, and change after change in the way we do everything from registering students to purchasing a book. It has been a lot of work, not just for Dr. Bob D'Alessandri, Provost Lang, Vice President Gray, and other senior administrators, as well as our regional campus presidents, but for all of you and for everyone involved in higher education in this country. I thank you each and every one for your personal contributions to our success.

As we have reported to WVU's Board of Governors, all of our financial indicators are moving in the right direction. WVU has received excellent bond ratings and clean audit opinions. Notably, for the past two years there has been no management letter, a rarity in the audit world. The full reaccreditation of WVU this year is evidence that we remained academically strong over the past ten years and also addressed every area of concern from the 1994 report of the site visit team.

Within West Virginia, WVU has been the only institution to receive the highest rating of "excellent" from the Higher Education Policy Commission's review of the compact reports each college and university must submit. In fact, in the context of West Virginia, I would say that we have clearly excelled in all categories of measurement.

I also think it is fair to say that we have begun to emerge as a very significant national university, recruiting quality students from all fifty states and ninety countries. We are demonstrating innovation in several new academic programs, advancing the quality of our student body, improving our athletic programs without a drain on the academic budget, creating more endowed chairs and professorships, and launching new research and economic development initiatives. Noteworthy among our collective achievements are:

- the attraction of $54 million to the Health Sciences Center research agenda in less than twelve months;
- the fantastic success of the biometric and forensic programs;
- the transition to being a university much more attentive to the needs of our students and parents;
- the successful completion of a capital campaign;
- the doubling by Dr. Cote and the men and women of Extension of the number of clients they reach, which now exceeds two hundred fifty thousand annually;
- our leadership in making West Virginia the first state with a Department of Energy Industries of the Future program;
- WVU's partnerships overseas, particularly in the College of Creative Arts and the College of Business and Economics (where we welcome Dean Sears to campus);
- the steady number of Truman and Goldwater scholars from WVU's student body;
- the revision of the general education curriculum by the faculty senate;
- the rededication to student life and academic enrichment programming;
- improvements in our libraries, including membership in PALCI;
- our basketball team's emergence as a student-centered, team-oriented program of class that captured admiration across the country;
- our standing as a national center for excellence in both biometrics and neurosciences; and
- the very recent launch of a new Web-based recruiting portal that yielded nearly one thousand users in just the first week, half of whom have already started the online application process as a result.

In addition, there are dozens, if not hundreds, of other achievements by faculty, staff, students, and administrators. We have done what we have done in the face of two unexpected and massive changes not foreseen in 1995: first, the tragedy and aftermath of 9/11 and the many ways it has affected higher education, and second, the most difficult change in the national financial markets since the Great Depression of the 1930s.

It is a tribute to our alumni and other supporters, as well our state and our university and all of its affiliates, that we raised the money we have raised privately and that we have maintained stability in a time of such financial turbulence.

We are truly grateful for the show of confidence and must remain inspired by their voluntary investment in the work that we do. We are also grateful to our congressional delegation, particularly Senator Byrd and Senator Rockefeller, as well as Congressman Mollohan, for all they have done to provide much-needed seed money for some of our most significant initiatives.

Now looking over the horizon, as we must do, we are facing yet another decade of change—ever-accelerating change of profound proportions.

First, globalization of the economy will continue, changing the relative position of nations. China and India will continue their rapid growth in economic importance. They will also continue to rapidly excel in higher education and research. Certainly our businesses, but also our universities, will have to adapt more quickly, seek to be more competitive, lower costs, provide better products and services, and above all be more innovative in a world that will expect lower costs and crave innovation.

In addition, the energy markets will change and grow significantly, and faster than expected. These changes will alter West Virginia's relative position in the United States and demand that our attention be given to every aspect of teaching, research, and service related to the production and distribution of energy and the attendant environmental concerns associated with its consumption.

In this climate, we must make sure that as a land-grant institution, we are part of a culture of innovation. We must ask ourselves hard questions that challenge the status quo and truly assess whether we can do more in order to adapt to world changes. WVU Tech's new President Charles Bayless has already identified energy as a key niche for innovation at Tech. During a speech, he reminded us:

> The United States is about 4.6 percent of the world's population, yet it uses 29.6 percent of the world's energy. As the rest of the world makes the transition from a labor economy to an energy economy, it will put increasing pressure on prices and make finding domestic energy even more important. The United States has less than 5 percent of the world's gas and oil reserves but about 25 percent of the world's coal reserves. Research into technologies such as coal liquefaction and gasification will allow WVU to be at the forefront in finding new, clean ways to mine and use coal to satisfy our nation's energy needs and create jobs in West Virginia.

Second, global security—or should I say, global insecurity—will play an ever-increasing role in the life of our nation and, hence, the life of our universities. The National Security Council's Global Assessment asserts, "At no time since the formation of the Western alliance in 1949 have the shape and nature of international alignments been in such a state of flux."[14]

As an example of how higher education, and particularly WVU, can adapt as the world changes with regard to international relations, I am pleased to announce a new program associated with the Department of Political Science in the Eberly College of Arts and Sciences, which has just welcomed its new dean, Dr. Mary Ellen Mazey, back to her alma mater. WVU will now offer an intelligence and national security program in the international studies program. This new program will be led by WVU professor and nationally established international studies scholar Joe Hagan. The curriculum will draw upon WVU faculty with expertise in foreign policy analysis, as well as experts from the intelligence community.

Such initiatives reflect the way in which higher education is expected to process changes in the external environment. WVU is already well positioned in many areas related to renewed national security interests. No doubt the national and international reputation of WVU's research and educational programs in these areas led to an invitation for me to join presidents and chancellors of some of the nation's more prestigious universities on the recently created National Security Higher Education Advisory Board under FBI Director Robert S. Mueller III.

I am honored to represent WVU's work and am already calling upon our campus experts to advise me. I also hope to learn about new opportunities and trends that will help us maintain a leadership role in this multidisciplinary field.

Third, our understanding of the mind, the body, and biomedical sciences will grow quickly and more rapidly than we can conceive, putting more pressure on us to provide an ever-increasing standard of health care. We will have to respond again with the same professional attitudes toward care and excellence with which we have responded to the challenges of the past decade. At the same time, increased competition for health care and education funding will be strong. The costs imposed on the nation by the changing nature of our military role in the world, as well as the need to respond to the recent natural disasters, may limit available funding.

As I was reminded at a health sciences retreat just last month, in this environment, the quality of our leadership and the quality of the services provided by health sciences will matter more than ever before.

Fourth, our higher-quality student body will have higher expectations of our programs and services, and our efforts to retain and recruit high-quality faculty will result in higher expectations for facilities, technology, salaries, and start-up packages. As a result, more will be required of administrators and staff as we continually strive to reduce bureaucracy and make investments in everything from technology to higher salaries.

Fifth, to meet the financial challenges of the next decade we will need to foster growth on our campuses in almost every way, which will challenge the communities in which we are located, as well as those of us who work on the campuses. Our experience over the past decade affirmed the belief that quality is prerequisite to our ability to grow. WVU's continued growth will be challenged by the same variables that challenged us over the past decade: shifting demographics, the competitive enrollment market, and resource capacity. The enrollment growth of the past ten years enabled our investments in infrastructure, salaries, and programs. We must manage the growth already achieved and continue toward the goal of 28,500 students on the Morgantown campus, 30,000 for the main campus that now includes Potomac State under newly appointed Provost Kerry O'Dell, and 36,000 for all WVU campuses.

Finally, as leaders of the institution, we must together manage the competing demands from the many different constituencies of our university. Ten years ago, I attended the Harvard School for New Presidents, which President Marie Gnage of the Parkersburg campus just attended. I asked the presiding dean, "Who owns the university?" He told me that mine was a question that should not be asked, let alone answered! His point was not to avoid the question, but to underscore how complicated the interests of a university are. Consider some of those with vested interests:

- 34,000 students at WVU statewide
- The more than 15,000 people who find their employment with WVU and its affiliates (5,800 on Morgantown's main campus alone)
- 165,000 living alumni

- Donors (50,000 to the capital campaign)
- Governor Manchin and state leaders, elected and appointed
- Federal leaders, elected and appointed
- Parents
- West Virginia taxpayers (from whom 25 percent of our budget derives)
- Patients (approximately 650,000 a year)
- Bond holders, who have loaned us hundreds of millions of dollars
- The academic program accreditation boards
- Federal grant makers
- Funding agencies
- Research partners
- Regional campus constituencies
- The 257,000 clients of WVU Extension
- Fans of our sports teams

And the list could go on. Every day, you and I, and ultimately our Board of Governors, must balance these many differing interests and do what is right for the university. This makes the leadership of our university today an enormously complex task for all those involved, not just its president.

With regard to salaries and benefits here at WVU, my message today is really quite straightforward. As I have said on many occasions, our goal is to take our classified staff to aspirational salary levels set forth in the statutory schedule and to offer our faculty and administrators very competitive compensation by national standards.

To attract the resources we need—both to build a better WVU and to reach our aspirational levels of compensation and fringes for everyone who works here—we must continue to adapt to changes in society that are shaping our environment. We must offer the marketplace, whether it is here in West Virginia or nationally, a higher and higher quality in all our services and programs. We must find ways to be more efficient at the same time. Toward that end, we appreciate the passage of Senate Bill 603 and thank Governor Manchin and the West Virginia legislature for their vision. We are working to implement the allowable changes in our business practices within the year timeline of the legislation.

We are different from other institutions in our state. That is why we are frequently called the flagship higher education institution. Our jobs are funded not just by state appropriations but also by the sale of auxiliary services, donations, research dollars, and tuition revenues.

In fact, many positions at WVU are totally funded from non-state appropriations. We need to keep this in mind. Since we are committed to increasing salary and fringe benefits for all employees, this makes the financial challenge at WVU greater than for other state institutions. Make no mistake about it; the salary increases we have given, nine out of the last ten years, were made possible by our collective efforts to improve our quality and our size at the same time.

We have improved our reputation among our constituencies, and we have increased our revenues as a result. This has enabled us to do what we have done without taking undue risks that could result in layoffs or jeopardize the quality of our offerings. We have not put the future of the university at risk, and we will not. This is a good place to work, and if we work together, we will keep it that way.

Because the perceived quality of our institution is so important to the future, our immediate goal is to not only adapt to the challenges that lie ahead but also to advance our national reputation. Our newly revised vision statement asserts not only that we will be student centered and meet society's changing needs but also that we will be an institution with a national reputation for excellence while doing so. We aspire to be nationally recognized for excellence in teaching, scholarship, discovery, performance, service, health care, athletics, and every other area of our collective endeavors. We will follow WVU's 2010 Plan, recently approved unanimously by the Board of Governors.

I want to publicly thank Provost Jerry Lang and Professor Larry Hornak for their leadership. I also want to thank everyone who served on the committees, all those who provided input, and the WVU Board of Governors for its guidance. The 2010 Plan has five primary goals:

- Attract and graduate high-quality students
- Recruit and retain high-quality faculty committed to the land-grant mission
- Enhance the educational environment for student learning
- Promote the discovery and exchange of new knowledge and ideas
- Improve West Virginia's health, economy, and quality of life

We are all fully aware that this will take funding. It will not be easy, but consider the fact that beginning in 1995, we reallocated $38 million from operating dollars to salaries and we shouldered millions more in base appropriation cuts and insurance cost increases. Yet we grew enrollment (by five thousand full-time students) and expanded sponsored projects and research (by 135 percent), which grew our resource base and enabled us to invest in technology, academic programs, new initiatives, libraries, university-wide salary and fringe benefit increases, and a renewal of the campus infrastructure.

I would also make special note that despite the significant budget challenges of the past ten years, and especially the past five, *USA Today* recently noted that WVU's in-state tuition rate is the tenth best among national flagship universities and fourteenth best for out-of-state tuition rates. WVU's tuition increases also ranked among the lowest in the country. Moreover, WVU has recently again been named to the list of *America's Best 100 College Buys* in higher education. What is important about this particular list is that only schools with above-average student academic credentials can be considered, and then the cost of attendance is valued. These two recent reports affirm that WVU has been an excellent steward of resources and maintained its land-grant responsibility to the people of West Virginia: offering a top-flight education while keeping costs down.

Upon this foundation of success and stewardship, we are well positioned to pursue the 2010 Plan goals. The implementation team has already started meeting because this 2010 Plan is only as good as the follow-through. We will have measures of our progress, and we will report those to the Board and to the campus community. If you have suggestions for metrics, I urge you to share those ideas with Provost Lang or Professor Hornak. We simply must keep the momentum going and turn the plan into a reality that we can be proud of in five years. I have every confidence that we will.

It is fair to say that our state's leaders and, increasingly, our national colleagues, are recognizing our ability at WVU to navigate the rough seas of the environment in which we must sail. In the end, perhaps what matters is not so much the destinations we have reached, or that we will reach, in our travels, but the purpose for which we travel—the noble purpose of making this world a better place. It is our mission, the purpose of our journey, which gives us all a sense of pride and satisfaction.

We are all privileged to be at West Virginia University as it crosses into the new millennium, at a time that is as challenging, and at the same time as satisfying, as any other in our 138-year history. It is a joy for me to travel with you, and as the designated leader of such a distinguished group of leaders, I thank you for your service to our university, our state, and our nation. I challenge you to navigate as well during the next decade as you did in the last.

As much as things change (and change has been a theme of this particular address), there are some things that do not. Universities have always been, and continue to be, the beacon of hope and understanding in our world. What happens in our classrooms and laboratories, as we educate tomorrow's leaders, carries on a long and rich tradition of education in this country. What happens in our hospitals and clinics literally saves lives and provides hope for our children's generation. What happens in the communities of West Virginia, when we promote solutions and develop the economy, carries on the land-grant tradition that sired this institution. These traditions of education, research, and service are enduring. In the 1920s, West Virginia's education secretary said that an institution such as WVU must seek to conserve all of the worthwhile knowledge that man has discovered and yet endeavor to enlarge the bounds of understanding. He said that the university turns the searchlight of the past upon the future to give glimpses of what is to be. Indeed, this notion is still the root of our mission, no matter how much the world changes.

I'd like to end with a video we produced to show at a large alumni gathering this past summer. It reflects on the past ten years and, I hope, reminds us all of why we are fortunate to work here at WVU—a special place in the hearts of so many.

NOTES

1   Henry Adams, *The Education of Henry Adams* (1907), quoted in Elizabeth Knowles, ed., *The Oxford Dictionary of Quotations*, 5th ed. (Oxford: Oxford University Press, 1999), 2.

2   Robert Zemsky and William F. Massey, "Toward an Understanding of Our Current Predicaments," *Change* 27, no. 6 (1995): 40.

3   Steve Ungavri, "TRIZ: Within the Context of the Kano Model or Adding the Third Dimension to Quality," *The TRIZ Journal*, October 1999, http://www.triz-journal.com/archives/1999/10/e/ (accessed January 25, 2007). See also Noriako Kano, N. Seraku, F. Takahashi, and S. Tsuji, "Attractive Quality and Must-Be Quality," *Hinshitsu: The Journal of Japanese Society for Quality Control* 14, no. 2 (April 1984): 39–48.

4   Alexander Martin, "Special Message and Report of Board of Visitors West Virginia Agricultural College" in *West Virginia University Report of the Board of Regents and the President, 1867/68–1896/97* (Wheeling, WV: John Frew, Public Printer, 1868), 12.

5   Mark Twain, *Life on the Mississippi*, (1883; Pleasantville, NY: Reader's Digest Association, Inc., 1987), 68–69.

6   Leo Tolstoy, *War and Peace*, trans. Constance Garnett (1869; New York: Modern Library, 2002), 690.

7   According to Morgan McCall, University of Southern California President Steven Sample attributes this story to Abraham Lincoln. See Morgan W. McCall Jr., *High Flyers: Developing the Next Generation of Leaders* (Boston, MA: Harvard Business School Press, 1998), 63.

8   Charles E. Hathaway, Paige E. Mulhollan, and Karen A. White, "Metropolitan Universities: Models for the 21st Century," *Metropolitan Universities* 1, no.1 (1990): 5.

9   Thomas Cahill, *How the Irish Saved Civilization: The Untold Story of Ireland's Heroic Role from the Fall of Rome to the Rise of Medieval Europe* (New York: Doubleday, 1995).

10   Cahill, *How the Irish Saved Civilization*, 196.

11   The College Board, *Trends in College Pricing 1998* (New York: The College Board, 1998).

12   William H. Willimon and Thomas H. Naylor, *The Abandoned Generation: Rethinking Higher Education* (Grand Rapids, MI: Wm. B. Eerdmans Publishing Company, 1995), 48.

13   William Blake, *The Complete Poetry and Prose of William Blake*, ed. David Erdman (Berkeley: University of California Press, 1965; revised edition 1982), 36.

14   National Security Council, *Mapping the Global Future: Report of the National Intelligence Council's 2020 Project* (Pittsburgh: Govt. Printing Office, 2004), 9.

TEN

A PLEA FOR PUBLIC SUPPORT OF HIGHER EDUCATION

2003

These remarks were given in the host city of a sister state institution located in the most southern reaches of West Virginia. Its president was present at the meeting. A second public college is nearby, and its president also attended. I was invited by townspeople, knowing full well that the event would include professors and staff members from the colleges located in the area. I decided to emphasize our common ground—the importance of higher education and its mission to serve the public. The remarks concluded with a plea for public support for higher education.

Since the dawn of civilization, special members of society have sought to capture the accumulated knowledge of mankind and pass it on to the next generation. These people are called scholars. Those of you who have studied the classics know that many older civilizations developed advanced scientific principles, conceptions of government, art forms, medicinal treatments, and technologies without which we would not be where we are today. The Egyptians, for example, gave us libraries, geometry, and engineering. The

Greeks gave us medicine and philosophy. The Romans gave us civic administration, road-building skills, and advanced systems of law. Others gave us writing, language, smelting, sailing, and more. The city of Athens, West Virginia, where Concord College is located, was named after the Greek city of Athens because it too is a symbol of learning, just as ancient Athens was to the Greeks.

Yet, believe it or not, all of this was almost lost, setting mankind back for centuries. When the Roman Empire fell into the abyss of the Dark Ages around the fifth century, A.D., the Barbarians sacked and burned the cities of the civilized world, including the temples and churches of learned clergy. In the flames, the lessons of history and science were consumed, going up in smoke, everywhere.

Everywhere, that is, except Ireland, where a Roman citizen of Britain named Patricius established a network of seminaries and libraries in Ireland that protected, preserved, and advanced the knowledge of prior generations. Patricius had been captured by the Irish while working on a farm in Roman England. His captors took him to Ireland, which was then a heathen and tribal environment. Patricius escaped from enslavement, became a priest, and vowed to return to Ireland to bring not just the word of God but also the accumulated knowledge of mankind.

Patricius was more than successful. During the years that followed his return, Ireland became the most civilized place in the Western world. Books from the ancient world were copied by hand, scholarly teachers were encouraged, and the moral lessons of prior generations were distilled and passed on to the next generation. When the Dark Ages ended, generations after Patricius's death, his intellectual descendants emerged from Ireland to repopulate England and Europe with the intellectual zeal that existed before the fall of mighty Rome. Great universities were founded later in Paris, Oxford, Rome, and Bologna.

Civilization was saved by one man and the people of one small island. Europe flourished, and its new states went on to dominate world commerce and trade because of their advanced technologies. You may have guessed by now that Patricius was later to become St. Patrick. His remarkable story is the foundation of Thomas Cahill's book, *How the Irish Saved Civilization.*

There are other examples of one man and one country making a difference in the world based on a commitment to scholarship and education. Where would America be if the early religious leaders had not decided to import the concept of the university to America, establishing Harvard and Yale? These institutions would educate not just our early clergy but also our early doctors, political leaders, and engineers.

Where would the nation be without the model of the University of Virginia, founded by Thomas Jefferson and supported by the people of Virginia, the same state that gave us William and Mary and Virginia Tech? Jefferson gave us the idea that the common man, not just landed gentry, should have the opportunity to seek a higher education, an idea that has made America what it is today.

Think, if you will, about the genius of the land-grant colleges, founded in the midst of the Civil War, upon the belief that America could not prosper without excellent colleges and universities everywhere. Land-grant colleges were founded using the proceeds of the sale of excess land owned by a nation that needed learned teachers, medical professionals, lawyers and judges, engineers, and agricultural scientists to move forward. Through the Morrill Act, America established public higher education as a priority. Our leaders lifted up higher education to move us out of the darkest period in American democracy.

WVU is one of the earliest land-grant colleges, founded by a new state in 1867 in the aftermath of a destructive civil war. WVU was asked to help this state grow and its people learn the lessons of history and science. It was established to advance the interests of the citizens of West Virginia and, in concert with other great state universities, to advance the interests of our nation.

In fact, based largely upon the great universities in every state of our nation, America has become the most powerful nation on earth—because its people are the best educated, and its universities are the best providers of education in the world.

Think of it: You and I live in history's most powerful nation during its most prosperous and powerful time. Our nation is strong because, taken together, our colleges and universities are the strongest in the world. WVU has survived and prospered through wars that have taken some of our best minds, depressions that drained our state of resources, and economic booms that demanded growth, which was costly to achieve. Through it all, our university has grown into an institution of influence and significance. We have grown into a university with three regional campuses and many distance learning centers; with a $150 million research enterprise; with offices in every county helping youth and communities through Extension programs that touch more than 130,000 citizens a year; with a commitment to continuing education; with our nationally acclaimed Robert C. Byrd Health Sciences Center and its two regional divisions; with law, engineering, journalism, nursing, medical, dental, pharmacy, and other professional development schools; and, most of all, with 32,000 undergraduate, graduate, and professional students who come from fifty states and one hundred countries.

Those who believe in and support American public higher education are currently facing another challenge. Over the past several years, billions of dollars have been drained from our budgets because of a lagging economy and shifting priorities, driven in part by the events of September 11, the rising costs of health care, and the high costs of crime. Last year, thirteen states cut the budgets of higher education. Caught with policies designed in and for a growing economy, state colleges and universities such as WVU have been faced with the realities of declining state support and growing enrollment. Faculty positions are going unfilled, staff are working to their limits, and administrators, against heavy odds, are looking for ways to keep our state colleges and universities nationally competitive.

WVU is an example of the challenge posed by growth. Our student body in Morgantown alone has grown by 3,200 full-time students in seven years. This growth has required new buildings, new technologies, and new investments in research centers and specialized faculty.

Because of the benefits of the Promise Scholarship program, more talented students are staying in West Virginia, and these students and their parents are demanding higher quality in the classroom. The average number of clients served by each of our Extension agents has grown from 700 to 1,100. Uncompensated charity care has grown to $44 million annually in our hospitals. Faculty salaries are losing ground, a difference of 5 percent during the past few years compared to our peers. We have fewer sports programs—the minimum required to compete in Division I—and we have nearly five hundred fewer full-time employees to handle the university's workload, which has significantly increased in the last few years. So, as you can imagine, we are genuinely concerned. Dr. Beasley, having been on the job since 1985, and Dr. Walker, having been at the job about a year, can give similar perspectives from their campuses.

All of our examples lead to the same conclusion. West Virginia has invested 136 years and literally billions of dollars in making WVU and the public higher education system what it is today. We dare not let its quality decline or its ability to serve be lessened. To do so would be to deprive our state of one of its hopes for a brighter future. Governor Bob Wise highlighted the importance of higher education in his State of the State address by suggesting favored status in the budget for higher education, the creation of an important and job-creating research fund, and modern management tools for our boards of governors. Indications are that our legislators continue to recognize the importance of higher education to our state and will give it priority during the legislative session this year.

I urge you, as people who obviously care about the future of this community and our state, to follow higher education policy, not just this year, but in the years to come. West Virginia must lift up higher education as a priority. We cannot continue to cut the foundation of our institutions' funding and increase service to West Virginia at the same time. We are dangerously close to falling behind the efforts made in other states. Other generations have been up to the task of building our higher education system, quality, and influence, even as they faced the challenges of a war-torn nation after the Civil War, the Great Depression, and economic booms. Are these challenging times? As we sit here today, they seem so. But I submit these times are no tougher than:

- starting West Virginia University as a land-grant college in the wake of the Civil War and adapting to its statewide role from its base in Morgantown,
- establishing Concord State Normal School solely through the support of five families in 1872 and developing the school until its accreditation in 1931, and
- launching Bluefield State College in 1885 as a black teachers' college and integrating the campus after 1954.

Consider the progress in just fifty years. These times are no tougher than those that sired our institutions throughout West Virginia; this is simply our time. I leave you with this question: How do we want history to judge our generation's leadership? Do we want to be seen as caring enough about the future to fund education? Our institutions and our state depend on us once again to rise to the challenge and emerge a stronger system of higher education.

We can all be a Patricius, simply by lifting up the value of education and sharing our passion for it with those in a position to help. We have no choice but to move either forward or backward. I hope you choose to help us move forward. West Virginia's future may depend on whether you stand up for higher education today.

ELEVEN

THE JOY OF TEACHING, INSIDE AND OUTSIDE OF THE CLASSROOM

2007

This piece was written toward the end of my service as president, after several years of teaching at our College of Law and nearly twelve years as president. By this time, I had arrived at a much deeper understanding of the values of the academy in general and the true meaning and impact of faculty diversity. I shared several versions of this message as letters and as a guest editorial prior to my departure.

For several years now I have taught a class called Lawyers and the Legislative Process. In it, students become familiar with lawmaking processes and learn the rather obscure art of bill drafting. The bills the students draft are sent to our state legislature's bill-drafting staff, and several have been enacted into law.

Recently one of my former students literally ran up to me during a convocation at the College of Law and blurted out, "President Hardesty, I use what you taught me every day." She then gave me a big hug. I was moved to tears, although I tried not to let it show. This young professional's comment meant more to me than words can express. I had arrived. To that future leader, I was considered first and foremost a university professor! A faculty colleague standing next to me cast a knowing glance on both of us as we spoke.

I know that I was only one of the many professors she encountered during her undergraduate years and during her three years at our law school. The faculty members at any public university are as diverse as the society that supports their work. Their diversity is part and parcel of the richness of the university community. One cannot truly appreciate a major university without contemplating the diversity of those who join its faculty ranks.

Perhaps a good point to begin is considering the different backgrounds, motivations, and preparation of those who work on college and university campuses in America. On our main campus alone, faculty from every state and about one hundred countries work side by side. They focus on 175 different programs of instruction and hundreds of different research, clinical, service, and extension projects. The academic institutions that prepared them for service include colleges and universities that are public and private, elite and open, small and large, rural and urban, foreign and domestic, residential and commuter, and every other manner of institution. Some are second- or third-generation faculty members. For them, the professorate is the family profession.

Others were drawn to the profession because of the transforming experience they themselves had in college. Others join academe because they are so drawn to a subject matter that they want to spend the rest of their lives learning more about it and sharing what they know with others. Some are on a mission—to transform the environment, to find a cure for a disease that took a loved one, or to represent indigent clients in a legal system that is hard for them to access. Others love to teach; they find their joy in the feedback offered by generations of students. Some join the academy immediately after completing their degree requirements. Others join in retirement or after finding their chosen profession was not what they thought it would be. Some are famous because of their writings and discovery. Others are obscure, known only to a few graduate students and colleagues in an obscure field. Some have fifty years of continuous full-time service on the same campus, and others are part-time or adjunct professors at several institutions within driving distance. Some are educated where they eventually teach, and others come from foreign lands seeking a new life in America.

The diverse backgrounds, motivations, and experiences of the faculty foster diverse attitudes toward almost everything in life. Enter a faculty committee meeting and ask, what is the purpose of undergraduate education? Ask the faculty senate which is more important to the university, public service or research and discovery? Seek a department's advice on this question: Should publication of research results be required for promotion after tenure is earned? Ask the deans, how shall we allocate the most recent discretionary gift? You will be amazed at the diversity of answers and the intensity with which there are offered. The differences will all be articulated with great skill and put forth with conviction, but the differences will be clear. The differences are driven by the nature of the respondents' backgrounds, motivations, and preparation for their life's work.

And yet, as diverse as they are, most faculty members have as much in common. Many—no, most—are very bright and have highly inquisitive minds capable of sustained and intense analysis and rational dissection of complex ideas. Most are hardworking and effective. Most value the faculty lifestyle, with its emphasis on intellectual achievement rather than accumulation of wealth. Many appreciate and utilize the university's cyclical calendar, taking the summer to do research, travel, pursue a second "profession" or a lifetime hobby, or just rest up from nine months of evening meetings and weekend activities. Nearly all value their academic freedom, which gives them the right, in most states, to speak out on issues related to their discipline without fear of reprisal. Many value the interesting mix of teaching, research, and service that their career tracks require. Finally, most members of the faculty truly enjoy being around young people and the youthful culture of campus life. It seems obvious to me that shared values mold the intense diversity of the faculty into a cohesive campus culture.

The tension between diversity on the one hand and cohesiveness on the other gives every public university and college campus attributes that I believe collectively advance the interests of the United States of America and the world in which we live. These attributes include critical examination of ideas, new and old; a healthy skepticism that advances scientific inquiry; a respect for those who are different; courage in the face of criticism; an innovative spirit; the courage to change when reason demands it; a willingness to stand up to authority, which advances democratic society; insistence on democratic processes in society; and much more.

A university is known by the life's work of each of its former students. Cardinal Newman said, "A university is, according to the usual designation, an alma mater, knowing her children one by one."[1] Because students achieve what they do in large measure because of the education they receive and the values they somehow acquire when enrolled in college, it is, in the final analysis, the faculty that define the modern American university. It is the faculty's diversity that has made American higher education the most important system of higher education in the world and attracted millions of people from other countries to our nation for their education. And, I would argue, it is this diversity that will keep it so, notwithstanding challenges for preeminence from institutions in other countries.

In the end, I am truly humbled that the small role I played in molding my former student's future was so evident to her. I am even more humbled to know that dozens of other teachers and professors also helped to mold her thought processes and skills. In the end, she decided who she would be, but it was those of us who were her teachers who collectively offered her the tools to make her own unique contributions to society. This interactive process between students and teachers is the defining characteristic, the essence, of a truly modern university. It takes place in the classroom, in the field, in the laboratories, and in the clinics. It takes place all over the university, in conversations both inside and outside the classroom. It is what sets a university apart from other institutions in society. It is why we must always strive to be a student-centered learning community meeting the changing needs of our society—diverse by its very nature, but uniformly committed to teaching and learning.

NOTES

1   John Henry Newman, *The Idea of a University: Defined and Illustrated* (1852; London: Longmans Green, 1896), 144.

TWELVE

INVOLVING PARENTS IN SUPPORT OF THE MISSION

THE WEST VIRGINIA UNIVERSITY MOUNTAINEER PARENTS CLUB

By Susan B. Hardesty

2006

A NOTE FROM DAVID C. HARDESTY JR.

In 2004, James A. Troha, a Ph.D. candidate at the University of Kansas, chose to submit a case study on the Mountaineer Parents Club in fulfillment of his dissertation requirement. According to Dr. Troha, the club has become part and parcel of a larger cultural transformation that was promoted through our commitment to becoming student centered; our vision of student-centeredness, and our subsequent integration of that vision, was a result of effective and symbolic institutional leadership and a thorough understanding of the students and families we serve. As the national chair and founder of the Parents Club at WVU, my wife, Susan, has traveled America as an advocate for parent support for student success. Her energy changed the face of WVU as the Mountaineer Parents Club grew from an idea to a thriving organization with a membership of fifteen thousand families. Because of her dedication, vision, and energy, she became a leading symbol, if not the embodiment, of our student-centered vision for the institution.

A NOTE FROM SUSAN B. HARDESTY, FOUNDER OF THE MOUNTAINEER PARENTS CLUB

David and I realized early in his presidency that there was not a vehicle to involve or to inform the parents of WVU students. It was clear to us that millennial students were raised by parents who were used to having answers, to being involved in decisions, and to having access to problem-solving resources. It was also clear that the cost of education was high and would continue to grow, and parents wanted accountability for their dollars spent. These remarks were offered at a meeting of the National Association of State Universities and Land-Grant Colleges in 2006. This was the second time I was asked to speak to the organization on the subject of parental involvement in support of student life and learning at a state university. Our Mountaineer Parents Club has been studied and benchmarked nationally many times.

The Mountaineer Parents Club was started by the president in 1995 as one of five initiatives to make WVU a student-centered institution. Because we had two college-age students of our own, and because I felt parental involvement was critical to student success, I was appointed to be the founder and champion of the organization.

At that time, only about fifteen organizations for parents existed. The premiere organization was at Texas A&M. I had learned about it from my sister, who had a student enrolled there at the time. She seemed excited about her son's school, in part because of her involvement in the Aggie Mothers' Club. While our concept was different, I had much to learn from the longstanding Texas A&M program, so during our first year at WVU, I visited with the "Aggie Moms" to learn about their organization. The organizers and volunteers were a tremendous help to us at West Virginia University.

We made several important decisions during the initial year of the Mountaineer Parents Club. First, unlike the Aggie Moms and other organizations for parents, membership in the Mountaineer Parents Club would be free, but families would have to join. Second, local clubs would be formed in areas with a high concentration of WVU students. This seemed natural to us because our Alumni Association was organized in the same way. Third, the logo of the club would be a gold heart surrounding the flying WV. The design means many different things to our parents and alumni, but the concept of love is prominent in the design. Finally, there would be an official administrative home for the club within the existing framework of WVU administration.

In that formative year, we developed mission and vision statements that have guided us. The mission of the Mountaineer Parents Club is to involve parents and other family members in programs and activities that result in continuous improvement of the student experience at West Virginia University. The vision of the Mountaineer Parents Club is to exceed the expectations of family members for the WVU experience, provide the information necessary for students and their families to pursue their life goals, and encourage family members to be active participants in, excited supporters of, and avid recruiters for West Virginia University.

The founding of the club required much hard work by many dedicated champions of the concept of parental involvement in undergraduate education. The first year, nine clubs were formed, and five hundred families joined. I traveled to each of the new clubs, assessing the needs of our WVU families.

One thing I learned during those visits was that parents wanted a direct telephone line they could call when they needed help.

I also learned parents were concerned about underage drinking on college campuses. They were concerned about travel to WVU; ground transportation to and from the Pittsburgh airport was costly and undependable. They worried about their students driving eight to ten hours alone to get to campus. Parents also felt the need to connect with other families in their area before classes started in the fall. We listened to their concerns and designed programs to address them.

Now, in 2006, after years of travel and hard work by dozens of dedicated employees and volunteer parents, the Mountaineer Parents Club has a membership of over fifteen thousand families, sixty-seven clubs all over the East Coast, seventeen state chairs to act as club liaisons in states with a low population of WVU students, and international chairs in Canada, Germany, and South America.

A parent advocate was hired in 1996 to answer a parent helpline, 1-800-WVU-0096. The advocate's job is to help parents support their students by providing answers and addressing concerns. The parent advocate, or university parent-oriented ombudsman, works in the president's office and is overseen by his chief of staff. Over thirty-five thousand calls have come into the helpline since 1996, and several times a month, the advocate now sends out *Parent E-News*, an electronic newsletter filled with pertinent campus information, to all Parents Club members.

Transportation to and from the Pittsburgh airport is now available and overseen by the Parents Club. In addition, the Parents Club, with assistance from local clubs, organizes buses for holidays to Erie, Buffalo, Philadelphia, Northern Virginia, central Maryland, Hagerstown, Allentown, Newark, and New York City. The reaction to this particular initiative has been decidedly positive. Here is what one mom e-mailed me:

My son is taking advantage of the bus at Thanksgiving. As a working mom, I truly appreciate this. I can't imagine the Sunday after Thanksgiving driving five hours and turning around and driving home to Buffalo. Thank you for this service, and I hope more families take advantage of it. With the price of gas, it is a great offer. This was a tremendous help to me, especially since I have all three of my kids in college. Thank you very much and Happy Thanksgiving!

—Mary Anne

An outgrowth of the initial suggestion that clubs plan an event in the summer has become the backbone of the local club efforts. During the summer of 2006, sixty-five summer send-offs were hosted by local clubs and state chairs. The WVU bookstore generously donated a two-hundred-dollar gift certificate to be given to one student at each send-off, and two tickets to the WVU Fall Family Weekend football game were also given to a family. A speaker from WVU attended every event. In addition to me, speakers included the president, the parent advocate, the director of the Parents Club, vice presidents, faculty members, staff, coaches, campus police officers, deans, resident faculty leaders, extension personnel, student leaders, and the Mountaineer. Building on a good idea, the local Parents Club chapters now host Winterfest events (like Bowl-watching parties or covered-dish dinners) for all WVU families in their area during the winter months. An additional two-hundred-dollar bookstore certificate is awarded during these events, as well as two tickets for a WVU basketball game.

The campus has embraced these events, and speakers from WVU have made over 650 visits to Parents Club events during the past eleven years. The impact of these events is significant; they provide wonderful venues for the sharing of parent concerns and solutions, they develop loyalty and school spirit, they allow students to connect with other students at WVU, and they give speakers from WVU the chance to meet directly with families in their hometowns.

Many personal connections have been forged and many problems solved without formal action on the part of the administration. I have personally made over 180 visits to Parents Clubs all over the East Coast, helping them get started, helping them restart when parent leaders graduated with their students, and speaking at summer send-offs and Winterfests. These visits to the hometowns of our students have given me the opportunity to relate to our families firsthand, to hear their concerns, and to hear their praises of various WVU programs.

Being able to share this information with the president has given him insight into what works and what needs attention. These efforts are part of an overall effort to make WVU's main campus, with a 2006 enrollment of over twenty-seven thousand students, feel like a much smaller academic community.

The number of parents attending the Fall Family Weekend has grown dramatically because parents feel they are also Mountaineers. Over six thousand discounted tickets were sold to parents for the 2006 football game, and over one thousand attended the pregame family tailgate buffet. Families expressed an interest in a similar weekend during the winter, so the Mountaineer Parents Club now hosts the Mountaineer Parents Club Winter Weekend for members. Several thousand families will come to campus each February for faculty lectures, a pizza party, and a basketball game.

The Mountaineer Parents Club has clearly raised the awareness of parental involvement's importance on campus. Deans now make an effort to include parents on their boards of visitors and on other planning committees. Over fifty student-centered programs have been put in place to improve student behavior, and parents have often been asked to serve on task forces dealing with behavior, housing, and safety issues.

Many parents volunteer their time to assist the club in delivering its programs. Over four hundred parents now hold a leadership position in their local Parents Club. These parents are invited to come to campus in the spring for the Mountaineer Parents Club University, which is a day planned to share the best practices of the clubs, hear from national speakers about college students and parenting, and learn from campus speakers about various student-centered initiatives.

David and I speak to parents at every Mountaineer visitation day and at every summer orientation session. Because of the Mountaineer Parents Club, parents feel empowered to ask questions, identify with us as WVU parents, and are eager to share their suggestions. Through WVU newsletters to parents, our parent electronic news and helpline, and WVU speakers at club functions, parents are now informed about various student-centered programs and WVU initiatives. They feel that they a part of the college experience and know how to get help for their students when needed. They have become actively involved in recruiting other students to WVU and are strong advocates for keeping their own children enrolled here. These tools of communications have helped us to improve everything from meal plans to financial aid forms. We have also been proactive in using these means of communication to seek parental involvement in changing campus culture and to disseminate important information, such as the conditions on campus after September 11.

Of course, administration of the club's activities requires a small staff. Initially, the Mountaineer Parents Club functioned under the WVU Alumni Association, but other homes have been tried. Finally, after studying the best possible fit, in 2006 the organizational home of the Mountaineer Parents Club was moved to WVU's Student Affairs division, with the director of the club reporting directly to the vice president. This decision was based on the common interests of parents, students, and the Office of Student Affairs. Student Affairs, which also houses undergraduate recruiting and orientation, has developed a great loyalty to parents since the club's founding, and it is a good fit for its administration. The director and her assistant will continue to help the local clubs and will ensure the continued success of the Mountaineer Parents Club.

The following e-mail, representative of the many notes we get from Parents Club members, helps us realize that we are meeting our mission and vision goals:

> The reason I am writing to you is to thank you for letting me share in our son's experience. I loved being a part of the Philadelphia Parents Club, where I chaired the student support committee. It made a HUGE difference. The biggest difference to me was that I felt more involved in his college life . . . Thank you so much. I will be very sad to see Tim leave WVU and hope that maybe someday he will be able to "give back" in some way. Thank you for a wonderful experience and God speed as you and President Hardesty journey on. Go Mountaineers!
>
> Sincerely,
>
> *Janis*

Many other universities have visited WVU to see how we do it and have asked why the Mountaineer Parents Club has been so successful. I tell them that our Parents Club has succeeded because the president believes in it and has made it a priority. He mentions the importance of parent involvement in every speech. He has supported my total involvement.

Has the Mountaineer Parents Club benefited West Virginia University? The answer is a definite *yes*! Looking back after over a decade, we have clearly learned that parents' demands for accountability can be managed in a manner that improves the university. We have learned that the president's vision of parental involvement in 1995 was right on the button. We have seen that the parents of millennial students, who were accustomed to guarantees, 1-800 numbers, complaint centers, and helpline operators, demand the same accountability of universities. They know that the cost of an education at our institution for a nonresident is about the same as the list price of a luxury automobile, and they expect value for their dollars spent on education. Our parents want to have answers when their kids call home, asking for advice. And kids do call home—often between classes! Our millennial students want their parents to have a WVU hat to wear; they want them involved (but not too involved), so the hometown Parents Clubs have been a perfect solution.

Parents have become our champions, our best recruiters, because they are informed and feel empowered. The honest input we have gotten from parents, through the Parents Club helpline and personal visits to clubs, has helped us improve WVU. We often hear about problems before they explode. Parents have helped us improve academic performance and behavior outside of the classroom. We have found that if we tell the families about all of the exciting programs, speakers, and other campus opportunities, they will tell their students. Just last week, I attended a lecture, and a student there told me his mother had called him and said he shouldn't miss it. The student did not know about the lecture, but his mother did because she had read about it in our newsletter. The more that parents know about the many efforts that WVU has made to be student centered, the more parents want their children to stay at WVU. Parents not only recruit, but they also help with retention.

Finally, there are several lessons I have learned on a personal level. The Mountaineer Parents Club has been a perfect volunteer role for me. As the spouse of the president and the mother of two WVU students, I have been able to contribute to the learning environment and student success without being seen as interfering. Because I was the perfect spokesperson to deliver the message that WVU cares about families, I have spoken at almost every Mountaineer visitation day and every summer orientation session for twelve years. Parents and students have identified with me from their first exposure to WVU. I have personally interacted with parents all over the East Coast. I have been in their homes, their churches, their libraries, their children's high schools. I know as much as anyone about the hometowns of our WVU students. This has given me credibility with the university community, parents, students, and the state. The university expresses its care and concern for students and their families through the Mountaineer Parents Club, and this has become a defining characteristic of my husband's presidency.

I will always be proud to be known as the founder of the Mountaineer Parents Club and look forward to watching the club thrive and meet the needs of WVU families in the years to come.

THIRTEEN

THE VITAL ROLE OF THE PRIVATE DONOR

WEST VIRGINIA UNIVERSITY'S RANDOLPH CANCER CENTER GALA

2007

University-development and fundraising professionals who work in the public university sector are fond of saying that no state university can be a great university without private support. I believe this to be true. Every year, volunteers at our Mary Babb Randolph Cancer Center hold a gala designed to encourage support for cancer treatment and research efforts at the center, which is part of the university's Health Sciences Center.

The gala's purposes are accomplished by informational programs and the support proffered to the center by those who attend. Every year, individuals are honored as part of the gala agenda, and in 2007, Susan and I were honored by the gala attendees. In these remarks, I tried to lift up the value of their work over the years on behalf of the university.

It is wonderful to be with you tonight and to be honored in such a special way. We thank you and all of those responsible for the evening. A few years ago, during the Building Greatness capital campaign that was conducted during my tenure as president, our foundation president was known to repeat the following phrase every time he requested support: "No state university can be a great university without private support." I know this sentiment to be true, for time and time again, I have seen the impact of private giving on different universities. Just think of the student scholarships, programs, buildings, and faculty support that you have helped to nurture. Each of you, and many others who share your dedication, have helped to make WVU a better place. In several ways, it is becoming a great university—a model state university—because of your support.

The university can spend only what it receives. Its sources of revenue are primarily state and federal subsidies, tuition, grants and contracts, and revenue from auxiliaries such as residence-hall charges and fees to support intercollegiate athletics. If one of these sources declines (for example, state support), other sources of revenue must be increased to make up the difference, or spending must be reduced. Without such actions, the quality of the university declines.

When Susan and I were students, public higher education was largely seen as a public good. It was supported so heavily that tuition was nominal, and the cost of attending minimal. This resulted from policy based on the proposition that the country needed an educated workforce and future leadership cadre in order to shape its economic future. Today, it is commonplace to say that public higher education is a private good; many believe that those who will personally benefit from an outstanding higher education should pay for it. This sentiment has led to a reduction of funding for public education as a percentage of state and federal budgets in recent years. The results have been clear: much higher tuition, increased student loans, and more limited access to higher education for millions of Americans. Similarly, state support for research has been strained. Private donations provide the infrastructure, personnel, and program money to move a vibrant research agenda forward.

Your donations have benefited many different aspects of the center's operations and, for that matter, the university's operations. Your motivations have been different as well. You come from different backgrounds, have different program targets for your support, and give in many different ways. But together you have made a difference by advancing cancer research and treatment in this country. You have shown a real determination to make sure that not just those with means have appropriate treatments available. You have also shown an interest in, and support for, treatments of the future.

Jay Rockefeller's father was noted for saying when we make charitable donations, we do so for several reasons. Among them is the fact that government agencies cannot possibly meet every need society identifies, that we see how meaningful our help is to those in need, and that giving affects our own lives. The information programs at this gala will help you to better understand the mission of the center and its good works. Many of you are cancer survivors and know full well of what I speak. We also think you have clearly helped to advance the first two thrusts of Mr. Rockefeller's statement: meeting societal needs and helping individuals.

Only you understand what your generosity has meant to you and your families. I trust for many of you that your philanthropic giving has given you a real sense of contribution to society as well as meaning to your life's journey. The many cancer patients we help through the center are clearly grateful for what you have done, as are the many fine faculty and staff of the center. On behalf of a grateful university, I thank you not only for your gifts but also for the spirit in which they were given.

FOURTEEN

THE ROLE OF WOMEN AT WEST VIRGINIA UNIVERSITY

By Susan B. Hardesty

1997

The spouse of a university president is often called upon to speak to university constituents. Many develop a project or area of interest and speak about it when giving public remarks. This was the case with my work on behalf of the Mountaineer Parents Club, about which much is written in this book. However, groups sometimes specify the subject matter for requested remarks. I was asked to speak to a group in West Virginia about the role of women at WVU. With help from many individuals, I developed this talk on women at the state's flagship university, from its founding through the end of the twentieth century.

—Susan Hardesty

Last weekend, WVU celebrated its 128th commencement. As I witnessed the ceremonies, it struck me how many women were honored for their achievements and for their advanced degrees. It also struck me how very different the world is for my daughter, who just completed her freshman year at WVU. One hundred years ago, at the dawn of the last millennium, our great-grandmothers were girdled, corseted, enveloped in yards of gingham and lace, precariously balanced on their pedestals. Graduation then was considered the most important social event at WVU, and the few women who graduated wore new white dresses during the ceremony. Ushers brought flowers and presents to place under their chairs.

If they were not women of means, our ancestors would have labored hard in a home where one in seven had a bathtub and none had electricity to power yet-to-be-invented vacuum cleaners or irons or washing machines. The pioneer women of WVU likewise faced their daily yearnings to learn with the same unforgiving odds, and it has been a real journey of discovery for me to learn about them in order to present this talk to you today.

I can't thank the Elkins Women's Club enough for requesting this topic— you who have always realized the value of higher education and nurtured that love in your colleagues and sisters. My research led me not only to share with you the accomplishments of WVU's first women but also the accomplishments of women on campus today. The old teacher in me knows that my job, in our short time together, will be to educate you—it will be your job to listen. I know from teaching that you may finish your job before I finish mine so let me know if that happens, and I'll try to wrap up quickly.

Our journey begins nearly 140 years ago at our historic Woodburn Circle, the heart of West Virginia University. It was there in 1858 that a stately private home was purchased along with twenty-five surrounding acres. It housed the Woodburn Female Seminary, a private girls school founded and operated by a church and its minister, the Reverend James R. Moore, and his wife, Elizabeth Irwin Moore. Woodburn Female Seminary flourished for nine years, serving girls from the region in primary and secondary education. However, the seminary and its brother school, Monongalia Academy, were sold to the state as part of an agreement to charter a new land-grant state university for West Virginia—a flagship institution to focus on teaching, research, and service for all.

WVU opened its doors in Woodburn Circle as the West Virginia Agricultural College in 1867, but girls from the seminary were not welcome. Opponents of coeducation argued that women would create problems with housing and its resulting "moral dilemmas," implying that women needed to be properly supervised, as in a home situation. Regent James Brown argued that women were not able to take care of themselves, from a moral standpoint, in a place like Morgantown. It is not known what inspired this opinion.

Elizabeth Moore, now widowed, had no choice but to close her girls school. Undaunted, she opened another school for girls in Morgantown in 1869, all the time keeping her eyes and heart on her old campus. Not long after, sympathetic faculty and upperclassmen at the new agricultural college began campaigning for a goal that would take them almost two decades to accomplish—coeducation. During the ensuing twenty years, women in the area continued receiving their education at Elizabeth's school, always with a watchful eye for regaining access to their old stomping grounds at Woodburn Circle.

But luck was not on Elizabeth's side, and she was dealt another blow. In 1873, women in the area had to watch helplessly as their old seminary building burned to the ground. Perhaps it was a blessing in disguise when sixteen years later they suffered the same fate when Elizabeth's second school was engulfed in flames. Opponents of coeducation could no longer argue that West Virginia women had access to higher education.

In June of 1889, just one and a half months later, on the recommendation of President Eli Turner, West Virginia University became coeducational, and ten pioneering women, ages sixteen through twenty-six, joined 189 men on the WVU campus. This past fall, women constituted 48 percent of the freshman class, which is quite an improvement over the 5 percent of 1889. Echoing the cruel attitudes we read about today on the campuses of our military acad-emies, the arrival of women was not greeted with warmth. Many of the faculty resented the women and opposed their presence on campus. No provisions had been made for their comfort or convenience. Their cloakroom was really just a basement room in Martin Hall with cold, hard benches and a row of metal wall hooks. One particular math professor crudely insisted on calling the women by their last names without adding "Miss," and no arrangements were considered for their social or athletic lives.

But these early pioneers were on a mission. Despite the adverse conditions, they were determined to claim the education they knew was rightfully theirs. They not only survived within the male-dominated system, they excelled, win-ning prizes in math, Latin, Greek, and literature. They also excelled in their vision and compassion. They were not only the mothers, sisters, aunts, and friends of West Virginia's women—they were role models. These bold women inspired future generations of women who would rally for women's right to vote and who would go on to conquer other barriers, entering the fields of teaching, law, medicine, domestic science, social work, and missionary work.

Twenty-four years after the chartering of the university, Harriet Lyon achieved one of the greatest successes. In 1891, she was the first woman to graduate from West Virginia University. Perhaps some of you, or your chil-dren, have stayed in Lyon Tower, a residence hall on our Evansdale Campus. It is but a small testament to her efforts. Elizabeth Moore Hall on our down-town campus also stands as a tribute, this time to the accomplishments of our founding mother.

Elizabeth and Harriet were not the only ones to make their mark on WVU. In 1895, Agnes Morrison of Wheeling was the first WVU law graduate. In 1897, Eva Boyers Hubbard started our art department, becoming the first of five women to join the faculty. In 1898, the first female student received a master's degree, and in 1899, WVU hired its first dean of women, Hannah

Belle Clark. In 1919, Livia Poffenbarger was distinguished as the first woman to receive an honorary degree at WVU.

WVU women were making progress on the social front as well. The first female campus organization was the Women's League, founded in 1897. The purpose of the league was to promote social relations among the women at the university by bringing all the women together on an equal basis. Then, through the women, the league hoped to bring the rest of the student body, meaning the men, together on equal terms.

Two national sororities, Alpha Xi Delta and Chi Omega, were chartered in 1905, and my sorority, Kappa Kappa Gamma, was chartered the following year. Also, women at WVU first attended a coed prom in 1922. It couldn't exactly be considered coed though—boys weren't allowed to attend until the following year.

According to the 1914 student handbook, the Board of Regents required that every social function held by students had to be chaperoned and held in university buildings. The 1925 publication of the rules and regulations for West Virginia University said that a woman could not be absent from town or spend the night away from her room without permission from the dean of women. Freshman women were only allowed to have one engagement or date during the first four nights of the week until 10:30 PM and a similar engagement on both Friday and Saturday nights, while junior and senior women were allowed an 11:00 PM engagement every night. It seems that many students today don't go out until 11:00!

Activities never diverted the women from their ultimate goal. They continued to succeed. In 1926, Ruth Wood was the first female WVU student to be nominated from Monongalia County for the House of Delegates. Carrie White became the first female recipient of an engineering degree in 1927, and in 1939, the WVU Alumni Association elected its first female president, just as Mary Lou Ballard was accepting the honor of being the first homecoming queen.

Interestingly, World War II gave WVU women a nudge in the right direction. In 1942, the student body president enlisted in the Navy, making Vice President Betty Head Baker the first female student body president. She graduated and went on to become not only a mother and a state senator but also an inspiration for her granddaughter, Erin Baker, who just completed her senior year at WVU as student body president. Another milestone came in 1945 when Victorian Louistall Monroe became the first African American woman to earn a graduate degree from WVU.

Rules during my days at WVU were still fairly strict. Dean of Women Betty Boyd was responsible for the supervision of campus women. Even in the '60s, missing curfews by as little as one to five minutes would result in a restriction, which meant staying in the dormitories for a Friday or Saturday night. Women were also given restrictions if they were absent from house meetings in the dorms or if they wore head scarves or curlers to the evening meal. All females were required to sign out of the dormitory for the weekend before going home, and then only after presenting proof of their parents' permission. A 1955–56 catalog states that freshman women were allowed to sign out to go to the library to study at night, but they had to report to the library proctor within ten minutes after leaving the dorms. Those were the days when women wearing Bermuda shorts were required to wear a coat and freshmen beanies were donned by both freshman men and women.

The year 1969 brought a period of radical change for WVU women when they won the battle for a no-hours policy. In 1972, WVU organized women's athletics to comply with Title IX regulations, and the marching band gave its first performance with women musicians participating. By the end of 1973 women were allowed to drink beer on campus, and wonder of all wonders, they were permitted to wear shorts to class.

One thing has never changed for women at WVU: a strong commitment to education. For instance, unlike Yale's, Harvard's, and Columbia's law schools, WVU's College of Law has been admitting women for over one hundred years. Although there were only fifty-five women graduates from the law school from 1899 to 1969, today 53 percent of the 1997 class are women, and they are led by a female dean, Terree Foster. Recent graduates currently serve as district court judges and federal magistrates. One woman has served as the U.S. attorney in West Virginia, another sits on the Supreme Court of Appeals of West Virginia, and numerous others work as partners and associates in law firms statewide.

Similar to the law school is the WVU medical program. From 1900 to 1960, woman constituted only 3 percent of the medical school population, but by 1996, 34 percent—183 out 537 graduates—were women. One recent female graduate is the director of the Harlem Hospital Center Pediatrics Department in New York City, and another is a pioneer in bone marrow transplantation. Yet another has become a professor of pediatrics and chief of neonatology at WVU. She is one of the few neonatologists in the country who has long-term clinical experience with drugs designed to help respiratory distress syndrome in premature infants. Pharmacy programs were first offered at WVU in 1914, and pharmacy became a college in 1936. By 1967, seven out of fifty graduates were women, and now that number has risen to two-thirds of the graduating class. Carmella Evans, a 1997 pharmacy graduate, was recently selected as one of twenty *USA Today* First Academic Team Scholars, chosen from thousands of nationwide applicants.

The Eberly College of Arts and Sciences graduates 60 percent of our students yearly, so this department too boasts some famous female success stories. They include Dorothy Dotson, a managing director of an international banking firm; Louise McNeill Pease, the poet laureate of West Virginia; and Jayne Ann Phillips, author of *Machine Dreams* and *Shelter*, both of which are set in rural West Virginia. A female graduate of the College of Agriculture and Forestry, Vivian Woofter, is currently responsible for the design and furnishings of all United States embassies; a 1978 female doctoral student in rehabilitation counseling is the director of the Federal Bureau of Prisons; and Rae E. McKee, the 1991 national teacher of the year, was the spokesperson for 2.5 million teachers in the United States.

The College of Creative Arts has produced many creative minds such as Joann Siegrist, known internationally for her work with puppets. Catherine Crotty is the pianist with the West Virginia Symphony, Patrice King Brown anchors the evening news in Pittsburgh, and Kay Goodwin currently serves as chair of the West Virginia System Board of Trustees, which governs WVU, Marshall, and the Osteopathic School.

Honors and accolades are increasingly the norm for WVU women. Both last year's and this year's student body presidents were women. Carolyn Connor is our twenty-fifth Rhodes Scholar, now completing her first year at Oxford University in England, and Anna Blobaum is our seventeenth Goldwater Scholar. Also on a fast track is Kristin Quackenbush, who was recently named the outstanding collegiate gymnast in the United States.

All of these women share a love of knowledge and of West Virginia. Their successes can be attributed to a variety of causes, but all of them have a common drive to succeed and a community of people supporting them along the way. West Virginia is that community, striving to make sure that never again will a woman be limited to the hard benches of the Martin Hall basement. Instead, she will always have an equal opportunity to rise to the top.

I really think that "community" is the operative word in today's times. That is what I have tried to instill in our Mountaineer Parents Club. For the more than three thousand families who have joined, we want to give them all the support they need to help their children succeed; we want them to feel connected to a community of people who share the same goals for their children. This sense of community, I believe, is the key to our club's success, and I believe it has also been the key to women's growth and achievement at WVU.

Our legacy truly parallels the national struggle women have waged for an equal voice. I was told once that a young woman was asked after an eye examination, "Have you had any trouble lately threading needles?" "No," she replied, smiling, "but I have had trouble reading the *Wall Street Journal.*" We certainly have come a long way from the time when it was a crime for a married woman to buy a sewing machine without her husband's consent, or when physicians were brought in to certify that women's physical and mental abilities were strong enough to withstand the pressure of introducing the typewriter to the workplace, and many predicted that women's minds would snap.

Our WVU women should be congratulated again and again for their past, present, and future accomplishments. I really love the words of Elizabeth Mertz, published in the *Radcliffe Quarterly*; see if you don't agree:

> When Aristotle wrote his books, when Milton searched for rhyme,
> did they have toddlers at their knees requesting dinner time?
> When Dante contemplated hell or Shakespeare penned a sonnet,
> did their preteen interrupt to say her shirt had ketchup on it?
> When Socrates was teaching youth and when Plato wrote,
> were they the ones to clean the mess the children made with Play-doh?
> Did food get bought when Darwin sought his Origin of Species?
> When Holmes donned his robes and gave wise opinions,
> was laundry piled four-feet high with socks mixed with linens?
> How much greater, then, the task of those who manage both,
> who juggle scholarship with child development and growth,
> and how much greater is the praise for those who persevere
> and finish their advanced degrees and take up a career!

I started by relaying a history that sometimes overwhelmed me because of the barriers and struggles its key players had to face. But happily, I can also tell you that WVU women had a chance to make history, and they did. WVU women have the opportunity to make a difference in this state and this country, and they are.

The actions, values, and lives of the women whose paths intersected with WVU are building a stronger society, one in which our common ground has helped drive legislation, goals, ideals, and dreams. Helen Keller once said, "One can never consent to creep when one feels an impulse to soar."[1] I am sure that if I were asked to give this talk to you again in a few years, WVU women would still be helping to make each other's dreams take flight. The clock will not turn back. The clock moves forever forward, and with it a history rich in vibrancy and optimism. Thank you.

NOTES

1   Helen Keller, speech to the fifth meeting of the American Association to Promote the Teaching of Speech to the Deaf, at Mt. Airy, Philadelphia, Pennsylvania, July 8, 1896.

Stewart Hall, constructed in 1902 to serve as the library, now houses the administrative offices of the university. The president's office is located in the tower and looks out over the downtown campus. Photo courtesy of WVU Photography Services.

The university president must develop relationships with public officials to serve the institution well. WVU President Harry Heflin, center, accompanied by student government President David Hardesty, right, welcomes Vice President Hubert H. Humphrey, Jr., in 1966. Photo courtesy of the David C. Hardesty Collection.

While at Oxford University as a Rhodes Scholar in 1968, Hardesty participated in the Queen's College Rowing Club. The Oxford experience influenced his personal development and later institutional programs to revitalize the undergraduate student experience. Photo courtesy of the David C. Hardesty Collection.

The Board of Governors oversees the university, including budgetary, policy, and curriculum issues. The president is accountable to the Board of Governors, which also has the responsibility of appointing WVU's president. Photo courtesy of WVU Photography Services.

President and Mrs. Hardesty react to the announcement that he has been appointed twenty-first president of WVU. The Inaugural Address describes their shared desire to serve their alma mater and their vision for WVU's future. Photo courtesy of WVU Photography Services.

Gerald Lang, Provost of WVU since 1995, counsels David Hardesty shortly before the 2006 State of the University address. As chief academic officer, the Provost advises the President, oversees the university in his absence, and manages operations. Photo courtesy of Bob Gay, *The Dominion Post*.

During the Inauguration, President Hardesty exchanges his crimson Harvard robe for a robe with the colors of West Virginia University, publicly displaying his allegiance to his undergraduate institution and the university he would serve for twelve years. Photo courtesy of Dale Sparks, *The Dominion Post*.

Cisco Chairman and CEO John Chambers ('71, '74) has been recognized as a distinguished graduate of West Virginia University and granted an honorary degree. He also delivered the university's 132nd commencement address. Photo courtesy of the David C. Hardesty Collection.

President and Mrs. Hardesty host students during at a 2003 honors reception at Blaney House, the president's home. Because WVU is a student-centered institution, the President often sought students' opinions regarding institutional priorities and recognized their accomplishments. Photo courtesy of WVU Photography Services.

During President Hardesty's tenure a new Recreation Center was constructed. This building provides recreation and exercise opportunities to ensure that students can develop the classical Greek ideal of "a strong mind in a strong body." Photo courtesy of WVU Photography Services.

The Bulger siblings are three stars of WVU Athletics. Marc ('99) was a starting quarterback at WVU, and now plays in the NFL. Kate ('04), right, is the third highest scorer in WVU basketball history, and now plays in the WNBA. Meg has scored 1,285 points with her senior season left to play. Photo courtesy of WVU Athletics.

The award winning WVU Marching Band, "The Pride of West Virginia," celebrated the ten-year anniversary of the Mountaineer Parents Club, which was founded and chaired by Mrs. Hardesty, at the WVU vs. East Carolina game in 2005. Photo courtesy of Chris Southerland, WVU Band.

WVU's 4-H programming and collegiate 4-H activities have earned national recognition, and President Hardesty was the first university president to serve as chair of the National 4-H Council. 4-H participants gain experience in public leadership through activities such as the Mineral County Fair. Photo courtesy of Ann Bailey Berry, WVU Extension Service.

Susan Hardesty founded the Mountaineer Parents Club to help parents connect with the university when she became first lady at WVU. In September 2005, Arts and Entertainment presented "An Evening with Bill Cosby" during Fall Family Weekend. Photo courtesy of the David C. Hardesty Collection.

The expanded and remodeled downtown Wise Library provides a state-of-the-art facility with research and computing resources for students and faculty. This modernized building preserves the ambience of the past in its comfortable reading rooms. Photo courtesy of WVU Photography Services.

Research is one of the primary missions of a university, and collaboration between students and faculty members is essential to a dynamic learning environment. Influential faculty members and administrators inspire the success of their students and colleagues. Photo courtesy of WVU Photography Services.

Extension Services uses the model of applied research for agricultural programs and other training such as structural fire fighting at its mobile fire lab. Engaging with the community to improve the State's welfare is a critical responsibility of land-grant universities. Photo courtesy of Wesley Nugent, WVU Extension Service.

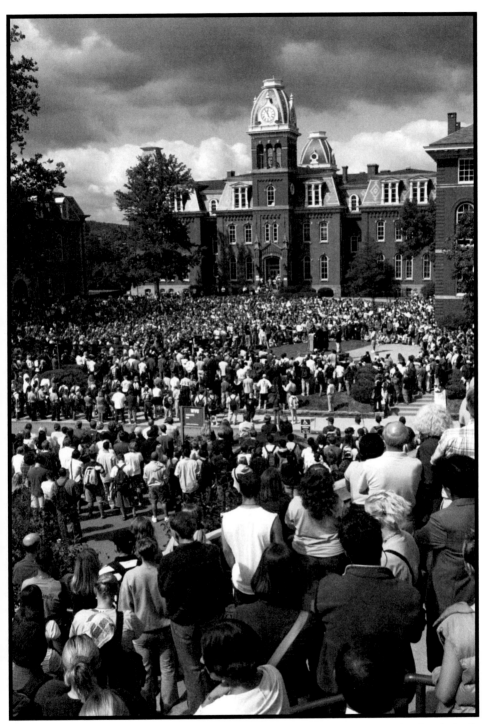

September 11, 2001, was a traumatic day for many members of the WVU community who lost friends, family members, and classmates during the terrorist attack. President Hardesty delivered an address to encourage the campus community at Woodburn Circle. Photo courtesy of Dale Sparks, *The Dominion Post*.

Philanthropists honored during the 2005 Woodburn Circle Society Induction Ceremony included Mike Puskar, Gerald and Carolyn Eberly Blaney, and George Farmer of the Hazel Ruby McQuain Trust. Donations have increased WVU's ability to attract students and faculty. Photo courtesy of Dale Sparks, All-Pro Photography.

The WVU Alumni Association's Loyalty Permanent Endowment Fund has helped more than 2,500 deserving students realize their dreams at WVU. Trustees, pictured with Hardesty, include Jimmy McCartney, General Earl Anderson, Steve Douglas, and Buck Harless. Photo courtesy of the David C. Hardesty Collection.

President Hardesty delivered a speech honoring four-star general Robert H. "Doc" Foglesong at his inauguration. A distinguished alumnus, Foglesong earned three degrees at WVU and is currently president of Mississippi
State University. Photo courtesy of WVU Photography Services.

Jerry West, another distinguished alumnus and legendary figure in the world of basketball, received an honorary degree in 2006, when he also delivered the commencement address to graduating WVU students. Photo courtesy of WVU Photography Services.

WVU's growth has contributed substantially to the regional economy. Shown at the groundbreaking ceremony for the Blanchette Rockefeller Neurosciences Institute are Governor Wise, Senator Robert C. Byrd, Senator Jay Rockefeller, NIH Director Dr. Zerhouni, VP for Health Sciences Dr. D'Alessandri, and President Hardesty. Photo courtesy of WVU Photography Services.

After returning to the United States from Iraq, former prisoner of war Jessica Lynch attended WVU. President Hardesty and Board of Governors Chair Stephen Goodwin introduced her to Senator Byrd. Photo courtesy of John Harrington.

In the public roles as president and first lady of WVU, David and Susan Hardesty officially welcomed elected officials including President George W. Bush. President Bush celebrated Independence Day on the WVU campus in July 2005. Photo courtesy of WVU Photography Services.

Presidents must garner support from public officials and educational leaders. After WVU graduate Brian Noland was appointed chancellor of West Virginia's Higher Education Policy Commission in July 2006, President Hardesty introduced him to Senator Byrd. Photo courtesy of Chris Southerland, WVU News.

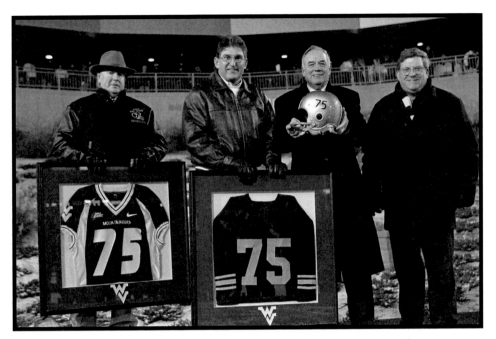

On November 24, 2005, Sam Huff's number became the first officially retiredfrom competition by WVU. Pictured left to right are Director of Athletics Ed Pastilong, Governor Joe Manchin III, Sam Huff, and David Hardesty. Photo courtesy of WVU Athletics.

President Hardesty and Governor Manchin cheer at the West Regional Championship against Louisville in Albuquerque, NM, on March 26, 2005. President Hardesty emphasized the importance of balancing athletics as a part of the undergraduate experience. Photo courtesy of WVU Athletics.

In 2006, the WVU men's soccer team went 15-3-3 and won the Big East regular season championship. Head coach Marlon LeBlanc won *Soccer America* national coach of the year honors. Photo courtesy of WVU Athletics.

Megan Metcalfe became the third female track and field national champion in school history by winning the 5,000-meter run in Sacramento on June 12, 2005. Photo courtesy of WVU Athletics.

Kevin Pittsnogle's 27 points against Louisville on March 26, 2005, helped lead the Mountaineers to the brink of the Final Four in the NCAA tournament before falling in overtime to the Cardinals. Photo courtesy of WVU Athletics.

Head football coach Rich Rodriguez was awarded the Gator Bowl Trophy on Jan. 1, 2007, after West Virginia won its second straight New Year's Day bowl game 38-35 over Georgia Tech in the Toyota Gator Bowl. Photo courtesy of WVU Athletics.

As figureheads and fans of the university, Susan and David Hardesty wore their blue and gold while cheering the Mountaineers at hundreds of athletic events during their many years of service to WVU. Photo courtesy of the David C. Hardesty Collection.

FIFTEEN

THE VALUE AND PERILS OF INTERCOLLEGIATE ATHLETICS

2007

In 1891, a group of WVU students ventured to a cow pasture outside Morgantown to face off against peers from nearby Washington and Jefferson College in a game that was fairly new and still evolving into the American football that we recognize today. It was not an auspicious start for WVU's athletic program—the Washington and Jefferson team won 72–0. As anyone who has heard of the Mountaineers knows, our athletic programs have evolved greatly.

In fact, throughout the United States, the growth of intercollegiate athletics has been explosive and now involves more than three hundred seventy-five thousand student athletes. While there are many obvious and important benefits to every college engaged in intercollegiate competition, there is concern among some college presidents and institutional board members related to the increasing cost of the programs, whose growth outstrips that of general university budgets. Campus leaders are also concerned about what they see as the increasing commercialism of college sports programs due to a variety of factors, including the very large number of TV channels available for paid program-

ming, the blurring of career paths and pay scales between university and profes-
sional teams, and the expanding use of agents by coaches. Some observers call
the increasing competition for proven coaches and the demand for more capital
investments and better facilities an arms race among the larger programs.

Fifteen years ago, the Knight Foundation Commission on Intercollegiate
Athletics made several recommendations to enhance the academic and finan-
cial integrity of Division I college sports.[1] Controversial at the time, the report
raised issues that are important to every college president.

During the past decade, I have served as a director of the Big East con-
ference, a member of the Bowl Championship Series Presidential Oversight
Committee, and a member of an NCAA presidential task force. And, as has
every sitting president at an institution with high-level intercollegiate athlet-
ics competition, I have also been involved for years in helping our campus
address many compliance, financial, strategic, and public relations issues, in-
cluding finding successors for very popular major sports coaches at WVU and
the reorganization of the Big East conference after three schools departed for
another conference.

In June 2005, I was appointed a member of the NCAA committee that even-
tually drafted a second major report on the future of intercollegiate athletics
called "The Second-Century Imperatives: Presidential Leadership—Institu-
tional Accountability." The report continues where the Knight Commission
reforms left off. "What remains will be done through an unflagging determina-
tion to see the reform efforts to completion," the report states, "and reap the
benefits of national academic policy based on sound data and good judgment."[2]
This report asks college and university presidents and their governing boards
to assert their authority in a serious effort to moderate the growth of athletic
budgets and to increase the transparency of athletic program budgets in order
to provide greater scrutiny of this important part of college life.

Toward the end of my tenure, the dean of the West Virginia University School of Physical Education, Dr. Dana Brooks, asked me to speak to one of his classes on the subject of presidential involvement in intercollegiate athletics. In the lecture (which was re-created from an outline I used for Dr. Brooks's class), I shared with future college athletic administrators one president's perspective on several issues related to intercollegiate athletics, in the hope that the discussion would lead to a fuller understanding of the value and perils of the intercollegiate enterprise in America. Many of the concepts were sharpened by experience, while others were speculative in nature. This lecture anticipated some of the findings of "The Second-Century Imperatives" report, which was being drafted at the time and which I have referenced in revising my speech for publication.

At the Harvard Seminar for New Presidents, which I attended the year after I was appointed president of our university, I asked a senior, experienced faculty member what sounded like a fairly straightforward question: "Who owns the university?"

"Young man," he replied, "that is a question that should never be asked, let alone answered."

I want to begin my lecture on presidential leadership regarding intercollegiate athletics with a simple proposition that is often lost on those who follow intercollegiate athletics. There are many owners of every university.[3] The athletic departments and the fans that follow their programs are certainly among those owners. Included in this group are the coaches and staffs of the sports programs, administrators, ticket holders, current and former players, media reporters and sportscasters, conference officials, NCAA officers and delegates, and others who have more than a passing interest in the sports programs that began here with a friendly football game with Washington and Jefferson College in 1891.

However, there are many other owners of the modern university, including state- and federal-policy makers, the appointed and elected members of governing boards, thousands of students and their parents, alumni of the colleges and schools, contributors, foundation grant makers, federal and state funding agencies, host communities, research partners, bond holders, patients, taxpayers, and many, many more. There are thousands of owners of every university. Each owner belongs to at least one of the university's many constituencies (i.e., groups who care about the university and its future and press their views upon the university's president).

The constituencies sometimes find themselves at odds with regard to the university's values, mission, vision, and goals. Even I am sometimes conflicted. As an individual, I belong to several constituent groups: I am a graduate, I have a child enrolled at the university, I make donations to our foundation, I am a sports fan and have been for forty years, I live in this town, I am a taxpayer, and I teach at the law school.

As a fan, I want to add a video scoreboard to our Coliseum, enhance the locker rooms in our football facility, buy a jet to ease the tiring recruiting trips for our coaches, schedule games on weekday nights when I like to watch TV with my family, invest in more talent in every staff position, award more scholarships, and do as much as humanly possible for our very fine athletic program. I firmly believe that most student athletes are getting a great education, learning self-discipline, and growing in maturity and wisdom. Sometimes I even want to e-mail myself in the president's office and complain that the university administration just doesn't do enough for some sports programs.

Other university owners support positions that would limit the emphasis on athletics found at many major universities. I identify with many of these positions as well. As a parent and taxpayer, I want to keep tuition and fees modest. As a faculty member, I want to make sure that academic programs continue to receive the highest campus funding priority. I want my students to be ready for class on the mornings after big games. I want to resist the pressure to increase funding for athletics so that the core mission elements of the university—teaching, research, and service—can be enhanced. As an alumnus, I want the student-centered values I hold dear to be maintained at the university. These concerns are addressed in the report of the NCAA presidential task force on the future of Division I intercollegiate athletics, *The Second-Century Imperatives: Presidential Leadership—Institutional Accountability*. This report focuses on ways to ensure the financial integrity of college sports and better integrate athletics with the academic mission of the institution.

As president of this institution, I do not have the luxury of looking at issues from the viewpoint of just one, or even a few, of the owners. It is my job to represent them all. It is my fiduciary responsibility to ascertain what I believe to be in the interests of the entire university, and all of its constituencies, and pursue those ends.

The modern university president is the chief executive officer of a complex organization. To the extent that athletics acts as a marketing arm of the university and represents the character of the university nationally—and to the extent that it affects the university's budget and values—presidents see it as their responsibility to be involved. "The reality for effective reform of spending and revenue-generating behaviors for intercollegiate athletics is this," the *Second-Century Imperatives* report states. "Each college and university must hold itself accountable for exercising its independent will as an institution of higher education. And it will do that best through well-informed, value-driven presidential leadership."[4] As part of that effort, I must be an advocate for and to all owners of the university, seeking to understand their points of view, all the while asking for their support of the university's strategic goals. As president, I have little choice but to do what I can to ensure the integrity of the university's finances, compliance with the rules by which we operate, and every owner's pride in the reputation of the institution.

One can argue, of course, that I have posed a false choice. One can easily suggest that intercollegiate athletics programs are made up of students, competing in a controlled environment, learning the lessons of life while being led by teachers called coaches, who are interested first and foremost in student welfare. As such, college sports are surely part of college life. On one level, this is true, and I strongly believe in the premise of intercollegiate sports. Yet many are concerned that commercialism is creeping into intercollegiate athletics at an alarming rate. One can make this case fairly easily. Some call the situation an arms race to conquer and outperform rival programs. The problem is that on most campuses, there is no bottom-line orientation such as that which one finds in a professional team. No one is trying to squeeze profits out of a public university. Some see this as a problem throughout the culture of academia: we tend to spend all of the resources we receive, from whatever source they are derived.

Athletic expenditures on most campuses are growing faster than the rate of growth in the general budgets of the entire university. This is true on our campus and true nationally. According to a recent *USA Today* article, at least forty-two of 119 Division I-A coaches now earn $1 million or more annually,[5] more than ten or fifteen times the average faculty salary. Television coverage generates significant revenues but requires games to be played on weekdays, sometimes before examinations and other important academic activities. Long-term bonds, binding future generations of taxpayers and tuition payers, are customarily issued to fund the building of beautiful sporting venues that rival professional facilities. Fans tune into talk shows that sell beer advertisements, and alumni write scathing letters to the editor castigating presidents and athletic directors who don't do their bidding.

As the *Second-Century Imperatives* report notes, "Intercollegiate athletics' greatest challenge often is its own success . . . The goal of intercollegiate athletics—to maximize the number of students who benefit from competing as part of their total educational experience—is jeopardized as the collegiate model drifts toward the professional approach."[6] The use of sports agents has crept into negotiations between administrators and coaches, and professional agents sign up student athletes, often improperly and long before they are mature enough to understand the import of their decisions. Athletic department budgets on some campuses are approaching, even exceeding, $100 million. And inevitably, the desire to win and be competitive, often encouraged by incentives, promotes behaviors that sometimes break the "rules of the game" and are often unethical.

Further, the lack of transparency leading to accountability is evident. Different philosophies of disclosure, different accounting definitions, and different methods of funding make comparisons between athletic programs at different institutions difficult. Often, departmental administrators, coaches, presidents, board members, and policymakers are hesitant to disclose the full cost of the programs to the general public, fearing backlash. Political pressure to support athletic programming over academic programming seems evident when legislators and opinion leaders openly criticize colleges for increasing tuition year after year, but remain quiet when expensive facilities are built and market-driven multimillion-dollar contracts are given to successful coaches.

The *Second-Century* task force participants were asked to chart a course of action that would protect the academy against excessive commercialism. The immediate reaction from some members was to impose limits on expenditures, in the same way limits have been imposed on competitive practices in recruiting, practice times, and other activities. But mandatory limits on the arms race seem unlikely at this point. Even when collective action seems logical, federal antitrust laws prohibit proactive efforts to control the spiraling costs.

While voluntary limits on spending seem far from becoming a reality, two courses of action seem to be acting as surrogates for decisions that would limit spending. The first is a national call for increased transparency and comparability of expenditures in order to make boards and legislators more aware of how much is actually being spent on athletics and how their athletic department budgets compare to those of other institutions. The second is the adoption of collective rules that protect student athletes and limit the impact of money on competition. Examples of the first strategy include initiatives of the *Second-Century* task force to suggest financial definitions and benchmarks for disclosure and comparison purposes. Examples of the second strategy include rule-based limitations on the number of scholarships that can be awarded for students to participate in various sports and the elimination of some of those scholarships if students fail to reach benchmark goals for academic performance, including graduation.

In the final analysis, the various owners of the university may reach a fair compromise. If the athletic enterprise begins to take too much of the university's private support, or taxpayer support, or if ticket sales put games beyond the reach of the average family following a state university team, the other owners of the institution will enter the fray, and self-regulation may take place.

In this debate, our culture of academic freedom and openness of debate and discussion may be an asset. On our campus, our faculty senate chair already has visited the athletic department to make a personal assessment of the self-regulation we practice. Collectively, faculty members around the country are forming national associations to question the direction of athletic departments and challenge the demands they make on the governing boards of their institutions. Taxpayer groups, and even members of the United States Congress, have expressed concerns that could lead to changes in federal and state tax laws that would impact the future of our athletic programs.

I am happy to report that at this juncture, our athletic department is well-managed and has a long history of respecting the academic enterprise through the adoption of rules, good communications, community input for decision making, and policies that have kept peace among the many owners of our university. The emphasis on student learning in WVU's athletic program is exemplified by the attitude of Men's Basketball Head Coach John Beilein, who once said, "I enjoy the process of seeing a young man grow both on and off the floor. To see him get it, to look in his eyes and have him say, 'I understand now, coach.'

That's what I coach for." The department and our fans seem to be owners that respect the rights of other constituents within the university community.

It is true, of course, that there is no easy answer to the question, who owns the university? But it does seem that more and more people around the country are asking this question and are intent on trying to answer it. Presidents will inevitably find themselves in the middle of these debates because the questions they raise will impact every aspect of institutional governance and decision making. The president's job, in the end, is to make sure that all owners are represented in the debate and that the final outcomes reflect the best decisions for the university.

NOTES

1   Knight Commission on Intercollegiate Athletics, *Keeping Faith with the Student-Athlete: A New Model for Intercollegiate Athletics* (1991).

2   National Collegiate Athletic Association, *The Second-Century Imperative: Presidential Leadership—Institutional Accountability* (Indianapolis, IN: NCAA, 2006), 11.

3   For more on the concept of a university's multiple owners, see Henry Rosovsky, *The University: An Owner's Manual* (New York: W. W. Norton, 1990), 261–262.

4   NCAA, *The Second-Century Imperatives*, 13.

5   Jodi Upton and Steve Wieberg, "Contracts for College Coaches Cover More Than Salaries," *USA Today*, November 16, 2006, http://www.usatoday.com (accessed January 10, 2007).

6   NCAA, *The Second-Century Imperatives*, 10.

SIXTEEN

THE MEANING
OF SOCIAL JUSTICE

It is broadly believed on university campuses that social justice and campus diversity are essential to a university's culture of respect and its ability to reach out to students and other constituencies. This chapter both defines social justice and discusses its practical applications on our campus.

CAMPUS STATEMENT ON DIVERSITY
AND CIVIL RIGHTS

1999

In 1999, our campus mounted a task force to reexamine the social justice programs at WVU. It served as a review of the campus commitment to equality of opportunity that had been firmly established by my predecessor, Dr. Neil S. Bucklew, WVU's twentieth president. At the conclusion of the task force's work, I drafted a statement related to our work in which I attempted to define the meaning of social justice in the context of our community and reaffirm it as a campus value. Below is an excerpt from that report.

I have come to believe that social justice is a set of ideas, policies, activities, and programs that have been generally embraced, both formally and informally, by the university community. In summary, they can be stated as follows:

First, the campus community shares certain values, centered on the intrinsic worth and dignity of every human being. Among these are a respect for law; freedom from fear; inclusiveness; a climate of opportunity for all community members; an absence of discrimination based on race, sex, marital status, pregnancy, age, ethnic origin, religious beliefs, sexual orientation, or disability; mutual respect based upon empathy and understanding; the recognition of merit; a sense of community and a feeling that the future should be shared by all of those in the community; accountability for actions; and the importance of diversity.

Second, our university engages in activities that foster these values. Among these are education, advocacy, communications, investigations, mediation, recruitment, networking, mentoring, advising, counseling, administration according to policy, policy development, community building, celebration, outreach, encouragement of diversity, cultural awareness activities, crisis management, and social activities.

Third, a variety of vehicles are used to achieve the ends sought. These include representative councils, task forces and groups, executive support and staffing, programs of various types, centers of education, research and service related to the programs and activities, academic offerings and credentials, awards and honors, policy enforcement, volunteer recruitment, and performance and entertainment options and groups.

Fourth, campus individuals, units, officers, and groups stand accountable for their actions. Accountability is achieved through clear job descriptions, clear charges to the councils and groups sanctioned and supported by WVU, clear goals and objectives to individuals and groups, periodic assessments of progress, an expectation of civility, enforcement of laws in an effective and timely fashion, and an expectation of voluntary compliance with laws by everyone in the university community.

Finally, there is a clear understanding that inherent tensions and challenges exist and must be managed effectively. The causes for the tensions are many, including conflicts caused by the tension or tensions between individual rights and collective or community rights, group identification and community identification, groups seeking different allocation of scarce resources, attempted communications among groups with different backgrounds and origins, historical prejudices, misinformation or a lack of information, and the evolutionary nature of policies and concepts.

THE IMPORTANCE OF DIVERSITY IN HIGHER EDUCATION
The Legacy and Future of Brown Versus the Board of Education

2004

As is often the case, foundation documents such as our social justice report (above) influence presidential statements for years to come. Below are remarks delivered at the WVU College of Law that incorporate the thinking outlined in the statement from our social justice task force five years earlier.

Fifty years ago, when the United State Supreme Court ruled that racially segregated schools were inherently unequal, Chief Justice Earl Warren noted that education is "the very foundation of good citizenship"[1] and a virtual prerequisite for achieving a successful career. The tragedy of segregated education lay in the human potential that was lost when young people were barred from high-quality education simply because of the color of their skin.

African American students were the victims of racist educational policies, but all students and teachers in segregated schools—black and white—missed out on the benefits of learning in a diverse community. Before the 1954 ruling, WVU admitted African American students only to graduate and professional programs not offered at the state's historically black colleges. Since then, we have endeavored to create a racially and ethnically diverse community that protects the rights of all students to receive a quality education.

Brown v. Board of Education paved the way for generations of African American students to receive quality education and fulfill their true potential. In turn, learning communities such as ours have been incalculably enriched by the presence of African American students, professors, researchers, and administrators. We would be a diminished community if not for the thousands of African American students who have passed through our doors. They include people such as Harvard University Professor Henry Louis Gates Jr., a graduate of Potomac State College; Judge Irene Berger, the first African American woman to be appointed to the circuit court bench in West Virginia; and WVU Vice President for Student Affairs Ken Gray, who has achieved the highest rank available in the U.S. Army Judge Advocate General's Corps. Our campus community would be poorer if we had never had the chance to utilize the wisdom of leaders such as Vice President Gray, WVU Parkersburg President Marie Foster Gnage, and School of Physical Education Dean Dana Brooks.

Today our faculty, staff, administrators, and students continue to work to create an ever more diverse and supportive learning environment, and in today's world, a commitment to diversity in education is more important than ever. In 1999, the American Council on Education endorsed a statement on the importance of diversity in higher education. The statement outlined four main benefits of creating a diverse learning community.

First, it said diversity enriches the educational experience by exposing us to unfamiliar perspectives and experiences. Second, it promotes personal growth and social harmony by challenging stereotypical notions and promoting critical thinking. Third, it strengthens communities by fostering mutual respect and teamwork. And fourth, it enhances our nation's economic competitiveness by tapping the talents and abilities of all our citizens.

Preparing students to live and work in the twenty-first century is the primary purpose of any university. Thanks to rapid technological advances, our world is quickly becoming an interconnected global village, and our students must learn to work in increasingly diverse settings. Kellogg Foundation President William Richardson has said that thriving in a multicultural setting will soon become a skill all employers will expect their employees to have mastered.

Research suggests that students actually learn better in a diverse educational environment. A 2000 American Council on Education report revealed that students who participate in racial and cultural awareness workshops or interact with diverse peers have better critical-thinking skills and are more open to diversity. Other research has shown that if college students socialize across racial lines and discuss racial and ethnic issues, they are more likely to have positive learning experiences, have an improved social self-concept, and be more satisfied overall with college.

At WVU, we promote multicultural awareness in a variety of ways, such as requiring all undergraduates to take at least one course focusing on a foreign culture or on minority or gender issues; offering such academic programs as a major in women's studies and minors in Africana studies and Native American studies; holding events such as Diversity Week and hosting educational programs tied to observances such as African American History Month and Women's History Month; honoring faculty, staff, and students who have acted as examples in treating all people fairly and compassionately; and maintaining a strong social justice program that educates faculty and staff on issues such as racism, sexism, homophobia, and disability awareness. Our social justice program rests on a belief that every human being has intrinsic worth and dignity and a unique vision to contribute to the community. We strive for something more than mere tolerance of our differences. Instead, we seek to build a community where people truly value different life experiences and seek out fresh perspectives.

While our university and our society have come a great distance in the past half century, much remains to be done to fulfill the promise of *Brown v. Board of Education*. As a research university, we have a responsibility to seek ways to fulfill that promise. For that reason, WVU's *Brown v. Board of Education* Fiftieth Anniversary Steering Committee is issuing a request for proposals for faculty and student research into equity and education. Projects should be aimed at analyzing progress toward equality, barriers, and potential methods for enhancing equity, particularly at WVU. The WVU offices of Sponsored Programs and Extended Learning will provide seed money of up to $7,000 for select projects. Proposals are due by October 4, and more information will be available on the WVU Web site starting tomorrow. The committee has also planned many educational events throughout the next year, and I encourage WVU community members to take part in as many of them as possible.

Nelson Mandela called education the most powerful weapon you can use to change the world. *Brown v. Board of Education* gave all citizens the right to a quality education. Fifty years later, it is up to each of us to use the educational resources at our disposal to create a world where people have a truly equal opportunity to succeed.

NOTES

1   Opinion for *Brown v. Board of Education*, May 17, 1954 (http://www.nps.gov/archive /brvb/pages/decision54.htm).

SEVENTEEN

PRIESTS
OF THE TEMPLE

As president, I was often called upon to deliver speeches that recognized the contributions of our graduates and other important members of our university community. I enjoyed these opportunities to share the stories of the individual men and women who make our university a world-class institution and who support each member of our community as if a family.

ENCOURAGING A NEW PRESIDENT
Recognition of an Exemplary Alumnus

2006

Eleven years after my own installation as president, I was called upon to provide remarks at the inauguration of Robert H. Foglesong, General, U.S. Air Force, Ret., as president of Mississippi State University. In those remarks, I tried to assure the audience that their new president understood their mission, had a vision for the institution, and shared their values. The remarks were brief and were made more precise by over a decade of experience leading WVU.

This is an important day in the history of this institution and its new president, and it is recognized as such around the country. It is a very hopeful day in the life of the university and a defining moment in your new president's life. My wife Susan and I have known Robert H. "Doc" Foglesong for about forty years—that is, since we were students together at West Virginia University. He has been an exceptional leader all of his life, and he will serve this university community well in the years to come. You are fortunate to have him as your president, and he is fortunate to have the honor of serving you. Congratulations to all concerned.

My mother was born and raised in Mississippi, and I was born here during World War II although I was raised in my father's hometown in West Virginia. In fact, my first cousin is a proud Bulldog, who married a fellow student here at Mississippi State. Your new president, who got his nickname, "Doc," from the fact that he has a Ph.D. earned in West Virginia, was born and raised in the Mountain State but now finds himself a citizen of Mississippi. Little did we know, those many years ago, that our lives and careers would bring us back together again as sitting presidents of public, land-grant universities in states for which we each have such a strong affinity.

It is a joy to be here, Mr. President, and to bring greetings from several of the constituencies who wish you well on this occasion. First, I am here today to offer greetings on behalf of America's college and university presidents and their institutions. Leading a large university is a complex job. It is also an incalculably important job because higher education is so vital to every aspect of our nation's wellbeing. American universities educate our future leaders, conduct research with life-changing potential, strengthen the economy, and create a brighter future for our entire society. I am pleased to welcome President Foglesong to this demanding and crucial role.

Second, I bring greetings on behalf of the land-grant community within American higher education. Mississippi State University was founded in 1878 pursuant to the Morrill Act, with donations of land sold to establish the institution. Mississippi State's statutory mission is, and has always been, to provide an affordable, accessible, excellent, and useful education to students from Mississippi and surrounding states. Later legislation created the Cooperative

Extension Service and charged land-grant institutions with applying research-based knowledge to improve citizens' lives. As the president of a land-grant university, I have experienced firsthand the importance of the land-grant mission, and I know that President Foglesong will honor the special commitment to society that is held so dear within the culture of land-grant universities.

Mr. President, I also offer greetings from your alma mater and your many friends in West Virginia. You earned three degrees from West Virginia University, and you have been honored as a distinguished alumnus many times. You have always been an enthusiastic Mountaineer and a great source of pride to our community. We are very proud of you today. Ladies and gentlemen, President Foglesong knows and exemplifies the importance of higher education and is a shining example of the contributions institutions like WVU and Mississippi State can make to the future of our states and nation. His life story is a tribute to the work of land-grant universities.

Finally, I bring greetings from my family to you, Doc and Mary, and your family. You will find, Mr. President, that you will travel the road ahead of you with your family and that they will share in your joys, accomplishments, challenges, and tribulations. It is not an easy road, but we can assure you that it is a journey with a very noble purpose. You and Mary will never doubt the meaning of your work here.

Mr. President, it is customary during a presidential inauguration to offer advice to the new president. Knowing your leadership skills, I hesitate to do so, but in the interests of tradition, here is my advice. At my inauguration, Dr. Charles Vest, another WVU alumnus who, at the time, served as president of MIT, offered advice that has remained in the forefront of my mind throughout more than a decade of leadership. Dr. Vest welcomed me to the "strange and wonderful" world of the American university presidency. Dr. Vest stressed all the roles that people expect us to play—scholar, politician, fundraiser, budget cutter, father, confessor, diplomat, negotiator, witty spokesman, expert on all things, sophisticated host, literary devotee, financial guru, friend to community leaders, inspiring public speaker, and towering public figure. Doc, you will wear many hats.

I also received related advice from former WVU President Dr. Harry B. Heflin. Dr. Heflin, who died last week, served as president when you and I were students. When I went to visit him after accepting the WVU presidency, I asked, "Dr. Heflin, what advice can you give me?"

"David," he said, "you can have the students upset with you, the fans upset with you, the faculty and staff upset with you, donors upset with you, the townspeople upset with you, the governor upset with you, and the legislature upset with you. Just don't get them upset with you all at the same time!" This was some of the best advice I ever received as president.

Embedded in the words of Dr. Vest and Dr. Heflin is a clear understanding of the nature of the American university presidency—it is a job that often requires leading change that disrupts the status quo. It is a job that requires one to seek and obtain the support of multiple constituencies if the job is to be done well. In this context, Doc, I will add my own advice: character matters—today as much as it ever has—and it always will. Fortunately for Mississippi State, your life is one lived in service and marked by integrity.

In the years ahead, Mr. President, you will find you and your colleagues facing predictable problems: you will be at work, every day, balancing budgets, growing enrollment, raising private money, and more. However, I can almost assure you that you will also confront challenges that are unimaginable to you now. For example, I could never have expected that, almost exactly six years after my own inauguration, I would stand in the same part of campus where I was inaugurated, speaking to a crowd of thousands. The second time, however, I was called upon to deliver comforting and hopeful words to a campus community heartbroken over the September 11 terrorist attacks on our nation.

Let me say to those assembled here today that I have every confidence that President Foglesong will surmount every challenge he faces. He will not only meet but exceed all the expectations this university and state have for him. More than anyone I have ever known, Doc Foglesong has a gift for grasping the big picture of any situation, asking the right questions, and suggesting the right course of action. He will lead with energy, vision, and character. He will maintain his customary approachable, down-to-earth interpersonal style. He will draw upon a lifetime of public service experience, during which he has demonstrated enormous personal courage and worked in nineteen countries, dealing firsthand with world leaders, managing multibillion-dollar budgets, and serving as a teacher and mentor to countless young people.

Mississippi State University will be an even stronger institution in the years ahead. Mississippi will be an even better place. And the nation to which he has already devoted a lifetime of service will benefit once again from Robert H. Foglesong's wisdom and determination. Congratulations, Doc and Mary, and congratulations to the Mississippi State community. You have both chosen well.

MAKING A DIFFERENCE
University Graduates' Contributions to Society

2004

In 2004, shortly before his death, Judge Charles Haden, a federal district judge for the Southern District of West Virginia, was honored at our College of Law when a professorship was endowed in his honor by his family and friends. Popular and respected, Judge Haden had served in all three branches of state government in West Virginia, and he was admired by men and women in both political parties prior to his elevation to the federal bench. His life was marked by service to his state and to his alma mater. At the dedication, I was called upon to speak on behalf of the university community. The ceremony was a tender moment for me because the honoree was a personal friend and mentor, and his health was declining rapidly.

Nearly 137 years ago, Alexander Martin, the first president of West Virginia University, offered remarks at his inauguration.[1] The college then consisted of $138,000 in assets, five faculty members, one administrator, and a few students.

Dr. Martin's excitement leaps off the page toward the reader of his speech. He talks of the important role the college will play in the life of our state. He dreams of the day when a few hundred students will constitute the student body. He talks of the need for private and state assistance to build the kind of university the state needs.

Dr. Martin predicts that Morgantown will become the state's intellectual center. He notes with pride that his college will spend over $40,000 in Morgantown every year. He predicts that the college will educate the professions in our state. He exhorts the faculty and board members who make up his audience to "erect a fabric which shall live through the ages, a monument of its enlightened liberality and an instrument of the highest good, till time shall be no more."[2]

Toward the end of his speech, he offers this exhortation: "Tell the young . . . of the state, that the college is for them and those who may come after them—that the state, the nation, and the world, in every department of life, stand in need of [those] with trained minds, cultivated tastes and sanctified hearts."[3] A few years later, the College of Law was born, and over the generations, our state's flagship university has produced thousands of young men and women trained in the law. They have become the lawyers and judges who have given the state the framework of law upon which democracy depends, without which no state can prosper.

I think Alexander Martin, who happened, like our honoree, to be a Republican and a Methodist, had men like Judge Haden in mind when he dreamed his dream: West Virginians, bound and determined to make something of themselves and to give most of what they became back to the state for the benefit of future generations. A double graduate of West Virginia University, Judge Haden has lived out the promise of the founders of the university, serving the interests of those in need of legal services, serving in all three branches of state government, and serving on the federal bench. Service to others has marked his career, and a remarkable career it has been.

All lawyers have role models, and Judge Haden is one of mine. He has been for thirty years. He was elected by the people of this community as their representative and served during what must be one of the golden periods of legislative activity in this state. Having served after him as state tax commissioner of West Virginia, I can tell you that as tax commissioner he hired some of the best civil servants ever to serve the state. His decisions were fair. Not a hint of impropriety was evident in his administration. He stood for equal treatment under the law and was popular, even as he collected taxes and levied fines.

As a West Virginia Supreme Court justice, he brought dignity and depth of thinking to our bench. As a federal judge, not only does he do the day-to-day work of the bench, but his peers have also deemed him worthy of leading them. His personal courage has been exhibited in his opinions and his personal life. His loyalty to his friends has been tested and found steadfast. His sense of humor is noteworthy and has helped his clients, his colleagues, and his friends through tough situations. He is a giving person, not a taking person. He is humble, not arrogant. He is a loyal and faithful husband and father. He is, above all, a man of integrity. And I would be remiss if I did not mention that beside him during his adult life has been a remarkable woman, whose own public service is, in and of itself, a testament to the nature of their household values. And he is a wonderful friend. Most of us in this room have sought his counsel and listened to his advice, and we have been rewarded, time and time again, for doing so. There is no more fitting honor for Judge Haden than to be recognized by his peers and the Bar of this state as a distinguished contributor to the fabric of West Virginia. He is one of the pillars upon which what is good in this state has been built. Toward the end of his speech, WVU's first president states his fervent desire that "those spectators reviewing this, and the intervening years, may see as little to disapprove and as much to commend as possible, and especially, when *the* day comes that shall present us at His Bar, . . . we may then receive the approving sentence—'Well done good and faithful servants.'"[4]

Thus, it is that today I join the founding president of our institution by saying to you, Judge Haden, and to you, Priscilla, and to those of you who made today possible, that the founders of West Virginia University would have been extremely proud and gratified by Judge Haden's life's work and by your generosity. You have lived out the founders' dreams, and today you make it possible for those dreams to come true for future generations of students of this fine college of law.

Well done, good and faithful servant.

CHARACTER MATTERS

Remarks at the Funeral of a Former President

2006

What follows is a tribute to Harry B. Heflin, the eighteenth president of West Virginia University and a close personal friend. The eulogy contains, among other things, advice for new college presidents and the assertion that college and university presidents are judged by their integrity and character, perhaps more than by any other attribute. Susan and I have always considered Dr. Heflin and his wife, Dora, inspirational people, primarily because their motivations always seemed to be student centered and grounded in the values of integrity and service to others.

When I was selected president of West Virginia University, one of the first people I called upon for advice was Dr. Harry B. Heflin, the man who was president of WVU when Susan and I were seniors there. Somehow I knew he would give me honest advice.

When I was student body president, Susan and I were invited to the Heflin's home and offered the rare opportunity to spend an intimate evening with WVU's first couple. It meant so much to us.

That year, Dr. Heflin encouraged and supported our student government as we conceived of and launched the first Festival of Ideas. He helped us get the vice president of the United States to speak as part of the program. He tolerated our desire to bring controversial experts on touchy subjects to our campus auditoriums. I also had traveled with Dr. Heflin to the state legislature to ask for more support for the university. So, we had been in his office, on the same platform, and in his presence many times. As student leaders, we felt his presence and listened as he taught the lessons of leadership. His wife, Dora, also was an influence on both Susan and me.

In fact, when I went to see him in 1995, we had already decided that we would try to treat every student body president as he had treated me and that we both would try to be as dedicated to students as Dr. Heflin and his wife were to us. I said, "Dr. Heflin, what advice can you give me?"

"David," he said, "you can have the students upset with you, the fans upset with you, the faculty and staff upset with you, donors upset with you, the townspeople upset with you, the governor upset with you, and the legislature upset with you. Just don't get them upset with you all at the same time!" This was some of the best advice I ever received as president. Embedded in his words was a clear understanding of the nature of the American university presidency—it is a job that often requires leading change that disrupts the status quo, a job that must seek and obtain the support of multiple constituencies if it is to be done well.

Last Sunday, I learned that Dr. Heflin once gave former WVU President Paul Miller essentially the same advice as they talked one evening about the importance of not doing too much too soon. He said Dr. Heflin told him, "Paul, I had a dream that found you the drum major of the WVU band, marching up and down Mountaineer Field. You are stepping high with bold and vigorous steps. Yet, strangely and gradually, individuals in the band keep dropping off and going into the stands until, finally, you are marching straight ahead by yourself." Such was "the quiet wisdom and fearless honesty of Harry Heflin," said Dr. Miller. Dr. Miller told me that this story has been passed on to hundreds at the Harvard School for New Presidents by a friend who teaches there every year.

It just so happens that I am now reading a book called *A Leader's Legacy*, by well-known leadership scholars Jim Kouzes and Barry Posner.[5] It is their summary of what they have learned through a lifetime of scholarship and experience. After Harry passed away and Dora asked me to talk today, several phrases in the book jumped off the pages at me:

People do not remember us for what we do for ourselves. They remember us for what we do for them.[6]

Exemplary leaders are interested more in others' success than in their own.[7]

Teaching is one way of serving. It's a way of passing along the lessons learned from experience. The best leaders are teachers.[8]

Everything leaders do is about providing service.[9]

So it is easy, looking back on Dr. Heflin's long and productive life, to discern one characteristic that marked his life: *Harry Heflin was a leader.* I dare say Harry Heflin was among the most respected leaders to ever influence higher education in West Virginia, and he influenced it for nearly seventy years. His experience alone made him an influential leader.

Having been born into a rural family and lived through the Depression, he understood the transforming power of education. Having been educated at Glenville State College, George Peabody College (now part of Vanderbilt University), and the University of Pittsburgh, he understood the diversity of the educational opportunities in America. Having taught in the public schools, having taught school teachers at the college level, and having served in the United States Navy training command, he understood effective pedagogy. Having served as a college vice president of finance, he knew the nuts and bolts of university administration. Having led the teacher education program at Marshall and having served as president of both Glenville State College (for seventeen years) and West Virginia University (on three separate occasions), he understood the nature and challenges of leadership at public colleges and universities. Having been a vice chancellor of the Board of Regents, he saw the big picture of the relationship between the state colleges and universities, and the people they serve.

Because of his experience and insights, he was able to coach, mentor, and guide the careers of literally hundreds of aspiring educational leaders. Moreover, Harry was a good judge of leadership talent. He was willing to follow fellow West Virginian Dr. Paul Miller to WVU, leaving a presidency to become a vice president for a man he admired. Dr. Miller said Dr. Heflin soon became a trusted advisor and "wise guide." Harry knew that who you work with is as important as the position you hold. He also appointed Fred Schaus as athletic director, launching the modern, nationally recognized athletic program we have today. In fact, dozens of men and women were personally recruited to public service and education leadership positions through Dr. Heflin's example and encouragement.

Harry, above all, recognized the importance that private and public investment in education—and especially in West Virginia University—can make in our state. In the words of former president Gene Budig, Harry Heflin came to "live for WVU, always believing in its relevance and might." His lifetime of experience and his common sense made Harry Heflin one of the most respected leaders ever to serve West Virginia higher education, and his influence as a leader extended beyond education. He was asked to serve on the state bar ethics committee, as a member of the Benedum Foundation Board, and in numerous other positions of trust. Even in the twilight of his life, his advice was sought by others attempting to lead as well as he did. He responded generously, asking nothing more in return but that those he advised should act in like manner.

Harry was honored many times in his life, with honorary degrees, membership in the Order of Vandalia, the naming of a building and scholarship programs in his honor, gubernatorial certificates of recognition, and plaques. He was asked to serve on several boards and to lead professional and civic organizations. But if he accepted a leadership role, he did it for the right reasons. Nothing pleased him more than to see his institutions or his students succeed. He was clearly in the tradition of presidents who view teaching as the defining characteristic of a great university. He was truly student centered.

Harry Heflin also had that uncommon ability to gauge accurately his place in history. From our conversations over the years, I came to believe that Harry Heflin saw himself as a trustee of human and physical assets that were amassed before he came to his various positions. I think he held fast to the knowledge that the important work of the institutions he served would continue after he left them. Dr. Heflin's commitment seemed to be to always advance the institutional mission and to serve during his time of trusteeship as best he could.

In fact, I don't think there was an arrogant or self-serving bone in Harry Heflin's body. His genuine humility, the related generosity of his spirit, and his clear commitment to the mission of public higher education are all part of his legacy of leadership that will influence West Virginia higher education for decades to come. In sum, Harry Heflin was an exemplary leader, possessing all of the timeless characteristics of enduring leadership. He leaves West Virginia a better place, and he leaves behind a leader's legacy worthy of our admiration and respect.

But there was something more important we admired about Harry than the way he led. It was the way he lived. There was his mountain-bred sense of humor. Here is a good example from Neil Bucklew, WVU's twentieth president: "Harry used to love to share a good story, and one joke we always laughed about had to do with the second time he was asked to come back as interim president. He really wasn't sure he wanted to; he and Dora were really enjoying time at their farm. Russ Isaacs was chair of the board at the time and really wanted Harry to serve as the acting president so he asked Harry, 'What can I do to encourage you to come back?' Harry said, 'Well, you can buy me a new tractor for my farm.' Russ said, 'Done!'" Of course, Harry never got that tractor, but he knew that all along. Neil used to kid him about how his tractor was doing. That was Harry: he always kept a good sense of humor about life.

Dr. Bucklew's story also shows Harry's sense of loyalty to those he served. I think he had a deep love for WVU. To his detriment sometimes, he was willing to be called back into service. While in that service, he felt compelled to make decisions that were not necessarily good for Harry Heflin but that advanced the interests of higher education. Former President E. Gordon Gee, who followed Harry as the nineteenth president of WVU, described this loyalty best: "Dr. Heflin was, in every sense of the word, a loyal Mountaineer. He willingly came off the field into the battle, like Cincinnatus, when called upon by his university."

There was also Harry's love for home and family. He loved home-cooked food. He loved the farm that was Dora's home-place, and he loved spending the summers there, working as hard as he had in his youth. And above all was his love for his family. His love for Dora Morgan Heflin began early in his life. Harry and Dora met in high school. They traveled through life together, moving from place to place and job to job. It is obvious to all of us that they were true partners, and it was obvious that Harry loved Dora every day during their over seventy years of marriage. To those who knew them, it was clear how much Dora molded Harry's work and character. This is the very nature of life-long marriages filled with love. And Harry's love of their only child, Morgan, and the grandchildren and great-grandchildren, was well known among his friends. Dora would tell friends stories about the family while Harry listened as long as she wanted to talk. His gentle demeanor and love of family were role models for all of us.

I think two traits marked Dr. Heflin's later years. These were intellectual curiosity and a sense of history. He read widely, stayed up with current affairs, and was not afraid to take on issues of substance when he gave presentations at meetings to his friends in the XX Club, a group of local men interested in matters of the mind. I especially remember one talk Harry gave called "Do You Remember?" in which he noted the changes in our society and societal values over a seventy-five-year period. I remember another in which he yearned for heavier public investment in higher education. How fortunate it is that Dr. Harry Heflin was with his family, his friends, and his community so long. His life was fruitful until the very end.

Always the teacher, Harry Heflin taught the lessons of service and life through example across his entire lifetime. Dr. Heflin stands as an icon of service to WVU and to higher education in West Virginia. He lived a long and full life, the kind of life the founders of WVU had in mind when they adopted our motto in 1867: "Add to your faith, virtue, and to virtue knowledge." Harry Heflin was not just a leader. He was a special kind of leader.

Dr. Harry Heflin helped me, and helped all of us, to understand the true meaning of the word "character." His very essence was there for all to see. He was totally transparent; there was nothing ambiguous about Harry Heflin. There was only Dr. Heflin's absolute belief in *always* doing the right things, *always* for the right reasons, and *always* for others. This is the true legacy Harry Heflin leaves for his family, his friends, his community, the higher education community, and every life he personally touched during his own long and wonderful life. Harry Heflin taught us that character matters—today as much as it ever has—and it always will.

Inspiring with Hope and Humor
Tribute to a Former Dean of Students

2004

There are, of course, "priests of the temple" who are or have been employed by the university and whose impact on the institution has been extraordinary or even transforming. Their stories embody the myths and traditions of the institution.

When they die, presidents are called upon to recall the person and, in doing so, recall the history of the university. I was faced with this task in 2004 when the Reverend Joseph Gluck, former dean of students, passed away after decades of service to West Virginia University. He had been my advisor and friend since I was a student leader, forty years earlier.

This past Christmas, amid the holiday greetings Susan and I received was a card bearing the image of Santa Claus and a sunflower. Inside, we found sunflower seeds, which had been lovingly gathered by hand so that we could have them for planting in the spring. Spring is here now, and the man who took the time and care to share that little bit of beauty with his friends is gone. But Blaney House will have sunflowers this summer, and West Virginia University will always have Joe Gluck, who in seventy years with WVU sowed seeds of wisdom, humor, and love that we will be reaped for generations to come.

West Virginian Natalie Sleeth wrote a hymn, a song of hope, that helps us to take some of the mystery out of death and to find meaning in things we cannot comprehend. She writes:

> In the bulb, there is a flower; in the seed, an apple tree;
> In cocoons, a hidden promise; butterflies will soon be free;
> In the cold and snow of winter, there's a spring that waits to be,
> Unrevealed until its season, something God alone can see . . .
> There is a song in every silence, seeking word and melody;
> There is a dawn in every darkness, bringing hope to you and me.
> From the past will come the future, what it holds a mystery,
> Unrevealed until its season, something God alone can see.[10]

None of us can ever hope to quantify the full scope of Joe Gluck's contributions to the world. We are all saddened to have lost his presence in our lives. I think, however, we should find the life of Joe Gluck a source of profound hope. His is the story of what one individual can contribute—to a university, a state, and its people.

Joe's association with WVU spanned more than half of our institution's history. Former President Gene Budig speculated that Joe had known more students than anyone in WVU history, and there is no reason to doubt it. In 1933, when Joe started work as a youth counselor at Jackson's Mill, America was in the depths of the Great Depression. Franklin Roosevelt had recently told citizens that they had nothing to fear but fear itself, yet economic recovery was still many years away, and a new threat loomed on the horizon: Adolf Hitler was taking power in Germany. A cleric in the American Baptist churches, Joe left Jackson's Mill in 1942 to serve as a chaplain in the U.S. Navy in the Central and South Pacific. Once again, he was doing what he did best, counseling and encouraging young people.

He returned to WVU as a veterans' coordinator in 1946, a time when former members of the military were pouring onto campus to pursue higher education with the help of the G.I. bill. He joined student affairs in 1948 and quickly became director, then dean of students, and eventually vice president. He provided guidance, as well as discipline, at a time when the university was empowered to act in the role of a parent. In this capacity, he saw the university through the 1950s—a time of integration, loyalty oaths for faculty members, and Sputnik-inspired attention to math and science curricula—and through the 1960s and 1970s as WVU's enrollment and facilities rapidly expanded, WVU's *in loco parentis* role faded, and women students earned the right to participate equally in university life.

By the time he retired in 1980, WVU enrolled more than twenty thousand students. In his new role as special counselor to students, he would reach out to new generations, the Gen Xers and the Millennials. Joe offered students a sympathetic ear. As he said, "I'm not always able to solve all their problems. But I am able to listen. Not many people listen." He often gave them advice on picking a vocation. It was one of Joe's most firmly held beliefs that everyone has a special God-given talent and that developing it and making it one's career was the key to a happy life. "When you've found that talent, you'll always have a happy day," he said. Working with young people was certainly Joe's God-given talent, and with it, he enriched WVU and the lives of its students.

If that was the only impact he had on WVU, we would be greatly indebted to him, but Joe's contributions went beyond helping individual students. He had a vision of student affairs at WVU that molded my opinions and those of other future leaders. He hired and guided people who made their own significant impacts on WVU's student affairs programs. He helped WVU secure important support from the Claude Worthington Benedum Foundation. Displaying his love of country, Joe helped to bring the mast of the USS *West Virginia* to campus. Displaying his spirituality, he offered the invocation at forty-two consecutive commencements. Displaying his spirit of generosity, he acted as the university's official Santa Claus for forty years. And displaying his spirit of "humorosity," to use the word he himself coined, Joe amassed a huge collection of jokes that he shared with friends. It is as a friend that I will remember Joe best. I first got to know him when I was a student at WVU, and through the years, I appreciated his wisdom and sense of humor.

I'm pleased to announce that, in memory of all the ways Joseph Gluck contributed to WVU, the university has acquired a beautifully sensitive portrait of him that will be displayed in E. Moore Hall as part of the university's permanent art collection.

The artist is Yvette LaFollette Mazza who, from 1972 through 1974, pursued and received a master's degree in art at WVU. During this time, she worked full time as Joe's secretary. The acquisition of the painting was made possible by a generous donation from Stu and Joyce Robbins from Old Greenwich, Connecticut.

Joe's devotion to WVU paralleled the immense pride he took in being a West Virginian. He considered himself the state's "head cheerleader"—and he became its chief defender when others made jokes about it. He possessed an innate understanding of West Virginia's people and had faith in them. He was truly one of West Virginia's "natural resources."

Joe's love of WVU and West Virginia were exceeded only by his love for his family. He was devoted to his wife, Margaret, and nursed her through a terrible illness before her passing in 2002. And his pride in his children, Susannah, Jody, and Christopher, was obvious.

Joe Gluck represented what Tom Brokaw has called "the greatest generation"—those whose early lives were shaped by the Great Depression and World War II. They shaped the destiny of our nation and raised the generation whose members are leading us today.

Joe Gluck shaped the destiny of this university. He made a difference in the lives of countless people who have gone on to great success using the lessons he taught them. He was the type of person who gave "the greatest generation" its name.

Last night on campus, we celebrated what volunteers and donors have contributed to WVU. Joe Gluck contributed his life. Joe once said, "My major help, and I hope the Lord will give me credit for this if I get there, is the word 'encouragement.' People need all the encouragement they can get." He showed us the effect one person can have on the world around him simply by reaching out to others with a loving spirit and good humor. If the life of Joe Gluck inspires each of us to do the same, his life's work will continue unabated, and as he would say, "Isn't that exciting?"

Reaching Around the World
Tribute to a Respected Faculty Member and Vice Provost

1999

Bob Maxwell was a special person. Charismatic, loyal to the institution, and dedicated to the teaching, research, and service elements of our mission, he was a teacher and a leader in every sense of the word. He was the epitome of a land-grant professor. Because of his travels to Africa, he changed lives on two conti-nents. Bob died tragically in Mozambique, one of the many countries he served as a visiting professor during his long career. A man of strong faith, he sought and taught peace around the world.

As Thanksgiving Day approaches, our university is thankful for the life of Robert H. Maxwell. We hope that our collective Thanksgiving service will be of comfort to Betty, Bob's family, and Bob's friends, for we share in their loss.

Susan and I are privileged to hold positions of responsibility and trust at our alma mater. We occupy them happily, knowing full well that we will re-ceive from our service more than we can ever give in return. Every day brings us far more joy than our combined labor merits.

Bob Maxwell was one of the reasons why we have found such fulfillment in our lives. His goodness inspired us. He seemed to understand us, and he frequently offered us words of encouragement. Bob's smile was infectious. His love for Betty and his family was obvious. His leadership talents appeared at every turn. His love of students and teaching were a tremendous example. My guess is that many of you—his family, colleagues, students, and fellow work-ers—share our view. We are all far better off for having known him. Bob was a complex and immensely talented man. Each of us could list many more of his positive attributes. We could each identify the characteristic that inspired us the most. As for me, I will remember Bob, most of all, for the loving spirit with which he served the world.

The hymnal of my church contains a hymn that is sung to Sibelius's well-known tune "Finlandia." Lloyd Stone wrote the words to the hymn, called "This Is My Song," during the dark period of our history just prior to World War II. The lyrics express the complex feelings of a man who loves his country dearly, yet recognizes that those in far off lands around the world, with whom we sometimes come in conflict, also love their homeland. The words of the first verse are as follows:

> This is my song, O God of all the nations,
> A song of peace for lands afar and mine.
> This is my home, the country where my heart is;
> Here are my hopes, my dreams, my holy shrine;
> But other hearts in other lands are beating
> With hopes and dreams as true and high as mine.[11]

Somehow, today I can visualize Bob and the heavenly host singing this plea for world peace. Like the author of the hymn, he was truly a man who loved his own land yet felt a call to serve others in far off places. He believed that they, too, deserved a future as bright as ours.

Bob loved America. His affection for his homeland was obvious to those who knew him. Bob also loved West Virginia and West Virginia University. While he was born, raised, and educated in Iowa and Indiana—he was always a farmer at heart—I think the mountains of Appalachia ultimately laid claim to him. The home that he and Betty built near Elkins is a physical manifestation of his commitment to the Mountain State. His emotional commitment to its people was even greater. As Maurice Brooks says in his book, *The Appalachians*, the mountains cast a spell over those who dwell within their shadows.[12] The people of the mountainous areas of the world may leave, but they always look back, longingly, at the peaks, and their ties are never severed.

From the time Bob and Betty joined the WVU family, his bonds to WVU and the people it serves were strong. While he often left to work in other countries, he always came home to its mountains and its people. Bob's affection for WVU and the people of our state may have been derived from the needs he identified as he visited with the people of rural West Virginia. He was close to this state's citizens; I would think that he was one of the more popular and recognizable professors ever to teach at WVU.

Bob was, for example, the leader of the Allegheny Highlands Project in Randolph and Upshur counties, a project that gave him an opportunity to lead scores of faculty. It was a project that gave him an understanding of mountain farmers that can only come from working closely with eighty families over a long period of time. Bob's tenure as dean, as director of Extension, and in other administrative positions put him in close contact with our state's leaders and numerous organizations. While his students came from everywhere, most of them came from the hills and valleys of West Virginia. Ultimately, Bob was inducted into the state Agriculture and Forestry Hall of Fame, and he was selected by its sponsors to provide leadership to that body. He was honored time and again, by professional organizations, West Virginia University, and his colleagues for leadership, for service, and for professional accomplishments.

Bob was popular. He was a man larger than life, with a grin that was infectious. He was known both on and off campus. He knew and fostered excellence in all that he did. He was always willing to serve when the cause was good and just. I asked Bob to come out of retirement at a time when the university badly needed him. He did so gladly, out of duty and commitment. It is the type of commitment that derives from a willingness to serve one's country.

Yes, Bob loved his nation and his adopted state. To paraphrase the psalmist, Bob Maxwell lifted up his eyes unto the hills, and there he found the inspiration he needed to be a leader. His particular type of patriotism gives stature, even nobility, to the professorate. The second verse of the hymn I described repeats the theme of the first:

> My country's skies are bluer than the ocean,
>
> And sunlight beams on the cloverleaf and pine;
>
> But other lands have sunlight too, and clover,
>
> And skies are everywhere as blue as mine.
>
> O hear my song, thou God of all the nations,
>
> A song of peace for their land and for mine.[13]

At a young age, Bob's sense of duty drew him to other nations, especially those in East Africa. His lifetime of service to people in these far-off lands eventually made a tremendous difference in the lives of the people who live there. It is a difference that is difficult to measure, but the impact is, and was, real. Beginning in 1960, Bob began a career of service to the people of Kenya, Botswana, Ethiopia, Malawi, Mozambique, Namibia, Swaziland, Tanzania, Uganda, and Zimbabwe. His service to Africa spanned his entire professional career. For example, Bob introduced the first vocational agriculture program into the secondary schools of Kenya. Years later, he helped to update higher education programs in Tanzania. He consulted widely on curricular and design programs throughout Africa, and while his service to other lands led him to the Czech Republic, Poland, and the Philippines, it is Africa upon which he made his mark abroad.

Bob died returning from Mozambique, where he had been helping the Catholic University of Mozambique to develop an agricultural curriculum for their new College of Agriculture in Cuamba. Mozambique is one of the world's poorest nations and has been destroyed by over twenty years of war. Importantly, he had involved the South African University of Pretoria in the project, and he was recognized in South Africa for his leadership. Because of the former animosity between Mozambique and South Africa, his role was that of a peacemaker. It was, in a sense, profound.

Don't underestimate Bob's work on the Mozambique project. The rector of Catholic University, Father Cuoto, said that Bob not only wrote the feasibility report for the project but also went with the rector to see the president of the republic to ask for money. He was friends with two presidents of the country, one of whom died on the same day that Bob passed away. The rector of the university wrote, "It is quite symbolic that Bob died in Africa, the continent where he devoted a lot of his life . . . It is true: Bob loved Africa . . . Bob Maxwell is an American with an African Heart . . . [T]he faculty . . . considers Bob Maxwell the 'protector of the whole project' . . . Bob Maxwell is alive and protects those who met him during his earthly life." In the same message, the rector sent love to "Mamma Maxwell," who also earned the love and affection of Mozambique.

On both continents, Bob Maxwell was a man of action; he was, in the words of the poet Longfellow, "up and doing / with a heart for any fate."[14] He was also a man of character, molded on the plains of the Midwest, in the mountains of Appalachia, and in the far-off lands of Africa. He was a man who loved both his family and his fellow travelers on this planet.

Today, a grateful university remembers Bob, knowing that, as the poet reminds us, great men leave behind them footprints in the sands of time.[15] In Bob Maxwell's life, there is a song of thanksgiving and hope for us. It is a song that his memory will always sing to each of us who knew him. It is a song of hope for peace in war torn lands. It is a song of goodness made manifest by selfless service. It is a song of the nobility of teaching, and the richness of university life. It is a song of thanks to master teachers. It is a song of peace for every part of the world.

Bob's song involves a strange mixture of talents. It is performed by men and women, black and white, accompanied on Appalachian instruments, playing African rhythms. But the voices of his choir unite in a strong message of "hearts united, learning to live as one." And in the midst of the voices, I can hear Bob Maxwell singing, his voice the clearest of them all.

NOTES

1   Alexander Martin, *Inaugural Address Delivered at the West Virginia Agricultural College* (Morgantown, WV: Morgan and Hoffman, printers, 1867).

2   Martin, *Inaugural Address*, 19.

3   Martin, *Inaugural Address*, 28.

4   Martin, *Inaugural Address*, 29.

5   James M. Kouzes and Barry Z. Posner, *A Leader's Legacy* (San Francisco: Josssey-Bass Publishers, 2006).

6   Kouzes and Posner, *A Leader's Legacy*, 10.

7   Kouzes and Posner, *A Leader's Legacy*, 10.

8   Kouzes and Posner, *A Leader's Legacy*, 10.

9   Kouzes and Posner, *A Leader's Legacy*, 14.

10   Natalie Sleeth, "Hymn of Promise," in *The United Methodist Hymnal: Book of United Methodist Worship* (Nashville, TN: United Methodist Publishing House, 1989), 707.

11   Lloyd Stone, "This Is My Song," in *The United Methodist Hymnal: Book of United Methodist Worship* (Nashville, TN: United Methodist Publishing House, 1989), 437.

12   Maurice Brooks, *The Appalachians* (Boston: Houghton Mifflin, 1965).

13   Stone, "This Is My Song," 438.

14   Henry Wadsworth Longfellow, "A Psalm of Life" (1838).

15   Henry Wadsworth Longfellow, "A Psalm of Life" (1838).

PART THREE

TEACHING MOMENTS

A PRESIDENT'S CALL TO ACTION

As every teacher knows, and as every college or university president knows, there are times when an opportunity presents itself to open the eyes of a student or, in some cases, to open the eyes of the entire university community. Such times often require immediate action, and, customarily, little time for preparation is available. The president is expected to speak to the issue at hand. I call these occasions "teaching moments."

EIGHTEEN

REMARKS AFTER SEPTEMBER 11

A teaching moment clearly presented itself during my presidency when the series of events we now call September 11 unfolded in New York, Washington DC, and rural Pennsylvania. By coincidence, my wife Susan and our assistants were in Washington DC on that fateful day and witnessed the events as they unfolded in our nation's capital. On subsequent occasions, I was called upon to reflect on the events of September 11. Two such opportunities afforded me the time for deeper reflection. The first was at a memorial one year later for the daughter of close friends who had died in New York. The second, five years later, was at a memorial service on campus.

Campus Memorial
After the Events of September 11

2001

Arriving home late on the evening of September 11, I was told in no uncertain terms by my primary advisors and by the student leaders on campus that I would have to advise the student body and the campus community as to how we should all process the acts of terrorism that had unfolded before our eyes on na-

tional television. The situation was made more complex by the presence of large numbers of students from the areas immediately affected (New York, Western Pennsylvania, and the District of Columbia) and by individual losses suffered by members of the university community. Without question, the challenge required a lifetime of learning and all the maturity that I could muster. On September 14 of that fateful year, with the knowledge that students on our campus needed help processing the events in their own minds, I walked over to the very place where I had been inaugurated—the lawn in front of Woodburn Hall—and delivered one of the most important and difficult public addresses of my lifetime.

Today we gather as a community. And today we realize just how large our community is. It includes the faculty, staff, students, alumni, and friends of the university and, of course, their families. We are also joined by community, state, and local officials and friends. We come from all over our nation and our world to be together here in West Virginia. Our roots are in all fifty American states and one hundred nations. It is strikingly clear that we live, truly, in a global village connected by common aspirations, commerce, television, the Internet, military and political alliances, easy worldwide travel, and the global nature of institutions of higher education like WVU.

At another university sixty years ago, Winston Churchill said, "The price of greatness is responsibility . . . If this has been proved in the past, as it has been, it will become indisputable in the future. The people of the United States cannot escape world responsibility."[1] How true these words ring today.

This week, America's involvement in the world led to human tragedy of the worst kind—thousands have lost their lives in a terrorist attack on the United States. We are only beginning to understand the magnitude of what has happened. The loss of lives and property is unimaginable. The implications are grave. Because of our national mobility and our connectivity, we all know, or know someone who does know, a family member or friend who has been injured or killed in the recent attacks on our homeland. Entire households have been lost. Flourishing businesses have suffered irreparable harm. Great futures have been extinguished. Accumulated wisdom and knowledge will not be shared. The suffering is great. Millions grieve as we gather here today. We all must share in the losses of those who have been touched by these terrible acts; they have our sympathy. This university—the entire university community—extends its condolences and prayers to all such people. Our hearts are open to them.

As we gather today, the issues presented to our leaders and to each of us are complex and multifaceted. What has happened saddens us, not only because of personal losses, but also because there has been a frontal assault on our way of life. Our liberty and freedom have been challenged. Clearly, the goal has been to dampen our spirits and patriotism.

But as surely as we must show our support of those who have lost their loved ones, we must also show our confidence in the future of democracies around the world. Men and women who valued freedom above all else founded the United States of America. In the words of Reinhold Niebuhr, "We were born to exemplify the virtues of democracy and to extend the frontiers of the principles of self-government throughout the world."[2] At a time of great tragedy during his own lifetime, President Lincoln said that our nation should be dedicated to the great task remaining before it, and that our nation must resolve that those who died to preserve our democracy shall not have died in vain.

As America grew as a nation, we changed, assuming greater and greater responsibility in the world. By 1943, when we faced the threats of the maniacal Nazis, Winston Churchill would say of the United States, "There is no halting-place at this point. We have now reached a stage in the journey where there can be no pause. We must go on . . . Tyranny is our foe, whatever trappings or disguise it wears, whatever language it speaks."[3] Later, when we struggled with conflicting values within our nation, Martin Luther King Jr. asked us to use our heritage and our anger to cause freedom to ring across America and around the world. It is now our time, and this is a time that tests our sense of mission and responsibility. The world looks on, awaiting our reaction to the tragedy we have experienced. Our national character is again being tested. Our response must be a clarion call for justice. For this reason, if no other, we must now summon all the determination our generation can muster in defense of the freedoms we enjoy. We have no choice if we are to truly honor those who have died as a result of terrorist activities within our country and beyond its borders.

This will be an effort unlike any before it. We will all be asked to do our part. It will require individual and collective discipline, and it will require individual and collective civic responsibility, bravery, and courage.

But we cannot act unjustly; we may even need to refrain from acting. Our university community includes many who belong to other nationalities. We must not harbor animosity toward our neighbors simply because they come from other places in the world. Rather, we must all do our part to foster the global peace we all seek. In the months to come, we will each be called upon to serve in ways we do not yet comprehend. We must each answer the call when it comes, however it comes.

And so today, we grieve for the thousands who have been needlessly lost. We all are deeply saddened, and we join fervently with the millions who pray for peace in the world. But even as we grieve, and even as we seek to under-stand, we will stand united in our search for justice. We must look into our own hearts and summon the individual and collective courage and strength we will need to keep America the home of the brave and land of the free—and keep the flame of freedom alive in the world. Because we are Mountaineers, we can do nothing less.

Montani semper liberi. Mountaineers are always free.

Remembering a Friend Lost on September 11

2002

One year after the September 11 attacks, I was invited to give the primary address at a prayer breakfast remembering all who died on that fateful day. Specifically, the event honored Mary Lou Hague, a young West Virginia woman whose family members have been our friends since we were students together at the university.

Good morning. I am honored to speak to you today. I am also humbled to speak to the impact of a tragedy so momentous in its scope and so painful to the individuals touched by it. It's difficult to find words that can bring any meaning to the senseless acts we witnessed one year ago. Today I want to suggest that out of the deepest trials and tribulations of life, we can each find a meaning that will give us hope. Yes, even in the depths of our pain and suffering, we can each find meaning that propels us forward. When we find meaning in our lives, we can accomplish great things under the worst of circumstances.

A year ago, a disaster of epic proportions shattered our nation. Thousands of lives were lost, and many Americans, including those in our own community, faced life's most difficult task: going forward when someone we love has died. Since then, our nation and our state have mourned additional lives lost to the horrors of war. Finding meaning in these tragedies can seem an almost impossible task, yet when we reflect on several other times in mankind's history when events threatened to rob the world of hope, we know that we can do more than just survive in such circumstances.

Our nation has, perhaps, faced no darker time in its history than 1863. The nation had been torn asunder by war, and its continued existence was very much in jeopardy. After two years of bloody conflict, no end seemed in sight. For three days in June, a battle raged in a Pennsylvania field that would leave tens of thousands of Confederate and Union soldiers—tens of thousands of Americans—dead, wounded, or missing. Five months later, President Abraham Lincoln stood in that battlefield and honored the dead by rededicating the living to the preservation of our country. Remember his familiar message, reminding us that our words are inadequate to consecrate ground that thousands of acts of bravery have already sanctified. Lincoln, urging the American people to turn sorrow into renewed purpose, said:

> ·It is for us the living, rather, to be dedicated here to the unfinished work which they who fought here have thus far so nobly advanced. It is rather for us to be here dedicated to the great task remaining before us—that from these honored dead we take increased devotion to that cause for which they gave the last full measure of devotion—that we here highly resolve that these dead shall not have died in vain—that this nation, under God, shall have a new birth of freedom—and that government of the people, by the people, for the people, shall not perish from the earth.[4]

Winston Churchill led Great Britain through one of its darkest hours during the early days of World War II, as that small island nation stood up to Hitler's aggression with little help from allies. As bombs rained down from above for months, the British people found the courage to continue living their lives. They took their inspiration from Churchill and his unswerving belief that great difficulties could lead to great action. When Harrow schoolboys added a special verse to the school song in honor of Churchill's 1941 visit, he asked them to amend the verse's reference to "darker days":

Do not let us speak of darker days; let us speak rather of sterner days. These are not dark days: these are great days—the greatest days our country has ever lived; and we must all thank God that we have been allowed, each of us according to our stations, to play a part in making these days memorable in the history of our race.[5]

As a leader of a people who had been oppressed for decades, Martin Luther King Jr. faced bigotry and even violence without giving into despair or losing sight of his goal of a world that judged people by the content of their character rather than by the color of their skin. Even as he began to sense that his own life would be cut short before his work's fulfillment, he urged his followers to find the strength to carry on.

"For," as he said on the night before his death, "when people get caught up with that which is right and they are willing to sacrifice for it, there is no stopping point short of victory."[6] His murder plunged many people into despondency and parts of our nation into chaos. When he learned of Dr. King's death, presidential candidate Robert F. Kennedy was preparing to address a largely black audience in Indianapolis. He accepted the difficult task of breaking the news to them and asked them to use the tragedy to reflect on the country's future direction. He reminded his listeners:

You can be filled with bitterness, with hatred, and a desire for revenge . . . Or we can make an effort, as Martin Luther King did, to understand and to comprehend, and to replace that violence, that stain of bloodshed that has spread across our land, with an effort to understand with compassion and love."[7]

Robert Kennedy himself would live barely two more months before being felled by an assassin's bullet.

The wave of violence that swept through the United States in the 1960s, while thousands died in Vietnam and we struggled with conflicting values at home, was another of our nation's darkest periods and another time when many people questioned how America would go forward. Gradually, the nation's people emerged from the divisiveness of that period and began the process of healing their wounds, as Americans have always done after dark periods in their history.

Clearly, it is possible for a nation to summon the collective courage to persevere even when faced with seemingly insurmountable obstacles, but how can we as individuals rediscover hope after suffering a profound loss? How can we move forward when faced with illness, violence, or the death of a loved one?

In the book *Man's Search for Meaning*, psychiatrist Viktor Frankl detailed his experiences in one of the cruelest and most heartless landscapes the world has ever known: a Nazi concentration camp. Most of those who arrived with him at Auschwitz were sent immediately to their deaths. Those like Frankl, who survived that first selection, were separated from their loved ones, stripped of everything they owned, fed barely enough to stay alive, beaten often, worked beyond endurance, and degraded in ways large and small. With no end to their suffering in sight, most quickly lost their belief in the future and their sense that life had any meaning. Frankl observed among his fellow prisoners that losing a sense of meaning and the will to go on was not an inevitable consequence of even the most profound suffering.[8]

In fact, those who were able to find meaning in their suffering were more likely to find the will to survive the experience, he noted. But even those who died had the choice of doing so with bravery and dignity. As Frankl wrote:

> We who lived in concentration camps can remember the men who walked
> through the huts comforting others, giving away their last piece of bread. They
> may have been few in number, but they offer sufficient proof that everything can

be taken from a man but one thing: the last of the human freedoms—to choose one's attitude in any given set of circumstances, to choose one's own way.[9]

Upon his liberation from the concentration camp, Frankl helped to develop a whole school of psychotherapy based upon these observations of human behavior. It is known as logotherapy, derived from the Greek *logos*, or meaning. Frankl identified its fundamental teaching with Nietzche's statement that he who has a why to live for can bear with almost any how.[10]

The meaning that we are meant to find in life is one that each of us can only discover by ourselves—indeed, within ourselves—Dr. Frankl asserts. It is a meaning that we fulfill day by day, in the choices that we make, the way we respond to others, and the way we accept the unacceptable reality of tragedy. "Even a victim of a hopeless situation," Dr. Frankl wrote, "facing a fate he cannot change, may rise above himself, may grow beyond himself, and by so doing change himself. He may turn a personal tragedy into a triumph."[11] Pain, while giving us an opportunity to ennoble ourselves spiritually, is not something to be sought: Dr. Frankl is clear on that point, as is fellow Holocaust survivor Elie Wiesel, who said, "Suffering confers no privileges. It all depends what one does with it."[12]

On a personal level, it can seem harsh to assert that those who have suffered a deep personal loss can find meaning in their suffering—at such times, just surviving from day to day can be a struggle. But most people, faced with such a loss, instinctively search for some way to mine whatever good is possible from it. That is why mourners so often set up charitable funds or pursue causes in their loved one's memory. That is why people who have experienced a loss, major illness, or serious problem—people who have become part of what Albert Schweitzer called "the fellowship of those who bear the mark of pain"—are often the first to reach out to people going through a similar tragedy.[13] Deep down, we realize there is meaning in rising to every challenge with which we are faced and in transcending our own pain in the service of others.

Even when people come face to face with their own imminent mortality, they grope to attach meaning to their situation. Schweitzer became seriously ill in his forties. His recovery filled him with the desire to alleviate the suffering of others, and he established a hospital in Africa for people who would otherwise have no access to medical care. When recovery is not possible, dying patients, like concentration camp inmates, nevertheless retain the choice of how they will face their deaths. In her book *Close to the Bone: Life-Threatening Illness and the Search for Meaning*, Dr. Jean Bolen describes the way illness bares our souls and removes all but the most important things from our field of vision. Dr. Bolen writes:

> If our character and development of soul is shaped by us over time in much the same way as clay is worked upon before it must go through the fire, then we are both the artist and the work itself. We are a work in progress until the final touch. How we respond when we suffer unfairly, shapes us—and what we do when we know we are dying makes a difference if we truly are spiritual beings on a human path.[14]

My message today is that we can find meaning even in the darkest times and unlikeliest places—from the Gettysburg battlefield to the bedside of a dying cancer patient. Where we find meaning, we find hope. And we can transform hope into action that helps other people and rescues us individually from our own despair. As Mother Teresa said, "We must grow in love and to do this we must go on loving and loving and giving and giving until it hurts."[15]

As citizens of the United States, we are fortunate to draw upon a long history of our forebears overcoming obstacles and rebuilding after disasters. In the past year, our nation has begun the process of healing and recovery from this latest devastation. If another crisis comes, we will be prepared to meet its challenges as well.

As president of a university, I find constant inspiration in the enthusiasm and resilience of our young people. WVU's students were deeply affected by last year's attacks. They stood in solemn silence at a memorial service that week. They raised money, and they lined up to give blood. Today, our students will have special observances to honor the memory of the September 11 victims. Their primary concern has been learning all they can about the circumstances of this tragedy and finding a way to move beyond it. They requested and enrolled in courses exploring 9/11-related themes. Observing their behavior this past year, I found that they are more patient. They seem to be caring more about each other. They have refused to let this tragedy limit their world's scope—they are as eager as ever to take to the skies and travel abroad.

This is a day for acknowledging our nation's tragedy. Today, and always, we grieve for the thousands who were needlessly lost. Today, and always, we join with the millions who pray for peace in our world. But even as we grieve, and even as we offer our prayers, we must look into our own hearts and discover for ourselves the meaning that we can take from this tragedy. We must reach out to our neighbors in compassion, and we must work to stamp out the intolerance that ferments into hatred and violence.

Fifth Anniversary of September 11

2006

Five years after the events of September 11, I was asked to offer a short message at a remembrance organized by our students. The perspective was different from the one in 2001, of course. But the images of September 11 were still very much in the minds of those who attended the event.

Five years ago, our nation endured a shocking and heartbreaking act of violence. Nearly three thousand people died. Many of them sacrificed their own lives in an attempt to save the lives of other people. When the campus community gathered for a memorial service three days later, we knew that two of the victims were part of the Mountaineer family—Chris Gray and Jim Samuel Jr., two successful young alumni working as brokers in the World Trade Center. Many of us also knew, by that time, that we had a personal connection to the tragedy or that we knew someone who did.

We on this campus shared the raw emotions that gripped our entire nation and people throughout the world: fear about what the future would bring, anger at people who could commit such an evil act, longing to do something—anything—to help the people suffering the most, pride in the heroism that so many displayed that day, and, above all, aching sadness.

Five years ago, it seemed we would never be the same. A lot has changed since then. We live in a time of war and have grieved many more losses. Many of the students who gathered for our first September 11 memorial service, who lined up to give blood, and who raised money for charities benefiting victims' loved ones have graduated and gone out into the world. Many of today's WVU students were in high school or even middle school in 2001 and have their own memories of that awful day.

Only time will tell how those who experienced September 11 and its aftermath in their youth will incorporate its lessons into their own lives. As a university president, I already have seen a flowering of thoughtfulness and compassion among today's young people. I have watched as their desire to serve and to understand the world around them has grown.

Today, however, I am most struck by how much has remained the same. This campus still welcomes students from Middle Eastern countries, and they are treated with respect and dignity. Our students travel the globe, and they come home safely. Peace remains a priority for the students on our campuses.

Our community remains diverse and welcoming. We still enjoy our freedom to gather, to express our thoughts, to learn. We don't live in fear. Over those who would control and limit our lives through acts of terror, we have prevailed. That is a testament to the human spirit, to the American spirit, to the Mountaineer spirit. *Montani semper liberi.* Mountaineers are always free!

NOTES

1   Winston Churchill, The Gift of a Common Tongue speech at Harvard, September 6,1943, in Winston S. Churchill, *Never Give In! The Best of Winston Churchill's Speeches* (New York: Hyperion, 2003), 357.

2   Niebuhr, Reinhold and Alan Heimert, *A Nation So Conceived*, London, Faber, and Faber, 1964, 123.

3   Winston Churchill, The Price of Greatness is Responsibility speech at Harvard, September 6, 1943, in Winston S. Churchill, *Never Give In! The Best of Winston Churchill's Speeches* (New York: Hyperion, 2003), 357.

4   Abraham Lincoln, The Gettysburg Address speech at Gettysburg, PA, November 19, 1863.

5   Winston Churchill, Never Give In! speech at Harrow School, October 29, 1941, in Winston S. Churchill, *Never Give In! The Best of Winston Churchill's Speeches* (New York: Hyperion, 2003), 308.

6   Martin Luther King Jr., I've Been to the Mountaintop speech at the Bishop Charles Mason Temple Church of God, April 3, 1968.

7   Robert F. Kennedy, On the Death of Martin Luther King Jr. speech in Indianapolis, IN, on Martin Luther King Jr's death, April 4, 1968, reprinted in *"An Honorable Profession": A Tribute to Robert F. Kennedy*, eds., Pierre Salinger, Edwin Guthman, Frank Mankiewicz, and John Seigenthaler (Garden City, NY: Doubleday and Company, 1968), 7.

8   Victor Frankl, *Man's Search for Meaning: An Introduction to Logotherapy*, trans. Ilse Lasch, 3rd ed. (1959; New York: Simon and Schuster, 1984), 75.

9   Frankl, *Man's Search for Meaning*, 75.

10   Frankl, *Man's Search for Meaning*, 9.

11   Frankl, *Man's Search for Meaning*, 147.

12   Elie Wiesel, remarks on presenting the Congressional Gold Medal to Elie Wiesel, speech at the White House, Washington, DC, April 19, 1985.

13   Albert Schweitzer, *On the Edge of the Primeval Forest* (1931; New York: Macmillan, 1961), 173.

14   Jean Bolen, *Close to the Bone: Life-Threatening Illness and the Search for Meaning* (New York: Scribner, 1998), 101.

15   Mother Teresa, *A Simple Path*, compiled by Lucinda Vardey (New York: Ballantine Books, 1995), 99.

NINETEEN

REMARKS TO NEW CITIZENS
OF THE UNITED STATES AT A
NATURALIZATION CEREMONY

2002

Several federal judges in West Virginia have invited me to make remarks to those becoming new citizens of the United States as part of the naturalization proceedings over which they presided. It will suffice to say that I am always honored to be invited to offer remarks to our newest fellow citizens, and on most occasions, I have chosen to focus on the elementary mandates of citizenship in our country.

The bright eyes, the faces of many different hues, the spontaneous tears, the applause from the families and friends, and the occasional cheers in the courtroom have convinced me that those being given the privileges of citizenship in our country clearly recognize the greatness of the country to which they belong upon taking the oath.

The version of the naturalization address below was delivered in the courtroom of the Honorable Judge Robert Maxwell, federal district judge for the Northern District of West Virginia.

Susan and I are delighted to be here today and to be among the first to welcome you to the status of "citizen of the United States of America." Because we are a great and powerful nation in the world, and because individual dreams can still come true in the United States, this is a great day for you. We are all happy for you and your loved ones.

It is also a great day for America. People from many other lands have joined Native Americans in influencing the development of the United States. There have been several great waves of immigration to the United States from other areas of the globe. Among these are the four immigrations from the British Isles, described so eloquently in David Fischer's book, *Albion's Seed*; these include the Cavaliers, the Quakers, the Puritans, and the Scotch Irish.[1]

British settlers were later joined by immigrants from France, Spain, Central Europe, Africa, Eastern Europe, the Caribbean, India, Pakistan, Asia, Mexico, South America, Latin America, and so many other portions of the globe. Each new wave of immigration has given our state and the United States connections with other lands. In fact, at West Virginia University today, we have students and faculty from over one hundred countries. All are a part of our university; all are part of our nation's fabric.

As these great waves of immigration come to the United States, the new citizens bring with them new customs, new values, new foods, new religions, new architecture, new skills, new literature, new music, and much, much more. America today is a land of diversity as well as opportunity. There is no one color, no one religion, no one political party, and no one anything that lays claim to ruling America. America belongs to all of us. Every citizen here today stands on equal ground.

The diversity in our nation has made us a nation that tolerates dissent, values debate, appreciates regionalism, fosters cultural identity, values political diversity, appreciates federalism, values different leadership styles, and values volunteerism.

As a result of our diversity, we are a nation in which good citizenship can take many forms. One of the great lessons of American history is that good citizenship has made us a great nation. Today, Susan and I want to speak to you briefly about what we consider to be five elements of good citizenship. We want to encourage you to do five things for your new nation.

First, be loyal to your new country. We hope you will study the United States, understand it, value its traditions, appreciate its good points, support it willingly with your tax dollars, and most of all, vote in every election. We hope you will make it a *personal* goal to vote in *every* election.

Secondly, volunteer for your new country. Alexis de Tocqueville wrote, in 1830, that America had already become a great nation, though only fifty years old, because its citizens volunteered. Volunteerism has always played a central role in American democracy. It maintains our quality of life, and more importantly, it maintains the quality of our government. Why? Because volunteering to help America does three things: First, government can't do it all, so our nation is stronger because some of its citizens and communities are taken care of through volunteer efforts. Secondly, volunteerism helps people in need. Finally, volunteerism makes each volunteer a better person by teaching us to appreciate other people. Together, American volunteers build a spirit or bond, which binds our democracy together. America is the world's strongest nation because millions of Americans volunteer.

Thirdly, help to lead your new country. Broad-based leadership is important to the United States. As a nation that has many regions, supports many levels of government, and depends upon a competitive free-enterprise system, there are opportunities for leadership in every corner of our land. Every individual can still make a difference in America. Remember, you have as much right to lead as any other person. Arthur Schlesinger, a noted historian from Harvard, once said that leadership involves several activities, and we hope you engage in all of them: observing your country, reflecting upon the policies that should follow, imagining what could be done to improve your country, inventing new solutions to problems, and communicating your views to others.[2] Part of this communication will be through the English language, which we hope you will master because your leadership will be more effective if you do. By this statement, I don't mean to imply that you should abandon your native language. Far from it. I only mean that our nation is held together, in part, by common language.

Fourth, support public education and the education of your family in your new country. West Virginia values education. We are approximately fourteenth in the nation in the percent of our tax base that we contribute to the support of public education in the elementary and secondary schools and higher education institutions of our state.

Education is one of the pillars upon which your freedom is based. It is your responsibility, and ours, to maintain it. Educate your children and grandchildren, and be an active participant in their education at all levels. Students, whether they are in kindergarten or are seniors in college, are more likely to be successful if their families take an active interest in their education. Know their teachers, visit their schools, read aloud to little ones, read a book that your high school or college student is reading, be familiar with the various services and programs available to them. It's not enough to say to a child who is struggling, "You can do better than that." Help them find a way to do better. Be active in the parent/teacher associations or college-parent organizations. The ultimate goal of these groups is student success—take advantage of the support they will give you and your student.

Finally, uphold freedom in your new country. We urge you to value freedom of speech and to exercise your right to speak out. We encourage you to value freedom of religion and to hold to your religious ties. We urge you to exercise your right to travel and mobility, to move around our nation, and to change employers if you so desire. Here, you are largely free to be all that you can be! Freedom is one of the great values of most American people, and we hope you will help maintain it.

Rome, once the most powerful nation on earth, fell in seventy-five years. We are now the most powerful nation on earth. We were not always that way. We have no God-given or natural right to stay that way. *We* must all work to maintain our status as a great nation—*all of us* must work to maintain that status. Our Declaration of Independence has a phrase: "*We* hold these truths to be self evident . . ." Our Constitution contains the phrase "*We* the People." Our historical documents are full of the word "we." "We" refers to all of the citizens of the United States. I am one. Judge Maxwell is one. Now *you* are one, too. Today we are citizens together. It is our job to continue to support America and to help keep it strong. You have chosen a wonderful country. Today it embraces you and welcomes you with open arms. We charge you to embrace America, just as it embraces you today.

Thank you, Judge Maxwell, for inviting us here today. It is an honor for us to be in your courtroom and to welcome America's newest citizens. Congratulations to each of you, and welcome, citizens of the United States of America.

NOTES

1   David Hacket Fisher, *Albion's Seed: Four British Folkways in America* (New York: Oxford UP, 1991).

2   Arthur M. Schlesinger Jr., *Cycles of American History* (Boston: Houghton Mifflin, 1986), 419–436, and especially, 422–423.

TWENTY

FINDING WISDOM IN THE
INFORMATION AGE

2006

I was asked on several occasions to speak to groups organized around religious beliefs. During my legal career, I had served as general counsel to my denomination, so such invitations were not unexpected. When I spoke to these groups, I tried to link the values of higher education with those of the world's great religions, attempting as I did to speak only for myself and not for the public university of which I was president.

The remarks below were delivered in our church on Laity Sunday, a day each year when a layperson is asked to deliver the message from the pulpit. The theme for my talk was "finding wisdom," and I wanted to emphasize the importance of searching for it. With knowledge and facts so widely available through the Internet, questions of evaluating information and applying it to life have become increasingly prominent.

As I was revising this speech for publication, an article, "The Older-and-Wiser Hypothesis," was published in the May 6, 2007, issue of the "New York Times Magazine."[1] Stephen S. Hall's report on research about wisdom suggests that the complex relationship between information, knowledge, and wisdom is a concern for many other members of my generation, as well as for those of us involved in higher education.

We have been told, again and again, that we live in an age of technology, an age in which accessing information is king. This time is customarily called "the information age." The younger you are, the more normal it seems. The older you are, the more amazing it seems. Among the most successful companies in the world are those that sort out and sell information using technology. Think about Google, Cisco, Microsoft, Yahoo!, and other technological giants of the corporate world. Think about television and radio networks, and e-mail and e-news. Think about the History and Discovery channels. Many are giants in the business world. The *Wall Street Journal* recently reported that Microsoft has $38 billion in cash reserves.

A decade ago, WVU graduate Bray Cary, then employed by NASCAR, spoke to WVU students in sport management. He told them that there would soon be five hundred open channels for TV because of a newly launched series of satellites. "The challenge for us," he said, "will not be how to get on TV, but what to put on all those empty channels." He correctly forecast channels for Spanish speakers and Thai speakers, and channels devoted to learning. He predicted TV programming segmented by religious preferences and age groups. He parlayed this insight into a NASCAR network, one that lets us watch the race and ride with our favorite drivers at the same time. This technology was unknown just two decades ago; its application was unforeseen just a few years ago. Today, NASCAR ranks with football and basketball as one of TV's biggest moneymakers, thanks to Bray Cary, a man who saw the information age coming more clearly than most of us did.

In my car now, I have a satellite radio, and I like it because I can listen just to the news, or sports, or '60s music, or talk shows with either conservative or liberal leanings. And I'll bet a lot of you love the search engines on the Internet.

During our Sweet Sixteen appearance this year, I "Googled" the last name of our star basketball player, Kevin Pittsnogle. Back came the information I wanted. On that day, there were over 350,000 references to Kevin Pittsnogle on the Internet. Last week, before a planning conference preparing WVU to deal with widespread bird flu if it attacks the United States, I asked the search engine to give me what it had on "pandemic flu." Back came the answer: Google knew of 215 million pieces of information about the possible bird-flu pandemic that I could consult. How am I supposed to process so much information?

Most organizations of importance, and many individuals, maintain Web sites and blogs on which they either sell or supply free-of-charge information to any interested reader. The information can be plain-vanilla or highly complex. It can be about a church, or it can be about the unseemly underbelly of society. It can be about peace in the world or how to build a bomb. It can be about maturely reported, legitimate news, or it can be the crazed opinion of an evil-minded person. It is all there, ready for consumption. Some Web sites offer us the opportunity to tell others all about ourselves. Facebook.com is one such site. People post personal information, list their preferences in life, publish their pictures, and even indicate how they can be contacted.

In short, we live in an information age in which information on any subject is freely available anywhere in the world, any time of the day, to about any interested person who is armed with rudimentary technological skills. When we built the new downtown library addition, we were forced to confront a reality: electronic information is now as readily available as written texts. Thousands of journals, important scholarly publications, are now online. Our faculty debated the emphasis that should be put on shelf space versus computing capability in the new library. Millions of dollars were allocated based upon that debate.

Further, the Internet has enhanced competition. A few years ago, I came across a Web site selling sports shoes. It asked me to put in my weight; favorite sporting activity; whether I was normal-, high-, or low-arched; and a number of other facts. I pushed a button, and—presto—three recommendations for shoes made by different manufacturers appeared, along with dozens of mail-order outlets across America where I could buy them. I compared prices, bought a pair on sale, and have worn them ever since. Unlimited choice and unlimited competition offered me a great choice.

However, this competition can drive us crazy, and a new word, "spam," has entered our vocabulary. We get electronic ads sent to us on a daily basis, and without the right protective technology, these spam messages can consume our e-mail capacity. Just as early factories in the industrial age utilized child labor and produced pollution, the modern information-technology products have birthed their own set of major societal problems. Stalking, terrorism, and the selling of pornography have been made easier because of information contained in cyberspace.

When my class attended our freshman convocation, Dr. Paul Miller admonished us to continue learning across our entire lifetimes. He said knowledge would double every ten years, so we would not be able to rely on the content of what we learned in college. There would be more history, more geography, more art, more science, and more of everything to learn. Was he ever right. Today, some think knowledge doubles as often as every year. The advances in biomedical science, the arts, engineering, and other fields make it clearly possible for content to advance beyond our capacity to learn it. We can't know all there is to know. We tell our students in law school, "We will teach you how to find the law and analyze it. We cannot possibly teach you the laws of every jurisdiction." We know this is true in every discipline.

So today we are focusing on the tools of learning, introductions to entire disciplines, the different learning styles we all have, and other tools for the toolbox of the information age. Even if we can find information about the subject matter we are exploring, it will often be conflicting. One of the biggest problems of the Internet is that it presents us with often exaggerated or false information. Lots of information and opinions are there for the asking, but how much is true? How much of it is false?

With this comes the possibility of conflicting values, supported by a reference to facts supposed to be true. We live in a world in which millions hold conflicting values, all supposed to be supported by the truth. Today, professional mediators recognize that there are conflicts that arise daily in our work and homes that are based on differences in strongly held values and misperceptions of values held by others. Perhaps this is why value differences can actually lead to discrimination and even violence. The talking heads on television are full of conflicting opinions, but in most cases, both sides are convinced they are right. No doubt is evidenced. No acknowledgment of another point of view is recognized.

Beyond finding out what is true, assuming that truth can somehow be ascertained, lurks an even deeper subject: How much of what we can learn is truly worth learning? What books are worth reading? What Web sites are worth visiting? What speakers are worth hearing? What information is relevant to me and my family? How much of what we can find out is wise? In short, how do we find wisdom in the information age?

The Greek philosophers pondered such questions, as did other early schools of philosophy, and biblical scholars. In my concordance, there are over six hundred references to the words "wisdom" and "wise" in the Bible. In fact, several books of the Bible are devoted to the topic, namely Psalms, Proverbs, and Job.

The question I am raising—"How do we find wisdom in the information age?"—is not a new one, but it is an important one. It is a question made much more difficult to answer in an age that is marked by so much information and so many value-laden opinions.

Wisdom has many definitions. One secular definition I like I found on the Web itself: "the ability to apply knowledge or experience or understanding or common sense and insight." In other words, wisdom is the ability to make sound judgments that withstand the test of time. A more biblical definition is found in Matthew: an attribute that God imparts to people who study his word. In Corinthians we are taught that Greek philosophical wisdom is not enough, and that we should look to Jesus for divine instruction as to what is truly wise. In Proverbs, wisdom is imparted to human beings as a "gift from God." One Bible dictionary I have says this about wisdom, based upon a study of Psalms and Proverbs:

> Wisdom seeks by observation, experience and reflections to know things in their essence and reality as they stand in relation to man and God . . . Wisdom proceeds from man, and is the product of his own experience and observation. But while it is a human effort, it recognizes that a good understanding is the gift of God, and it postulates the fear of God and obedience to his commands and its first principle.[2]

Whatever wisdom is, I know that I need it, and I believe most of us need it. My father-in-law was a wise man. He used to say that the world was backwards. He lamented the fact that young people needed experience before they could get it and older people often found the wisdom late in life that they needed when they were young and raising a family. In an age in which we are bombarded with so much confusing, false, and conflicting information, wouldn't it be good to be wiser? Wouldn't we and our children, our parents, our clergy, and our closest advisors all benefit from wisdom? Knowing the right thing to do is of vast importance, not just to us as individuals, but to this church, to our denomination, and to the entire world. Just think of the difficult and imponderable questions we face today. My guess is that right now everyone in the church is struggling with, or at least wondering about, an issue that doesn't seem to have an easy answer. I think we all know we need to find the answers to life's most vexing problems. The real question is, how do we find wisdom in the information age?

I firmly believe that knowing we need wisdom is the first step in finding it. Our search for wisdom has to begin with humility, a belief that we don't know all there is to know, and that we can and should try to learn more every day. In many ways, education and the ability to accumulate and analyze data and opinions are critical tools in the information age, as is our own sense of what is right and wrong. These tools come only with constant study—perhaps as a result of a lifetime of learning, as Dr. Miller suggested.

The second step in the search for wisdom is asking for help with our search. We can seek help through reading the Bible, which is, in many respects, the collective wisdom of the ages, and through conversations with those who have somehow obtained more wisdom than we possess. We can seek help in the pulpits, Sunday schools, and counseling sessions of our churches. We can seek help in our relationships with friends and family who love us. We can seek help by directly asking God through prayer.

The third step in our search for wisdom is having the courage to accept its mandates once we find it. Put another way, we often know the right thing to do but don't have the courage to accept the pathway the truth often leads us to. Courage is another topic for another day, but I am sure you know what I mean. We have often done what we should. We have often not done what we should. The difference is having the courage to do what is right when we know what is right. In the end, as the Bible suggests, wisdom must be humbly sought by each man, woman, and child, with all the help we can elicit. And in the end, I suggest that you will know it when it is given to you.

Yes, we live in an information age. It is an age that presents us with difficult and sometimes imponderable problems. Discerning the right thing to do today is often not easy; doing the right thing is often not easy. After thinking it through, I have come to the conclusion that if we seek it—and ask for help, with God's help—we just might find the wisdom we need to live the kind of life God wants us to live, even in the information age.

NOTES

1   Stephen S. Hall, "The Older-and-Wiser Hypothesis," *The New York Times Magazine.* 6 May (2007): 58–66.

2   "Wisdom," *The New Westminster Dictionary of the Bible*, ed. Henry Snyder Gehman (Philadelphia: The Westminster Press, 1970), 1002.

TWENTY-ONE

CHAMPION FOR YOUTH
DEVELOPMENT PROGRAMS

Relationships are built over time, but they are invaluable to public universities. They can result in increased enrollment, political support, private support, job opportunities for students, and more.

I was involved in scouting in my youth and later led a university that sponsors the 4-H programs in its state. Eventually, I served as chair of the National 4-H Council, a private, not-for-profit organization supporting the National 4-H movement, which is housed in the Department of Agriculture and administered nationally by land-grant universities.

Because of these ties, I was often asked to speak at events sponsored by youth development organizations. When I did, I always tried to emphasize the importance of the youth organization to which I was speaking and to enhance the relationship between it and higher education.

In speaking to these groups, I tried to lift up points of pride in their history and endorse the goals and objectives of the organizations. My remarks from two of those events follow.

THE IMPACT OF THE 4-H PROGRAM ON YOUTH DEVELOPMENT IN THE UNITED STATES

2005

The following speech was delivered, in a variety of forms, to a number of youth development groups. I emphasized the importance of youth development opportunities in enabling the cultivation of future leaders. While president of a land-grant university, which supports 4-H activity in the state and is a national leader in 4-H programming, my lifelong involvement with youth development culminated in becoming chairman of the National 4-H Council Board of Trustees.

No doubt most of you here tonight were involved in a 4-H club, pledging your head to clearer thinking, your heart to greater loyalty, your hands to larger service, and your health to better living. Perhaps you were also a Boy Scout and pledged to keep yourself physically strong, mentally awake, morally straight, and offered to do a good turn daily. Perhaps you were a member of YMCA or some other youth development organization. If so, modern research indicates you were, indeed, fortunate. In fact, you are probably here tonight because of what developed you, positively and holistically, during your formative years. Tonight I want to talk about recent research related to positive youth development, specifically in the context of the 4-H movement. I have become exposed to this research as the result of my membership on the National 4-H Council.

4-H AND LAND-GRANT UNIVERSITIES

What we know as 4-H is a program of land-grant universities, such as WVU. In fact, WVU has been a leader in the movement since the program's inception over one hundred years ago. Today, about fifty-five thousand people are involved in the program in West Virginia, and about 7 million are involved across the nation. West Virginia has always been a leader in 4-H. Consider these facts:

- The first local 4-H camp in the nation was started in West Virginia in 1915.
- Black students were involved for the first time that year in Pocahontas County.
- The first 4-H state camp in the nation was started at Jackson's Mill in 1921, and in the next several decades, it became a model for the rest of the nation under the guidance of an extension agent named W. H. Kendrick. Today, Jackson's Mill represents an investment of the entire state and has helped to educate thousands of young West Virginians over the years.
- In 1926, Mr. Kendrick published *The 4-H Trail*, which, like the scoutmasters' handbook, is a guide for fostering positive, holistic development in young people.
- 4-H clubs exist in every county in West Virginia, and other 4-H programs reach communities—large and small, urban and rural—in many ways, from clubs, to programs designed to stop smoking, to summer nutrition education programs.
- In the early 1960s, research at WVU began a movement in the study of youth development called "life-span development," and the resulting research influenced teachers across the nation for years.
- In 1966, Mildred Fizer became the first woman in the country to head a state program of 4-H, right here in West Virginia.
- To celebrate one hundred years of 4-H, five West Virginians were inducted into the national 4-H Hall of Fame. In the same year, a state 4-H Hall of Fame was founded, and one hundred West Virginians were honored.
- And, in 2005, I became the first college president to chair the National 4-H Council, a group dedicated to raising public and private money for 4-H and providing leadership to the youth, volunteers, and professional faculty involved in 4-H across the nation.

THE VALUE OF THE 4-H PROGRAM

The contribution that 4-H has made to West Virginia and the nation is enormous according to two recent research efforts, one conducted at the USDA and the other at Tufts University. Among the many contributions of 4-H is the positive development of the youth involved, their brothers and sisters, their parents, and their communities. Since its founding a hundred years ago, the program has helped to develop millions of young people into responsible citizens and leaders, lowered the incidence of risky behavior, increased volunteerism and service in our communities, and delivered valuable training and education outside the classroom. In fact, the impact of the 4-H program has shaped modern America by changing its communities in a positive way. In a recent speech on our campus, Cathann Kress, the national director of 4-H within the USDA, told us, "The pioneers who shaped 4-H . . . began with not just the intention of changing youth but with the belief that changing youth would change our nation."[1] It has done just that.

Why does a program designed to reach young people after school accomplish so much? One reason is that the 4-H program operates under the guidance of research- and service-based state universities across the United States. It is supported on a consistent basis by funding from the USDA, state and local governments, and private funds. It is led by professionals in the field of positive youth development.

Another characteristic that makes 4-H so successful is that in 4-H programs, young people learn by doing and serving, not just by listening. In so doing, they not only learn, but they also help their communities become better places to live.

We now know that not all students learn best the same way. Some do fine with books. Others have different learning styles, such as learning by doing. Learning by doing fosters both learning and action. According to Kress:

We discovered along the way not only that the 4-H model of experiential education, of learning by doing, was very effective in developing youth mastery of skills and knowledge, but more important, that youth were highly effective community change agents who led by example and were themselves transformed by the experience of influencing others and their communities.

Because of the impact of youth in 4-H, over the past hundred years, 4-H has become a change agent in America. Land-grant university knowledge is derived from research and scholarship, and it has been transferred to communities by teaching children how to do things better and encouraging them to share what they have learned. Today, we call this "service learning" on our campuses, and our students can even get college credit for helping their communities solve problems. Examples of 4-H changing the country range from efforts to teach young people better food-production methods during World War I, to smoking-cessation programs in recent years. During the early decades of this century, young people were actually taught the latest farming methods and asked to teach them to their parents. 4-H demonstration projects, like livestock raising, are actually a means of disseminating the latest science at the grassroots level.

Another reason 4-H works is its underlying philosophy that the young people of America will develop into contributors across their lifetimes, so the program molds those involved into skilled leaders with a caring and generous attitude. Adolescence has a bad connotation in some circles and is seen as a negative time, ranging from, say, age ten to age twenty.

Recent research by Dr. Richard Lerner at Tufts University has shown that this need not be the case.[2] Young people can have a very positive and productive youth if they are exposed to the right environment and nurtured appropriately. According to Dr. Kress, students have basic needs we can all understand:

they want to belong to a group, to have a relationship with a caring adult, and to acquire and master skills that make them feel empowered. Young people will meet their basic needs in one group or another, and it is clear that which group they choose makes all the difference in the world.

The question becomes whether the groups to which they belong, and the skills they acquire, will be positive in their development and lead them to be useful to society.

The young want to feel empowered, and the more empowered they feel, the more independent they become. As they become independent and exercise leadership, they become more involved and caring, or as Cathann Kress says, generous. The length and intensity of their relationships are even more important than originally thought, and the relationships that are formed and maintained over time determine the value system of the emerging adult. Perhaps this is what our parents were saying when they warned us to make friends with the right people.

To paraphrase the Tufts study, young people will certainly develop; the question is, what environment will meet their basic needs?[3] Thus, according to Kress, we can derive from positive youth development research and one hundred years of 4-H what she calls the "Essential Elements of 4-H." Here they are:

- Belonging to an inclusive group led or coached by a caring adult in a safe environment
- Mastering skills and knowledge that students find interesting and useful
- Developing the independence of thought that leads children to envision themselves as active participants in the future and gives them a feeling of self-determination
- A spirit of generosity toward the community and others

The Tufts study takes a similar tack and calls this set of characteristics the five *c*'s: competence, confidence, character, caring, and connection.[4] When young people develop these characteristics, they become positive contributors to the community and engage in less risky behavior.

In sum, university research now shows that 4-H is the kind of environment that, over time, leads to better development, better character, better citizenship, and better problem-solving skills in the hands of young leaders. Collectively, those involved influence society in a very positive way. We call this "positive youth development," and it was highlighted, along with the Tufts study, in a recent *Newsweek* article.[5] We all benefit from young people's significant contributions to society. Positive youth development leads to service projects, volunteerism, demonstration projects, and the passing on of lifetime skills. Conversely, risky behavior results in the absence of positive youth development. In fact, in the absence of positive youth development, isolation or even destructive behavior can result.

THE POLICY IMPLICATIONS OF RECENT RESEARCH

Policymakers have to conclude that youth are resources to be developed, not problems to be solved. According to Dr. Lerner, it is now clear that young people thrive when their inherent basic needs are aligned with the developmental assets in their communities.[6] Positive youth development opportunities, according to Lerner, must be available, affordable, welcomed in the culture, and competently provided. The positive results his research found increase with the breadth and intensity of student involvement.

In reality, young people are involved in a variety of groups. Each group teaches some behavior and provides opportunities to develop character or skills, positive or negative. Obviously, students in poor environments suffer, but even in such environments, 4-H programs can achieve substantial results for the youth involved and the communities in which they are located.

Amazingly, we need not wait decades for the results. Lerner found that 4-H participants were making real contributions to society by the time they were in the sixth grade if they had been involved with 4-H for two years.[7] He also found that such students were significantly less likely to engage in risky behavior, such as smoking. The obvious conclusion is that positive youth development programs are high-quality investments for communities.

SOME THOUGHTS FROM A LAYPERSON

From my recent exposure to the 4-H program, I would offer some conclusions, although, not being a psychologist or sociologist, I do so with great humility: Investing in positive youth development helps the young people involved develop their own skills, giving them a better head start in life. This is good for them, their families, their communities, and their country.

Similarly, such investments deter risky and negative behavior, which can be costly to society. Development will take place one way or another. If we don't pay attention to positive youth development programs, we will pay attention to the negative outcomes of our failure to do so. Developmental years need not be negative. In fact, they can be quite positive. Positive youth development adds social capital to our communities. Young people can make a difference while they are young. The return on investment is immediate. They can do volunteer work, serve on boards, and help those in need.

We need to think differently about our students; they are tremendous assets that can be deployed. The best youth development organizations are backed by caring adults, informed by research and disciplined ways of doing things.

Investments should be long term. In fact, Dr. Kress suggests that short-term programs can often be destructive because they let our young people down just as they are making progress. When you get right down to it, positive youth development can be extended across a lifetime. What could be better than developing your intellect, taking care of your health, helping others through your deeds, and trying to be a loyal and caring friend?

CONCLUSION

In 1926, W. H. Kendrick argued that the two greatest outcomes that 4-H could bring about were a vision of life's possibilities and a way to realize the fullness of that vision. While Kendrick was talking about helping young people navigate the troubled waters of their environment, I think his recipe is good enough for us older fellows to consider for ourselves.

With its roots in education theory, religion, and the real virtues of early American rural life, 4-H seems as relevant today as it was during its formative years. It is being applied in the cities and suburbs of American, not just in rural areas, and modern 4-H is finding a following among young people and adults who care about them.

More importantly, the holistic and positive youth development organizations in our community are clearly worthy of our support. Researchers are now finding that what the founders of the 4-H movement intuitively knew to be true has a strong basis in scientific fact. Allow me to close by asserting that the 4-H programs of America are just one example of the true genius of those who envisioned the land-grant university some 143 years ago, when President Lincoln, in the middle of a terrible civil war, took time to sign the magnificent Morrill Act. Far from being outmoded, today's 4-H programs, led by land-grant universities, are needed now more than ever.

THE TRAIL TO EAGLE

2004

These remarks were delivered at a ceremony during which I was designated a Distinguished Eagle Scout by the Boy Scouts of America, forty-three years after I became an Eagle Scout.

They call it the "Trail to Eagle." It may begin with a nurturing mother in a Cub Scout Den before the fifth grade, or later after the boy has entered high school.

It may be traveled in a rural community or one of America's largest cities. It may be traveled with one's father or with men who have no children. The trip always involves boys seeking to be men and men who care about youth development. It teaches traditional values such as common courtesy, trustworthiness, and loyalty to friends and country. It uses outdoor activities to teach teamwork and leadership, and it uses indoor skill-building to explore careers and lift up intellectual achievement.

It teaches habits that are good for our economy, such as self-reliance, planning and organizational skills, diligence, and hard work. It teaches habits that are good for our families, such as loyalty, friendliness, and helpfulness. In an age of obesity among young people, it fosters fitness and wellness. Through adventure, it teaches respect for the environment and how to handle potentially dangerous tools such as fire and knives. It introduces almost every conceivable subject matter—geology, geography, orientation, medicine, communications, history, animal science, and everything else from astronomy to zoology.

At a time when learning comes easy in a young person's life—but only if it is welcomed—the Trail to Eagle makes learning fun and exciting. In short, the journey along the trail prepares one for academic pursuits and career advancement—for a lifetime of learning. Success is available to every traveler, regardless of one's economic background, religious preference, or race. If the trail is traveled well, the joy of learning is experienced and embraced, and success is celebrated time and time again along the trail. In fact, along the way, success is increasingly expected. As a result, self-worth is enhanced, and leadership roles are sought out and played well on the stage of an early life.

When the day comes to end the journey, the traveler learns that, in fact, the journey will never end. Traveling along the Trail to Eagle will be a part of the traveler's life until the last campfire. Service to others and the life well lived are values embedded in the very psychological makeup of most awarded an Eagle. In 1926, at a scouting convention in London, our founder, Lord Baden-Powell, asked his listeners to close their eyes and imagine the end of their lives. He asked this haunting question: "Will each life have been well lived in service to others?" The answer must be yes, and it is grasped by almost every Eagle Scout.

My own journey began in a den put together by my mother and her friends, and it took my friends and me through the entire scouting program, including service as a staff member for several years at the old Central West Virginia Council's Camp Mahonegon, in Upshur County. During that part of my journey, I made life-long friends and had significant opportunities to develop my leadership skills. My Eagle certificate was signed by President John Kennedy. My journey was traveled with my brothers Ben and John, whose own certificates were signed by President Johnson and President Nixon, respectively. My sister grew and succeeded equally in the Girl Scouts. My parents were involved all along the way, providing support and love as we all learned to "do our best to do our duty." Today, we all live useful and productive lives.

My journey on the Trail to Eagle has continued long after I was awarded the badge by my scoutmaster. It has led me along trails I could not have imagined for myself when I was a scout. I have met presidents of the United States and the queen of England, studied in world class universities, visited forty countries, and fully participated in three domains of society—government, law, and education. My journey prepared me for servant leadership in numerous organizations. It taught me to be happy alone in the hills of Appalachia and to find joy traveling with large groups of university supporters at Bowl games. It prepared me for the joy of teaching students in my law class. It taught me how to build a team culture that manages budgets totaling well over $1 billion a year, and it helped prepare me to deal with adversity in my professional and personal life. Along the way, I learned, in the words of Lord Baden-Powell, that "the real way to get happiness is by giving out happiness to other people."

I am, of course, honored to be designated a Distinguished Eagle Scout. I thank my nominator and the selectors at the national office. Thank you for reminding me again of the important role scouting has played in my life. But in my heart, I know that throughout our state and nation there are many Eagle Scouts more deserving than I. I am but their surrogate, a humble example of the great underlying and lasting contributions of scouting to our state and nation. For the honor you have bestowed on me, I thank you. But I thank you even more for supporting scouting. You are building better communities in West Virginia. You are, in fact, building a better America, one boy at a time.

My understanding of the importance of scouting was advanced recently when I heard Cathann Kress, the national leader of the unit within our government that oversees the 4-H program, speak at West Virginia University. She articulated far better than I can how vital youth development is in today's America. She pointed out the critical importance of teaching young people character, wellness, leadership, and interpersonal skills. While she focused on 4-H, she could have been talking about the Boy Scouts, the Girl Scouts, the Boys and Girls Clubs of America, the YWCA, Junior Achievement, or one of many other youth development organizations.

America needs young people who know that citizenship is expected of every American. America needs young people who can find adventure and excitement without the dangers of drug abuse. America needs young people who know how to lead and know how to follow. America needs young people who value fitness and seek to live wholesome lives. America needs young people who care about others and respect the diversity of our nation today. In fact, America needs us all to support, in every way we can, every youth development organization, including, most assuredly, the Boy Scouts of America.

About a hundred years ago, in the twilight of the nineteenth century, Lord Baden-Powell launched a movement that would help make his native England and the United States of America what they would become in the twentieth century. Today, we find ourselves at the dawn of another century, the challenges of which seem more perplexing and difficult than those that Baden-Powell's generation faced. It seems clear to me that the Trail to Eagle formula he suggested to build character, fitness, leadership, and interpersonal skills is even more important in today's world than it was in the world of the last century. So I say to you, without reservation, "Scouting Now! More Than Ever!"

NOTES

1   Cathann Kress, speech at West Virginia University, September 30, 2004. The points Kress made parallel her PowerPoint Presentation, "Essential Elements of 4-H Youth Development," available at http://www.national4-hheadquarters.gov/library/elements.ppt.

2   Richard Lerner et al., "Positive Youth Development, Participation in Community Youth Development Programs, and Community Contributions of Fifth Grade Adolescents: Findings from the First Wave of the 4-H Study of Positive Youth Development," *Journal of Early Adolescence* 25, no.1 (2005): 17–71.

3   Lerner, "Positive Youth Development."

4   Lerner, "Positive Youth Development," 23.

5   Barbara Kantrowitz and Karen Springen, "A Peaceful Adolescence," *Newsweek*, April 25, 2005: 58–60.

6   Lerner, "Positive Youth Development."

7   Lerner, "Positive Youth Development."

TWENTY-TWO

CELEBRATING VOLUNTEERS

FIRST ANNUAL CONFERENCE ON
VOLUNTEERISM

1979

These remarks were delivered at the First Annual Conference on Volunteerism, which was held at Jackson's Mill. I wrote and delivered this speech when I was state tax commissioner, because our governor, John D. "Jay" Rockefeller IV, was unable to attend the conference. At the time, I was a volunteer on behalf of West Virginia University, and my remarks seek to capture my sense of fulfillment from my volunteer activities and to remind the volunteers in the audience that their efforts are important. Some twenty-five years later, when serving in the United States Senate, Senator Rockefeller and his family helped to establish and fund the Blanchette Rockefeller Neurosciences Center at West Virginia University, once again exhibiting the family's commitment to volunteerism and philanthropy described in these remarks.

First, I wish to certify (that's a lawyer's term for "I really mean it") that Governor Rockefeller is ill this morning. He has lost his voice, which is a terrible thing for a chief executive, especially a political office holder. I was with him in Marion County at a meeting to discuss community development projects when his voice faded away, like an old soldier. He wishes he could be here. He gladly accepted your invitation and is disappointed that it is simply impossible for him to be here today. And so, he has sent the state's tax commissioner as a substitute. I cannot resist reading to you my favorite sickness excuse, which was written by a British bricklayer who was unable to report to work:

Dear Sir:

When I returned to the workplace this morning, I found that the storm which had occurred during the night had blown a number of bricks from the top of the wall where the mortar was still soft.

I immediately set about to repair the damage.

I filled a large wooden barrel about half full of bricks, tied a rope to the barrel, climbed to the roof, secured a pulley to a beam, cantilevered the beam from the roof, and strung the rope through the pulley.

I climbed back down to the ground, seized the free end of the rope, and raised the barrel and bricks to the roof. I then used the bricks from the barrel to repair the damage.

When I finished this task, there were bricks remaining in the barrel. There were also bricks at various points on the roof from the earlier construction. In order to clean up the work site, I placed these bricks in the barrel. Climbing back down, I seized the free end of the rope and proceeded to lower the barrel and bricks to the ground.

At this point, I made the unfortunate discovery that the combined weights of the barrel and bricks was greater than my own.

As the barrel started down, I started up. Halfway up, I met the barrel coming down. It struck me on the left side of my head, breaking my left jaw. The

barrel continued on toward the ground, I continued on toward the beam, striking the top of my head on the beam, and mashing my fingers in the pulley.

When the barrel hit the ground, the bottom broke out, the bricks spilled
out, and now I was heavier than the barrel. I started down. The barrel started
up. Again, we met at midpoint, this time breaking my left ankle.

The barrel continued on toward the beam; I continued on toward the
ground, falling on the sharp bricks that had spilled from the barrel and cutting
myself severely.

At this point, I must have lost my presence of mind, for I let go of the rope.
The barrel came down, striking me on the other side of my head, breaking my
other jaw, and therefore, sir, I respectfully request sick leave.[1]

I would like to make only three brief, major points, which I hope will stimulate your thinking at this conference. I do so knowing that most of you in the
room today are dedicated volunteers. You are familiar, in large measure, with
the goals and aspirations of your organization in particular and volunteerism
in general. The first point I would like to make was made by the governor's father, John D. Rockefeller III, who was frequently looked to as a spokesman for
America's volunteers. The volunteer sector is vital to America's strength and national character. As you know, the Rockefeller family has had a strong, unwaver-
ing belief that America, as a nation, should share its prosperity and should participate, without the hope of personal gain, in the improvement of the quality
of life of the citizens of America and other nations. Governor Rockefeller began
his public-service career as a volunteer—an antipoverty worker—and while it
sounds unusual for a Rockefeller to live in a trailer in Emmons, West Virginia, it
would not come as a surprise to someone who knew of his family's dedication.

Mr. Rockefeller frequently noted that thousands of indispensable American
institutions depend on voluntary contributions of time and money for their
survival. Toward the end of his life, he was deeply concerned about what he

saw as an erosion of the influence of volunteerism. In an important article on the subject, he identified three estates, or sectors, in American life: the public, or government, sector; the private, or business, sector; and the volunteer sector, which comprised the millions of people engaged as volunteer workers.[2] He was concerned that, in our nation, individuals sometimes have a tendency to turn to government to finance, direct, and maintain many of the services that were once the sole province of the volunteer sector. This loss of spirit, which is often reflected in a decline in philanthropic giving, is based on a fallacious assumption that there will always be millions of dollars from the government to do what volunteers do not. Mr. Rockefeller, therefore, suggested that leaders in America should always concern themselves with the welfare and vitality of all three sectors in order to restore and maintain the vitality of our unique American spirit.

Although written sometime ago, these thoughts ring true today. Perhaps more than most, I was impressed by the events and debate surrounding Proposition 13. During that debate, the *Washington Post* surveyed a cross section of the American public and found that, while 70 percent of Americans felt the tax load they bore was fair, only 34 percent felt government spent funds prudently and in a cost-effective manner.[3] It was then that a wave of government budget cutting began at all levels. Most observers expect this wave to continue. It has resulted in less certainty about the availability—especially at the federal level—of funds to support government programs of all kinds.

There is, of course, an appropriate and important partnership between volunteers and government, which seeks to improve the quality of lives in West Virginia. We in state government are very much aware of volunteers' contributions to programs centered on government. Among those state agencies that use volunteers are the Departments of Health, Welfare, Natural Resources, Culture and History, Emergency Services, and Economic Development; the

Commission on Aging; and our Library Commission. Volunteers with these agencies have considerable influence on directing the resources of government toward needs they help to define. Many other state programs are designed to improve the quality of life we enjoy, but none of these programs should or can become a substitution for volunteer efforts. In that sense, our partnership is limited. We are and should be mutually supportive, but those in government and those in volunteer organizations have roles that should not become completely merged.

Why? Because volunteers are free to choose how they will use their resources. It is this freedom that brings about unique and important contributions to sectors of our society that are not touched by government. In this way, volunteer efforts are often more innovative, more soul searching, and more substantial than government's efforts can ever hope to be. And so, volunteerism's place in America is more important today than it has been for decades. It is the volunteers of our society, united by a common goal of improving the quality of life, who can assert the soul, the heart, and the mind of our nation in the days ahead. We cannot—and we should not—allow America's volunteers to become an endangered species. There are many lives in our nation and in distant lands that depend on your work and your spirit of service without expected personal gain.

I might add that one can never underestimate the image of Americans that is fostered by volunteer work; we are seen as a generous and moral people. Twice this year I traveled to Japan with the governor on behalf of the state to promote the sale of West Virginia coal in the country and to interest foreign investment in West Virginia opportunities. I was most impressed by the acknowledged contribution that Americans, led by John D. Rockefeller III, made in helping a badly wounded and demoralized people regain their economic strength and national self-confidence through volunteer work. Today that nation collectively feels a deep obligation to our country. And most impressive of all is the belief that our nation is a humanitarian one—a view that is shared by those who have experienced the work of America's volunteers.

All of you know and have experienced the work of volunteers in West Virginia and in the towns where we live. Whether it be in distant lands or in our own community, the benefits of volunteer work are obvious. In summary, I simply wish to stress that we need to maintain a vigorous and growing volunteer sector in the years to come.

Secondly, as one who is not a "professional" volunteer, I would like to commend you for undertaking this conference. This conference is an important event for several reasons. First, I think it will serve to enhance skills you must have to be effective. Management, communication, and organization are important to your mission. They are the tools by which you accomplish your objectives, and they are the characteristics by which you are judged by a large number of those who observe your work.

Whether it is large or small, any organization is, or should be, interested in doing its job well. The public's perception of how effectively and professionally you accomplish your goals is important to your success. Volunteer projects range from one-on-one counseling to the management of multimillion-dollar undertakings. The skills you will learn at this conference are important to every one of those projects. More importantly, the skills are equally applicable to any project. In the coming decade, one of the most important skills for volunteers and for those in government will be the ability to assess community needs and to set community priorities for the public and volunteer sectors. The explosion in demands for social services arising out of the last decade, together with the limitations on government spending in the future decade, will mean that it will be crucial for us to carefully assess the needs of our citizens and to decide on priorities for our combined efforts to improve the quality of life in America.

In the past decade, the personal income of West Virginians has risen dramatically. We are perceived by many as the "Cinderella State" because of the strides we have made. In large measure, it is up to you, the volunteers of West Virginia, to build on West Virginia's new-found confidence and to use your improved organizational skills to ensure that West Virginia's new-found prosperity is matched by a new-found sense of moral and cultural well-being.

It is this challenge that strikes me as the most important aspect of this initial conference on volunteerism in West Virginia: the challenge to renew your dedication, the challenge to redefine and reexamine your objectives, and the challenge to initiate a new spirit of cooperative volunteerism in West Virginia life.

On behalf of the governor and myself, I commend you for attending this conference and wish you well.

Thirdly, through the words of Erma Bombeck, I wish to express a sentiment I feel quite strongly today. This great lady of humor and humanity said:

Volunteers are like yachts.

No matter where they are, they arouse your curiosity. Who are they? Where do they come from? Why are they here?

They could stay moored where it's safe and still justify their being, but they choose to cut through the rough waters, ride out storms, and take chances.

They have style. They're fiercely independent. If you have to ask how much they cost, you can't afford them.

Volunteers and yachts have a lot in common these days. They're both a part of an aristocratic era that is disappearing from the American scene. They're both a luxury in a world that has become very practical.

Day by day, the number of volunteers decreases in the country as more and more of them equate their worth in terms of dollars and cents.

Three years ago I did a column on volunteers in an effort to point out that they don't contribute to our civilization. They ARE civilization—at least the only part worth talking about.

They are the only human beings on the face of this earth who reflect this nation's compassion, unselfishness, caring, patience, need, and just plain loving one another. Their very presence transcends politics, religion, ethnic background, marital status, sexism, even smokers vs. nonsmokers.

Maybe, like the yacht, the volunteer was a luxury. And luxuries are too often taken for granted.

One has to wonder. Did we, as a nation, remember to say to the volunteers, "Thank you for our symphony hall. Thank you for the six dialysis machines. Thank you for sitting up with a 16 year-old who overdosed and begged to die. Thank you for the hot chocolate at the Scout meeting. Thanks for reading to the blind. Thanks for using your station wagon to transport a group of strangers to a ball game. Thanks for knocking on doors in the rain. Thanks for hugging the winners of the Special Olympics. Thanks for pushing the wheelchair into the sun. Thanks for being."

Did the media stand behind them when they needed a boost? Did the professionals make it a point to tell them they did a good job? Did the recipients of their time and talent express their gratitude?

It frightens me, somehow, to imagine what the world would be like without them.[4]

And so, like Mrs. Bombeck, on behalf of the governor and those he represents, I say thank you.

It is very fitting that this first conference has taken place during the great American holiday season, for it is during this time of the year that we should renew our willingness to share and our sense of thanksgiving for the gifts we have been given. It is your willingness to serve that has been your greatest gift—and it is the tradition of giving in the past that gives volunteerism its greatest opportunities in the future.

NOTES

1   Irish folk story published in *Reader's Digest* in 1937.

2   John D. Rockefeller III, "In Defense of Philanthropy," *Business and Society Review* 25 (1978): 26–29.

3   Barry Sussman, *Washington Post*, October 1, 1978, Monday, Final Edition, "Poor Government Service Is Target of 'Tax Revolt'; 'Tax Revolt' Targeted at Poor Service," A1.

4   Attributed to Erma Bombeck.

TWENTY-THREE

ENCOURAGING STUDENT SUCCESS

As a university president, I gave prospective students, their parents, and educators advice about preparing for college. While the essential message may be similar, my remarks must be shaped to the specific situation of the listeners. Each of the following three speeches is intended to help future students adjust to college life, but one is directed to the students, the second to their parents, and the third to their teachers and guidance counselors.

IT'S NOT ALL ABOUT BRAINS
Advice To Students

2002

These remarks were presented, in many variations, to high school students, to students being inducted into honoraries on our campuses, and to various convocations at other institutions. The speech below was given at a convocation at Glenville State College, a sister public institution.

The theme is that success will be determined by integrity, the development of time management skills, and persistence, not just by intelligence. I was given a relatively brief time to make my point to this group of students from rural Ap-

palachia, many of whom were the first in their family to attend college and who, like other college students from humble circumstances, were anxious about college. It was my task to give them the confidence they needed to get off to a good start. As the reader will note, with the institutional president's encouragement, I suggested to the faculty that focus is a good habit of mind for members of the faculty as well as their students.

If I have learned one thing about getting ahead in life, it is this: stay focused. Before I begin my message to the next class of students, let me just say to the faculty here that maintaining a focused commitment to those served by our institutions is more critical this year than ever before.

For faculty members across West Virginia—and, indeed, across the nation—I know that these are worrisome times. In West Virginia, we are facing budgets cuts, and we are not alone: forty-six states have had to cut back due to the current economic downturn. In this environment, it is important for us to avoid thinking too much about these financial concerns and to concentrate instead on addressing the needs of those we serve—students, parents, communities, employers, patients, clients, and others.

By doing the best we can for them, we can demonstrate higher education's value to the state of West Virginia and encourage government investment in higher education to continue over the long term. We can't let tough times distract us from focusing on the needs of our students by focusing instead on ourselves. Throughout higher education, we are facing these problems together, and if we all stay focused on those we serve, they will become our advocates, and with their help, we will overcome the challenges we face.

Students, you must also stay focused—on your goal of completing your college education and preparing to begin a successful career. I want to stress to you today that when it comes to success in college and in life, it's not all about brains. *The New Shorter Oxford English Dictionary* defines the brain as "the mass of substance contained in the skull of humans and other verte-brates; this organ as the seat of sensation, motion, or human speech, the or-gan of thought, memory, or imagination; intellectual power; a clever person."[1] Looking from the outside, I am sure that many of your friends think that you achieved today's recognition because you are blessed with "brains" or "gray matter" or "native intelligence." To be sure, because your parents are here to-day, I want to pay tribute to your genetics, your inherited capacity. Surely your genetic makeup has a lot to do with innate reasoning ability. You have also had good preparation and, in many cases, a wonderful home environment.

Your education and environment also contribute to your mental capacity, so I'm told. You have the gift of intelligence, and you certainly have academic talent. But my message to you today is, it's not all about brains. Success in life, academic or otherwise, takes more than intellectual capacity. You all know very bright people who have failed in their careers and personal lives. Have you analyzed why they have failed? You know people of modest intelligence who have been wildly successful. Have you analyzed why they have succeeded?

So, it is fair to ask, "President, if it's not all about brains, what is it all about?" Well, I would submit success is about the following:

First, it is about having goals and objectives and a willingness to sacrifice to achieve them. I don't know any successful person who did not work hard to get where they are. And the only way to learn to work hard is to practice.

Second, it is about time-management skills. We all have the same twenty-four hours at our disposal each day, and those who can establish their priori-ties properly do better than those who cannot.

Third, it is about integrity and trust. These attributes sustain your relation-ships and cause opportunities to come your way.

Fourth, it is about emotional intelligence and interpersonal skills. In one of his books, Howard Gardner of Harvard addresses some of the primary at-tributes of leaders coming from this form of intelligence.[2] These skills and abilities make you more confident, give you emotional stability, and create connectivity with others who can help you enhance your own work.

Fifth, it is about good health and living habits. Included in this category is the balance between your work life and your personal life. We all recognize the importance of recreation and relaxation.

It is about stability in your personal and family relationships. The "static" created by disruptive relationships can alter the road to success and make staying on course difficult. It is about lifetime learning and study. We live in an information age where knowledge doubles every four years. It is about taking risks, seizing the day, and being entrepreneurial. The key is understanding the risks, not avoiding them. It is also about fortune or fate. We expect to hit some bumps in the road, and we expect some bumps to be removed without our interference.

Finally, it is about—perhaps most of all—finding meaning in your life. Success has to do with enjoying your work. Confucius said that if you find a job you love, you will never work a day in your life. Victor Frankl wrote in *Man's Search for Meaning* that people your age are looking for meaning in their lives. Well, everyone looks for meaning in their lives, and when they find it, success comes naturally. Note that each of these attributes is a habit that, with practice, you can develop. So, I wish you the best in all that you do. Remember, it's not all about brains: it's a lot about you and your habits of mind.

PREPARING FOR SUCCESS IN COLLEGE
Advice for Parents

2007

As the impact of the Mountaineer Parents Club demonstrates, students benefit greatly from the support and encouragement of their parents. Many parents are influential in their children's decisions to apply to college, and their involvement contributes greatly to success in college. Because I believe parents are important to students and to the university, I have reached out to them and attempted to provide them with the information they need to support their children. This essay, published in the "Book of Experts" guide of the "State Journal," offers parents suggestions about how to prepare their children for college and facilitate their success at the university as well as after graduation.

All parents want the best for their children, and most parents believe that a college education will launch their children into successful, fulfilling careers. As a university president, I often hear from parents who want to know how they can increase their children's college readiness.

Parents are right to be concerned. Higher education is a vital prerequisite for entering most careers, and the earnings gap between those who have and have not completed college continues to widen. According to the College Board report, *Education Pays*, the typical full-time worker with a college degree earned 62 percent more than the typical worker with only a high school diploma. As educational attainment increases, so does the earnings differential.

Considering the value of a college education, it is understandable that parents want to do all they can to help their children prepare for college. As an educator, I focus my advice on the academic preparation that enables students to enter college and, more importantly, to graduate from college. I suggest that parents encourage their children to follow these four practices to enhance the odds for college success.

TAKE RIGOROUS COURSES

A U.S. Department of Education study released this year found that the rigorousness of a student's high school curriculum is the strongest indicator of postsecondary degree completion, regardless of the major a student pursues.

ACT Inc. recommends a high school core curriculum including four units of English and three units each in math, science, and social studies. Their research has shown that students who complete this core curriculum have a better chance of enrolling in college, are more likely to stay in college, are less likely to need remedial coursework in college, and typically earn higher first-year grade point averages than do students who do not take the core curriculum.

Students who exceed the core curriculum have even higher college freshman-to-sophomore retention rates. When possible, high school students should consider taking Advanced Placement or International Baccalaureate Program courses. Since many institutions accept these courses for college credit, students can save time and money in college. More importantly, the experience they gain doing college-level coursework will increase their overall college readiness. Ideally, students should start planning a college-preparatory curriculum in middle school. By taking algebra in eighth grade, for example, they will be prepared to take higher level math in high school.

BUILD STRONG STUDY HABITS

Parents can do their children a great service by helping them develop good study strategies and time-management skills. When students enter college, they suddenly find themselves with the freedom to manage their own time and make their own choices about when and how much to study. If good study practices have become a habit by the time they graduate from high school, they are more likely to make good choices as they manage their time in college.

I always tell incoming WVU students that they should study at the same time and place every day so the practice becomes a habit. Study means engaging in careful, critical thought that leads to the understanding of concepts encountered in classes and assignments. Parents should also remind their college-bound students that attending class is the most important thing they can do to increase their chances of academic success in college.

EXTEND LEARNING BEYOND THE CLASSROOM

Participating in extracurricular activities in high school can broaden students' interests, develop their leadership skills, and make them more attractive candidates for admission to the college of their choice. A report from the National Center for Education Statistics demonstrated that youth who participate in extracurricular activities have better school attendance levels and higher levels of achievement. Students have to realize, however, they cannot do everything. Their studies must remain their first priority.

BECOME STUDENTS OF THE WORLD

Above all, parents should strive to help their children become lifelong learners—people who are curious about the world around them, comfortable interacting with people of various backgrounds, able to find and evaluate information, and able to communicate their thoughts clearly and effectively.

By encouraging a love of reading in their children, parents can make their children's lives not only more successful but also more pleasurable. Reading about current events and discussing them as a family will increase children's awareness of the great issues of our time. Reading about other cultures and traveling as much as possible will increase young people's ability to thrive in a global marketplace.

Developing a capacity for lifelong learning in children will help them succeed in college, but it will also do much more. By giving them perspective, wisdom, and joy, it will help them live truly successful lives.

TWELVE ATTRIBUTES OF A QUALITY INSTITUTION
Advice to Educators

2005

These remarks were delivered at a meeting of our campuses' academic leaders with counselors, faculty, and principals of West Virginia's public school system. It is this kind of exchange that I believe will truly build the higher-education/ public-education bridges of understanding that public officials seek. In these remarks, I tried to establish reasonable expectations for those we serve. In other speeches, I encouraged superintendents of school districts to clearly state for the higher-education community what we should rightfully expect of their school districts. Our mutual goal should be to find ways to exceed the reasonable expectations we have thus established.

At this conference, we have learned a great deal about what our university expects of the graduates of your high schools. But our relationship is a two-way street; I would like to discuss with you the other side of the equation—what students should expect from colleges and universities. During their college searches, students will consider institutions that vary widely by mission, size, location, and other qualities. I believe that whatever the type of college they are considering, students should look for twelve characteristics that help to define excellence in undergraduate education.

The first expectation should be opportunities for middle and high school students to visit campus and learn how to prepare for college. Colleges should encourage prospective students to visit campus by making it as easy as possible for students and parents to tour campus and talk to faculty members and current students. At WVU, our gateway to campus is the Visitors Resource Center, which uses cutting-edge interactive technology, as well as knowledgeable tour guides, to introduce guests to the university.

Colleges should also offer many opportunities for high school students—and even middle and elementary school students—to participate in campus activities, including academies for high-achieving students, camps, and educational experiences such as the WVU College of Engineering and Mineral Resources' annual Pumpkin Drop. Youth should feel welcome at campus athletic events, lectures, and cultural events. These opportunities to visit campus help build a young person's interest in attending college.

The second expectation should be informative recruiting with sufficient information to determine whether the student and college are a good fit. During the recruiting process, the institution should provide plentiful, accurate information that allows the student to determine if the institution is a good fit. In addition to an informative view book and Web site, the college should have knowledgeable admissions counselors who can answer any question a student or parent might have, from information on a specific program, to advice on which residence hall to pick, or how to finance a college education. You should expect admissions counselors to be readily accessible in a variety of ways. WVU counselors attend college fairs throughout the region, meet with prospective students at the Visitors Resource Center, and staff special Mountaineer Visitation Days on campus. They are reachable, of course, by phone and e-mail and can even be instant messaged.

Recruiting and admission are the first steps in a young person's college career. Of course, it takes more than a smooth and friendly recruiting process to make a great institution, but the presence of such a process makes it easier for students to find out if they and the institution are a good fit. An affordable cost is one necessary component. When assessing affordability, students and parents should carefully consider financial aid and scholarship opportunities as well as tuition costs. Above all, they should consider the quality of the degree and the future earning power it is likely to command. A student's priority should be earning a good degree, not necessarily a cheap degree.

This past fall, we welcomed three students from Hedgesville High School who were each attracted to a different aspect of WVU. One was looking for a strong journalism school. One was looking for an excellent engineering program. All three had ideas about the kind of extracurricular activities they wanted to pursue. Two were looking forward to participating in the university Honors Program. The unusual thing about these students is that they are triplets—Paul, James, and Sarah Braswell. Their search for a university that fit their needs is similar to that of students everywhere; a good recruiting process helps students find the institution that is truly right for them.

Third, you should expect an excellent start: a meaningful orientation for students and parents the summer before the freshman year. At WVU, students and parents begin the college experience by attending New Student Orientation, a day-long summer program that familiarizes them with the campus and with academic and student-life expectations. New students also have the option of participating in Adventure West Virginia, a wilderness orientation program that combines activities such as rock-climbing, whitewater rafting, and backpacking in some of the state's loveliest locations with fireside discussions on strategies for excelling academically and socially at college. Discussions are led by highly successful WVU students, and the program is directed by Greg Corio, a WVU graduate who enjoys sharing his passion for West Virginia with our newest students.

Fourth, I would look for a strong first-year program that develops skills needed for college success and excites students about learning. High school students should be sure that any college or university they are considering offers a supportive first-year experience. The foundation for a successful college experience is the freshman year. I believe this so strongly that, as many of you probably know, I made strengthening WVU's first-year experience one of my first priorities as president. A first-year program should complete students' orientation to college and help them develop skills they will need for success in the first year. It should also excite the student about learning, in and out of the classroom.

Collectively, WVU's first-year programs are known as Operation Jump-Start, and they have contributed to improved academic performance and first-year retention. When new WVU students arrive on campus, they attend the Jump-Start Academy, a three-day program that includes discussion of substance abuse, safety, relationships, and other concerns that are vital to students' well-being, as well as further discussion of academic responsibilities. The day before classes start, freshmen attend New Student Convocation, a rite of passage that welcomes them to the WVU academic community and introduces them to the responsibilities and rewards of learning at the college level.

All WVU freshmen must take University 101, an orientation course that teaches skills crucial to success in college, such as time management, note taking, and test preparation. University 101 activities are integrated with residence hall programming. In the residence halls, WVU students have access to resident faculty leaders, or RFLs—faculty members who live near the residence halls and share meals and advice with students. RFLs also oversee cultural and recreational events that create a sense of community among residents.

Parental involvement is also crucial throughout the college experience, but particularly in the transition from high school to college. My wife, Susan, leads WVU's Mountaineer Parents Club, which connects parents to campus life. Proving that parents do desire involvement in their children's education, the club has grown to include thirteen thousand families. WVU also employs a parent advocate to respond to callers who seek advice or offer suggestions through our toll-free helpline.

Fifth, but of ultimate importance, you should seek and find academic excellence: a breadth of academic offerings and quality faculty. Once they arrive on campus, students expect—and have the right—to find outstanding academic programs and talented faculty. Academic quality is clearly one of the most important characteristics that students and parents seek in a higher-education institution. But how can they evaluate academic quality?

Rankings, such as those published by *U.S. News & World Report*, are one way. These rankings do provide a handy snapshot of some academic quality indicators. But over the years, many experts—including Gerhard Casper, former president of perennially high-ranking Stanford University—have criticized the rankings for the false precision with which they seem to quantify what is in many ways unquantifiable—the quality of a university.

Instead of relying solely on rankings, I would encourage students and parents to ask certain questions of each institution they are seriously considering. These questions help to define academic excellence.

First, is there a wide range of academic offerings? This may not be important to a student who knows exactly what program he or she wishes to pursue, but many more students are undecided and often end up graduating in a major far different from the one they initially found interesting. In fact, they may find themselves drawn to a discipline they did not even know existed before they started college.

For most students, a college or university that offers enough majors to enable wide-ranging career exploration is desirable. This is one advantage of a larger campus—it gives students room to explore a wide range of academic interests.

Second, do faculty members have a reputation for excellence? Have they won awards for their teaching? Have they published their research in prestigious peer-reviewed journals? Do the most renowned professors on campus actually teach undergraduate courses on a regular basis? What is the average student-faculty ratio? Do current students and recent alumni speak favorably about their professors? When students need extra help, are faculty members accessible? Are students required to synthesize their knowledge through some kind of capstone project before graduation? Do the professors teach students not just specific vocational skills—which quickly become out of date—but how to think?

Third, are academic support programs in place to help students succeed? Such programs include tutoring services, availability of advanced learning technologies, special programs for at-risk students, and enrichment programs for high-achieving students. Does the campus regularly host thought-provoking, high-profile lecturers, as WVU does during its annual Festival of Ideas?

No one should enroll in any college or university without seeking the answers to these questions about academic quality.

Next, I would look for wholesome out-of-classroom learning opportunities. Out-of-classroom learning activities are extremely important to college students. The right kind of extracurricular activities provide a healthy balance to a student's schedule. These activities enable students to hone leadership and interpersonal skills that will serve them well in any career. Extracurricular activities also help to distinguish some student résumés from those of other candidates when they are applying for jobs after graduation.

When choosing a college, students should consider how wide-ranging the extracurricular activities available are and the degree to which students are encouraged to get involved. At WVU, students can participate in intramural and intercollegiate athletics, fraternity and sorority life, student government, artistic exhibits and performances, and more than 350 student organizations that focus on everything from religion and politics to community service and professional development.

Colleges and universities should also provide positive recreational opportunities that help students resist pressure to spend their free time engaging in risky behavior. Our WVUp All Night program attracts thousands of students each weekend for free food, concerts, dances, movies, and other activities in the Mountainlair student union building. Our Student Recreation Center is a campus hotspot, where students swim, run, lift weights, play basketball, rock climb, and otherwise improve their health and well-being. Students and parents should expect a similar investment in student recreation opportunities from any quality college or university. They should also accept nothing but the highest standards for campus safety.

Next, I would look for service and research opportunities that help students accomplish meaningful tasks while in college. Students should look for an institution where they can start living their dreams long before they graduate—where, through partnering with faculty members on meaningful research and service projects, they can learn by doing. WVU undergraduates have documented the struggles of cancer patients for an Emmy-winning documentary, built an environmentally friendly SUV that placed tenth in a national competition, and presented research at international scientific conferences. These opportunities enrich a student's education and provide a boost in the job market after graduation. As a student who participated in the cancer project said, "In job interviews, instead of trying to convince people of what you can do, you can say, 'Look at what I've done.'" Students should look for a college or university where they can start gaining valuable experience right away.

Every campus experience will be enhanced by racial, ethnic, and economic diversity and an atmosphere of respect for others. Students and parents should look for an institution with a diverse campus environment and a commitment to celebrating everyone's varied contributions and viewpoints. A diverse campus environment makes it easier to prepare for a diverse workplace, but this is not the only benefit of campus diversity. An American Council on Education report revealed that students who interact with diverse peers show measurable gains in their critical thinking skills. Other research has shown that socializing with others from diverse backgrounds improves learning outcomes, social self-concept, and satisfaction with the college experience. A college or university that attracts students from around the world gives students a priceless opportunity to learn about other cultures.

At WVU, we strive to integrate diversity into our curriculum and extracurricular activities. Our core curriculum requires students to take a course focusing on a foreign culture or on minority or gender issues. For students who want to explore further, we offer an Africana studies minor, a women's studies major, and a Native American studies minor. The WVU President's Office for Social Justice offers training for faculty, staff, and students on many diversity issues. We hold an annual Diversity Week that includes lectures, films, and arts presentations celebrating a wide range of cultures. The university also presents awards to faculty, staff, and students who have acted as examples in treating all people with fairness and encouragement.

You should also expect familiarization with the global community. This is a matter of growing importance. Colleges and universities must prepare students to live and work in the twenty-first century. Our world is more inclusive than it was even ten years ago, in large part because of the growth of the information superhighway. Our students can speak to people in other countries at the click of a mouse. When they become professionals, they are likely to participate in "virtual work teams" with people whose first language is not English.

The workplace is quickly becoming an interconnected "global village," and our students must learn to work with increasingly diverse markets. Kellogg Foundation President William Richardson once said that the ability to thrive in a multicultural setting will soon become another form of literacy that all employers will expect their employees to have mastered. It is essential that institutions help students develop a global awareness.

In upcoming months, WVU students will study pottery in China, fashion design in Italy, Eastern European religion and society in Hungary, and digital photography in Mexico. Offering study-abroad programs such as these—as well as opportunities to learn from faculty members from other countries and to take courses focusing on world issues—is a hallmark of an institution that can help students develop a world vision.

Next, the university you choose should have a reputation in the job market and job placement opportunities. Most people regard higher education as the path to a satisfying career. When choosing a college, students should consider whether an institution will actually help them fulfill their career expectations.

To do this, institutions must not only offer job search support but also have a high enough profile to attract recruiters from Fortune 500 companies and other top employers to campus. They should also have a reputation for academic excellence so that a degree from the institution has value in the eyes of potential employers. I encourage students and parents to find out all they can about the employers who recruit on campus and the jobs that recent graduates have received.

I would also look for facilities conducive to learning. A college or university cannot be judged solely on the basis of its facilities, but any university that fails to make continued investments in its learning facilities is unworthy of consideration by prospective students. The campus visit is an important part of the college search process, and nearly every such visit includes a tour of campus facilities.

A collection of shiny new buildings or venerable ivy-covered halls may be impressive, but are they really a sign of a quality institution? Students and parents may need to dig a little deeper to evaluate institutional facilities. Across the country, and particularly in West Virginia, the past few years have been difficult for higher education. Budgets have been strained, and many worthy initiatives have been competing for scarce dollars. In such an environment, it is difficult for an institution to find resources to invest in academic facilities. Such investment is crucial, however, to maintaining an environment where faculty and students can engage in learning and discovery.

WVU is 138 years old, and keeping our facilities up-to-date has not always been easy. We have managed, however, to invest in our facilities to create a top-notch living and learning environment. In recent years, we have built a state-of-the-art library and a technologically sophisticated life-sciences building. We have renovated other libraries and upgraded athletic and performing-arts facilities. We recently broke ground for an addition to our agricultural-sciences building, and will be renovating three academic buildings on our downtown campus.

Finally, you should seek a university where you can find a longterm commitment to fostering lifetime learning, pride, and support for higher education. Students should look for an institution with which they can make a lifelong connection; they should find a place where they can receive continuing education throughout their careers. A school should have an active and enthusiastic alumni base and a community where a graduate always feels at home. The college they choose should also help them develop a commitment to lifetime learning. With a foundation of analytical and communication skills and an excitement about discovery, people can continue to learn, explore, and create throughout their lives. Giving students the tools to do this is the most important job of any educator.

Dr. Cathann Kress, who provides leadership for youth development at 4-H national headquarters, has outlined the essential elements of 4-H youth development as positive relationships with caring adults, opportunities for belonging, experiences with hands-on learning, opportunities to master problem-solving skills, and opportunities to value and practice service to others. These elements, you will note, are also very similar to the five promises that Governor and Mrs. Manchin have said West Virginia must make to its young people—a caring adult, a safe environment, a healthy start, a marketable skill, and an opportunity to serve the community. I believe these elements are also an essential part of a college education.

The costs of college have increased rapidly in recent years. In some cases they are truly astounding—Brown University recently announced new tuition rates exceeding $40,000 per year. A college education could soon cost $200,000 or more at some institutions. The most expensive colleges are not necessarily the best. No matter what college they are considering, students and parents must do their homework and evaluate it carefully. I believe the criteria I have outlined for you will give them a basis for doing that, and I hope you will share them.

Institutions that meet these criteria are institutions that care about students. At WVU, our feelings for all our students is analogous to the feelings across West Virginia for our Sweet Sixteen basketball team. We take pride in our students' successes, and we support them through any setbacks. We would glory in a victory tomorrow night, but we will not be disappointed if the men's basketball team loses in the Sweet Sixteen. The effort, determination, and character they have shown in their incredible postseason run are true indicators of student success. We try to build and nurture those qualities in all of our students as they make the journey from high school students to independent, productive citizens. In improving the lives of our state's young people, we are proud to be on the same team with you.

NOTES

1   *The New Shorter Oxford English Dictionary* (New York: Oxford University Press, 1993).

2   Howard Gardner, in collaboration with Emma Laskin, *Leading Minds: An Anatomy of Leadership* (New York: Basic Books, 1996).

TWENTY-FOUR

SUPPORTING PRODUCTIVE COMMUNITIES

Economic development has become an important part of the service element of the mission of public universities. The following speeches were written in the hope that they would encourage and be supportive of West Virginia's economic efforts.

SO, YOU WANT TO BE AN ENTREPRENEUR?

2001

In recent years, universities have been asked to foster a spirit of entrepreneurialism among our students and to teach entrepreneurialism on our campuses. In 2001, I wrote this article for the "State Journal," a newspaper devoted to the business community. My goal was to define the entrepreneur and to offer examples of the entrepreneurial spirit as exhibited in the lives of many of our graduates. Five years later, we enrolled students who were interested in this subject in a new entrepreneurship major within our College of Business and Economics. The article was well received, as much for the positive attitude it displayed toward the business community as for the exact content of the message.

A popular television show asks each of its contestants to aspire to be a millionaire. By answering a series of questions, those lucky enough to appear on the show can accumulate a million dollars, or even more. If only it were so simple to become wealthy in the real world! Outside the television studio, attaining economic prosperity requires the creativity and hard work of people we refer to as entrepreneurs.

One thing about the real-world process, though: those who often attain wealth through entrepreneurial activities create wealth for many other people who become associated with them in the process. Entire communities share in the prosperity, not just one lucky person. Today's American culture, filled with stories of dot-com fortunes, inspires many college students to become entrepreneurs. In West Virginia, a recent study encourages the state to foster entrepreneurship, arguing that entrepreneurs can accumulate wealth while diversifying the state's economy.

We want entrepreneurs, yet very few people know what it means to be one. What are they, anyway? How do we encourage them? Can our school system and our colleges and universities create them? To be sure, the entrepreneurial spirit includes a willingness to take risks: to lay out one's own money in the hopes of making a profit. The classic example of the entrepreneur is a small-business person who offers a product or service addressing a market need or niche.

Craig Underwood, for example, saw an opportunity to create a company specializing in frequent-flyer "air mile" programs. Bill Hinchey recognized a need to create an easier way to test for substance abuse. Bray Cary saw a way to match up NASCAR fans and television. Today, these former West Virginia University students are success stories who return to campus frequently to urge students to do their "own thing."

Entrepreneurs are also active inside well-established businesses. Within large companies, business units are sometimes given a certain amount of "risk capital" and told to create new business lines in hopes of increasing the parent company's profits. Big accounting firms have created consulting firms; chemical companies based in commodity products have entered specialty chemical businesses; newspapers have bought television stations and offer Web-based services.

Government entities such as NASA and the U.S. Defense Department reward creative risk-taking by entrepreneurs working within them. So, too, do state universities.

George Bennett, a WVU graduate, encouraged the university's senior staff to create "greenhouses"—experimental units where the normal rules do not apply and risk taking is rewarded. As a result, WVU faculty in English, engineering, business, and economics have proven their entrepreneurial spirit in a variety of successful endeavors.

There is no common social or educational background among entrepreneurs. Women living in small-town Appalachia have started successful companies making quilts. Artists working in new genres have succeeded in the music business. Broadcast journalists have developed new programs and segments targeting specific audiences. Educators involved in research have created opportunities in private, for-profit undertakings. New mousetraps, and better ones, are offered up every day, in every community in the country.

These successes show that it is not what you do, or the size of your organization, that makes you an entrepreneur. You might have no money to work with, or lots of it. Bill Gates, Steve Jobs, John Chambers, and other high-tech gurus built profitable businesses from entrepreneurial activities. Now their companies have money, yet every day, they take new entrepreneurial risks. The money you risk does not even have to be yours. Lots of new businesses are funded by banks, investors, and venture capitalists.

So what is it, then, that drives the entrepreneur? I think it is the ability to observe society objectively, to discern—better than other people—a true need, and match it with a solution that makes common sense. Certainly it is about money and having the means to develop an idea. But more than anything, entrepreneurship is about offering others something they really need.

When I commuted long-distance for seventeen years, I was just waiting for a cellular telephone. The law firm I belonged to was revolutionized by computer-driven database search engines. A small tractor shaved hours off my gardening time. Geographic information systems technology helps outdoors enthusiasts find their way on lakes and mountains. Someone came up with the highlighter for students and the laptop computer for traveling executives. Hotels specialize in serving travelers on a budget, or on an unlimited budget. And on it goes.

Given that entrepreneurial activities have great value, we in education should be creating ways to teach entrepreneurship. But, can entrepreneurial talents be taught? The answer is yes. Educators need to note what entrepreneurs have in common and point out these characteristics to our students. We can systematize the principles of entrepreneurship and teach them, and we can encourage the entrepreneurial spirit with the right initiatives. Several ideas come to mind:

- Ask role models to share their experiences in a variety of forums.
- Look to the future by sharing demographic information and trends.
- Teach "servant leadership" skills. Introduce diversity and global awareness as values, and encourage travel.
- Assign "capstone" experiences that integrate several courses of study.
- Encourage education outside the classroom and lifelong learning.
- Study the lives of others through biography.
- Reward risk taking and thinking, not just results, in nontraditional ways.
- Teach listening skills.

- Share the importance of learning to write and speak clearly.
- Urge students to consider trying to start a "business" while in school.
- Value all forms of intelligence, not just analytical ability.
- Reward hard work as well as intelligence.
- Teach independence of thought and critical analysis.
- Teach organizational and time management skills.

This list is incomplete, but I hope it encourages the reader to contemplate the truth that in every classroom, tomorrow's entrepreneurs are waiting for encouragement. It is up to all of us to teach them to seize the opportunities that arise every single day. Entrepreneurs take risks and "invest," to be sure. But even more, they serve society. They thrive on change, and they focus on success. When we needed better farming methods, we started agricultural colleges. When we needed industry, we started schools of engineering. When we needed to win the race into space, we increased our emphasis on math and science in our schools and colleges. When we needed something in America, we got the job done.

Today, we need self-starting, need-meeting entrepreneurs. We can get this job done, too, right here in West Virginia.

CAN WE GET IT RIGHT THIS TIME?
Thoughts on Economic and Community Development

2001

This speech was delivered in 2001 to a group interested in economic development in Greenbrier County, West Virginia. I delivered much the same message on several other occasions. It is a very frank speech in which I tried to confront several economic realities as they existed in our state at the time. I am pleased to report that our economic condition has improved considerably in recent years.

At the time this speech was written, all of us at WVU were listening to the many pleas of our state's leaders to involve ourselves in economic development. I had just read two books on West Virginia history, cited in the text, that had stimulated my thinking on the subject. I tried in this and other related speeches to suggest ideas of what could be done. More importantly, I tried to remind the audiences that our state's economic strategies were sometimes lacking in the past and that all of us in positions of responsibility should feel the pressure to "get it right this time."

As I indicated in this speech, West Virginia has many natural resources, such as water, that can provide the foundation for the state's economic future if they are managed well. In recent years, these resources have become even more valuable. In fact, as I prepared this manuscript for publication, an article about the value of water was published, "Water for Profit," which again suggested to me the economic potential of West Virginia's natural resources for the next century.[1]

TODAY'S BATTLE CRY—ECONOMIC DEVELOPMENT!

Today, the bipartisan battle cry in West Virginia is, "Economic development!" For most (admittedly not all) public leaders in the Mountain State, almost any policy or condition that leads to increased tax revenue, job growth, or general economic development is deemed worthy of support. Manifestations of the cry include:

- creation of a nonpartisan, state-sponsored, economic development organization;
- mandated focus of the state's institutions of higher education on workforce education, technology transfer, and job-creating research;

- the focus of the state's CEO organization, the West Virginia Roundtable, on economic development;
- the creation of community- and region-based economic development organizations; and
- your own interest in the subject.

The reasons for the unity of purpose seem sound: relatively low state per capita income, relatively high unemployment and underemployment, declining population growth rates, declining rates of growth in state tax revenues, an out-migration of young people, and troubled city budgets. Several state business concerns—especially in the chemical and manufacturing sectors—are showing a diminished presence in West Virginia. High percentages of college students from West Virginia leave the state upon graduation, lured by higher pay elsewhere. The reasons for the current condition of our economy are well understood:

- The diversification of the national economy away from manufacturing companies and toward the service and information technology industries
- The consolidation of U.S. industries, reducing the numbers of headquarters in West Virginia
- The globalization of competitive markets, resulting in the movement of plants "off shore" to lower-cost locations
- Mechanization, resulting in a reduced workforce
- Competition, sometimes excessive among the states, causing companies to move from one state to another

Blame is freely assigned by all concerned. Labor, management, politicians, scholars, media gurus, working people, retirees, and economic professionals all seek to lay the causes of the situation at the feet of others. Policy analysts, elected leaders, and almost everyone who attends a cocktail party or church social have proposed solutions to "the problem," including workforce development, tax incentives, restrictive legislation, and election law reforms.

Regions within our state feel the results of the economic transition differently. Our Eastern Panhandle, North-Central West Virginia, the Greenbrier Valley, and the Potomac Highlands seem to be doing well. But other parts of the state are suffering from economic anxiety and decline. The regions seem to send conflicting messages to our leaders and sometimes fight over limited state resources. A recent state-sponsored study has suggested a responsible course of action, which is being widely looked to as "the solution." There are doubts, of course, but no one has a better answer. Now the question becomes, can the state afford to fund the recommended actions, or even a partial solution?

THE BATTLE CRY OF A HUNDRED YEARS AGO—ECONOMIC DEVELOPMENT!

The cry for economic development in West Virginia has been heard before—just as fervently and with even more conviction. In his 1998 book, *Transforming the Appalachian Countryside*, WVU professor Ronald L. Lewis notes that commercial development of our region was part of the culture of its exploration and settlement.[2] It finds its roots in the royal charters granting land to commercial enterprises, western migration, and the frontier spirit of its settlers.

In preindustrial West Virginia, during my Great-Grandfather Hardesty's generation, there were at least two economic areas, "one in the settled farm and town sections around the periphery and broad river valleys, the other in the underdeveloped wilderness back counties that made up about two-thirds of the State."[3] Thus, Morgantown on the Monongahela; Charleston on the Kanawha; Harpers Ferry on the Potomac; Lewisburg on the Greenbrier; Wheeling, Parkersburg, and Point Pleasant on the Ohio; and even Weston and Clarksburg on the West Fork are of a different origin than Elkins, Beckley, Richwood, Madison, Webster Springs, and similar towns.

The battle cry was heard first around 1880 and lasted until 1920, when "West Virginia officials promoted the exploration of [natural resources] . . . as the surest road to economic development and the railroad as the most efficient for delivering economic growth."[4] There was logic—even patriotic fervor—in the battle cry: the national slogan was "westward ho!" and national policies fostered the connection of West and East by rail. President Lincoln, according to historian Stephen Ambrose, was a railroad lawyer and advocated the developmental potential of the new form of transportation.[5] He supported the East-West connection, which was completed in 1869 shortly after his death.

The B&O and C&O crossed West Virginia as part of the western expansion, connecting railroads within West Virginia. By 1880, the connectors and main lines afforded access for the timbering operations and mines of remote West Virginia to national markets.

The natural resources of the state were phenomenal: "Two thirds of West Virginia was still covered by ancient growth hardwood forests. . . . The Wealth of the virgin forest invited exploration, and the American ideology of unrestrained expansion, a federal policy of cheap land, and notions of linking civilization with open country" supported unrestrained expansion.[6] The timber was so mature (ten feet in diameter, and 100 to 150 feet high) that a single tree could make enough lumber to build several houses in rapidly expanding East Coast cities. The settlers in "rural" West Virginia wanted a way to escape a barter economy and acquire cash. Moreover, "pioneers considered trees an encumbrance on the land they wished to farm, and they sought the quickest and easiest way to get rid of them."[7]

Towns had grown up around cattle markets (e.g., Lewisburg), and rural mountain people had always shown a willingness to enter into commercial arrangements. In fact, the woods were always used to the maximum economic advantage of West Virginia's pioneers.[8]

While capital was being accumulated by both business and government, it had, prior to 1880, been invested primarily in the early towns of the state (e.g., Wheeling). By the turn of the twentieth century, capital, both outside and inside of West Virginia, was accumulated and ready to be deployed for a reasonable return in the back counties. Liberal and progressive writers supported its deployment, including professors at West Virginia University.[9] Our state's founders were largely supporters of economic expansion, and by 1900, the "entire machinery of State government" was used to that end.[10] Urban areas of the country were supportive of natural resource development. The mills and factories of urban America added value to our timber and coal. As a result, strong links between parts of West Virginia were established with Pittsburgh, Baltimore, New York, and other eastern cities.[11]

The laws of West Virginia increasingly protected entrepreneurs and fostered economic growth.[12] Much of the land in West Virginia was aggregated in a few landowners, as it had been since colonial times.[13] West Virginia was the legal equivalent of modern Delaware by 1900. The work ethic of West Virginians was also noteworthy; development was bipartisan. "No better example . . . can be found than the leaders of the two political parties . . . Henry G. Davis (Democrat) and his son-in-law . . . Stephen B. Elkins (Republican)."[14] Optimism was the mood. In 1902, Granville Davisson Hall, a state founder, wrote:

Under the census of 1900 West Virginia numbered near a million souls, and now, a year later, no doubt the million mark has been reached. Its statistics show an even larger growth in commerce and development. Among the coal-mining States, it is already third, and the production steadily increases. In no State in the Union has the tide of prosperity risen higher. From all sources— the local press, private correspondence, newspaper intelligence, the testimony of tourists and visitors—comes the uniform report of an opulent, unprecedented development, present and prospective, of the natural riches of this region, so long locked from the world of business enterprise by the repulsive policy of Old Virginia. While these last pages are being written, a local paper comes to hand with the statement that sixty-three railroads are at this time [November 1901] ... proposed and under construction within the State, ranging in length from ten miles to sixty.

The same paper contains the Thanksgiving proclamation of Governor White, wherein he says:

> We are truly a favored people among the nations of the world, and the citizens of no State in the Union have more abundant reason for thanksgiving than those of West Virginia. Our national prosperity has been very great, and we have been shielded from pestilence and distress. Our State has probably been blessed above all others in the progress of material development and in the increased production of the great riches with which God has favored us.
>
> The happy geographical position of West Virginia, her genial climate; her riches in soil, coal, stone, timber, iron and oil, will make her another Pennsylvania in industry, wealth and population; and her fine school system, crowned by the university at Morgantown, assures an intellectual growth adapted to the natural aptitude of her people.[15]

THE GOOD, THE BAD, AND THE UGLY

The turn of the century was a prosperous time in West Virginia. The timbering of the virgin forests, opening of mines, creation of glass and steel industries, and expansion of oil and gas industries created enormous collective wealth and tax revenues. On West Virginia University's campus, Stewart Hall (the library), engineering and chemistry buildings, Women's Hall, Chitwood Hall, Purinton House (the president's home), and many other buildings were erected, seemingly sparing no expense. Whole new colleges (Potomac State, West Virginia State, West Virginia Institute of Technology) were started. Banks were established, some with major trust departments. County courthouses reflected prosperity, as did the new large houses and even mansions in almost every town.

By the early 1900s, Henry Gassaway Davis had become a candidate for president of the United States, and in 1922, John W. Davis was a candidate for president of the United States. In 1911, President Taft visited West Virginia University. The professions grew to serve the state.[16] Entertainments were developed, of which WVU college football, local live theaters, and community bands are examples. The times were good, and many prospered, including thousands of immigrants brought into West Virginia to feed the wildfires of prosperity. These were the times of my grandfather.

But the good times were fleeting, and by 1920, almost all of the virgin timber was gone, and one-fourth of the state had been burned.[17] Towns that had miraculously sprung up were gone. Agriculture, a major reason for the land-grant charter of West Virginia University, had declined precipitously.[18] Farmers, lured by cash, took part-time jobs or moved off their farms altogether; some lost their farms or sold them and went to work for wages.[19] Erosion was common, and streams and rivers were polluted.[20] Navigable waterways were disrupted.[21] Politics was changed forever; in fact, politics and the economy had merged.[22] Laws had been skewed to favor capital. Crime had risen.[23] It had become obvious that "development" did not necessarily mean progress.

And then, the Great Depression rolled over our state, as Lewis says, "like a dense fog."[24] Its impacts on the coal fields are legendary. These were the days of my father's youth. He was raised in a large house built by his father on the prosperity of the early 1920s. In 1950, after the Depression and the war, he converted it to apartments and moved to a smaller home. After the depression, public works were of increasing importance to West Virginia. Since 1940, West Virginia has been at the mercy of the national economy, despite occasional economic boosts brought about by war, national energy shortages, and new investment. When I was West Virginia's state tax commissioner, I was told by department personnel that "when the nation gets a cold, West Virginia gets pneumonia." This has been my world.

As a result, many West Virginians in politics, education, and even the media today exhibit regionalism, conflicting views of economic history, myths of blame and responsibility, and disinterest in public policy. Again the battle cry is for "economic development," spurred not by optimism, patriotism, or ideology, but by anxiety and even desperation. This must not be the world of my children, and so I raise the question for the current generation of West Virginia's leaders—can we get it right this time? At the dawn of the twenty-first century, will we make the decisions that can put us in the main stream of prosperity in the most powerful nation on earth, at its most prosperous time?

THE CHOICES WE MUST NOW MAKE

It seems evident that the lessons of West Virginia's economic history point to several choices our generation can and should make:

Learning from the Past

First, we need to heed the lessons of history. This implies that our understanding of Appalachian history should be emphasized and deepened. Consider the importance of applying Dr. Lewis's insights to another natural resource—water. Tonight we sit on the banks of a major river, but Washington is reaching the limits of growth unless it finds additional water.

Already utilities are considering water impoundments in our state as private property, to be sold and exported at will. Consider energy generation as well, 70 percent of which is exported from West Virginia. Acid-rain legislation closed northern West Virginia mines. The absence of national dialogue on en-

ergy is striking—the debate has urban–rural overtones. As cities allow subur-
banites to drive their Lincoln and Cadillac SUVs to work, we close our mines.

Knowledge of Regional Differences

Second, we must recognize regional differences and adopt policies that per-
mit the strengths of each region to emerge. Our regions have deep roots in
history. Our founders were led by men like Granville Davisson Hall and
Marmaduke Dent of northern West Virginia. Commercial interests of the
northern part of the state dominated the first constitutional convention and
early state government but were dislodged in the late 1870s by another region's leaders, those whose cultural and economic roots lay with the planters
of the confederacy. Geography, topography, roads, and rivers also lay at the
roots of our regional diversity, which has been exacerbated by differences in
businesses and waves of immigration.

State policies will have to recognize these differences and perhaps even cus-
tomize solutions for some areas, like the Northern Panhandle, that will not,
and should not, be applied in other regions like southwest West Virginia. Legal,
even constitutional, changes may be necessary. The drive for sameness and
"uniform and equal" in almost everything has been taken too far—in education, state government, and local government—based largely on limited state
resources and distrust of local government, which finds its roots in our political
history. While other states have local school districts and home rule, our state
has a centralized system of school governance and centralized taxation.

Tax policies that are "uniform" by constitutional law can work well in the
interior and penalize the border counties, where over half of our people live.
Tax incentives have favored capital investment (1968–1980) or job creation
(1985–2000), but only on a statewide basis, without regard to the differences
evident in the regions. One size doesn't fit all.

There must be something in our policies for every region. Our regional visions should collectively include treating education as a growth industry; bolstering tourism and retirement communities; and developing broadband communication-based industries, sustainable forestry, clean power generation, value-added manufacturing, software development, clean coal technologies, and new segments of our traditional chemical industries. The visions must also include safe and caring communities, effective school systems, excellent health care, and responsible government.

The technology revolution has reached Morgantown, but it will have to reach every region of the state. If it does, education and jobs can be transported to former coal towns as easily as coal was transported to the East Coast. The vision for each region will have to be shared across regions, which means that our business, government, and education leaders will need to find common ground. This is a cause worthy of funding by charitable foundations.

Looking to Ourselves

Third, we must seek our own solutions, abandoning national trends in favor of policies that work for us. Our historic ties to other centers of influence have caused us to look elsewhere for solutions. Legislators copy ideas from southern and western states, and colleges and universities seek to emulate the Ivy League and Big 10 institutions. Sometimes reliance on other's ideas ("best practices") works. Sometimes reliance on others is misplaced. Trying to copy other states' tax structures is a good example.

Out-Migration

Fourth, we must stop the exodus of state leaders resulting from out-migration. Company headquarters have closed in West Virginia, and we are now heavily reliant on businesses traditionally national or international in scope. We will need to foster a new generation of leaders and entrepreneurs. To do so

will require a number of steps as well as cultural change. We also need to favor incentives that support indigenous businesses and foster the relocation of
headquarters to West Virginia. What is it worth to have the headquarters and
leadership of a major corporate entity in West Virginia? Arguably, it is at least
worth disproportionate tax credits.

Diversity

Finally, we will need to encourage diversity and be open to many voices. Our
naturalization ceremonies are full of talented new citizens born in other countries—their spirits must be allowed to soar. Women must be welcomed in
politics and management—they are more than half of our population. Young
working people must occupy center stage in policy development. For this to be
done, their voices, guided by new forms of technology and new ways of thinking, must be integrated with our own.
The people of each region must learn more about those of the other regions.
In short, new people must be welcomed to our communities. They need to be
recruited to city councils, school boards, nonprofit organizations, clubs and
churches, and political organizations.

In some ways, we are a people of close communities. In a sense, this is good
and results in a safe and stable state. But when close becomes closed, we go
too far. The power tradition in our state tends to favor the few. It must become
more inclusive. Our eighteenth-century backwoods ways, our nineteenth-cen-
tury political monopolies, and our twentieth-century "old boys" networks are
not working. The twenty-first century has to make room for anyone with talent,
vision, leadership, skill, and determination. We have had enough brain drain—
we need more brain gain.

When Doherty and Summers wrote a history of WVU in 1982, they titled it *West Virginia University: Symbol of Unity in a Sectionalized State.*[25]
Throughout our history, WVU has struggled, as the state has struggled, to

maintain a leadership role. From its disadvantaged location, with limited resources, it has been the most influential engine of progress in the Mountain State since its founding.

Today, its role is more central than it has ever been. The leaders at WVU feel the pressure to "get it right this time." We hope others do as well.

Leading Economic Change in America's Communities

2004

After nine years as president, I was invited back to the community where I had previously worked to speak at the annual meeting of the community foundation. I had served as the volunteer chair of the foundation before becoming president. The topic was volunteer leadership of positive change in the communities of our state; many of these communities are struggling to establish new industries and quality job opportunities.

The subject matter you have assigned me is a bit daunting: what is the role of leadership in changing our community?

Over the years, I have read dozens of books on topics related to leadership. My library is filled with biographies and history books that take a serious look at leaders. I have also had wonderful opportunities during my career to meet and confer with many of the men and women who study leadership for a living. I am around leaders in many domains of expertise, including political leaders, college presidents, coaches, labor leaders, and business leaders. We talk a lot about the subject.

But to be honest, most leadership literature and most conversations about leadership focus on leaders who have a position and who are charged with leading a specific type of organization such as the army, a university, a hospital, a governmental unit, or a business.

The challenge of leading a civic community is really much more complex. Communities contain many different cultures, citizens with different goals and aspirations, and many different organizations, each with their own leaders. Facilitating change in a community seems to me a more difficult leadership challenge than leading a single organization.

I want to suggest that community leadership is a four-step process. Those four steps are:

- Building the case for change
- Establishing a clear vision for the community
- Empowering others to act in furtherance of the vision
- Celebrating those who advance that vision

Let me begin with James McGregor Burn's famous 1976 definition of leadership: motivating others to act in their own self-interest. More recent authors suggest that change is always involved when people lead. To paraphrase one writer, change is about leading people from A to B. Think of Lincoln and King; both changed America. One had an official position of governmental leadership, the other did not. But things were different after they led, and our society is better because we moved from A to B with their leadership. Burns's look at famous leaders in many different domains suggested to him that leadership involves calling on others to act in a way that is good for them in the long run. He argues that the best leaders educate those they lead. He is also well known for the notion that in leadership settings, people often take turns leading. He suggests that great leaders stand on the shoulders of those they lead.[26] Burns would argue that good leaders are, first and foremost, good teachers.

It seems to me that if community leaders are intent on changing things, they must first build the case for change. Community leaders seeking transformational change should speak out loudly and clearly on why change is needed. This is a teaching mission. Leaders must spend time stating clearly why it is in the community's best interest to change. Sometimes this takes years.

Jon Meacham, editor of *Newsweek*, recently spoke at a WVU forum in Charleston about the principal characters of his new book, *Winston and Franklin*. Recalling their uncanny ability to speak with candor and in simple, straightforward language, he reminded us of the importance of clarity of message when change is being sought, no matter how complex the issue is—whether it is world peace or city zoning.

In 1996, at a press conference and at dozens of subsequent meetings, I announced our intent to change the culture of the campus community. The campus was not sure that it wanted to hear the message—we were challenging belief systems and years of an embedded culture.

It took years to get the point across—years of speaking, years of meetings, and years of public forums. It took the help of many people from within the WVU community. These leaders were committed to change and shared our belief that we needed to change if we were going to survive in the competitive environment that is higher education. We all became patient champions for change.

The point is that cultural change requires us to enlist the help of others who believe a better state of affairs can and should be realized. One final note on this point—community change advocates must be people with the perceived moral authority to speak on behalf of the community, and they must speak the truth, without pulling punches and yet without arrogance. They need to come from all sectors of the community and say clearly what is wrong. In the end, I think you will be surprised at how fast a community can change once there is a collective will to change it. In sum, when change is required, articulate the need, enlist help of others who are respected, be clear, and do not mince words.

NECESSARY CHANGES

This brings up the next logical question:

* What changes are needed?
* Where do we want to go?
* What needs to change?
* If this is A, where is B?

For change to occur, a collective vision of the desired future state of things must be held out in front of the community that is being asked to change, and that vision must be a more desirable state than the current situation. Vision has enormous power to motivate change. Think of JFK: "We will put an astronaut on the moon and return him safely to earth within this decade." Think of Martin Luther King Jr.: "I have a dream today that my four little children will one day live in a nation where they will not be judged by the color of their skin but by the content of their character."

ESTABLISHING VISION

How do we establish that vision? At the heart of every successful vision for any community is a collective determination to serve the real needs of that community. True vision is always needs-based. People respond to a vision when they believe it would meet their needs if the vision were realized. Visions are forged in the crucible of public debate among persons of goodwill who yield their own beliefs to a bigger and better idea when it is put forward, no matter who puts it forward. The Kanawha Valley has proven that when it has a vision, it can get the job done.

Just one note of caution: one lesson of leadership we have learned at WVU is that when change wants to happen, we must let it happen. Our nugget of an idea was the vision that we could be more student centered. We suggested a few things, but we have accomplished much more than we dreamed of because many were involved in further refining and defining the vision and making it their own. Other leaders emerged from inside, and outside, the university community. They were not held back or constrained. In fact, they were encouraged. Their vision was built on our original vision,which led to an even bigger vision.

Perhaps the foundation, or a group of organizations, could sponsor a visioning process for the community, extended over many months. If so, the coordinating group should be truly representative and ably led by persons who care more about the future than the past. The organizers should be given a clear charge to ask questions of importance:

- Who needs to be involved in shaping the future of our community?
- What are the challenges we face?
- What would the Valley look like, feel like, and, in fact, be if it were a better place?
- What changes need to be made in order to make this a better place than it is today?
- How long will it take us to change?
- Who should be involved?
- What are appropriate mile markers on the road to our future?

Heifetz and Linsky, in their book *Leadership on the Line*, remind us that there are really two kinds of changes: technical change and adaptive change. Technical changes are ones that authorities can accomplish if we but identify the needs. They address things that can be fixed, such as when people say, "We need a stop light here! We need more parking there! We need a new park here! We need a new road there!" To accomplish technical changes, authorities simply apply current know-how and go to work. On the other hand, adaptive change requires us to change ourselves and often the way we think.

Adaptive change is what some would call cultural change. If the closeness of a community has eroded, the job of changing the community is an adaptive one—it requires a transformation of the culture:

- We need to listen and communicate better.
- We need to include new faces in our organizations.
- We need to examine the way we govern ourselves in this community.
- We need to redefine our community to include others previously omitted.

We need to ask:

- Are we spending public and private money on the right things?
- Do we value education enough?
- Do we need to be honest with our political leaders?
- Do we need to lessen the acrimony when we debate—and reintroduce civility and respect while increasing our passion and commitment?
- How can we be recognized as hosting America's best capital city?
- Can we be known as a city with a surplus of leaders, all committed to the common good?

The vision will need to have some details and some specific goals and objectives. But more than anything else, it will need to harness people's imaginations. It will need to help people see what they can become if they can but change their own patterns of behavior and think in new ways. A good vision will contemplate some fixes, to be sure, but a powerful vision will contemplate the community changing its own character. The exact nature of your vision is something only you can define, but it is clearly within your grasp. I can promise you this: the very act of trying to define that vision will change the community for the better. Victor Frankl, in *Man's Search for Meaning*, asserted that if we find the why's in life, the how's will take care of themselves.[27] When a visioning process really works, people will understand the need for change. The changes, both technical and adaptive, will follow.

Let me address the final points together, because both are derived from what I consider to be essential elements of what we call human nature. A vibrant community will both empower its major constituencies to act in furtherance of the vision and celebrate good examples of those who, by their actions, represent achievement of the vision.

We all like to have some say in our own future, and we appreciate it when others help us achieve our dreams. Moreover, we all like to be praised, and we experience joy when others celebrate our successes. People work harder when they are praised than when they are criticized. People innovate when empowered, and they stagnate when they are overmanaged. The more they are praised, the more motivated they become. These two fundamental aspects of human nature, while obviously true, are often overlooked.

One obvious lesson of these truths is that we need to look around every community in West Virginia to see if we are doing everything we can to empower those who want to make something of themselves and their communities. Laws may need to be changed. Linkages must be forged. Collaborations must be fostered. We may just need to get out of the way of those who have the will to succeed; and once individuals and organizations succeed, we need to include them—not just our traditional leaders—in our celebrations.

Our WVU campus community offers awards every year to outstanding teachers, students, administrators, alumni, donors, and staff members. Giving awards takes time; choosing from among deserving candidates and planning effective celebrations takes time. But many people and organizations are honored because many people help lead WVU. In the Morgantown area, one hundred people are honored every year for their innovative spirit and achievements. I have never heard of some of these people before the awards are announced, but their lives and their work are important. I should know of them, and the local paper tells me about them.

Our awards hold up positive examples for others to see. They reward excellence with honors and sometimes cash. They encourage young people and gratify older ones. Ask yourself if you are doing enough to recognize and reward innovation in the Valley. Perhaps you are. Perhaps you are not. I just know this: celebration pays big dividends. In the words of leadership writer James Kouzes, who will be the keynote speaker at next month's leadership conference, sponsored in part by WVU, "People become exhausted, frustrated and disenchanted . . . It's part of the leader's job to show appreciation for people's contributions and to create a culture of celebration."[28]

There is so much more to say and no more time to say it. Let me just leave you with this final thought: founding West Virginia in the aftermath of a civil war that divided our state was not easy. Transforming Charleston and the Valley from a frontier town to an economic engine around the turn of the twentieth century was difficult. Getting this region through the Depression was extremely challenging. Leading the Valley through World War II was a struggle. Unifying the community in the 1960s and 1970s presented major challenges. And beginning the Greater Kanawha Valley Foundation with just a few early contributions and amassing $105 million in assets was not easy. We live in hard times, but they are our times. Others have faced their challenges. We will face ours.

To conquer our challenges, we must recognize the need to change and create a compelling vision that contemplates an optimistic and positive future. We must involve and empower others, including those who have not been involved before, to act in furtherance of the vision, and we must reward and celebrate the successes that will inevitably follow. Thank you for honoring me with this invitation. I know the greater Kanawha Valley; as Winston Churchill said, you will never give in. The Greater Kanawha Valley will be a better place because of your determination to make it so.

NOTES

1   Alex Stuart, "Water for Profit," *CFO* 23, no. 2 (February 2007): 40–45.

2   Ronald L. Lewis, *Transforming the Appalachian Countryside: Railroads, Deforestation, and Social Change in West Virginia, 1880–1920* (Chapel Hill, NC: University of North Carolina Press, 1998).

3   Lewis, *Transforming the Appalachian Countryside,* 7.

4   Lewis, *Transforming the Appalachian Countryside,* 7.

5   Stephen Ambrose, *Nothing Like It in the World: The Men Who Built the Transcontinental Railroad, 1863–1869* (New York: Simon and Schuster, 2000).

6   Lewis, *Transforming the Appalachian Countryside,* 3, 5.

7   Lewis, *Transforming the Appalachian Countryside,* 27.

8   Lewis, *Transforming the Appalachian Countryside,* 35.

9   Lewis, *Transforming the Appalachian Countryside,* 53.

10   *Manufacturers' Record* (1906), quoted in Lewis, *Transforming the Appalachian Countryside,* 57.

11   Lewis, *Transforming the Appalachian Countryside,* 81.

12   Lewis, *Transforming the Appalachian Countryside,* 107.

13   Lewis, *Transforming the Appalachian Countryside,* 85.

14   Lewis, *Transforming the Appalachian Countryside,* 213.

15   Granville Davisson Hall, *The Rending of Virginia: A History,* ed. John Edmund Stealey III (1902; Knoxville: University of Tennessee Press, 2000), 614–615.

16   Lewis, *Transforming the Appalachian Countryside*, 193.

17   Lewis, *Transforming the Appalachian Countryside*, 5.

18   Lewis, *Transforming the Appalachian Countryside*, 8.

19   Lewis, *Transforming the Appalachian Countryside*, 262, 9.

20   Lewis, *Transforming the Appalachian Countryside*, 146.

21   Lewis, *Transforming the Appalachian Countryside*, 277.

22   Lewis, *Transforming the Appalachian Countryside*, 234.

23   Lewis, *Transforming the Appalachian Countryside*, 205.

24   Lewis, *Transforming the Appalachian Countryside*, 290.

25   William T. Doherty Jr. and Festus P. Summers, *West Virginia University: Symbol of Unity in a Sectionalized State* (Morgantown: West Virginia University Press, 1982).

26   James MacGregor Burns, *Leadership* (New York: Harper and Row, 1978), 443.

27   A paraphrase of Friedrich Nietzsche, quoted in Frankl, *Man's Search for Meaning*, 9.

28   James M. Kouzes and Barry Z. Posner, *The Leadership Challenge: How to Get Extraordinary Things Done in Organizations* (3rd ed.; San Francisco: Jossey-Bass Publishers, 2003), 19.

PART FOUR

EDUCATION AND EXPERIENCE

PREPARING FOR LEADERSHIP

While the vast majority of individuals approach the academic presidency after a lifetime of teaching and academic administration, there are other avenues for those who aspire to lead an institution. In addition to law, successful candidates have come from charitable foundations, elective politics, government, business, and other fields. There appears to be no definitive path to the academic presidency. According to a survey published in the November 2005 issue of the *Chronicle of Higher Education*:

> [F]or all the demands on presidents, the position does not require the grasp of a discrete body of knowledge or the attainment of a specific degree. There is no clear route to the presidency, and the job has been filled successfully, and unsuccessfully, by scholars, business leaders, fund raisers, lawyers and priests. Almost a third of the respondents to the survey came to the presidency from the position of provost or chief academic officer, 22 percent from a presidency elsewhere, and 22 percent from a nonacademic vice presidency at a college or university. While those results indicate that a traditional academic background is still preferred, the high number of nonacademic administrators who

become presidents reflects the growing focus on legislative relations, fund raising, and other external issues.[1]

According to the 2007 American Council of Education survey of college presidents, the typical background of higher-education presidents has shifted a bit in recent years, with 31.4 percent having served as a chief academic officer or provost and 21.4 percent having served as a president prior to their current appointment.[2] Fewer presidents move directly to their role from a position as a faculty member, chair, or senior academic affairs executive. Successful candidates must be prepared for the rigors and demands of the office despite the differences in their backgrounds.

The ACE survey indicates that over 85 percent of presidents are over fifty and under seventy, reflecting both the maturity and energy the office demands.[3] The *Chronicle of Higher Education* survey identifies the challenges of the job today as fundraising, dealing with public officials, budgeting, governance, faculty matters, enrollment concerns, alumni relations, and the overall pace of the job.[4] Of these challenges, fundraising, financial management, community relations, and strategic planning occupy the most time.[5]

The selection process seems to ferret out people who understand the mission of the institution with which they are matched, have credentials and experiences that are appealing to the selection committees, have the skills of modern leadership, and who have the values honored within the institution and the academy.

On a few public occasions, I have reflected on my own preparation for leadership positions. Like other leaders, I was prepared by the values I was taught by my parents and other family members; a very fine formal education in the public school system and at West Virginia University, Oxford University, and Harvard Law School; my work as a professional; and my firm belief in the transforming value of public education, including public higher education.

One of my mentors was the former chancellor of the University System of West Virginia, James Rowley. When I decided to submit my resume for consideration, he advised me to think deeply about the nature of the academic presidency and my own unique preparation for it. This is advice I readily pass on to others interested in the academic presidency today. Preparation for the modern presidency is both a set of experiences and a set of attitudes and habits of mind. These can be acquired in any number of ways.

Below are a few of the speeches and essays in which I have reflected on what prepared me for the presidency of a major public university. In a couple of cases, the reflections are intensely personal, but I feel certain that they are reflective, at least in their tone, of the thoughts of others as well.

TWENTY-FIVE

REFLECTIONS ON OUR JOURNEY TO SERVICE

Most leaders believe that the experiences of early life and, most importantly, their family environment—whether positive or negative—strongly influence their attitudes toward life, their willingness to learn, their willingness to stand under the strong spotlight that leadership attracts, and much more. I first began reflecting on this topic during my undergraduate years, when I wrote a paper for Dr. Leonard David, one of my public-speaking professors, entitled "The Influence of Fathers on Their Sons in British Oratory."

More than anything else, our parents' lives were lived to give us the opportunity to attend college and become contributing members of society. This they did, and as they did so, the values they held were evident. These values have greatly influenced our lives and the lives of our children.

DAUGHTER OF THE YEAR
West Virginia Society of Washington, D.C.

By Susan B. Hardesty

1997

I delivered these remarks in response to being designated Daughter of the Year by the West Virginia Society of Washington, D.C. David received the Son of the Year award on the same night. We were the first couple honored at the same time in the history of the society. The West Virginia Society is one of many groups in Washington that provides events where expatriates gather for conversation, and to consider the needs of people back home as well as the contributions of their states to the collective leadership of the nation. Attendees include persons born or raised in the various states or working in or around Washington in various government offices.

Typically, the West Virginia Society asks the honorees to reflect on their lives and the role that West Virginia institutions, friends, and families played in their development.

—Susan B. Hardesty

David and I have traveled a long road together. This is the first time we have been honored as a team. We are grateful to the West Virginia Society for this honor and want you to know that we are proud to be West Virginians and proud to be serving West Virginia together.

After thinking about tonight for many months, I realize that my message is really quite simple: West Virginia is one big community. That community feeling is the reason we are here tonight. West Virginians care about one another. Time and time again, I have seen West Virginians join together voluntarily to support one another, and I have often been the beneficiary of that support.

The first West Virginians who taught me to care about other West Virginians were my parents, Carolyn and Clifford Brown. My parents bled gold and blue, and they instilled in me pride in West Virginia and its flagship university. I was raised a faculty brat in Morgantown where my father began his WVU career as a student during the Depression and went on to become an assistant director of the WVU band. He completed his career in Morgantown thirty-five years later as the assistant dean of the College of Creative Arts.

I attended the WVU Elementary Laboratory School, also known as "the Little Red School House," which was a tiny two-room school next to the old basketball coliseum where "Hot Rod" Hundley and Jerry West played. We were encouraged to think and to achieve in that little school. There were fewer than fifty students. Student teachers "practiced" on us, psychology students analyzed our responses to ink spots, and we were among the first second graders in America to be taught French as an experiment by the WVU Language Department. I remember loving school, feeling successful, and knowing by fifth grade that I wanted to teach elementary music.

Our home was always filled with WVU students my father advised and faculty members who were family friends. Most of my friends were university children. I well remember my mother debating which white gloves she should wear to a tea that President and Mrs. Irvin Stewart were hosting. She was active in Campus Club and the Music Club, was an elementary school teacher, and never missed a WVU concert or ball game with my father. My father was keenly aware of campus politics as well as statehouse activities that affected education.

I grew up loving West Virginia. I have memories of little things that developed that sense of pride. I don't ever remember a trip when our family didn't pass the time in the car singing West Virginia songs. My father often sang us to sleep by singing the alma mater. My parents, who were from Fayette County, Pennsylvania, were proud to be West Virginians and were always optimistic about our state's future. I remember my father working very hard to make sure that my remarks to the state legislature when I was governor of Girls State were appropriately laudatory of West Virginia.

My parents were close partners, just as David and I are. They were, therefore, very happy when I met David during our freshmen year at WVU, and they were even happier when we married five years later. David and I went through school together at WVU. We were both leaders. We were lucky to mature together and remain close during that maturation. We grew to love our alma mater together, marrying in Morgantown in 1968. Our reception was held at the newly built Mountainlair.

During the first years of our marriage, we lived in England and in Boston, and we were able to view our state from outside. There was hard work and excitement in our years abroad and in New England, but there always was that tug—that nudge—to get back to the mountains, to the seasons, and to our families and the people of West Virginia. It's that same tug that we hope our two children, and many other children, will feel. In fact, I think it is that tug that motivates West Virginians living in Washington to gather together on nights like tonight and to serve their state while living away from it. We are one big community of West Virginians who care about each other.

I want to tell you about three incidences in my life when I have witnessed West Virginians working together and volunteering in this spirit of community. I have been an educator all of my life—first as a music teacher and later as a special education teacher. I have taught in several school systems: Morgantown; Oxford, England; Lexington and Woburn, Massachusetts; Charleston; and Jackson County. My professional work has led me to see the value of volunteerism in our society, and I have tried to volunteer my time and leadership in projects that would enrich educational experiences.

My interest in music and education led me to stay connected with WVU's College of Creative Arts. In 1985, while driving home from Charleston to Ripley, David and I talked about how exciting it would be to bring the Mountaineer marching band to Charleston for a concert. We wanted everyone in the Kanawha Valley to experience the thrill of "the Pride."

I mentioned this idea to Phil Faini, the highly energetic and successful dean of the Creative Arts Center. He could have said, "No, we can't possibly move four hundred band students just for a concert. No, the band never does a sit-down concert outside of Morgantown. No, there's not enough money." But those of you who know Phil know he said, "That's a great idea. Let's do it!"

With the help of volunteers, and funding from Russ Isaacs and several others, the first annual WVU band concert in Charleston was launched. For the past ten years, Mike Perry and BankOne have completely funded the Keynotes Concerts in Morgantown and Charleston, and the concerts are now a part of WVU Days. More than 82,800 West Virginians have attended those concerts. A more important number to note is that 481 groups of high school and junior high band students have attended these concerts and been inspired by the Pride. This concert is now organized by WVU, but the groundwork for this highly successful program was originally laid by a group of volunteers—selling tickets door to door, contacting band directors from their home phones, and developing advertising strategies over the kitchen table. The concert is truly the result of West Virginians joining together to support a community project.

Another project with which I have been identified demonstrates again this sense of community. My professional work in special education interested me in literacy, which in turn led to an interest in the Read Aloud program founded by Jim Trelease of Springfield, Massachusetts. The premise of Read Aloud is that if children are read to at an early age, they will develop a love of literature and a thirst for knowledge. The Read Aloud West Virginia program was started in Kanawha County around 1986 by Mary Kay Bond and a group of volunteers, many of whom I had met during my volunteer days in Charleston.

Following their lead, I saw a need for this program in Jackson County. In the spring of 1988, I approached ten community leaders in Jackson County to ask for their help. Every single one of them said, "Yes!" By the time school children finished the fall semester that year, we had 155 volunteers from the community reading aloud in almost every elementary classroom in Jackson County. Ministers, doctors, grandparents, school board members, the mayor, bankers, retired school teachers, the superintendent—all of them reading aloud to school children and making the statement that reading is fun and worth all the work it takes to become a reader. The program quickly spread to nearby counties. Because of the work of volunteers all over West Virginia, a grant was eventually secured from the Benedum Foundation to develop a statewide Read Aloud program under the umbrella of the West Virginia Education Fund. Almost every county in West Virginia now has a Read Aloud program improving literacy in West Virginia and totally driven by community volunteers.

Over the past two years, I have been most closely identified with another volunteer-related effort. I owe it to my sister Nancy, a WVU graduate now living in Houston, who came home to visit us shortly after David's nomination. She brought video tapes of the Aggie marching band with her. Her son goes to Texas A&M, and she thought we'd like to hear their band. She made us watch the tape for two hours, and while we watched, Nancy talked and talked about Texas A&M. She knew everything there was to know about the Aggies because she was a member of the Texas A&M Mothers Club. She was an "Aggie Mom."

Right then, David and I realized we had nothing like this at WVU. We had no way for parents, especially non-WVU parents or parents who had never attended college, to connect with their students or with the university. How were they supposed to know where to park, how to ride the PRT, where their students could get tutoring help, where the good apartments were, what concerts were available for their students? How could they learn about the history and traditions of our flagship institution?

We knew that night that if David was appointed president, we would create an organization that would help connect parents with the university so they could be supportive of their students. After a year and a half, I can proudly report that we have nearly three thousand families who have joined the Mountaineer Parents Club.

We have clubs in twenty-five counties in West Virginia and twenty-one clubs throughout Maryland, New Jersey, Pennsylvania, Ohio, Virginia, and New York—all chaired by parent volunteers who have called me and said, "I want to start a Mountaineer Parents Club in my town."

When speaking to the Board of Visitors of the CAC last year about the Parents Club, a member of the board spoke up and asked if there was a club in Washington, DC. When I responded, "No, not yet," she said, "Well, there is now. I'll start one for you!" My warmest thanks to Edna Falbo, your society's chair, for chairing our DC club.

Last month I mentioned in our Parents Club newsletter that we'd like to have WVU parents around the country serving as state chairs to help parents in their states connect with each other and with the university. Within two weeks, volunteers had called from Oregon, Delaware, Connecticut, Florida, Illinois, Massachusetts, South Carolina, Utah, Ohio, and Virginia.

WVU parents are networking with each other, hosting faculty members for club programs, coming to campus together for athletic and cultural events as well as special campus tours, and are now beginning to recruit students and their parents. I am happy to report that there is now a place for parents at WVU. This effort truly demonstrates that West Virginia University families want to be involved and want to be a part of the WVU community. We at WVU value them and want them to be at the heart of our efforts.

Even more importantly, the Mountaineer Parents Club has become a vital part of David's efforts to create a student-centered university. Right from the start, parents are working as vital partners to give each of our students every possible chance to succeed. We are sending a strong message at WVU: you are never alone. David has helped us get the Parents Club started, but then again, he has always helped me do what I really wanted to do. He has been West Virginia's best gift to me. He has guided me, encouraged me, challenged me, liberated me, and supported me since we met as WVU freshmen thirty-four years ago. We have loved each other's families and have shared many smiles and tears together while raising our two children, Ashley and Carter.

David has set a high standard for our family. I love the phrase, "Character is what you are when no one is watching." I can tell you that David's character is the finest of anyone I have ever met. I see David when no one is watching. I am proud to be the president's spouse and welcome the opportunities that David's position has opened for me to serve my university. By honoring us together, you recognize that we are a family working together for West Virginia, just like many of you here tonight.

Thank you for honoring me and for helping me to realize how very fortunate I am to be in West Virginia, at our university, with my family, doing something that is so meaningful and fulfilling to me.

I spoke of the songs of West Virginia that my family sang as we traveled. I want to end with one that says it all:

I want to wake up in the morning
Where the Rhododendron grows
Where the sun comes a-creepin'
Into where I'm a-sleepin' and the
Songbirds sing hello.
I want to wander, through the wild woods

Where the fragrant breezes grow

And drift back to the mountains,

Where the Rhododendron grows.[6]

I am proud to be from West Virginia and am deeply grateful to be recognized as your Daughter of the Year.

SON OF THE YEAR

West Virginia Society of Washington, D.C.

1997

In 1997, Susan and I were the first couple honored together as Daughter and Son of the Year by the West Virginia Society of Washington, D.C. This recognition caused me to once again reflect on the support I have received during my lifetime by the people of my state, my family, my friends, my teachers, and my mentors.

There is a new showplace for West Virginian arts and crafts at the Beckley exit of the West Virginia Turnpike. It is called Tamarack, after a pine tree, and it is advertised as offering "the best of West Virginia." Tamarack sells only the best—juried arts and crafts. These special products are offered at commensurate prices to customers who patronize this innovative outlet for mountain artisans.

As I pondered why you would honor me tonight, I looked back on my life and came to the conclusion that I must have been truly blessed by "the best of West Virginia." I am absolutely delighted that you would honor Susan and me. We are humbled to be the center of your attention. But I truly believe that it is not me, or us, but rather our beloved state that is the object of your affection. For if I am anything, I am the product of the best our state has to offer.

First, I come from a really good, even wonderful, West Virginia family. It is not particularly famous and certainly not rich. It has its share of rogues and failures, with a sprinkling of shining stars. In the recipe of genetics and experiences that make it up, it offered me as much love, wisdom, and nurturing as any family could.

My dad's family hails from Shinnston, where it has lived for many generations. Coming to the United States when it was still colonies, in 1775, our ancestors have worked in West Virginia since long before it was a state. My father is, more than anything else, a man of character. I have never known him to cheat or lie to another human being. He was raised during the Great Depression, served in World War II with five other siblings who reached adulthood, and worked hard all of his life. He has been a town councilman, a small business man, a government inspector, a faithful employee, a library volunteer, and a loyal churchman of the same church his family attended since its founding. He is not college educated, but like many of his generation, he knows the value of education and has always impressed it upon his children.

My mother was born in the Deep South—Mississippi to be exact—and came to Shinnston from modest circumstances with a heart as big as one can imagine. She met Dad while studying nursing during the war and came home with him to West Virginia to be part of a large and imposing family. She raised four children from their marriage and worked as the town's nurse both before and after her children were raised. To her own detriment, and everyone else's delight, she was and still is full of empathy, sympathy, and caring. She loves everyone. Most everyone loves her.

These wonderful parents gave their children many gifts—a strong work ethic, a family reputation for honesty and the desire to maintain it, a sense of civic responsibility, family loyalty, a sense of the true importance of friendship, respect for older people, a sense of obligation to young people, a love of travel, and, above all, a sense that one can achieve goals through hard and honest work.

We grew up modestly, amid family triumphs and failures. But we were given love that I can only imagine is the "best of West Virginia," if not the best in the world. This love is a great reservoir of strength for me and my two brothers and sister today, and will be until we die.

Secondly, I came from a great community in the Mountain State—one of the best: Shinnston. It mounted many community-based youth organizations, like the church groups and Boy Scouts of which I became a part. In these groups, I sprouted my "leadership wings." In Shinnston, decisions had long-term impacts. In time, good decisions paid dividends, and bad decisions had adverse consequences. In Shinnston were role models and mentors who continue helping me to this day. In it were people of different countries, ethnic backgrounds, and creeds. They taught me not just to appreciate, but to look for the contributions of those who were different from me.

Consider these words about her father by Meredith Sue Willis, my childhood friend—now a celebrated author living in New York:

> To my father, Shinnston, West Virginia, represented grand new vistas. This was the great world to him in a way city people can hardly imagine. Shinnston had folks from Syria and Spain and Yugoslavia. Shinnston had a mansion on a hill built by an Italian immigrant, and a dark little shop in town where an elderly Jew repaired shoes. My father says the first day he was in Shinnston, he met Dave Hardesty, who told him: "We have a real tall man here in town named Short, and we have a little short man named Long. There's a black man named White and a white man named Black." A town of wonders: everything was possible.
>
> My father's stories of boyhood and growing up in West Virginia have a tone of nostalgia. . . . The Shinnston boyhood stories are like an intense, Technicolor version of the *Our Gang* comedies. Oh, the funny things they did. The jokes they

played. Those Scotch-Irish Hardestys and black Junior Mayfield and the Italian Romeos. It seems in my father's stories that the world is populated by boys, and all the boys are equal in the rough-and-tumble of their adventuring.[7]

Shinnston was a dying town, economically speaking, when I was growing up. People were leaving as the mines and plants of West Virginia closed, but the habits of success formed over many generations were still there—civic pride, a sense of communal caring for every member of the community, and an obligation to future generations. Fortunately, my town survived and has even made a comeback of sorts. Today, it raises up new generations of young people as it raised mine. This community helped me become what I am. I am immensely grateful to it and its people. Sometimes I feel like the whole town nurtured me to maturity.

Third, I was given a fine education in West Virginia. The public school teachers I had were very good, especially in history, speech, social studies, and English, subjects that have proven critical in my career. I got an old-fashioned education, which included Latin and French, science and math. It was "sturdy" in a sense—it gave me the abilities I needed to succeed. It also gave me the opportunity to play football, be in a band, serve as a student leader, and sing in a choir. It was an education that I am not sure one can get as easily today. When I speak to groups in Shinnston, I still ask those who were teachers when I was in school to stand for applause. Several always come to hear me speak, as if I could have something to say to them. In fact, I still use the lessons they taught me every day.

I went on to the state's flagship university in Morgantown, after considering briefly West Virginia Wesleyan and an out-of-state school. It was a good—no, a great—decision for me. I was taught by good faculty, but more importantly, I was instilled with the belief that I could be what I wanted to be. True or not, I believed it. I eventually had the audacity to run for student body president, and I won. This led to my being selected a Rhodes Scholar and then to degrees from two internationally recognized universities, Harvard and Oxford.

Today, as it did thirty years ago, WVU takes the youth of fifty states and a hundred nations long distances, from "I can't" to "I can." There was richness in my experience at WVU. I took classes from a former president, Irwin Stewart, and got to know several faculty members very well. I met students from around the country and around the world. I was challenged to think and to serve. Again and again I was exposed to different people and different ideas. Today I am greatly influenced by the notion that certain elements of a good education are timeless and beyond the reach of current circumstance. I believe in public education to the core of my being, and I am deeply indebted to it. I want each man and woman of our current student body to feel the same way in thirty years.

Fourth, West Virginia has afforded me the best opportunities for growth as a leader and as a professional, primarily through the efforts of friends and mentors. I was helped along my career by many people and their generosities. Some, such as Mike Benedum and William J. Maier, you may have heard of. Their philanthropy helped to fund my education.

But there were so many others—people who opened doors of opportunity and windows of new horizons for me—all in West Virginia. My partners in the practice of law in Charleston showed me how to achieve world class excellence in an Appalachian setting. My clients—as diverse as the United Methodist Church, the West Virginia Bankers Association, big companies, start-up businesses, and young people in big trouble—taught me the true joy of service to others. Public servants in West Virginia, like Jay Rockefeller and Gaston Caperton, gave me the opportunity to fulfill my burning desire to put my education to work in the service of my state. Others, like Robert Byrd, help me to serve my state today. In my current position I have come to deeply respect, appreciate, and celebrate our congressional delegation. They too are the best.

My closest personal friends are a treasure to me, and they include many of my generation who have themselves achieved much in serving others. As I seek to do my best for West Virginia, West Virginians including my brothers and sister, Glen Hiner, Hank Barnett, Joe and Kay Goodwin, Harry Heflin, George Bennett, Howard Hardesty, my colleagues at WVU, and the leadership of your society still mentor me and push me toward making WVU all that it can be, by urging me to be all that I can be.

There was a turning point in my career when I had to decide where I would spend my professional career. It didn't last long, but it was there. I—I should say, "we"—decided to come "home to West Virginia." What a good choice it was. I have never wanted for opportunity because there is so much to do. There are not really enough of us to do it.

I feel truly optimistic about West Virginia. I am lucky to feel so closely attached to it and to be identified with its future. If I could give each young person in our state the feeling that they could find their opportunity in "our home among the hills," I would. Opportunity lies within the spirit of each individual, and I am convinced that it also resides collectively within the people who now make up the leadership of our state.

Finally, but mostly, I was given a gift from God when Susan agreed to be my wife. She is truly a woman of great strength, who has grown stronger with each year of our marriage. Like all couples, we have faced some truly difficult times together. But we have shared much joy together. I know that I would not be here tonight but for her constant love and artful persuasion.

The daughter of a WVU faculty member of some forty years, she shares with me a love for WVU, West Virginia, and our current calling—and for us, it is a calling. People are attracted to her generous personality and amazing capacity for work. She has always been a wonderful volunteer, friend, and leader. Sometimes I am amazed she married me. When people say that I am a "perfect fit" for WVU, as they sometimes do, I know what they mean. They mean that

Susan so complements my skills that my own frailties are often overlooked in an effort to keep Susan happy. She, too, is truly "the best of West Virginia." Of that I am certain.

Our marriage led to the creation of a family, and I want to say that I learn from my children each day. They are special. They keep me centered. I love them so much! In their sorrows and joys I am constantly reminded of my obligations not just to them but also to the twenty-nine thousand other young people who are students at our university. Together Susan and I have raised Ashley and Carter, grown to maturity, obtained five college degrees, traveled extensively, met the queen of England and presidents of the United States, faced serious illnesses and tragedies, moved from place to place, and gone from job to job. We've made mistakes together. We've been lucky together. But we have always done it together. I can't imagine being president of our alma mater without her.

So, in my life, I have encountered the "best of West Virginia." I humbly hope that you will take under advisement several potential lessons in my story, which has been repeated thousands of times in our state. Love, community, family, service to others, civic responsibility, and friends helping friends are at the core of true success for our nation and, I believe, true happiness for its citizens. Certainly young people can be shown the way to success by caring people who take the time to be a mentor, teacher, and role model. And as importantly, opportunity is available wherever and whenever we individually and collectively decide that it should be available.

NOTES

1   Rita Bornstein, "The Nature and Nurture of Presidents," *The Chronicle of Higher Education* 52, no.11(2005), http://chronicle.com (accessed November 17, 2006).

2   Audrey Williams June, "Presidents: Same Look, Different Decade," *The Chronicle of Higher Education*, February 16, 2007: A35.

3   June, "Presidents: Same Look, Different Decade," A35.

4   Bornstein, "The Nature and Nurture of Presidents."

5   June, "Presidents: Same Look, Different Decade," A35.

6   Traditional West Virginian folk song.

7   Meredith Sue Willis, *The Mountains of America* (San Francisco: Mercury House, 1994), 4–5.

TWENTY-SIX

REFLECTIONS ON UNDERGRADUATE GROWTH

FOR THE 125TH ANNIVERSARY OF WOODBURN HALL

2001

Every state university has its own set of traditions and a history of which its alumni are justifiably proud. These are held most dear by undergraduates. Presidents are often called upon to recall and memorialize institutional traditions and values and in doing so, lift up significant faculty, stories, programs, buildings, events, and alumni in the life of the university. As president, I was presented with such an opportunity in 2001 when I was invited to speak at an event celebrating the 125th anniversary of West Virginia University's signature building, Woodburn Hall.

In preparing these remarks, I relied on a variety of historical sources, including "West Virginia University: Symbol of Unity in a Sectionalized State," by William T. Doherty Jr. and Festus P. Summers, and other sources mentioned in the text.[1] I also had just received and read a copy of the "1900 Monticola," the university yearbook, which an alumnus gave me to present to the West

Virginia collection in our library.[2] *The collection is a rich source of information for those interested in the history of Appalachia, the state of West Virginia, and the university itself. I also relied heavily on my own understanding of the importance of undergraduate education at the university. Susan and I were students at West Virginia University from 1963 to 1967, during the presidency of Paul Miller and the acting presidency of Harry Heflin. It was an exciting time for young people in general and college students in particular.*

At WVU, we were fortunate to be exposed to wonderful teachers and mentors, inside and outside the classroom. I eventually became student body president. As I mentioned in my inaugural address decades later, I went to the university from the public schools of a small town in West Virginia and left four years later, prepared for the rigors of Oxford and Harvard. My story has been repeated millions of times across America in other states and at other public land-grant universities.

West Virginia University has produced twenty-five Rhodes Scholars, of which I was the sixteenth. In the 1980s, several were asked to reflect on the impact that West Virginia University had on their academic preparation and leadership potential. The themes of my response offer a personal glimpse of the importance of undergraduate education at West Virginia University.

By that time in my career, it was apparent to me that West Virginia University had been the right choice for me. Had I gone to the university in a different year; had the university been in a different stage of development; had the students, faculty, and staff not been of a particular mold, then my career, both at the university and elsewhere, would have followed a much different course. For me, West Virginia University was the right institution at the right time. Not for several years would I realize how fortunate I was to have followed my intuition.

I was interested in government, politics, and law, and so I majored in political science. In the College of Arts and Sciences, housed for well over a century in Woodburn Hall, I found an academic challenge that I could meet, but only if I put forth effort. I particularly remember courses taught by professors John R. Williams, Wesley M. Bagby, John F. Stasny, Leonard Davis, and Irvin Stewart. By my senior year, I felt that I was grasping the essentials of the material presented to me in class and gaining insights that would serve as the basis for future academic work. Gradually, I matured and developed academically. In another institution, the academic challenge might have been too great; in others, not great enough.

There was another, and perhaps even more important, sphere in which I developed at the university. I will call it personal growth, and I believe that all individuals who have attended a university look back on the time they spent there and sense this growth. To me, the university seemed large, diversified, full of energy, and perhaps even cosmopolitan. I met new friends from around the state and country and a few from around the world. These friendships, which were developed early in my career at the university, broadened my interests and heightened my awareness and understanding of people.

Like many other students of that era, I was drawn to campus activities and service projects. These led to student politics, which resulted in my becoming student body president. Each of these new activities gave me an opportunity to assume responsibility and learn about people. It was while I was serving in student government that I met another group of university people who helped shape my life. These included the many students with whom I was associated and also Harry Heflin, Joseph Gluck, and many others involved in the administration of university life. Like many graduates, I have concluded that the college experience offers invaluable opportunities for personal development.

When I left the university, my sense of pride in West Virginia and its major university bordered on chauvinism. Like many of my classmates, I left the state for several years to pursue graduate degrees. Also, like a growing number of West Virginians, I returned to West Virginia after finishing graduate school. The impact of West Virginia University on my life was enormous. The university shaped my future academic career (and, hence, my working career) and my personality during four very formative years of my life.

The remarks that follow were filled with emotion because they caused me to reflect on our undergraduate years at the university and the enormous power every university has to transform young lives and develop young people into future leaders and contributors to every sector of society.

Homecoming at WVU is rarely considered complete without a visit to Woodburn Circle, and when I enter the university's signature building, Woodburn Hall, I have the special feeling that most graduates experience when they truly "come home" to their alma mater. I had so many classes here, I made so many friends here, I dreamed so many dreams here, and I learned so much here. In many ways, Woodburn Hall is, for me, not only a symbol of the university but also a symbol of all that gives richness to university life. Since its construction just a few years after the founding of the university, Woodburn Hall has been identified with what is good about WVU.

West Virginia University was founded in 1867, the same year as Howard University, the University of Illinois, and the University of Minnesota. It opened with 122 students and 274 books. At the time of the founding, the state was controlled by the Republican party. In August 1875, about the time Woodburn Hall was built, a new Board of Regents met in Martinsburg. The new group fired the first president, Alexander Martin. According to one board member, it was "pure coincidence" that all of the professors who were reelected to the faculty were Democrats while all of those invited to retire were Republicans. Thus, Woodburn Hall opened with a "wild" beginning, in the midst of controversy.

By 1900, times were better. The College of Civil Engineering and Mining was started here to support the industrialization that was occurring in our nation. Also by the turn of the century, a physicians' training program began with the establishment of the WVU School of Medicine, which offered two years of medical school. The research program gave rise to many pranks concerning cadavers and fostered innovative methods to frighten unsuspecting students out of their wits.

Women were not left behind. They were admitted to every department in the university (except the military) by 1897.

The early years of the university must have been thrilling. By 1901, Granville Davisson Hall wrote, in a book called *The Rending of Virginia,* that WVU had achieved flagship status.[3] Distinguished scholars like Oliver Perry Chitwood formed the faculty.

At about the turn of the century, the north wing of Woodburn Hall was completed in time to get ready for the war years that followed. ROTC was formed in 1916 to aid in the war effort, and it has been present on campus ever since. Roughly 2,700 students served in the "war to end all wars." Sixty years later, I attended ROTC classes on the top floor of Woodburn Hall.

Shortly after the turn of the century, Woodburn Hall was joined by Purinton House (the president's home[4]), and the library was moved to a new building (now called Stewart Hall). It is perhaps the most elaborate and durable building ever built on campus. WVU even built an observatory situated above the top of North High Street. This permitted WVU's faculty to observe the sky, and it permitted the students to observe the townsfolk.

Residential living required extracurricular activities, and by 1900, WVU had been playing Pitt in football for five years. The class cheer was "Boom-a-la, boom-a-la / Rah-rah-reck / Nineteen hundred's right on deck!" The students of the early twentieth century walked out of Woodburn in 1919 to watch WVU footballers play perennial rivals Rutgers, Maryland, and Pitt. We still play them today. My great-uncle, Clay B. "Mud" Hite, was on that team with the great Ira Errett "Rat" Rogers, our first all-American. My aunt used to say, "If it had not been for Mud blocking for Rat, he would not have been an all-American." By 1925, enrollment at WVU had grown to 2,300 people and the "new" Mountaineer Field was built. Over seventeen thousand fans attended the inaugural game, which was a 14–0 victory over Penn State. Go Mountaineers!

As West Virginia University grew, so did the campus. The chemistry building was built in 1925 to ease the pain of Woodburn's crowded classrooms. It could accommodate two thousand students at a time.

The location of the university has always been problematic to some. When the state was founded, the bigger cities got the capital, the prisons, and the mental institutions. The university was relegated to Morgantown, which was essentially a small village. Talk of moving WVU to southern West Virginia persisted well into the 1920s, but the state capitol burned and people up here started talking about moving the capital north. That put an end to that discussion, and Woodburn Hall remained at the heart of the university, then fifty years old.

By the 1930s, Americans were experiencing the Great Depression, but the magnificent Wise Library was opened to serve Woodburn's students, among others. It's interesting to note that the WVU book collection outgrew Stewart Hall in just under thirty years. I wonder how long the new library addition, now under construction, will last.

As the nation headed into World War II, WVU was again a center for the training of soldiers (one of the first few institutions selected as a training site during the war). Our patriotism has always been part of Woodburn Hall's heritage and evident to the leaders of the United States armed forces, who helped to place the mast of the USS *West Virginia* just across the way.

The 1950s were a period of dramatic change and growth at the university, overseen by one of its most dynamic leaders, President Irvin Stewart. I was fortunate to have him for a graduate-level class in Woodburn Hall. Susan went to teas at Purinton House when she was a child; and on occasion, she helped to pour punch while wearing her white gloves. During the '50s, Woodburn Hall again sowed new seeds. Brooks, Armstrong, Hodges, and Eisland halls were built along with others. In November 1950, a student organization called "Mountain" established the Mountaineer statue festival fund to commission a dignified symbol of a mountaineer. It is striking to me that it took twenty years to raise $15,000 for the statue that now stands near here.

By the way, about the same time, in 1958, the School of Engineering joined the space race after Sputnik. I remember a neighbor's garage door opening when Sputnik went over and how concerned all the academic leaders in the country were that we had fallen behind. This feeling was partly responsible for the election of John Kennedy. Math and science were increasingly emphasized. By the 1970s, West Virginia had launched the computer era on campus, and in 1975, it formed the Network for Educational Computing. Eventually, a new science, called computer science, grew out of the statistics department at WVU.

Susan and I were here from 1963 to 1967. The 1960s saw protests and demonstrations about student rights, civil rights, and the Vietnam War. Some of the demonstrations occurred on the lawn outside this hall. I can remember debating with the likes of professors Wes Bagby and John Williams over the merits of American policies. Students were interested in service but also in testing authority. It was a wonderful time to be on the college campus, and Woodburn Hall is where I had most of my classes. To get the students from Woodburn Hall to the new Evansdale campus, the university opened the PRT in 1975. It was one of the largest single federal expenditures on a university project ever. The first phase alone cost $128 million.

For more than fifty years, members of the alumni body and students gathered on the lawn of Woodburn Hall before going down to the old stadium for football games. In fact, West Virginia was increasing its prominence in all sports. It was during the 1950s and '60s that basketball reached new heights, with the likes of Gale Catlett, "Hot Rod" Hundley, Rod Thorn, Jerry West, and others playing on our campus. By 1975, West Virginia beat North Carolina State in the Peach Bowl, led by Rhodes Scholar and quarterback

Danny Williams. And, oh, the students of Woodburn Hall—the debaters, the researchers, the scholars, the student body officers, and so many others! They went on, and will always go on, to become the leaders of our state and nation. I doubt if there is a hall in the United States that can claim more Rhodes, Truman, *USA Today*, and Goldwater scholars per square foot.

All in all, Woodburn's rich heritage and long line of distinguished faculty members inspire us all. It's not the church but the faith that matters. It's not the stadium but the team spirit that is important. And it's not Woodburn Hall but what it represents that inspires us all as we sit here today. I was inaugurated as WVU's twenty-first president in front of Woodburn Hall, and I have to admit that every time I come into this building, I conjure up how far I have come since first walking through its hallways as a student. I'm truly humbled to be the president of an institution where so many have traveled as far, and many further.

In 2000, five years after coming to WVU, Susan and I decided that we would commission one of West Virginia's talented artists, Sally Rowe, to make a quilt for us. It hangs here today. Taking months to construct, it comprises two thousand pieces of cloth that form an impressionistic image of Woodburn Circle. The quilt is titled *Woodburn Circle 2000*. That we chose this gift for each other in the millennium year says more than I could possibly put into words about our feelings for Woodburn Hall: we love the place! And like so many of you, we love this place because we love the university and cherish its transforming qualities. This is truly a university where greatness is taught, and where greatness is learned, thanks in large measure to the people and programs of Woodburn Hall.

NOTES

1   Doherty and Summers, *West Virginia University*.

2   *The Monticola: West Virginia University 1900* (Morgantown, WV: Acme Publishing, 1899).

3   Granville Davisson Hall, *The Rending of Virginia: A History*, ed. John Edmund
     Stealey III (1902; Knoxville: University of Tennessee Press, 2000), 615.

4   While Paul Miller was president (1962–1966), a new residence was purchased
     for the university president. This building is now called the Blaney House in
     honor of philanthropists W. Gerald and Carolyn Eberly Blaney.

TWENTY-SEVEN

REFLECTIONS ON THE OXFORD EXPERIENCE

RESIDENTIAL EDUCATION AS PREPARATION FOR LEADERSHIP

1987

Like thousands of other students over the past several hundred years, I was deeply influenced by the rich educational experience of attending Oxford University, where I studied and was awarded a degree in philosophy, politics, and economics. With the passage of time and the luxury of reflection, I realize that my experiences at Oxford likely played a large role in formulating my efforts to better integrate the inside classroom activities with the outside life of the university I later led.

My wife Susan and I visited my Oxford tutor, Geoffrey Marshall, who is mentioned in these remarks, three times after leaving Oxford—once during a private trip to England before we had children, once with our daughter when she graduated high school, and once with a group of forty-five university donors on a trip to England we titled the "Road to Oxford." All three trips were both heartwarming and highly motivational.

Dr. Marshall inspired me more than words can convey. It is fair to say that his faith in my potential (he called me a "diamond in the rough from Appalachia") and his determination to help me through the rigors of Oxford's academic demands transformed my life. His influence on my leadership was present every day of my presidency.

At the University of Charleston (West Virginia) in the mid 1980s, I was invited to reflect on Oxford's contributions to higher education at a gathering of faculty and students interested in the Rhodes Scholarship and other postgraduate fellowships. The remarks I offered are set forth below.

My presidency, the Oxford experience, and other influences on our leadership team led to major initiatives designed to make the university more student centered. Our agenda included the assignment of tenured faculty to live and work as resident mentors and coaches in our residence halls, the construction of a health-and-wellness center, refinements to the Honors College, and the launching of Lincoln Hall, a residential college. Many more student-centered efforts (that is, programs designed to foster students' academic success and develop them as leaders) were adopted at West Virginia University as it grew larger and larger at the turn of the century.

These programs all sought to build community within a larger university. I was greatly assisted in these efforts by Dr. David Stewart, an Oxford don (professor and tutor) who understood and shared my vision and helped to develop it. Although skeptical when he came to my first focus group on residential education, he became champion of the program and told me as I was writing this book that these remarks should be seen as a "foundational document" for the residential college system we have initiated.

Our efforts were overseen and funded by the university provost, Dr. Gerald E. Lang, and the vice president for student affairs, Maj. Gen. Kenneth Gray, U.S. Army, retired. These three men and those they led were tireless proponents of our student-centered vision for the institution we led, which was eventually formally adopted and incorporated in our planning efforts. It defines our vision as follows:

> West Virginia University is a student-centered learning community meeting the changing needs of West Virginia and the nation through excellence in teaching, research, service, and technology.

This statement appeared on the back of my business cards during my presidency and served as the basis for dozens of public addresses, including several that are reproduced below.

Participating in a collegiate gathering on a cool winter night and talking about Oxford University and its contribution to higher learning is a nostalgic experience for an American Oxonian. The tutors at Queens College would approve, for thinking about ideas outside the lecture hall is encouraged at Oxford, especially if the discussion is preceded by sherry and small talk. Dr. Geoffrey Marshall, my academic advisor—or as he was called at Oxford, my "moral tutor"—would be especially interested in my participation tonight. Dons cherish the thought of one of their scholars returning to the colonies as an ambassador of Oxford's awesome intellectual influence.

Christopher Hobhouse, in his book *Oxford*, reports that the first recorded events related to Oxford took place around 700 AD.[1] The university had its beginnings some four hundred years later, and the room to which I was assigned when I "went up" to Queens College was constructed in about 1775. Queen's College was established in 1344, long before Columbus discovered America.[2]

It is difficult for one person to describe the breadth of the Oxford experience. Every American man and woman who has been blessed with the opportunity to take up residence at Oxford University must be filled with vivid impressions related to the experience. Oxford is one of the world's great universities. It is certainly a crucible of Western intellectual thought, and its historic significance is renowned. Its architecture is inspiring; its student body is cosmopolitan. In short, the sights and sounds of Oxford bombard the brain of one who takes up residence there during the impressionable college years.

Many British philosophers have talked about the importance of sense impressions—sights, sounds, smells, and the like—and how we come to know about things from them. It is said that one philosopher approached the precipice of insanity because he could not be sure he really knew anything. Tonight I share his confusion, for sorting out and making sense of my own Oxford experiences has not been easy. To top off the challenge, "Oxford is a dangerous place to write about," argues James Morris, who found his thoughts on Oxford, contained in his book, *Oxford*, subject to much criticism by others familiar with the university and its history.[3] To make it easy for me and less confusing for you, I will only offer my impressions of the Oxford experience. I will leave it to those more familiar with the subject matter to determine their veracity.

Some months ago, quite by chance, I had occasion to review two similar views of the purposes of an education. In 1964, Dr. Grayson Kirk, then president of Columbia University, delivered an address entitled "Responsibilities of the Educated Man."[4]

Dr. Kirk identifies four responsibilities of the university-educated person: to endeavor to achieve clarity and precision in the spoken and written word; to develop a sense of values and the courage with which to defend them; to make every effort, honestly and objectively, to understand our society and to comprehend what separates it from others; and to look squarely at the world and its problems with courage and hope, not with fear and rejection. These being the outcomes, it seems fair to assume that Dr. Kirk's view was that a college or university ought to produce these results. Nearly twenty-five years later, Derek Bok, the president of Harvard, set forth in his book, *Higher Learning*, his view of the purposes of the liberal arts education:

Undergraduates should acquire an ample store of knowledge . . . They should gain an ability to communicate with precision and style, a basic competence in quantitative skills, . . . one foreign language, and a capacity to think critically and clearly.

They should become acquainted with the important methods of inquiry . . . and develop an awareness of other cultures . . . They should acquire lasting intellectual and cultural interests, gain in self-knowledge, and ultimately be able to make sound choices about their future lives and careers . . . They should achieve greater social maturity and acquire tolerance of human diversity.[5]

To accomplish these outcomes in just a few years seems an impossible task for any faculty, and it would appear to challenge any student to the limits of human capability, prompting me to remember a wonderful story about Winston Churchill.

It has to do with a complaint made by a woman from the Temperance League. She claimed that he had consumed enough alcohol during his lifetime to fill half of the large hall in which he was standing. The story ends when he slowly turns his gaze toward the ceiling and answers with the very Churchillian phrase "So much to do, so little time."

Nevertheless, it does seem fair to ask how Oxford measures up to the standards set by Kirk and Bok. It also seems fair to summarize their view by saying that higher education should teach one to think, communicate, appreciate, honestly evaluate, and contribute. It is with these criteria in mind that my impressions of the Oxford experience are offered for your consideration.

If Oxford encourages attainment of any academic skill, it encourages precision in one's use of the English language. Precision of word and thought is not only taught in English class; the emphasis extends throughout every aspect of university life. For example, consider the number of professors of philosophy at Oxford. I don't know the exact number, but my impression is that there are more philosophers gathered at Oxford than at any other university.

Throughout the centuries, philosophers at Oxford have studied the meaning of life through the meaning of words. For example, moral philosophers have taken great interest in concepts like "ought," "right," "good," "justice," and "liberty." Logic has also been a part of the basic Oxford curriculum, and illogical use of the language is frowned upon, not only by professors of logic, but also by the rest of the academic community. This emphasis on the study of philosophy means that precision of thought (and expression) is expected and, for the most part, achieved.

Oxford is well known for its debating society, the Oxford Union. The classic Oxford debating style puts great emphasis on persuasion, of course, but style and word play are the real delights of the live audiences at the Union.

Every Thursday night, one may observe that those invited to debate at the Union are accomplished at plying the spoken word. The intimacy of the tutorial system also encourages attainment of a higher level of writing and speaking skills. Each term, students are assigned a few subjects to master. They are then given weekly or biweekly assignments to author a paper related to each subject. These papers are read to the dons, or teachers, who then offer up a critique. Inasmuch as only one or two other students are present (and often only the don and one scholar are present), lack of clarity stands out like Pinocchio's nose.

The method of testing encourages clarity and precision. Generally speaking, the tests are not set, or made up, by the same teachers who are helping "tutees." Rather, a panel of professors writes exams designed to determine students' understanding of basic concepts. Exams are offered at the conclusion of one's stay at Oxford, during a week-long or ten-day period called "schools." It helps to know how to write at exam time, since it comes only once or twice during one's tenure at the university. Moreover, if the examiners are unclear about a student's comprehension of the subject, they may require an oral examination—or as it is called at Oxford, a "viva." It is said that the best of those awarded highest honors, or "firsts," are applauded at the conclusion of their viva.

The tutorial system also breaks down barriers to student–faculty fraternization. Since exams are rarely set by those teaching during an exam period, students are not viewed as engaging in unethical conduct if they get to know the dons. In fact, many dons seem to like students and appreciate the intellectual and social contact they have with them. It is not at all unusual for tutors to invite students to dinner, sherry, and small seminars. Despite Oxford's size, undergraduate education there is very collegial—more like a small, exclusive graduate school than an undergraduate school grinding out degrees.

Obviously, the Oxford tutorial method and the school's system of testing encourage critical thinking. The ability to think through a problem and communicate one's thoughts on plausible solutions is assumed by graduation—in fact, long before. The ability to think is the essence of the traditional Oxford education. It should not amaze us that nearly one-half of England's prime ministers, including the current "Iron Lady," have graduated from Oxford University.[6]

Oxford's brand of teaching is expensive and is available to only a few. Historically, only the rich and those studying for the clergy with the help of the church could afford to attend Oxford. Gradually, numerous scholarships were developed, including those for foreign students (like the Rhodes). However, today, significant numbers of poor and middle-class students are able to attend Oxford. Obviously, admissions standards are high, and highly motivated students seek admission. Cambridge University is built on a similar foundation, which gives rise to the commonplace that the training ground for England's leaders is "Oxbridge." (Notice that Oxford is mentioned first; the word is not "Camford.")

Because of its traditional role as a crucible of leadership for the British Empire, leadership training and "values" education are traditionally acceptable at Oxford. In the same way that use of the language is stressed in every aspect of university life, certain leadership skills and basic values are assumed by the time one "goes down" from the university—that is, by the time one graduates. While it is often held that Oxford teaches liberal views, I don't think this is true. Oxford teaches the values associated with higher learning, not a particular political philosophy.

One of these values is the obligation of educated people to participate in leadership. This belief that everyone has a responsibility to take part in some aspect of civic leadership is taught in several ways.

One example is the way Oxford teaches sports. It is helpful, in this context, to know that Oxford University is a federation of smaller, largely independent colleges. For the most part, each college has its own residence halls (usually built in quadrangle fashion), library, chapel, dining hall, teaching rooms, and sports facilities. This means that Oxford has numerous teams engaging in squash, cricket, tennis, rugby, rowing, and the like.

Although Oxford has prestigious varsity teams, at the college level, competition is intense, and sporting skills are taught by students, not professional coaches. The opportunity to participate in rewarding college sporting activities is widely available. Participation in college sports carries an obligation to teach younger or newer participants and, if called upon, to lead the team or crew. This means that Oxford is full of captains. The same phenomenon extends to other activities such as student government, theater, and social activities.

It is also true that the academic skills Oxford stresses are those needed by leaders. Primary among these are the ability to communicate and the ability to analyze and solve problems. It is said that there is no political training ground like Oxford University, but Oxford trains leaders in every field of human endeavor. Moreover, like any other great university, Oxford attracts to its halls, or self-selects, students with great potential to lead. Such students have an inclination to participate by leading rather than by watching.

Another value Oxford stresses is an appreciation for the truth. This value is an outcome of the academic emphasis on logic and philosophy and Oxford's

clerical roots. Oxford students and dons appreciate insights into difficult issues. Good solutions are appreciated. Somehow, one seems to acquire other
values at Oxford: an appreciation for right over might, an understanding of
the intrinsic dignity and worth of every individual, an appreciation for different cultures, and an appreciation for those who fight the good fight. The
tradition of seeking a rational basis for morality contributes to these values.
The melting-pot quality of Oxford's student body also does a lot to open young
eyes, as does the size and diversity of Oxford city's population.

All in all, Oxford passes the tests for a good education set forth by the two
American college presidents. Emphasis on quality for over a thousand years
has had beneficial side effects. One of the world's great libraries is at Oxford.
Scholarship abounds. Understandably, industry in Oxfordshire has flourished.
The international influence of Oxford over the past several hundred years has
resulted in rich endowments.

Other aspects of Oxford's pedagogy have been exported to the elite
American schools—Harvard, Yale, the University of the South, and many
others. The leadership-training tradition has fostered many scholarship programs throughout the world; the Rhodes, Fullbright, Guggenheim, Marshall,
Truman, and (at West Virginia's Marshall University) Yeager scholarship programs offer special opportunities for students to at least experience some of
the Oxford model. Perhaps more importantly, the values that Oxford stresses
have been emulated by all of academia in some respects, from the pageantry
of the graduation to an avowed dedication to the truth.

In closing, I would submit that Oxford's values and skills should be and
are the same values and skills that should be taught at American colleges and
universities. The values and skills that Oxford teaches have as much relevance
for us here in Appalachia as they do in England. What Oxford does, in general
terms, is not unique.

What is unique is that what it does, it does so very well.

NOTES

1   Christopher Hobhouse, *Oxford* (London: B. T. Batsford Ltd., 1948), 1.

2   For further details, see Christopher Hobhouse, *Oxford* (London: B. T. Batsford Ltd., 1948) and *Handbook to the University of Oxford* (Oxford: Clarendon Press, 1966).

3   James Morris, *Oxford* (London: Faber and Faber, 1965), 7.

4   Grayson Kirk, "Responsibilities of the Educated Man," in *The University of Denver Centennial Symposium: The Responsible Individual and a Free Society in an Expanding Universe*, ed. Fred Hoyle (Denver: Big Mountain Press, 1965).

5   Derek Bok, *Higher Learning* (Cambridge, MA: Harvard University Press, 1986), 54–55.

6   Margaret Thatcher was the prime minister of England when these remarks were written.

TWENTY-EIGHT

LEADING LAWYERS

WHY LAWYERS LEAD IN AMERICA

1995

Most of my formative professional years were spent as a lawyer in a firm that served a wide variety of clients. I was also appointed tax commissioner of West Virginia by then–Governor Jay Rockefeller. At the time, the post was customarily filled by a lawyer because of the commissioner's role in making tax policy and administrative determinations pursuant to that policy.

Toward the end of my legal career, after twenty years of experience, I began to reflect on the legal profession, the impact it has on society, and on the preparation of leaders in America's complex system of government and voluntary associations. This essay on why many lawyers find their way into leadership positions in American society was originally published in "The West Virginia Lawyer" shortly after I became president of West Virginia University in 1995, and it was read primarily by other lawyers.

I have given it to every member of my seminar, titled "Lawyers and the Legislative Process," since I began teaching it in 1998. The remarks are included here because in writing this essay, I was clearly speculating on what had prepared me, a "nontraditional president," for my position as president of a major university. Since then, I have met several lawyers who have found their way into positions of academic leadership. Many share my view that the skills lawyers develop are excellent preparation for leadership positions across a variety of fields of expertise. Prior to the publication of this article, I benefited from the editorial comments of law professor John Fisher, who later became dean of the College of Law at West Virginia University.

Lawyers lead in America and always have. Abraham Lincoln, for example, assumed numerous positions of leadership during his career. In fact, Donald T. Phillips's popular, recent book on Lincoln and leadership[1] prompted me to begin thinking about the subject of this article—lawyers who lead—and hence the title, "Leading Lawyers." What sparked my interest in the topic is the number of instances in which lawyer-leaders are found outside the profession. One would expect to find lawyers leading law firms, the judiciary, the adjutant general's offices, the attorney general's offices, corporate law departments, law schools, and the offices of public defenders. But colleges and hospitals? Banks and labor unions? Industry and business?

In the introduction to his definitive textbook on the law of property, A. James Casner of Harvard Law School writes, "It is an observable fact that through some combination of chromosomes and professional training lawyers tend to come to the top of the barrel in the shaking and jolting of competition for authority."[2] Consider for a moment the wide variety of fields in which lawyers lead or have led in America: government, politics, diplomacy, business, higher education, societal reform, the volunteer sector, the nonprofit sector, business and industry, and labor organizations, to name just a few. In nearly every field, lawyers have risen to the occasion and provided that elusive spark we call "leadership."[3]

The literature of leadership is proliferating, happily, and helping us to understand what leadership is and why it comes about.[4] Some of the work is serious scholarship and directed toward whose who are serious students of the subject, such as college teachers and scholars, and think tanks and strategic-planning offices around the country. More is popular writing, designed to feed a national preoccupation with new leadership skills, traits, and habits.

Why do lawyers, regardless of their gender, race, socioeconomic background, ethnic origin, and law school often find themselves in a position to lead? What follows is a speculative list of suggestions that begin (but only just begin) to answer the question.

First, leaders must be able to think clearly, and most lawyers do. Legal education and the practice of law foster thinking skills across a lifetime. The ability to comb through documents, analyze oral presentations, and evaluate physical evidence, looking for "truth," often translates into marketable skills for a leader. Moreover, since law school is, in large measure, an academic exercise, the notion that fashioning complex abstract ideas and translating them into action can be accomplished by the same person is not uncomfortable to lawyers.

For years, in many law schools, first-year students were asked to read K. N. Llewellyn's essay (originally lectures) on our law and its study, *The Bramble Bush*.[5] Llewellyn introduced law students to a variety of topics related to the study of law, one of which was the important role that logic plays in successful lawyering. Consider this passage from his essay:

> The rules that you derive from putting cases together are therefore *rules not merely of description but of ought*, major premises from which one concludes that if the rule is correct, a particular further case ought to be so decided and not otherwise; to which is added an implication in fact that the judge in a future case will be on his job. Now on the level of *predicting* what will in fact come to pass, clearly there are three places to attack your rule as you thus set

it up. One may attack it by challenging your logic: you have slipped in your reasoning . . . or you may have so built your alleged rule that it fails to cover some of the cases before you, or cover some of them contrary to their holdings . . . or, and finally, one may attack you on your implication about future judges; you may have picked a premise perfectly all right and your future judge may kick over the traces.[6]

Not all commentary about how lawyers are taught to think is so esoteric. Consider the following passage from *The Making of the Country Lawyer*, the autobiography of noted trial lawyer Gerry Spence, who asserts there may be a lawyer's way of analyzing problems:

I listened to the dean's initiating speech with mounting anxiety so heed my words, gentleman—there were two women in the class—and *learn to think like lawyers*. Then he cast us his most generous smile, and bestowed on us his first assignment in contracts.

Think like lawyers the dean had said. I wondered how a lawyer was supposed to think. Logically, without passion, I supposed. Think with thoughts unconnected to emotions. Drive out all feelings for law was a science and science was feelingless law. And, like science, law could not be understood by the unscientific mind. I therefore set out to *think like a lawyer*.[7]

Second, lawyers learn to communicate: in writing, orally, and nonverbally. The closing argument, the able brief, the serious interview, the gestures in cross-examination, and other activities continuously hone a lawyer's communication skills. Like critical thinking, these skills often improve during the course of a career.

Think of the Gettysburg Address as an opening argument, made in an effort to heal a nation bound up in a potentially catastrophic civil war.

Howard Gardner of Harvard University argues persuasively that communicating, primarily through stories and examples, is the primary tool of leadership. He defines leaders as "persons who . . . markedly influence the behaviors, thoughts and/or feelings of a significant number of their fellow human beings."[8] Gardner emphasizes again and again the importance of storytelling in leading, citing numerous examples of effective storytelling as effective leading when accompanied by actions that embody the story told.

Moreover, good communicators are attracted to the law. Again, Gerry Spence:

I had never known a lawyer, never met one, never seen one, even at a distance. No lawyers ever went to the Methodist Church so far as I knew. I had never been in a courtroom. I had no idea what lawyers did. I had never heard of Clarence Darrow. But Abraham Lincoln was a lawyer, and he had become president, and so were Jefferson and Madison, and I thought Roosevelt was probably a lawyer, too. All great men were lawyers. I had never heard of a doctor or veterinarian or a teacher or a preacher who became president. Even when my voice was cracking like a one celled radio at three in the morning, my speech teacher, Miss Velma Linford, insisted that I possess this wonderful voice, and that someday I would become a great public speaker. I believed her . . . [L]awyers speak in the public. They speak to juries and they become politicians and speak to whole crowds of people. So, on analysis, there wasn't any doubt about it: the law was for me.[9]

Lawyers are lifetime learners. Further, law and leadership both reward a classic liberal education, although one is not required for either law or leadership. Knowing something about history, government, philosophy, economics, science, math, foreign languages and cultures, and similar core subjects is not necessary, but it is useful for both practicing lawyers and leaders. Perhaps this is because both must learn across their lifetimes. Perhaps it is because lawyers and leaders must relate well to numerous constituencies.

Of course, the ability to think and communicate well are closely related. Consider a portion of Professor Casner's charge to first-year students, wherein he comments on a lawyer's ability to think and communicate more effectively as a result of legal training:

> A lawyer's useful field of operation is one in which the legal ingredient is large, and to this ingredient the lawyer brings professional knowledge as well as the basic abilities; but the fact that the nonlegal ingredient is frequently dominant and the further fact that the situations in which a lawyer's help is solicited are many and varied give the lawyer the habit of tackling new problems with confidence and skill, regardless of their nature.
>
> Our listing of the basic qualities is the following:
>
> Fact consciousness. An insistence upon getting the facts, checking their accuracy, and sloughing off the element of conclusion and opinion.
>
> A sense of relevance. The capacity to recognize what is relevant to the issue at hand and to cut away irrelevant facts, opinions, and emotions which can cloud the issue.
>
> Comprehensiveness. The capacity to see all sides of a problem, all factors that bear upon it, and all possible ways of approaching it.
>
> Foresight. The capacity to take the long view, to anticipate remote and collateral consequences, to look several moves ahead in the particular chess game that is being played.
>
> Lingual sophistication. An immunity to being fooled by words and catch phrases; a refusal to accept verbal solutions which merely conceal the problem.
>
> Precision and persuasiveness of speech. That mastery of the language which involves (a) the ability to state exactly what one means, no more no less,

and (b) the ability to reach others with one's own thought, to create in their minds the picture that is in one's own.

And finally, pervading all the rest, and possibly the only one that is really basic: self-discipline in habits of thoroughness, an abhorrence of superficiality and approximation.

These are not qualities which spring naturally from family background plus a liberal arts education. You will be shocked at your deficiencies in all of them as your professors will point them out. But be not dismayed, for the qualities can be acquired and developed; and the law schools of this country are in the business of doing precisely that.[10]

Third, lawyers, generally speaking, have a knowledge, however rudimentary, of the structure of leadership institutions: the branches of government, the rules of conducting business, and normally, the difference between right and wrong. They get this information in law school and by practicing law, and it is cumulative. For decades, one well-known capstone course at Harvard Law School was called The Legal Process. It was taught over the years by Dean Sacks and a number of other guiding lights of the law. In it, lawyers were taught to discern the most appropriate forum for lawmaking (the legislature, the courts, administrative bodies, etc.) and asked to debate the most appropriate forum for dispute resolution of various types of issues.[11]

Lawyers also are able to cross over and into other "domains of expertise,"[12] meaning that their work often puts them in contact with, and gives them empathy for, persons working in fields other than law. This talent increases as lawyers practice their profession. The counsel who is asked to draft an agreement between a contractor and a local government, for example, has to empathize with the cultures of both to do a good job. The litigator, during the course of his or her career, might obtain an intimate view of, and often come to understand, the true nature of dozens of occupations.

Next, for many lawyers, there is a convergence of public and private interests in leadership activity. For example, activities like serving on a school board, doing a talk show, or heading a citizens' reform effort lead to name recognition in a jurisdiction that often overlaps with the public forums that contain potential clients. Before lawyer advertising, leadership activities were considered legitimate ways to become better known.

Further, men and women with charisma often self-select into the profession, in the way that those skilled in math select engineering or those with proclivity in science become doctors. The reasons men and women have or don't have charisma are mysterious, and must include both innate and learned talents to motivate others, serve others, and communicate, whether they are acquired before or after attending law school. What is charisma? In the words of two authors (writing about the college presidency):

> Charismatic leadership, the single most effective form of leadership is based on the admiration and liking that people feel toward an individual. The charismatic leader has an extraordinary ability to inspire trust and confidence . . . This is not the charisma of divine inspiration, a special gift, grace, or talent that some have and most have not, but rather a quality of trust and confidence that almost anyone can honestly cultivate.
>
> Despite popular opinion, charisma and public presence are neither genetic nor intuitive, but simply the ability to inspire trust and confidence. Bass, in his authoritative *Bass and Stogdill's Handbook of Leadership* . . . concludes that charismatic behavior can be taught and learned and public presence developed. Anyone of reasonable intelligence and with motivation can develop charismatic characteristics. Age, gender, race, height, weight, and other obvious personal characteristics have little or nothing to do with the ability to develop and use charismatic influence. Virtually anyone of reasonable intelligence and strong motivation can accomplish it.

Many factors contribute to charisma: sincerity, appearance, focus, confidence, wisdom, courage, sensitivity, discipline, vision, reliability, and strength.[13]

Next, busy lawyers, like busy leaders, learn to manage numerous initiatives at the same time. Executive education courses sometimes include "inbox" exercises that teach students to learn from and manage written information they receive. Billing by the hour, working on a number of matters simultaneously, and being able to change thought patterns quickly are talents that are useful to busy executives and to lawyers—and hence to leaders.

There is, of course, the fact that lawyers hold a special status in society. The status is conferred by state and federal law, normally after competition of an exam, and sometimes after an apprenticeship. Interestingly, the exam that makes one eligible for the status is called "the bar," albeit for reasons other than its implied exclusivity. Despite their protestations to the contrary, Americans tend to accept status as one criterion of leadership, whether gained by credentials, wealth, fame, or other means. Status, of course, is a two-way street, and no doubt every new member of the bar has some sense of obligation that attends the granting of his or her status as a "member of the bar."

Lawyers have held special status in America since its founding. The status of the profession was noted by Alexis de Tocqueville in his famous treatise on American society, in which he speculated as to why lawyers achieve such status:

The special information that lawyers derive from their studies insures them a separate rank in society, and they constitute a sort of privileged body in the scale of intellect. This notion of their superiority perpetually recurs to them in the practice of their profession; they are the masters of a science which is necessary, but which is not very generally known; they serve as arbiters between the citizens; and the habit of directing to their purpose the blind passions of parties in litigation inspires them with certain contempt for the judgment of the multitude. Add to this that they naturally constitute a body; not by any previous understanding, of by any agreement that directs them to a common end; but the analogy of their studies and the uniformity of their methods connect their minds as a common interest might unite their endeavors . . .

The government of democracy is favorable to the political power of lawyers; for when the wealthy, the noble, and the prince are excluded from government, the lawyers take possession of it, in their own right, as it were, since they are the only men of information and sagacity, beyond the sphere of the people, who can be the object of popular choice. Lawyers belong to the people, and to the aristocracy by habit and tastes; they may be looked upon as the connecting link between the two great classes of society . . .

In America, there are no nobles or literary men and the people are apt to mistrust the wealthy; lawyers consequently form the highest political class and the most cultivated portion of society. If I were asked where I would place the American aristocracy, I should reply without hesitation that it is not among the rich, who are united by no common tie, but it occupies the judicial bench and the bar.[14]

Obviously, leaders must also deal with disputes relating to personnel, policy, vision, and interpretation of rules and regulations. If lawyers traffic in anything, it is dispute resolution in the courts, mediation, arbitration, and the like, and dispute avoidance (through good contracting). Again, consider the sage advice of Llewellyn advising young lawyers:

What, then, is this law business about? It is about the fact our society is honey combed with disputes. Disputes actual and potential; disputes to be settled and disputes to be prevented; both appealing to law, both making up the business of law. But obviously those which most violently call for attention are the actual disputes, and to these our first attention must be directed. Actual disputes call for somebody to do something about them. First, so that there may be peace, for the disputants; for other persons whose ears and toes disputants are disturbing. And secondly, so that the dispute may really be put at rest, which means, so that a solution may be achieved which at the least in the main is bearable to the parties and not distinguishable to the looker-on. The doing of something about disputes, the doing and charge, whether they be judges or sheriffs or clerks of jailers or lawyers, are the officials of law. What these officials do about disputes is, to my mind, the law itself.[15]

There are many, many more similarities and overlapping skills and aptitudes that lawyers and leaders, in a variety of contexts, share: the ability to work collegially, the ability to organize, media relations skills, an ability to work without close supervision, and so forth. The list goes on and on. Of course, not all lawyers lead. Some simply do not have the opportunity. I seem to remember that Homer said, "Fate is that thing no man born of woman can escape." Tolstoy urges us to never underestimate providence:

> When the apple is ripe and falls—why does it fall? Is it because it is drawn by gravitation to the earth, because its stalk is withered, because it is dried by the sun, because it grows heavier, because the wind shakes it, or because the boy standing under the tree wants to eat it?
>
> Not one of those is the cause. All that simply makes up the conjunction of conditions under which every living, organic, elemental event takes place. And the botanist who says that the apple has fallen because the cells are decomposing, and so on, will be just as right as the boy standing under the tree who says the apple has fallen because he wanted to eat it and prayed for it to fall. The historian, who says that Napoleon went to Moscow because he wanted

to, and was ruined because Alexander desired his ruin, will be just as right and as wrong as the man who says that the mountain of millions of tons, tottering and undermined, has been felled by the last stroke of the last workingman's pick-axe. In historical events great men—so called—are but labels that serve to give a name to an event, and like labels, they have the least possible connection with the event itself.

Every act of theirs, that seems to them an act of their own freewill, is in an historical sense not free at all, but in bondage to the whole course of previous history, and predestined from all eternity.[16]

Perhaps more to the point, however, is the fact that, like other occupations and professions, law today fosters significant specialization, sometimes resulting in a narrowness of purpose and outlook, an unwillingness to empathize, and motivation to excel in a field rather than promote the public's interest through public service or another leadership activity. There are other barriers to a lawyer's entry into the arena of leadership as well: lack of vision and motivation, fear of technology, lack of independent thinking, the lure of lucrative work within the profession, and the psychic income of serving clients within the confines of the law—one of the major domains of expertise that has its own status and remunerations within our society.

Suffice it to say, however, that lawyers often lead, skillfully crossing domains of expertise to motivate and guide others to act in their own self interests. And they are likely to continue doing so in America. Furthermore, the need for lawyers to lead has never been greater, given the complexity of the modern marketplace, the importance of good leadership to capitalism, and fragmentation of society's values and visions.

Shouldn't society, through bar and law school activities, be made aware of the skills lawyers can bring to circumstances requiring leadership? Can't lawyers begin to project to the general population the imagery of "servant leader" in the same way that M.B.A. holders promote themselves as "excellent managers"? In recent years, attempts to restore faith in the legal profession have fostered a wide variety of programs, from stricter ethical requirements to media campaigns designed to improve the image of lawyers. Perhaps public recognition that lawyers are well qualified to serve as leaders, and try to do so ethically, can help restore trust in the profession, making it one of the recognized bridges between domains of expertise in our society.

Lawyers are part of the glue that holds America together, not just in the courtroom, but in the boardroom, the schoolroom, the community center, the legislature, the executive mansion, and academe as well. Lawyers have always led. Let's recognize that fact, clearly, and assert that they always will, because they are prepared by their inclination and training to do just that!

NOTES

1   Donald T. Phillips, *Lincoln on Leadership: Executive Strategies for Tough Times* (1993).

2   A. James Casner and W. Barton Leach, *Cases and Text on Property,* 3rd ed. (Little Brown, 1984), 2.

3   Congressional leaders (Senator Robert C. Byrd, Congressman Bob Wise, and Congressman Alan Mollohan), diplomats (John W. Davis), college presidents (Gordon Gee, the author), state legislators (e.g., Speakers of the House of Delegates Robert Kiss, Charles Chambers, Clyde See, and Joseph P. Albright), volunteers (John McClaugherty, John Hoblitzell, Sue Farnsworth, Cathy Armstrong, and David Todd), business leaders (A. Michael Perry and Ralph Bean), labor leaders (Davitt MacAteer), and many, many other members of the bar have put their leadership talents to work on behalf of others in West Virginia.

4   For an excellent compilation of readings on leadership, see J. Thomas Wren, *The Leader's Companion: Insights on Leadership Through the Ages* (Free Press, 1995).

5   K. N. Llewellyn, *The Bramble Bush: On Our Law and Its Study*, 5th printing (1975).

6   Llewellyn, *The Bramble Bush*, 7.

7   Gerry Spence, *The Making of a Country Lawyer* (New York: St. Martin's Griffin, 1996), 223–224.

8   Howard Gardner, in collaboration with Emma Laskin, *Leading Minds: An Anatomy of Leadership* (New York: Basic Books, 1996), 8.

9   Spence, *The Making of a Country Lawyer*, 147–148.

10   Casner and Leach, *Cases and Text on Property*, 2–3.

11   The materials have now, fortunately, been published. See Henry M. Hart Jr. and Albert M. Sacks, *The Legal Process: Basic Problems in the Making and Application of Law* (West Publishing Company, 1994).

12   I have borrowed this term from Gardner, *Leading Minds*.

13   James L. Fisher and James V. Koch, *Presidential Leadership: Making a Difference* (American Council on Education, 1996), 38, 41.

14   Alexis de Tocqueville, *Democracy in America*, trans. Harvey C. Mansfield and Delba Winthrop (1835–1840; New York: Knopf, 1993), 273, 275–76, 278.

15   Llewellyn, *The Bramble Bush*, 12.

16   Leo Tolstoy, *War and Peace*, trans. Constance Garnett (1869; New York: Modern Library, 2002), 690–691.

TWENTY-NINE

THE EDUCATION OF A VOLUNTEER

REPORT OF THE CHAIRMAN TO THE UNIVERSITY SYSTEM BOARD OF TRUSTEES

1991

Alexis de Tocqueville, in his classic book, "Democracy in America," written in the early 1830s, predicts that America will become a great nation because of, among other things, the penchant of its citizens to form themselves into voluntary associations.[1] He clearly saw the critical importance of the not-for-profit sector to the health and prosperity of the United States.

For years prior to my appointment as a university president, I served in a variety of leadership positions in volunteer organizations. Perhaps the most challenging position began in 1989 when I was appointed to the first chair of the University System Board of Trustees by the Honorable Gaston Caperton, then governor of West Virginia and now president of the College Board. Other appointees included leading executives of business, labor, and the volunteer community. The governor assembled an extraordinary group of leaders to lead the newly created governing board for the state's four graduate institutions, and as

the systems first chair, I was faced with a variety of foundational organization
and leadership challenges, including speaking for such a distinguished group.
As we addressed these issues, we all grew in many ways, especially in our under-
standing of higher education issues as the new century approached. In the piece
that follows, a final report to the board in my capacity as chair, I memorialized
the lessons we learned in our first two years as a governing board. The gover-
nance system has since been changed, but the lessons learned by our group were
very representative of lessons learned by all governing board members.

Years later, I came to realize that leadership skills are often nurtured and
developed in the volunteer sector. As a volunteer for the university system and
two other organizations—the Greater Kanawha Valley Foundation and West
Virginia Business Roundtable—all of which I chaired, I was given the opportu-
nity to learn from leaders in the private sector and to understand more deeply
the role and importance of the not-for-profit sector in the United States. One
can easily see from the remarks below that my understanding of financial is-
sues, social justice, and the importance of remaining student centered clearly
advanced during my service on the University System Board.

In the original production of *Peter Pan*, the pirate captain took several opportunities to make his "dying speech," apparently out of fear that when the
time came for him to die, he would not have time to get what he had to say
off his chest.

Although the Board of Trustees of the University of West Virginia System
will continue when I step down as chairman, I thought nevertheless that it
would be appropriate for me to share with you a few observations about our
board and its institutions.

It is my hope that these observations will serve to chronicle our progress
during the past two years and contribute, in a small way, to the progress that I
am sure the board and system will make in the future.

THE NATURE OF OUR SERVICE ON THE BOARD OF TRUSTEES

To begin, I would note that we are not alone in our search for the answers to the many probing questions we have been asked. On Sunday, June 2, 1991, the *New York Times* carried a major article entitled "Higher Education Feels the Heat." The author, Anthony DePalma, indicates that currently in America "there is a fundamental rethinking about what colleges do and how they ought to do it."[2] Says Mr. DePalma:

> The turmoil has made the campus less a retreat from reality than an immersion in it. The average tenure of a public college president is now less than four years. The overwhelming majority of faculty members retire before reaching the mandatory age of 70. And students have grown increasingly discontent. Diversity has bred divisions and alliances by minority grouping. And there is no escape from the complex politics on campus, the forum for the debate over "political correctness" and whether it stifles free speech.[3]

While Mr. DePalma is referring to the questions now being asked in Washington and other states, no less serious questioning is taking place here in West Virginia. First addressed during the debate preceding the passage of Senate Bill 420 two years ago, the questions related to the role and mission of higher education in West Virginia have continued during our tenure as trustees. Numerous study groups and our board have examined basic questions: Should colleges and universities be awarded a special place in society? Are the missions of our institutions clear? How should public monies be allocated among the various institutions in West Virginia? What new programs are needed? Are our faculty and staff adequately paid? How large should our system be? What is the proper mix of students? Is the current role of collegiate athletics proper? What is the proper role of the medical education establishment in West Virginia? Is there social justice on our campuses? How fast should tuition increase? What is the proper role of state government in governing higher education? The lengthy list of difficult questions and the discussions that followed have been some of the defining characteristics of our first two years as trustees.

Governor W. Gaston Caperton III, to whom we owe the honor of serving as trustees, has devoted substantial personal effort to educational matters. His personal interest has been demonstrated by his efforts to pass Senate Bill 420, his personal involvement in our selection, his appearances before our board and joint meetings of our board with the Board of Directors of the State College System, and personal contact with us related to governance issues. The governor's interest is indicative of the public's interest in higher education in West Virginia and its impact on the people of our state. All in all, we bear both a heavy and a visible responsibility as trustees.

Last month I came across the collected works of Robert Frost—specifically his poem entitled "Stopping by Woods on a Snowy Evening." These oft-quoted verses end with the following words:

> The woods are lovely, dark and deep,
> But I have promises to keep,
> And miles to go before I sleep,
> And miles to go before I sleep.

As I read the poem, it seemed to me that the challenges we faced in 1989 as a new board, individually and collectively, were indeed "lovely, dark and deep." We had a lot to learn about the complex and sometimes mysterious problems of higher education, but we have been rewarded and challenged beyond our expectations.

THE REWARDS OF SERVICE

First, we have had the opportunity to meet hundreds of students from the system campuses and to hear about their hopes and aspirations. The talent we have seen has given us hope that their aspirations will be realized. We have also come to know the two students who served as members of our board very well. One was a nontraditional student and one was a traditional student. We have learned firsthand the viewpoints of the two types of students that now constitute our student population.

The faculty on our university and college campuses has been represented before the board and its various committees on dozens of occasions since we took office. We have come to know the richness of their backgrounds; their dedication to teaching, research, and service; and the gap between their average pay and what they truly deserve to receive. We have come to know that the term "classified staff" comprises many different types of job classifications and individuals. We have also come to recognize the importance of their role in delivering services to our students and faculty, as well as the fact that for many, the average pay, like that of the faculty, is below what they deserve.

We have also come to know many presidents and senior administrators on our college campuses. While the statistics suggest that their tenures will be brief, it is clear to me that we are blessed by the service of leaders who have truly exceptional abilities. We have come to know the demands of their offices, especially the demands on a college or university president, and how they can conflict and become almost unbearable. We have developed great appreciation for the boards of advisors. By giving generously of their time and wisdom, they exert a very positive influence on the institutions they represent.

Finally, I think we have come to realize the significant challenges facing our chancellors and others in the higher-education central office. These have been years of turmoil for the higher-education officials in our state, and it is clear to me that they have been as motivated by a desire to serve others as they have been driven by legal mandates.

Aside from the people we have met, the "woods" have been "lovely, dark and deep" with respect to the issues we have discussed. Former trustee Rachael Worby, Trustee James, and others have raised our consciousness with regard to our need to focus on the issue of social justice on the campuses. We have given these issues priority, but perhaps more importantly, we have each been made more aware of the work that remains to be done in this area.

Several members of the trustees, especially Trustees Perry and Powell, have continued to focus on the ways we can give West Virginians access to our colleges and universities. We have come to learn that "access" programs can also be programs of "excellence." That student enrollment in the institutions of our system has been increasing and is now well in excess of forty thousand is both encouraging and reassuring.

We have also come to see how much the people of West Virginia care about their colleges and universities. From simple expressions of support for our athletic teams, to the significant financial commitments of those supporting the current capital campaigns, we have witnessed this commitment. Perhaps more importantly, we have noted how much our elected representatives care about what goes on at the university and college campus. It is important for us, as I will mention later, to nurture this caring attitude and to guide its direction.

We have also come to appreciate, more than before, the richness of the higher-education community in America. While most of us have had experiences on the college and university campuses as students, faculty, staff, administrators, or supporters, the governing board has a unique perspective. Its decision processes give us an inside look at the diversity, talent, and challenges of the campuses. The "campus community" now means something more special to me, and I am sure that it does to you as well.

We have also learned that those who preceded us on the Board of Regents were good stewards. The foundation its members left us was very solid. Despite the desire for change in the governance structure, the public was well served by the dedication and leadership of our predecessors.

We have also come to see that the mission of the university system is as broad as higher education itself. Within our system, we have enormous diversity: community college programs, junior college programs, regional campuses of a major university, a graduate school focusing on nontraditional graduate students, a graduate school focusing on a single professional program, a regional university of significant potential, and one of the nation's fine land-grant comprehensive research universities. Because of this variety, we have been exposed to an unusually wide range of issues.

Thus, while our trip through the higher-education landscape has sometimes seemed overwhelming, it has, at the same time, been worth it. I am sure that in the two years we have served, we have gained new respect for the responsibilities we bear. It is not surprising that we are called "trustees," for we exercise positions of stewardship as well as positions of leadership. We are part of a tradition that finds its roots in the ancient universities of Oxford, Paris, and Bologna and is an important part of the American democratic experience.

OUR EARLY ACCOMPLISHMENTS

When we assumed our positions as trustees, it was clear to us that we had "promises to keep," because expectations were very high following the passage of the legislation that created our board. Before we could act, however, we had to organize ourselves. We did so by taking a fresh look at our organizational requirements. The prior organizational structure was not taken for granted. These early activities consumed far more time than I would have thought, but they will, I am certain, bear fruit in the years to come. Already I can see the benefits of your labors as our committees have begun to function quite smoothly and as our meetings, while occasionally involving controversial decisions, have proved to be surprisingly efficient.

Consider the breadth of what we have accomplished administratively: We have designed a job description for a chancellor, established a chancellor's office, hired an interim chancellor, and hired a permanent chancellor. We have established an agenda format that brings before the board the issues of the day, greetings from the leaders of our state, and higher-education information that can be shared with others. We have established a new philosophy of governance and put it in writing. This new philosophy of governance essentially calls for the creation of strong institutions, bound together in a system with a common purpose and a clear mission. Under the leadership of Trustees Goodwin and McMillan, we have created mission statements for each of our institutions and for the system as a whole, and we have begun the process of delegating issues that are appropriately local concerns back to the campuses.

We also forged an initial relationship with our state government and its first secretary of education and the arts. We have established a joint meeting format for use with the Board of Directors System. We have considered and acted upon the application of the West Virginia Governmental Ethics Act to our system and demanded, I believe, a high standard of ethical conduct from our system's employees.

We have accomplished all of this through unanticipated effort on your part, including loyal attendance at board meetings, committee meetings, special meetings, and retreats. Perhaps above all, the debates we have had (and there have been many) have been civil in tone. You seem committed to the idea that our collective wisdom is better than our individual ideas. I have been truly amazed at the contribution that each of our trustees is capable of making in a debate or discussion of the issues. The variety of perspectives, the different thought processes, and the absolute dedication to do "the right thing" has inspired me, as your chairman, at every meeting.

Having organized ourselves, we considered the various issues that came before the board. Some came routinely, and others arose out of special circumstances. We now see that our time was spent on topics of the type and nature that other governing boards around the country are also addressing.

Consider also the large number of administrative topics we have addressed and which are of vital importance to those in our campus communities: the TIAA-CREF reforms, the oversight of distance education facilities, the improvements in our capital project management policies, adjustments to our resource allocation model, the review and revision of several policy bulletins, two presidential reviews and the presidential review process, the concept of a "regional campus," the adoption of a clinical track faculty-appointment model, the beginning of research corporations for our two major universities, the acquisition of a farm at Potomac State, a stadium and fine arts center at Marshall University, a new science building at the West Virginia School of Osteopathic Medicine, an enormous amount of construction at West Virginia University, and much more. Our supervision and consideration of these projects and issues would not have been possible without the leadership of our committee structure. We are all truly indebted to each of the board members who have made a special effort as chair of one of our regular standing or special committees, especially Trustees Goodwin, Hoblitzell, James, McMillan, Perry, Todd, and Worby.

During our tenure, legislative appropriations to the university system increased 10.5 percent in the aggregate. This is not an insubstantial amount, given the overall condition of our state and national economies. In many states, decreases in appropriations are being implemented this year.

One of our major accomplishments has been to demonstrate a sense of concern about social justice on our university and college campuses. In doing so, I believe we are helping America prepare for a tomorrow that will be as diverse as it will be complex. Members of our board have attended a variety of conferences related to the subject and continue to help educate our system about these issues. Perhaps more importantly, we have dedicated a substantial portion of our moral leadership to these issues. Our adoption of policy statements addressing social justice issues is evidence of our increased commitment, as is the leadership given to this board by people whose souls are utterly committed to social justice in America.

Most recently, we have sought to address the series of issues surrounding medical education in our state. I think it is important for us to note, in retrospect, that we have really tried to address at least four issues simultaneously: the need for more doctors in rural areas of our state, the need to improve health care and health care delivery for West Virginians, the need to allocate precious resources effectively in order to support medical education in our state, and the need to address how medical education can be best undertaken in our state. These four distinct goals have often become confused, and as the governing board for three medical schools in a small state, we have been at the vortex of the confusion. My own sense is that there is a growing consensus that will lead to an appropriate resolution, one that recognizes the important role of our institutions and the special role they must play in addressing the health care needs of West Virginians.

In this regard, we have begun to look at new ways to coordinate the efforts of our medical school complexes. Perhaps the best demonstration of what can be achieved when all institutions work together is our "system" application to the Kellogg Foundation for a substantial grant to explore new ways of teaching the healing arts in off-campus clinical settings. Out of many national competitors, we have been chosen to receive a grant. Our medical schools can take great pride in this achievement.

The Caperton Plan for Health care (and implementing the Kellogg Grant), announced yesterday, reflects our input and deserves our most serious consideration and support in the coming months.

Finally, we have become more sensitive to the importance of the relationship between the university system and the public schools. That we play a major role in the preparation of teachers and other school personnel for West Virginia at both the undergraduate and graduate levels is a matter given high priority. Our advocacy of the Advanced Placement Program and the In-field Master's legislation and our approval of the baccalaureate program in Elementary Education at WVU–Parkersburg are indicative of this priority.

THE YEARS AHEAD

Yet the board has "miles to go before it sleeps." I think that our recent retreat helped us to identify the issues the board needs to address in the coming years. I am personally excited about the possibility that the board will focus attention during the next few years on student concerns and student-related issues: tuition, our resident–nonresident mix, guidance and counseling, access, special programs of excellence, student athletics, recruitment, and so forth. The lifting up of these concerns for special consideration by the board should not in any way detract from, or diminish the board's efforts to continue to serve the people of the state (for example, through economic-development efforts) or its efforts to help pursue knowledge (through our basic and applied research activities). I feel strongly, however, that every governing board like ours must keep its eyes on the students it serves. Our governing board must never lose sight of the wonderful things that happen when a mind, young or old, is expanded and when new vistas of human potential are opened through a college education.

Our advocacy on behalf of higher education must get stronger. While mid-year budget cuts now seem to be a thing of the past, we have been forced to meet substantial increased costs of operation. Some of these increases resulted from actions of state government; others resulted from the increased costs of goods and services provided. Moreover, the percentage of the general revenue budget in West Virginia represented by our system dropped slightly during our tenure, from 9.7 percent to 9.6 percent. The board must make the case for supporting all of higher education in every forum: state government, Congress, and in the boardrooms of charitable foundations and private sector businesses.

In this regard, I hope that the board will address its communications tools in the coming months. The board can and must do a better job of communicating its goals, the particular strengths of each institution, the richness of college life (to which I have alluded), and the needs of the university system (and, indeed, all of higher education) to the body politic in general and, in particular, to those in a position to be of assistance to higher education. In the past, we have focused on communications with the governor and state legislature. I believe our communications must also be directed toward Washington, the private sector, and the citizenry of our state. As I have indicated, I firmly believe that the people of West Virginia care about their colleges and universities. They need to know that their colleges and universities care about them, too.

As part of its goal to improve the quality of our efforts, I hope the board will continue to recognize the importance of recruiting talented people. As importantly, I hope the board can focus on empowering talented people to realize their potential. In this regard, the board must always recognize the importance of attracting, retaining, and giving support to high-quality leaders for our campuses and the office of the chancellor. This will require special attention on the board's part, attention that I believe we have exhibited in the two presidential searches and the two chancellor searches we have conducted to date. Our commitment must be to attract the best possible person to each open position over which we exercise the power of appointment.

It is customary to say that public higher education should serve the needs of the people who support it. I hope the board will keep its commitment to this commonsense notion and will, from time to time, assess its progress in a way that will make it accountable, not only to the legislature that created it and the people who support higher education in West Virginia, but also to the traditions of higher education institutions that have now survived over one thousand years. The board must never forget that at the base of its "trusteeship" responsibilities is an obligation to provide efficient management and positive, enlightened leadership for higher education. I believe we have made tremendous strides toward this end.

Recently, the president of Yale, Benno Schmidt Jr., noted that today the core values of the university—freedom of speech and expression, the primacy of truth, and the quest for knowledge—are being examined.[4] He argues that the university community must constantly strive to demonstrate that it is extraordinarily important to the future of our society. For us to demonstrate that our institutions are indeed special, we, as a board of trustees, must constantly strive to demonstrate:

- that we accept our position as one of "trust,"
- that we understand our mission and believe in it,
- that at the core of our being is a respect for all people—not just the ones on our campuses,
- that our decisions are driven by a strong desire to do what is right, not by expediency, and
- that we believe colleges and universities are, indeed, special places in our society.

SUMMING UP

In conclusion, I am reminded of my father's wisdom that the best way to move a large pile of coal from one place to another is one shovelful at a time. Each step we have taken has been manageable and sometimes modest in scope. Looking back on our first two years of operation, however, I feel that we have accomplished much of which we can be proud. Trustee Joe Powell is fond of saying that he tries to stand "shoulder to shoulder" with his chairman and the other members of the board. Even when we have had differences, I have never felt anything but support for the common goals we collectively forged. You have made a tremendous effort in terms of time, emotional energy, and moral commitment. To each of you I am grateful.

On your behalf, I extend our mutual thanks to Governor Gaston Caperton for our appointments; to the state legislature for its ratification of our appointments, interest, and support of the university system; and to the hundreds, even thousands, of individuals who have worked during the past two years toward the goal of transforming higher education in West Virginia.

Our period as trustees together has been one of the most rewarding periods of my life. While we have more promises to keep, and more miles to go before we sleep, I am proud of what we have accomplished together in just two years.

NOTES

1   Alexis DeTocqueville, *Democracy in America*, trans. Harvey C. Mansfield and Delba Winthrop (1835–1840; Chicago: University of Chicago Press, 2002).

2   Anthony DePalma, "Clash of '91; Higher Education Feels the Heat," *New York Times*, June 2, 1991, http://www.nytimes.com/ (accessed January 10, 2001).

3   DePalma, "Clash of '91."

4   Benno Schmidt Jr., "The University and Freedom," *Academe* 73 (Winter 1992): 14–18.

BRINGING CLOSURE, TIME TO SAY GOODBYE

A LETTER OF FAREWELL TO THE UNIVERSITY COMMUNITY

2007

During my tenure as president, I wrote a quarterly letter to our alumni and friends that appeared in the "West Virginia University Alumni Magazine." This was the last such article, which both Susan and I signed.

At commencement in recent years, at the end of the ceremony, a graduating student from the School of Music has been asked to sing "Time to Say Goodbye" ("Con Te Partiro" in Italian) to the graduating students. Made famous by Andrea Bocelli and Sarah Brightman, the song's only words in English are "Time to Say Goodbye." The rendition always stirs emotions, not only among our graduating undergraduates, graduate students, and first professionals, but also among the family and friends present and the faculty, staff, and administrators in the audience. Students share a special emotion as they are about to leave the university that transformed them and enter a new phase of their lives. We love the song because of its extraordinary beauty and because of its poignant message. At that special time to say goodbye, we are reminded of why we have served our university—it transforms the lives of its students and serves communities, our nation, and our world through its teaching, research, and service mission.

The time is rapidly approaching when it will be time for us to say goodbye. While we will remain in Morgantown, we will be stepping aside to allow new leadership to guide the university and to allow ourselves a much-needed respite from the rigors and demands of the modern American university presidency.

As we leave, we know that the university is a much different university than the one at which we arrived in 1995. WVU today is made up of campuses, farms, forests, extension offices, medical facilities, and partnerships and networks all across West Virginia. New academic programs, growth in enrollment, more robust research and service agendas, new campuses, a new health care system, Eastern Panhandle and Clarksburg hospitals, a stronger athletic department, new technologies, larger dependence on private funds and tuition dollars, and the changing nature of global competition in the education market have made our alma mater a much more exciting and complex institution.

Thanks to the work of a very strong and stable leadership team, the university is in sound financial condition, notwithstanding the significant financial challenges of the past decade. An innovative and vibrant parent organization, a strong alumni association, and a strong private foundation have achieved similar milestones. Most believe the reputation of the institution has advanced nationally and internationally. One national leader has called WVU a "model land-grant institution."

We are saying goodbye to the university community with enormous grati-tude to the students who have worked hard to pay for and achieve a WVU degree and who have been our inspiration every day. We also say goodbye to their families who have worked with us every day to improve the university and to help develop a more student-centered culture at WVU.

We are saying goodbye with the certainty that many thousands of faculty, staff, students, administrators, volunteers, donors, state- and federal-office holders, policymakers, and others have worked with us to advance the mis-sion of the university on all of its campuses and to achieve global excellence that is valued in a competitive market. We offer our thanks to each and every person with whom we have served. So many have worked so hard to accom-plish so much.

We are saying goodbye with a full understanding that challenges lie ahead for the next president. Salaries and job descriptions must be made and kept competitive if we are to succeed in a market for talent that is global at a time of widespread retirements. WVU's agenda will likely include activities that improve the lives of every West Virginian. Growth will be necessary, and on some campuses, it will have to be managed to the benefit of our host commu-nities and neighbors. Increased private giving will play an important role in our future. New efficiencies will have to be found. Of course, other challenges lie ahead, but they will no doubt be identified, confronted, and mastered by the next generation of leadership.

But in the final analysis, as we say goodbye, we have come to realize that every university's agenda constantly changes. Having known all presidents of the university since Dr. Irvin Stewart, who served the university with his wife Florence for twelve years (from 1946 to 1958), we know that we have been privileged to hold positions of trust for such an extended period at a very spe-cial moment in time—the turn of the century, the dawn of a new millennium.

Our job has been to advance the university as best we could as it marched into the twenty-first century, knowing full well that future leaders will do the best they can to serve the university in the centuries to come.

It is time to say goodbye. We leave with joy in our hearts and thankful both for the education we achieved at our alma mater and the extraordinary honor of serving it.

David C. Hardesty Jr., '67
President

Susan Brown Hardesty, '67
Founder, Mountaineer Parents Club

CONCLUSION

Assembling the speeches, articles, and essays contained in this book and introducing to you the occasions on which they were written have reminded us of how a busy personal and professional agenda seems to compress time. It hardly seems possible that we took on our positions at this university twelve years ago.

During that time, our campus has witnessed the education and emotional and intellectual maturation of thousands of undergraduate, graduate, and professional students. Our personal journey has included a huge array of people, events, travels, and experiences.

Both the university and the society it serves have changed. The impact of the events of September 11 on our campuses serves as just one example of how intimately related universities are with the world they serve. Surely we have come to realize that we live and work in a global economy, and we are not insulated from the political, social, and competitive forces influencing global society.

The period has been one of enormous transition for American higher education. Parents and students have demanded accountability through their legislatures, and subsidy funding has been withdrawn in favor of grants, vouchers, scholarships, and other forms of direct payments often tied to direct benefit and performance. Technology has changed everything from how we teach to how we communicate. Revolutions in science have stimulated whole new research efforts. Much, much more has changed in our society.

As our society has changed, our universities have changed. The change was reluctant at first, but gradually campuses across America realized that because universities are public institutions, if society changes, so must the institutions that serve society. This has caused campus leaders to focus on leading change and change management. The times have rewarded both leaders and campus constituencies who are willing to change.

Part of the change that has been rewarded is the acceptance of modern business practices and strategic planning. Our business officers have been up to the task. The environment has been constantly monitored, administrative and management processes have been modernized, priorities have been established, and goals and objectives have been shared. These efforts, together with a lesser share of state and federal spending, have caused the campuses of public institutions to become more and more efficient. Regardless, the teaching, scholarship, research, and service activities of the university have become even more robust in recent years. Focusing on change has lifted up the eternal value of leaders and leadership to any organization. Leaders serve to form teams, mentor, coach, provide hope and vision, celebrate accomplishments, encourage performance, provide an explanation of meaning in work, teach, and engage in a variety of other tasks that move people toward common ends.

In the context of today's environment, diversity, intellectual capacity, and adaptability emerge as powerful tools for universities, which collectively serve as powerful social and economic engines in today's world. As we emphasize in the "Afterword," the modern university constantly changes as it serves and adapts to the needs of our world.

As even the casual reader will note, I have quoted Winston Churchill liberally throughout my tenure. In retrospect, I realize that my reliance on his word craft is related to my conception of one of the more important skills a modern president must possess: the ability to articulate insights and concepts that are important to each university.

In many respects, therefore, this has been a book about the power of words. As I indicated in the chapter on intercollegiate athletics, the modern university has many owners, all of whom are tied to and even vested in the past, present, and future of the university. The president must somehow give voice to all owners, even if they are in conflict. And while giving voice to competing and conflicting interests, the president must also emerge first among equals, the one clear voice of the university. It is the president who must define the mission, vision, values, and goals of the university, all of which must somehow seem eternal in a world marked by constant change.

APPENDIX 1

TIMELINE OF SPEECHES

Year	Event	Chapter
1963–7	David C. Hardesty and Susan Brown attend WVU as undergraduate students	
1968	David C. Hardesty and Susan Brown marry	
1979	Celebrating Volunteers	Chapter 22
1987	Reflections on the Oxford Experience	Chapter 27
1991	The Education of a Volunteer	Chapter 29
1994	Can Education Be Run Like a Business?	Chapter 6
1995	David C. Hardesty appointed President of WVU	
	Getting Started (The Inaugural Address)	Chapter 8
	Leading Lawyers: Why Lawyers Lead in America	Chapter 28
1996	A Student-Centered Vision (State of the University Address)	Chapter 9
1997	Staying on Track: Piloting River Boats, Wiggling Free, Finding Waldo, and Following in the Footsteps of St. Patrick (State of the University Address)	Chapter 9

Year	Event	Chapter
	Daughter of the Year: Reflections on our Journey to Service (Susan B. Hardesty)	Chapter 25
	Son of the Year: Reflections on our Journey to Service	Chapter 25
	The Role of Women at West Virginia University (Susan B. Hardesty)	Chapter 14
1999	Campus Statement on Diversity and Civil Rights	Chapter 16
	Reaching around the World (Tribute to a Faculty Member and Vice Provost)	Chapter 17
2000	Leading Change	Chapter 7
2001	The New University (State of the University Address)	Chapter 9
	Campus Memorial After the Events of September 11	Chapter 18
	Reflections on Undergraduate Growth	Chapter 26
	Can We Do It Right This Time? Development in West Virginia	Chapter 24
	So, You Want to Be an Entrepreneur?	Chapter 24
	Leading Economic Change in America's Communities	Chapter 24
2002	Remarks to New Citizens of the United States at a Naturalization Ceremony	Chapter 19
	Remembering a Friend Lost on September 11	Chapter 18
	It's Not All About Brains (Advice to Students)	Chapter 23
2003	Ten Characteristics of a Highly Effective Organization	Chapter 2
	A Plea for Public Support of Higher Education	Chapter 10

Year	Event	Chapter
2004	Lifelong Learning for Leaders and Organizations	Chapter 3
	The Importance of Diversity in Higher Education	Chapter 16
	Inspiring with Hope and Humor (Tribute to a Dean of Students)	Chapter 17
	Making a Difference (Contributions of University Graduates)	Chapter 17
	The Trail to Eagle: Scouting Now! More Than Ever	Chapter 21
2005	Quality Matters (State of the University Address)	Chapter 9
	Leader Overload	Chapter 5
	Twelve Attributes of a Quality Institution (Advice to Educators)	Chapter 23
	The Impact of the 4-H Program on Youth Development in the United States	Chapter 21
2006	Recognizing Lessons Learned at the Turn of the Century, (State of the University Address)	Chapter 1
	Fifth Anniversary of September 11	Chapter 18
	Involving Parents in Support of the Mission (Susan B. Hardesty)	Chapter 12
	Building Leadership Capacity	Chapter 4
	Finding Wisdom in the Information Age	Chapter 20
	Character Matters (Remarks at the Funeral of a Former President)	Chapter 17
	Encouraging a New President (Recognition of an Exemplary Alumnus)	Chapter 17

Year	Event	Chapter
2007	The Joy of Teaching, Inside and Outside of the Classroom	Chapter 11
	The Value and Perils of Intercollegiate Athletics	Chapter 15
	The Vital Role of the Private Donor	Chapter 13
	Preparing for Success in College (Advice for Parents)	Chapter 23
	Bringing Closure, Time to Say Goodbye	Afterword

APPENDIX 2

THE NUMBERS AT WVU
1995–2006

	1995	2006
Headcount Enrollment (main)	21,517	27,115 (expect 27,600 for 2007)
Headcount Enrollment (all campuses)	28,944	34,637
FTE Enrollment (main)	19,300	25,678
FTE Enrollment (all campuses)	24,960	31,271
Research/Sponsored Projects Funding	$64.1 M	$142.9 M

	1995	2006
Extension Participant Contacts	122,225	645,183*
Foundation Assets	$183.0 M	$991 M as of June 30, 2007
Foundation Endowment	$140.2 M	$430 M as of June 30, 2007
Patients Admitted to WVU Hospitals	12,818	21,091
Uncompensated Health Care provided by WVU Hospitals, including charity and bad debt	$26,301,272 (includes University Health Associates)	$48,559,335 (does not include University Health Associates)
Number of families in the Mountaineer Parents Club	0	17,500 (July 1, 2007)
Operating Budget (Expenses) Includes WVU Main Campus including HSC, Research Corporation, Potomac State College, and WVU-Parkersburg.	$413,203,000	$693,860,000 (also includes WVU Institute of Technology and CTC at WVUIT)
Revenue	$430,642,000	$737,254,000
Total completed and approved construction expenditures, 1995-2007		$708,000,000

* Counting methods have been normalized across programs and counties, resulting in more accurate data.

BIOGRAPHICAL

INFORMATION

SUSAN BROWN HARDESTY is the daughter of a faculty member at West Virginia University, from which she graduated with honors in music education and to which she returned as an active spouse of the president. She also earned a master's degree in special education from the West Virginia College of Graduate Studies (now Marshall University Graduate College). During her career, she taught at a private school in England and in the public schools of Massachusetts and West Virginia. An active volunteer and advocate for the arts and education throughout her life, she embraced volunteer leadership of her alma mater. Foremost among her volunteer activities for her alma mater were her efforts to found the Mountaineer Parents Club, an organization of fifteen thousand families that has been honored many times for its work in support of undergraduate students at West Virginia University, and activities related to charitable fundraising for the university and its host community's United Way.

DAVID C. HARDESTY JR. served as president of West Virginia University, his undergraduate alma mater, from 1995 until 2007. While a student, he served as WVU's student body president. He also holds degrees from Oxford University (which he attended on a Rhodes Scholarship) and Harvard Law School. Prior to becoming a university president, he practiced law, served in the cabinet of West Virginia Governor Jay Rockefeller, and was an active volunteer leader in his home state. Hardesty's presidency was noted for its student-centered emphasis, rapid growth in enrollment, research activity and endowments, and expansion of the economic-development mission of the university. While he was president, Hardesty served as chair of the National 4-H Council and as a member of several task forces and committees related to higher education and intercollegiate athletics, including the Bowl Championship Series Presidential Oversight Committee. He also served on the National Security Higher Education Advisory Board. He has been a frequent speaker at meetings sponsored by a number of national organizations, most often on the subjects of cultural change and leadership. He has served on a number of civic, not-for-profit, and corporate boards and commissions. He currently is a tenured professor at the College of Law at West Virginia University, where he teaches courses related to the legislative process and bill drafting.

President and Mrs. Hardesty met at WVU while they were students. They have two adult children and have been married since 1968.

REFERENCES AND
CITED WORKS

Ambrose, Stephen. *Nothing Like It in The World: The Men Who Built the Transcontinental Railroad, 1863–1869*. New York: Simon and Schuster, 2000.

Blake, William. *The Complete Poetry and Prose of William Blake*. Ed. David Erdman. Berkeley: University of California Press, 1965; rev. ed., 1982.

Bombeck, Erma. "A Tribute to Volunteers." *Good Housekeeping*. 1970.

Bornstein, Rita. "The Nature and Nurture of Presidents." *The Chronicle of Higher Education*. 52, no. 11 (2005). http://chronicle.com (accessed November 17, 2006).

Bolen, Jean. *Close to the Bone: Life-Threatening Illness and the Search for Meaning*. New York: Touchstone, 1998.

Bok, Derek. *Higher Learning*. Cambridge, MA: Harvard University Press, 1986.

Brokaw, Tom. *The Greatest Generation*. New York: Random House, 1998.

Brooks, Maurice. *The Appalachians*. Boston: Houghton Mifflin Company, 1965.

Bruch, Heike and Sumantra Ghoshal. "Beware the Busy Manager." *Harvard Business Review*. 80, no. 2 (2002): 62–69.

Burns, James MacGregor. *Leadership*. New York: Harper and Row, 1978.

Butler, Timothy and James Waldroop. "Job Sculpting: The Art of Retaining Your Best People." *Harvard Business Review*. 77, no. 5 (1999): 144–152.

Butta, Jim. "Mountaineer Fans Invade Jacksonville." *Wheeling (WV) Intelligencer.* January 1, 2007: 17.

Cahill, Thomas. *How the Irish Saved Civilization: The Untold Story of Ireland's Heroic Role from the Fall of Rome to the Rise of Medieval Europe.* New York: Doubleday, 1995.

Casner, A. James and W. Barton Leach. *Cases and Text on Property.* 1950; Boston: Little, Brown, 1984.

Churchill, Winston S. *Never Give In! The Best of Winston Churchill's Speeches.* New York: Hyperion, 2003.

The College Board. *Trends in College Pricing 1998.* New York: The College Board, 1998.

Collins, Jim. *Good to Great: Why Some Companies Make the Leap . . . and Other Don't.* New York: HarperCollins Publishers, 2001.

De Gues, Arie P. "Planning as Learning." *Harvard Business Review.* 66, no. 2 (1998): 70–74.

DePalma, Anthony. "Clash of '91; Higher Education Feels the Heat." *New York Times.* June 2, 1991. http://www.nytimes.com/ (accessed January 10, 2001).

DeTocqueville, Alexis. *Democracy in America.* Trans. Harvey C. Mansfield and Delba Winthrop. 1835–1840; Chicago: University of Chicago Press, 2002.

Doherty, Jr., William T. and Festus P. Summers. *West Virginia University, Symbol of Unity in a Sectionalized State.* Morgantown: West Virginia University Press, 1982.

Drucker, Peter F. *Classsic Drucker: Essential Wisdom of Peter Drucker from the Pages of The Harvard Business Review.* Boston, MA: Harvard Business School Publishing Corporation, 2006.

_____. *The Effective Executive.* New York: Harper and Row, 1966.

_____. *The Essential Drucker: Selections from the Management Works of Peter F. Drucker.* New York: HarperBusiness, 2001.

Frankl, Victor. *Man's Search for Meaning: An Introduction to Logotherapy.* 1959; 3rd ed., trans. Ilse Lasch, New York: Simon and Schuster, 1984.

Football Bowl Association. "Overview." http://www.footballbowlassociation. com/overview.html (accessed January 25, 2007).

Frost, Robert. *The Poetry of Robert Frost.* Ed. Edward Connery Latham. "Stopping by Woods on a Snowy Evening." New York: Holt, Rinehart, and Winston, 1969, 224–225.

Gardner, Howard. *Frames of Mind: The Theory of Multiple Intelligences.* New York: Basic Books, 1983.

Gardner, Howard, in collaboration with Emma Laskin. *Leading Minds: An Anatomy of Leadership.* New York: Basic Books, 1996.

Gladwell, Malcolm. *Blink: The Power of Thinking Without Thinking.* New York: Little, Brown, 2005.

Hall, Granville Davisson. *The Rending of Virginia: A History.* 1902; Ed. John Edmund Stealey III, Knoxville: University of Tennessee Press, 2000.

Hall, Stephen S. "The Older-and-Wiser Hypothesis." *New York Times Magazine.* May 6, 2007: 58–66.

Hallowell, Edward M. "Overloaded Circuits: Why Smart People Underperform." *Harvard Business Review.* 83, no.1 (2005): 54–62.

Handbook to the University of Oxford. Oxford: Clarendon Press, 1966.

Hardesty, David C., Jr., "A Response to President Yates' Essay: *Vision, Transparency, and Passion.*" *University Presidents as Moral Leaders.* American Council on Education. Ed. David G. Brown. Westport, CT: Praeger, 2006, 129–134

Hardesty, David C., Jr., Lawrence S. Cote, and Larry LeFlore. "Changing Campus Culture." In *Handbook of Applied Developmental Science: Promoting Positive Child, Adolescent, and Family Development through Research, Policies, and Programs.* Vol. 4. Eds. Richard M. Lerner, Donald Wertlieb, and Francine Jacobs. Thousand Oaks, CA: Sage Publications, 2003, 13–34.

Hathaway, Charles E., Paige E. Mulhollan, and Karen A. White. "Metropolitan Universities: Models for the 21st Century." *Metropolitan Universities*. 1, no. 1 (1990): 30.

Heifetz, Ronald A. and Marty Linsky. *Leadership on the Line: Staying Alive through the Dangers of Leading*. Boston: Harvard Business School Press, 2002.

Hobbhouse, Christopher. *Oxford: as It Was and as It Is Today*. 1939; 4th ed., London: B. T. Batsford Ltd., 1948.

House, Jack. *Winston Churchill: His Wit and Wisdom*. London: Hyperion Books, 1965.

June, Audrey Williams. "Presidents: Same Look, Different Decade." *The Chronicle of Higher Education*. February 16, 2007: A33–35.

Kano, Noriako, N. Seraku, F. Takahashi, and S. Tsuji. "Attractive Quality and Must-Be Quality." *Hinshitsu: The Journal of Japanese Society for Quality Control*. 14, no. 2 (April 1984): 39–48.

Kantrowitz, Barbara and Karen Springen. "A Peaceful Adolescence." *Newsweek*. April 25, 2005: 58–60.

The Kellogg Foundation. *Returning to Our Roots: Executive Summaries of the Reports of the Kellogg Commission on the Future of State Universities and Land-Grant Colleges*. Washington, DC: National Association of State Colleges and Land-Grant Universities, Office of Public Affairs, 2001.

Kirk, Grayson. "Responsibilities of the Educated Man." In *The University of Denver Centennial Symposium: The Responsible Individual and a Free Society in an Expanding Universe*. Ed. Fred Hoyle. Denver, CO: Big Mountain Press, 1965.

Knight Commission on Intercollegiate Athletics. *Keeping Faith with the Student-Athlete: A New Model for Intercollegiate Athletics*. 1991.

Kouzes, James M. and Barry Z. Posner. *The Leadership Challenge: How to Get Extraordinary Things Done in Organizations*. 3rd ed. San Francisco: Jossey-Bass Publishers, 2003.

_____. *A Leader's Legacy*. San Francisco: Jossey-Bass Publishers, 2006.

Lerner, Richard et al. "Positive Youth Development, Participation in Community Youth Development Programs, and Community Contributions of Fifth Grade Adolescents: Findings from the First Wave of the 4-H Study of Positive Youth Development." *Journal of Early Adolescence*. 25, no.1 (2005): 17–71.

Lewis, Ronald L. *Transforming the Appalachian Countryside: Railroads, Deforestation, and Social Change in West Virginia, 1880–1920*. Chapel Hill: University of North Carolina Press, 1998.

Llewellyn, K. N. *The Bramble Bush: On Our Law and Its Study*. 1930; New York: Oceana Publications, 1975.

Martin, Alexander. *Inaugural Address Delivered at the West Virginia Agricultural College*. Morgantown, WV: Morgan and Hoffman, Printers, 1867.

_____. "Special Message and Report of Board of Visitors West Virginia Agricultural College." In *West Virginia University Report of the Board of Regents and the President, 1867/68–1896/9*. Wheeling, WV: John Frew, Public Printer, 1868.

McCall, Jr., Morgan W. *High Flyers: Developing the Next Generation of Leaders*. Boston, MA: Harvard Business School Press, 1998.

McCarthy, Bernice. *4MAT in Action: Creative Lesson Plans for Teaching to Learning Styles with Right/Left Mode Techniques*. Oak Brook, IL: Excel Inc., 1981.

McCauley, Cynthia D. and Ellen Van Velsor, eds. *The Center for Creative Leadership Handbook of Leadership Development*. 2nd ed. San Francisco: Jossey-Bass, 2004.

McGregor, Douglas. *Human Side of Enterprise*. New York: McGraw Hill, 1960.

The Monticola: West Virginia University 1900. Morgantown, WV: Acme Publishing Co., 1899.

Morris, James. *Oxford*. London: Faber and Faber, 1965.

Mother Teresa. *A Simple Path*. Comp. Lucinda Vardey. New York: Ballantine Books, 1995.

Nagy, Laszlo. *250 Million Scouts*. Chicago: Dartnell Publishers, 1985.

National Collegiate Athletic Association. "Composition of the NCAA." http://www1.ncaa.org/membership/membership_svcs/membership_breakdown .html (accessed January 27, 2007).

National Collegiate Athletic Association. *Executive Summary of The Second-Century Imperatives: Presidential Leadership—Institutional Accountability*. Indianapolis: NCAA, 2006.

———. *The Second-Century Imperatives: Presidential Leadership—Institutional Accountability*. Indianapolis: NCAA, 2006.

National Security Council. *Mapping the Global Future: Report of the National Intelligence Council's 2020 Project*. Pittsburgh: Government Printing Office, 2004.

Newman, John Henry. *The Idea of a University: Defined and Illustrated*. 1852; London: Longmans Green, 1896.

New Shorter Oxford English Dictionary on Historical Principles. 5th ed. Oxford: Oxford University Press, 2002.

O'Toole, James. *Leading Change: The Argument for Values-Based Leadership*. San Francisco: Jossey-Bass Publishers, 1996.

The Oxford Dictionary of Quotations. 5th ed. Ed. Elizabeth Knowles. Oxford: Oxford University Press, 1999.

Phillips, Donald T. *Lincoln on Leadership: Executive Strategies for Tough Times*. New York: Warner Books, 1993.

Rosovsky, Henry. *The University: An Owner's Manual*. New York: W. W. Norton, 1990.

Salinger, Pierre; Edwin Guthman; Frank Mankiewicz; and John Seigenthaler, eds. *"An Honorable Profession": A Tribute to Robert F. Kennedy*. Garden City, NY: Doubleday and Company, 1968.

Schmidt, Jr., Benno. "The University and Freedom." *Academe*. 73 (Winter 1992): 14–18.

Schweitzer, Albert. *On the Edge of the Primeval Forest and More from the Primeval Forest: Experiences and Observations of a Doctor in Equatorial Africa*. 1931; New York: Macmillan, 1961.

Smart, Bradford and Geoffery Smart. *Topgrading: How Leading Companies Win by Hiring, Coaching and Keeping the Best People*. Paramus, NJ: Prentice Hall Press, 1999.

Spence, Gerry. *The Making of a Country Lawyer*. New York: St. Martin's Press, 1996.

Stuart, Alex. "Water for Profit." *CFO*. 23, no. 2 (February 2007): 40–45.

Surowiecki, James. *The Wisdom of Crowds: Why the Many Are Smarter than the Few and How Collective Wisdom Shapes Business, Economies, Societies, and Nations*. New York: Doubleday, 2004.

Tolstoy, Leo. *War and Peace*. 1869; Trans. Constance Garnett. New York: Modern Library, 2002.

Twain, Mark. *Life on the Mississippi*. 1883; Pleasantville, NY: Reader's Digest Association, Inc., 1987.

Ungavri, Steve. "TRIZ within the Context of the Kano Model or Adding the Third Dimension to Quality." *The TRIZ Journal*. October 1999. http://www. triz-journal. com/archives/1999/10/e/ (accessed January 25, 2007).

The United Methodist Hymnal: Book of United Methodist Worship. Nashville, TN: United Methodist Publishing House, 1989.

Upton, Jodi and Steve Wieberg. "Contracts for College Coaches Cover More Than Salaries." *USA Today*, November 16, 2006. http://www.usatoday.com (accessed January 10, 2007).

Welch, Jack with Suzy Welch. *Winning*. New York: HarperBusiness, 2005.

Wiesel, Elie. *Night*. 1958; Trans. Marion Wiesel. New York: Hill and Wang, 2006.

Williams, John A. *West Virginia and the Captains of Industry*. Morgantown: West Virginia University Library, 1976.

Willimon, William H. and Thomas H. Naylor. *The Abandoned Generation: Rethinking Higher Education*. Grand Rapids, MI: William B. Eerdmans Publishing Co., 1995.

Willis, Meredith Sue. *The Mountains of America*. San Francisco: Mercury House, 1994.

Wilson R. S., L. L. Barnes, and D. A. Bennett. "Assessment of Lifetime Participation of Cognitively Stimulating Activities." *Journal of Clinical and Experimental Neuropsychology* 25 (2003): 634–642.

"Wisdom." *The New Westminister Dictionary of the Bible*. Ed. Henry Snyder Gehman: Philadelphia: Westminister Press, 1970, 1002.

Wren, Thomas J., ed. *The Leader's Companion: Insights on Leadership through the Ages*. New York: The Free Press, 1995.

Yukl, Gary. *Leadership in Organizations*. 5th ed. Delhi, India: Saurabh Printers, 2002.

Zemsky, Robert and William F. Massey. "Toward an Understanding of Our Current Predicaments." *Change* 27, no. 6 (1995): 40–49.

INDEX

4-H programs, 268–76, 279, 306

Abu Ghraib, 48
Adams, Gail Galloway, 144
Allen Hall, 139
American Council on Education, 211, 212, 303, 336

Baden-Powell, Lord, 277, 278, 279
Bagby, Wes, 360
Baker, Betty Head, 194
Baker, Erin, 194
Ballard, Mary Lou, 193
Bammel, Lei, 131
Bayless, Charles, 156
Beilein, John, 62, 206
Benedum Foundation, 225, 231, 343
Bennett, George B., 3, 17, 135, 310, 351
Berger, Irene, 211
Berra, Yogi, 48
Blake, William, 148
Blaney House, 229, 362
Blaney, Carolyn Eberly, 229, 362
Blobaum, Anna, 196
Board of Visitors, 344
Bok, Derek, 79, 101, 366, 367
Bolen, Jean, 250
Bond, Mary Kay, 342

Bowles, Rice, McDavid, Graff and Love, 71
Boyd, Betty, 194
Brokaw, Tom, 232
Brooks, Dana, 201, 211
Brooks, Maurice, 94, 235
Brown, Carolyn, 340
Brown, Clifford, 97, 340
Brown, James, 191
Brown, Patrice King, 196
Bucklew, Neil, 100, 140, 142, 208, 226, 227
Budig, Gene, 41, 225, 230
Burns, James MacGregor, 25, 26, 54, 325
Byrd, Jack, 92
Byrd, Robert C., 92, 108, 155, 350, 385

Cadran, Ann, 117
Cadran, Erika, 117
Cadran, Robert, 117
Caesar, 36
Callen, Basil, 93
Caperton, W. Gaston, III, 109, 121, 350, 387, 390, 400
Cary, Bray, 261, 309
Caveney, Brian, 125
Chambers, John, 310
Charan, Ram, 60, 67

Churchill, Winston, 7, 8, 28, 34, 36, 84, 242, 243, 246, 332, 367, 406
Cicero, 37, 96
Civil War, 167, 170, 276
Clark, Hannah Belle, 193
College of Agriculture and Forestry. See Davis College of Agriculture, Forestry, and Consumer Sciences
College of Agriculture, Forestry, and Consumer Sciences. See Davis College of Agriculture, Forestry, and the Consumer Sciences
College of Business and Economics, 16, 110, 132, 308
Collins, James, 61, 62, 63, 65
Colson Hall, 142
Comminger, Henry Steele, 100
Commission on Aging, 285
Conner, Carolyn, 108, 140
Conner, Jack, 108
Conner, Margo, 108
Cote, Lawrence S., 131
Creative Arts Center, 139, 342
Crotty, Catherine, 196
Cuoto, Father, 237

D'Alessandri, Robert, 153
David, Leonard, 338
Davis College of Agriculture, Forestry, and Consumer Sciences, 143
Davis, Estelle Conaway, 143
Davis, Gladys Gwendolyn, 143
Davis, Henry Gassaway, 317, 319
Davis, John W., 319
de Tocqueville, Alexis, 257, 381, 387
Dehart, Robert, 98
Dent, Marmaduke, 321
diversity, 43, 50, 51, 171, 172, 174, 208–13
Doherty, William T., 323, 354
Dotson, Dorothy, 195

Drucker, Peter, 28, 49

effective organizations, characteristics of, 25–30
    questions for diversity, 51
    questions for leaders, 53
Elizabeth Moore Hall, 192, 232
Elkins, Stephen B., 317
Esposito, Pat, 114
Evans, Carmella, 125, 195

Faini, Phil, 97, 98, 342
Falbo, Edna, 344
Festival of Ideas, 222, 302
Fischer, David, 256
Fisher, Jennifer, 57
Fisher, John, 374
Foglesong, Robert H. "Doc", 14, 214, 215, 216, 218
Foster, Ruel, 92, 103
Foster, Terree, 195
Frankl, Victor, 29, 64, 248, 249, 293, 330
Frost, Robert, 20, 390

Gardner, Howard, 42, 92, 292, 377
Gates, Bill, 310
Gates, Henry Louis, Jr., 211
Gault, Stan, 47
Gee, E. Gordon, 16, 227, 385
Gladwell, Malcolm, 68
Gluck, Joseph, 229–33, 356
Gluck, Margaret, 232
Gnage, Marie Foster, 42, 158, 211
Goldwater Scholar, 23, 125, 196
Goldwater Scholarship, 23
Goodwin, Kay, 196, 351
Gray, Chris, 252
Gray, Kenneth, 80, 85, 153, 211, 364
Great Depression, 155, 170, 230, 232, 319, 347, 359

Greater Kanawha Valley Foundation, 331, 388

Haden, Charles, 219–21
Hagan, Joe, 157
Hague, Mary Lou, 245
Hall, Granville Davisson, 317, 321, 358
Hall, Stephen S., 260
Hallowell, Edward M., 59
Hathaway, Charles E., 130
Heflin, Harry B., 3, 95, 138, 217, 222–28, 351, 355, 356
Heifetz, Ronald A., 29, 35, 66, 328
Hinchey, Bill, 309
Hiner, Glen H., 2, 351
Hite, Clay B. "Mud", 358
Hitler, Adolph, 230, 246
Hobhouse, Christopher, 365
Hood, Ed, 47
Hornak, Larry, 161, 162
Hubbard, Eva Boyers, 192
Hundley, "Hot Rod", 44, 125, 340, 360

Jobs, Steve, 310
Johnson Scholars, 16
Johnson, Florence Highland, 15, 16
Johnson, Lyndon, 278
Jones, Reg, 47

Kalbaugh, Trish, 124
Kellogg Foundation, 3, 8, 80, 109, 212, 304, 396, 417
Kendrick, W. H., 270, 275, 276
Kennedy, John F., 27, 72, 77, 131, 278, 360
Kennedy, Robert F., 247
King, Martin Luther, Jr., 243, 247, 327
Kirk, Grayson, 366
Kouzes, James M., 21, 24, 64, 223, 331
Kress, Cathann, 271–73, 275, 279, 306

Lang, Gerald, 120, 131, 153, 161, 162, 364
Laskin, Emma, 92
leader overload, 56–69
leader overload, causes of, 61–68
leader overload, signs of, 58–60
leadership capacity, 46–55
leadership team, 10, 25, 38, 46, 56, 78, 81, 84, 86, 364, 402
leading change, 78–86
leading change, lessons learned, 83–86
learning organization, 37
learning organization, ways to create, 37–44
LeFlore, Larry, 78
Lerner, Richard, 272, 274
lessons learned, 9, 25, 53, 83, 105, 224, 388
lessons learned, recognizing, 11–24
lifelong learning, 44, 32–44, 296
lifelong learning, benefits of, 35–37
lifetime learning. See lifelong learning
Lincoln, Abraham, 126, 243, 246, 276, 316, 325, 374, 377
Linsky, Marty, 29, 35, 328
Llewellyn, K. N., 375

management team, 3, 43
Mandela, Nelson, 213
Marockie, Henry, 76
Marshall, Geoffrey, 363, 364, 365
Martin Hall, 192, 196
Martin, Alexander, 100, 164, 219, 220, 357
Martin, Chris, 42
Massey, William F., 113
Maxwell, Robert, 238
Mazey, Mary Ellen, 16, 156
Mazza, Yvette LaFollette, 232
McCarthy, Bernice, 27
McCauley, Becky, 23

McGregor, Douglas, 49
McNerney, James, 47
Meacham, Jon, 326
Mertz, Elizabeth, 197
Michael, Vivian Davis, 143
Miller, Francena, 139
Miller, Paul, 32, 37, 95, 138–40, 148,
  223, 225, 263, 266, 355
Monroe, Victorian Louistall, 194
Moore, Elizabeth Irwin, 190, 191
Moore, James R., 190
Morris, James, 366
Morrison, Agnes, 192
Moses, Herman, 115
Mother Teresa, 250, 254, 419
Mountaineer Parents Club, 19, 26,
  79–81, 106, 116, 117, 145, 176–85,
  189, 196, 293, 300, 344, 345, 412
Mueller, Robert S., III, 157

Nardelli, Robert, 47
NASCAR, 261, 309
Naylor, Thomas H., 81, 144
Nazi, 7, 243, 248
Newman, John Henry, 174
Nixon, Richard, 278

O'Dell, Kerry, 158
O'Toole, James, 4, 27
Office of International Programs, 16
Oglebay Hall, 117, 142
Operation JumpStart,, 129, 130, 144,
  300

Patricius, 136, 137, 166, 167, 170
Peale, Norman Vincent, 28
Pease, Louise McNeill, 195
Percival Hall, 139
personnel, thinking about, 49, 50, 51,
  52, 53
Phillips, Jayne Anne, 195

Phillips, Margie, 20
Pittsnogle, Kevin, 262
Plato, 36, 197
Poffenbarger, Livia, 193
Posner, Barry Z., 21, 24, 223
private donors, 186–88
Promise Scholarship, 169
Proudfoot, Chad, 57

Quackenbush, Kristin, 196
Quigley, Amy, 138

Read Aloud, 342, 343
Rector, Jerry, 92
Research Corporation, 142
Rhodes Scholar, 108, 124, 140, 196,
  350, 355, 360
Rhodes Scholarship, 92, 108, 364, 412
Richardson, William, 212, 304
Robert C. Byrd Health Sciences
  Center, 108, 109, 168
Rockefeller, John D. "Jay", IV, 155, 188,
  281–84, 350, 373, 412
Rockefeller, John D., III, 283, 285
Rogers, Ira Errett "Rat", 358
Roosevelt, Franklin, 230
Roosevelt, Theodore, 57
Rowley, James, 337

Samuel, Jim, 252
Satterfield, David, 98
Schlesinger, Arthur, 257
September 11, 2001, 149, 168, 182,
  218, 241–53, 405
Shaw, Buzz, 53
Showalter, Kenneth, 111
Smart, Brad, 48, 49
Smart, Geoffery, 48, 49
Smith, Julie, 61
social justice, 43, 208–13, 304, 388
St. Patrick, 124, 136, 137, 167, 408

Stasny, John F., 356
State School Board, 74, 77
Stewart Hall, 15, 318, 358, 359
Stewart, David, 130, 364
Stewart, Irvin, 111, 132, 340, 350, 359, 403
Stone, Lloyd, 234
Summers, Festus P., 323, 354
Surowiecki, James, 51

Tolstoy, Leo, 126, 383
Troha, James A., 176
Truman Scholarship, 23, 128
Turner, Eli, 191
Twain, Mark, 22, 125

Underwood, Craig, 309
university, student centered, 80–82

Vance, J., 15
Vanderslice, Tom, 47
Vest, Charles, 125, 216, 217
Warren, Earl, 210
Weete, John, 142
Welch, Jack, 47, 62, 66
West Virginia Business Roundtable, 71, 72, 76, 388
West Virginia State School Board Association, 71
West Virginia University Alumni Association, 117, 147, 178, 182, 193
West Virginia University Extension Services, 14, 84, 96, 109, 119, 131, 151, 168, 169, 172, 180, 216, 235, 270, 402
West Virginia University Foundation, 125, 134, 152
West Virginia University Student Recreation Center, 139, 141, 303
West Virginia University, role of athletics, 199–207

West Virginia University, role of women, 189–98
West, Jerry, 44, 94, 125, 140, 340, 360
White, Carrie, 193
Williams, John, 360
Willimon, William H., 81, 144
Willis, Meredith Sue, 348
Wimmer, Terry, 125
Wise Library, 359
Wise, Bob, 169
Wood, Ruth, 193
Woodburn Circle, 149, 190, 191, 357, 361
Woodburn Hall, 91, 142, 242, 357, 359, 361

Yates, Albert, 79
Yukl, Gary, 65
Yura, Michael, 132

Zemsky, Robert, 113